Time Capsules

Time Capsules

A Cultural History

by
William E. Jarvis

McFarland & Company, Inc., Publishers
Jefferson, North Carolina, and London

Library of Congress Cataloguing-in-Publication Data

Jarvis, William E., 1945–
Time capsules : a cultural history / by William E. Jarvis.
p. cm.
Includes bibliographical references and index.

ISBN 0-7864-1261-5 (softcover : 50# alkaline paper) ∞

Time capsules—History. 2. Civilization—History.
I. Title.
CB151.J37 2003
909—dc21 2002011400

British Library cataloguing data are available

Cover photograph: Time Capsule of Cupaloy, Westinghouse East Pittsburgh Plant, 1938 *(Westinghouse Historical Center, Pittsburgh, PA)*

Manufactured in the United States of America

McFarland & Company, Inc., Publishers
Box 611, Jefferson, North Carolina 28640
www.mcfarlandpub.com

This book is dedicated to my wife Mary Ann Hughes
and to my daughter Anna Jarvis.
(The dining table is free now!)

It is also dedicated to all those who have deposited
something to a distant future — and wondered why...

Contents

Introduction: The Time Capsule Experience

> *A container used to store for posterity a selection of objects thought to be representative of life at a particular time ("time capsule,"* The Oxford English Dictionary, *1989).*

> *For two years Fairgoers have gaped at the capsule, gleaming at the bottom of its open well. One day this week, from a huge, hot cauldron, 500 lb. of petroleum pitch, chlorinated diphenyl and mineral oil were poured into the well, to act as a packing indefinitely resistant to moisture and soil acids. On the stroke of noon, the well was sealed. A crowd of spectators bared their heads. A bugle sounded taps. The capsule started its long journey through time ("5000 year journey," 1940, p. 59).*

What's going on here? A time capsule, the 1938 New York World's Fair's Westinghouse Time Capsule of Cupaloy (rechristened as "Time Capsule I" in 1964), was finally having its burial site, the "Immortal Well," sealed up in 1940 ("5000 year journey," 1940, p. 59; Hyman & McLelway, 1953, pp. 194+; "Scientific events," 1940, pp. 280–281; Youngholm, 1940, pp. 301–02). Such time capsule burials can trigger a response of solemn respect, or even criticism or outrage when someone's favorite artifact, written message, cultural icon or historical relic is not included in the "canon," the pile of relics and records tucked away for a few decades, centuries or millennia. The 1938–AD 6939 Time Capsule noted above is a classic modern time capsule, with both a deliberate deposit and a definite target or retrieval date scheduled at the time of that deposit.

This book is a cultural history of time capsules and many widely-related time-information transfer experiences. Time capsules in a narrowly defined sense are deliberately sealed deposits of cultural relics and recorded knowledge that are intended for retrieval at a given future target date. We will examine formal and popular cultural aspects of these repository vessels, practices and phenomena, tracing the modern time capsule's functions from its ancient Mesopotamian and Egyptian foundation deposit origins. We will follow the changes in these more than 5000-year-old traditions from *deliberately indefinite* deposits of 3000 BC to the AD 1876 invention of *target-dated* deposits. Contents and specifications of nineteenth, twentieth and twenty-first century time capsules will be analyzed. Their origins are rooted in primal, ancient activities including dedication rituals such as the commemoration of ancient Near Eastern building projects. More recent kinds of time capsules have been deliberately deposited for targeted retrieval on specified dates. Some have even ridden on interstellar probes into deep space. The deliberate preservation of "ancient" writings is also one of the key functions of time capsules we'll consider. Interpretive historical aspects of a wide variety of time capsule phenomena will be discussed. Time capsules are treated here as significant attempts to transfer cultural information across the millennia. They are notable popular cultural curiosities. Time capsules are historical carnivals of relics, oddities and mementos. They are also potentially significant formal records of our world's civilization to distant futures.

We will distinguish many varieties of real time capsules and time capsule–like experiences. There are a wide variety of time capsule types: Earth- and space-based, ancient or modern, informal ("popular") or official projects, those with humorous intent and otherwise, pretend exercises and real-physical items, "short" term (approximately 100 years or under) and longer term (1000 years or more). Ancient foundation deposits, cornerstone ceremonies, centennial and bicentennial time capsules, time capsules sealed by schoolchildren for ten years, 5000-year time capsules sent off with great hoopla by great promoters, and scientists' space-time capsules are all are part of the great projects of sending messages to the future. Archaeological finds and "let's pretend," notional time capsules ideas can evoke "as-if" time capsule experiences. We can also imagine fictional time capsules as literary devices and will look at all these forms of imaginary time capsules and time capsule–like experiences as well.

Over the ages, time capsules have captured the popular mind, and never more so than in the recent turn of the millennia. What is the meaning of the increase in time-consciousness and time capsule activity? Time capsules are about sending out slices of our time to the future. There seems to be something deeply reassuring about partaking in the ancient urge to dedicate or commemorate buildings, events, places and people by deposit rituals. Time capsules are also about the fun and challenges of actually planning for the future's retrieval of our messages and objects by the "foreign culture" of the future. There have been time capsule–type experiences ever since humans have measured time, characterized the past as distinct from the present, or saved items for later consideration. "Capturing a moment in time" implies the changes that time can bring to any world of any given time period. The deeply human impulse to mark a time as distinctive is clearly far older than the beginning of formal written chronology. Recording lunar cycles and seasonal passages is probably at least as old as our species. Keeping some kind of calendar, in song or verbal observation alone, even if not recorded as a marked physical medium, is a quintessential human cultural activity. "I mark time, therefore I am" could be humankind's motto.

Time Capsule Milestones in World Chronology

800,000 Years BP (ca.) "Before Present": Stone tools noted in archaeological record of Africa and Southeast Asia.

8000 BCE "Before Common Era": This baseline "start" date ca. 10,000 years BP is commonly noted as the beginning of planned, brick-built, agriculturally supported Neolithic town sites in Western Asia. It serves as a convenient "power of ten" millennia chronological measure backward in time "benchmark date" for "chronological thought experiments."

4241 BCE Egyptian priestly early calendrical start date in world technical chronology. In 1936, Jacobs featured its zero baseline date for the "beginning of civilization" in his Crypt project's yesterday-midpoint-tomorrow chronology.

3000 BCE (ca.) Assumed by Westinghouse and Osaka Time Capsules' senders to be the beginning of Mesopotamian and Egyptian civilization's written records, metallurgy and planned city-temple building precincts. Formal foundation deposits common in archaeological record.

100 BCE (ca.) Jingu Shrines sacred precincts are first constructed, Ise, Japan.

30 BCE Ptolemic Dynasty of Alexandrine Egypt ends with death of Cleopatra VII. Hellenistic–West Asian culture areas are fused to Roman culture and politics by Augustus Caesar. Vernacular as well as formal foundation deposits in Graeco-Roman archaeological record.

690 CE "Common Era": Jingu Shrines sacred buildings' replication cycle begins, Ise, Japan.

1220 Salisbury, England, Cathedral cornerstone dedication rituals recorded (Julian Calendar dates).

1248 (August 14) Dedication service for the rebuilt Cologne, Germany, Cathedral. Actual hollowed-out repository with a variety of contents, including account of the ceremony, consecrated waxen saintly images, coins and unspecified items apparently typical of the time of deposit. This 1248 CE Cologne foundation deposit ritual and its repository's contents have all of the features of the modern indefinitely deposited cornerstone or foundation practices.

1361 (July 29) York, England, Cathedral. Cornerstone dedication ceremony recorded.

1500 (ca.)–1900 (ca.) Deposits in fireplaces, windows, walls and foundations. An early seventeenth century English child's shoe, found behind a child's room's wooden paneling, is a typical building resident's protection deposit.

1851 The "Crystal Palace" Great Exhibition, Hyde Park, London, England, opens as first major world's fair. Railroads and sea steam transport developments continue.

1876 Philadelphia Centennial Exposition, Fairmount Park, Philadelphia, USA. "The Century Safe," first modern deliberately deposited, target-dated time capsule, was exhibited at a World's Fair. Charles D. Mosher's later Chicago "Memorial Time Vault," 1876–1905, was conceived from his photographic exhibit at the Exposition.

1923 "King Tut's Tomb" worldwide craze begins, later inspiring Jacobs' Crypt project.

1923 Tokyo Earthquake occurs and memorial name scrolls of victims are dedicated for 10,000 years in a Buddhist temple, inspiring Jacobs' Crypt notions.

1935 Dr. Thornwell Jacobs, Oglethorpe University President, first discusses a project that will become the Crypt of Civilization on Campus.

1936 Jacobs announces his Crypt of Civilization project, with the year 1936 as the 6177-year midpoint between the Egyptian calendar start date of 4241 BCE and his Crypt's target date of 8113 CE.

1937 G. Edward Pendray interests Westinghouse Co. in a "time bomb" project for the 1939 New York World's Fair.

1938 Pittsburgh, Pennsylvania. Westinghouse Time Capsule vessel takes shape.

***1938** Flushing Meadows, New York City: "The Time Capsule of Cupaloy" is lowered into its "Immortal Well" on September 23, the autumnal Equinox. "Time capsule" term is coined for this first (multi-) millennial time capsule deposit's (5001-year) target date.

1939 The New York World's Fair, Flushing Meadows, Queens, New York City, opens.

***1940** Crypt of Civilization is sealed for 6117 years as the longest targeted time-spanning time capsule.

***1957** "MIT Time Capsule," 1957–2957 CE, was buried on the MIT Campus on June 5 near its Compton Laboratories.

***1964–65** "Westinghouse Time Capsule II of Kromarc" exhibited at the 1964-65 New York City World's Fair site and was buried ten feet *north* of the Westinghouse 1938 Time Capsule I, both to be opened in 6939 CE along with Time Capsule I.

***1970** Osaka Prefecture Castle Grounds, Osaka. Deposited after exhibition at the EXPO 70 World's Fair, the twin Time Capsules are sealed, "no. 1" for 5000 years, "no. 2" for regular centennial retrievals until 6970.

***1973** "State of India Time Capsule," Red Fort, Delhi, India, 1973–6973, was "pulled out of the running" only a few years after its 1973 deposit for Nation's twenty-fifth Independence Day.

1976 U.S. Bicentennial celebrations included the opening of the 1876 "The Century Safe" (now called "The Centennial Safe"). Numerous new time capsules are sealed, including Reynolds Metals Co.–designed time capsules such as the U.S. NARA Bicentennial Time Capsule in Washington D.C.

1977 Two Voyager Record space-time capsules begin an interstellar journey from Earth for perhaps 10,000 years or more.

***1979** "Rice/Tree/Burial Project," ArtPark, New York, Time Capsule, 1979–2979 CE: 1000-year deposit near Buffalo, New York.

***1982** "BBC Time Capsule" is buried until 3982 CE at the historic Castle Howard, Yorkshire, England, U.K.

1993 Latest reconstruction-destruction in Jingu Shrines' sacred buildings' 1200-year-long replication cycle takes place Ise, Japan.

**Between 1938 and 1982, these* eight *time capsules were deliberately deposited for a retrieval on a target date at least 1000 years after their deposit-sealing date.*

2000 Osaka Expo 70 Time Capsule "no. 2," the "Centennial" capsule, has its first opening after the 1970 initial deposit of "no. 1" and "no. 2," and is later resealed for the first of its 100-year periods.

2076 U.S. Tricentennial: The Bicentennial Time Capsule, 1976–2076 is targeted to be opened by the U.S. National Archives. Other Reynolds Metals Inc. time capsules for the various U.S. states are slated for reopening too.

6939 CE "Common Era": The Westinghouse Time Capsule of Cupaloy ("Time Capsule I") is targeted for retrieval on the autumnal Equinox, along with the 1965 Time Capsule II deposit.

6970 CE The Osaka Expo 70 Time Capsule "no. 1" is targeted for retrieval in this year after 5000 years of deposit. Osaka Expo 70 Time Capsule "no. 2," the "Centennial" capsule, will also be opened after its last 6900 CE resealing.

8113 CE Target date designated for the opening of the Crypt of Civilization deposited at Oglethorpe University, Atlanta, Georgia, May 25, 1940.

10,000 CE This "Tenth Millennium" Common Era benchmark chronology date is one possible "Notional Futurescape of a Distant Tomorrow."

12,000 CE This "Twelfth Millennium" Common Era benchmark date is another possible such "Notional Futurescape's Distant Future," ten millennia ahead. It is a convenient "power of ten" chronological measure for potential time capsules and other "benchmark chronological thought experiments."

CHAPTER 1
How Time Capsules Work

Why create time capsules? There are at least four good reasons: First is just the fun of putting together a time capsule and actually sending off a sealed-up sample or bit of our present time. Anticipating a capsule's future reception can be fun, and receiving a real time capsule can be fun too. A second motive is the ancient "participation mystique" of playing a part in archetypal, ceremonial, commemorative rituals that have been deposited at least since the beginnings of Sumerian civilization over 5000 years ago. They may even date back to the West Asian Neolithic pre-metallurgic cultures of ca. 8000 BCE. Third, these transactions make significant socio-cultural commemorative celebrations for individuals, families, communities, business and all sorts of organizations, events and even whole eras. Finally, people seem to enjoy complex philosophical and technical challenges of what to, or how to, send or receive artifacts and linguistic messages between a past and a future.

These are real, physical causes of time capsule–like experiences, whether we receive "time capsules" from past (human) world-periods in the form of libraries, archives and archaeological traces, or from physical capsule vessels. But even just an intent to do a time capsule collection can be an interesting thought experiment; it's fun to entertain the notion of an imaginary time capsule and wonder what we would put away in it. With these notional, "as-if" time capsules a variety of fictional, metaphorical, "let's-pretend" wish lists have been called "time capsules." An encapsulation might be an as-if, "just imagine" idea, or consist of an actual physical vessel and contents.

What makes a real physical time capsule? This is necessary to understand before considering their "as-if," pretend relatives in detail. Real, literal time capsules are physical deposits, items in containers, objects or sites. We will emphasize here such salient features as the information transfer character of time capsule cases and phenomena, with their communication, information and interpretation dimensions. We will examine time capsule approaches to historical communication as potentially significant trans-millennial information transactions. Finally, we will compare time capsules' terminology in a variety of disciplines such as archaeology, museology, space sciences, environmental studies and preservation technologies.

Cultural, Historical and Information Transfer Functions of Literal Time Capsules

Time capsules can be high points of human artistic, cultural and technical-material civilization. Their unique combination of archival-historical record and archaeological-deposit dimensions may be their most interesting aspect. Such vessels and notions play a dual role of reflecting world-images for our own cultural era to ponder and for the "possible futures" we imagine. Time capsules can be significant information transfer attempts across centuries, millennia — and revealing evidence for our self-reflection too. Major time capsule projects are technical challenges of the highest order, but are simultaneously capable of inspiring widespread public interest, awe or controversy. Time capsules can embody the highest technical and cultural aspirations of civilization, like the World's Fairs where they are sometimes exhibited. They are commonly featured as institutional publicity promotions, public relations activities, carnival-type attractions, or even the very familiar, *de rigueur* civic commemorative rituals. They are convenient devices (literal or metaphorical) for us to commemorate hopes and evidence by leaving them for possible futures. Influential groups of twentieth century savants and promoters organized a few noteworthy time capsule projects and attempted to preserve them for future recipients. More often, people have been content to seal up smaller cultural samples, multitudes of which serve as "garden-variety" time capsules— modest shorter span memorials.

Today's foundation deposit and cornerstone repositories are survivals of the kinds of dedicatory, "votive" founding of sites and buildings. Those consecrations and commemorative founding rites are the antecedents of our modern (post–1876) time capsule deposits and rituals. A major subset of such foundation dedication practices involves ritual behaviors specifically focused on foundation stones and other key structural features of buildings. The term "foundation rites" can apply to either building-related or non–building-related "founding" ceremonies, including ribbon-cuttings and inaugurations of exhibitions, parks, bridges, etc. No building structure need be involved for a founding, dedication rite to be staged. Even if not associated with celebrating a lower foundation structure or even the ceremonial roof topping of a building, these rituals are founding or foundation in this broader dedicatory sense. We will use this meaning of "foundation deposit rite" in the larger sense as any dedication custom or "founding" ceremony. Those ancient practices have much in common with today's time capsule experiences, as seen in the ancient functions of those depositions. There are significant differences between them too. Archaeological exhibits and interstellar space probes have been dubbed "time capsules." Space-time capsules are much like the commonplace cornerstone repositories of relics. Cornerstone deposits and space-time capsules differ from classic modern time capsule phenomena and projects, primarily because the former lack definitely fixed target dates. All these deposited messages and other contents are capable of inspiring the awe, humor, curiosity, historical insight and controversy catalyzed by a time capsule. Until the last quarter of the nineteenth century, commemorative cornerstone repositories (the descendants of ancient foundation depositions) were the only deliberate deposit, time capsule–type phenomena. These deliberate depositions for targeted opening dates prescheduled at deposit are a relatively recent historical phenomenon, since only 1876. It all started with two projects exhibited in 1876 at the Philadelphia (U.S.) Centennial Exposition (Diehm, 1882; Viskochil, 1976, pp. 95–104).

The Massachusetts Institute of Technology campus has three very interesting kinds of time capsules. Each of these deliberate deposits is a distinctive type of capsule. One is a "millennial" spanning (with a *deliberately* targeted retrieval date of 1,000 years in the future) time capsule. Another is a "centennial-type" capsule (i.e., for 100 years or less) for a targeted 50-year span. A third sort of capsule is an *indefinitely* buried vessel without a targeted retrieval date. It is a foundation deposit–type time capsule. Even though this third vessel has a larger "time cargo," it is *not* a true, i.e., target-dated time capsule, in the modern sense. These "centennial-millennial" distinctions and various target dated *vs.* indefinite characteristics will be examined in greater detail. These factors distinguish these three deliberate time capsule deposits from one another. A true millennium-spanning target-dated MIT time capsule was buried near the Compton Laboratories on June 5, 1957, for a 1000-year period ("Cardinal and Gray," 1957, pp. 506–507). It's a ten-inch diameter, 24-inch long glass container with a few relics. Another, the 50-year-span targeted MIT time capsule, is late for its scheduled retrieval. It is weighed down not just figuratively by history but literally! It still has the 36,000 pound Cyclotron's core magnet deposited on top of it (Lovinger, 1998; *10 Lost Time Capsules*, 1991; *The 9 Most Wanted Time Capsules*, 1999; Remington, 1954, pp. 16–17). Our third example is a 150-lb. encyclopedic specimen buried May 5, 1966, in McDermott Court under Alexander Calder's "stabile" sculpture "The Big Sail" (Shrock, 1965, pp. 195–208.) Geologist Robert Shrock collaborated with H. E. Edgerton on it in 1966. It has a 14-volume science-technology encyclopedia, a few other books and some technical exhibits. This larger vessel has no scheduled opening date. It is more a foundation deposit and is not, strictly speaking, a modern-type time capsule because it lacks such a prescheduled target date. It is at risk of being opened prematurely, perhaps before the antiquarian significance of its contents are appreciated after the passage of millennia.

It is a curious coincidence that pioneer "freeze-frame" high-speed photographer Harold E. Edgerton was a prime mover on the 1957 MIT millennium-span time capsule and helped initiate the 1966 indefinite foundation deposit buried under the McDermott Court "Big Sail." These two deposits froze cultural images of his time, providing "snapshots" of it for posterity. "Doc" Edgerton's strobe photography techniques produced memorable photos, including a bullet in half-transit shattering a light bulb, a drop of milk crown-shaped in mid-splash and a graph-like plot of a bouncing white ball's multi-exposed images up and down. His team provided imaging services for the multi-frame study of the early instants of U.S. atomic test explosions. His interest in photographically "freeze-framing" captured moments of time was paralleled by figuratively "freezing time" in time capsule projects.

What is and is not a time capsule? How best to define basic categories of time capsule–like experiences? They can be defined as items deliberately sealed in containers and scheduled for retrieval on a specified target date. They are usually deposited with specific customs. They are generally intended to commemorate examples of a present life-and-times culture pattern to a (presumably very different!) possible future time. Time-span may range from a few decades to many millennia. Time capsule sending efforts can be challenging technical preservation and coordination projects of the highest order, or they can be simple, casual affairs. There is no absolute, black-and-white set of logical defining criteria available to guide us in the time capsule realm. Like many other cultural activities of humanity, time capsule phenomena are a "fuzzy set" ("non–Aristotelian type") logical category. The defining boundaries of a time capsule experience are not always clear-cut, "either-or," absolutely defined phenomena, and can be viewed through many lenses. Time capsules can be "anything that encapsulates time" (Smithsonian Center for Materials Research and Education, 2000). Defining what does and does not constitute the boundaries of "encapsulation" and what represents any given time can be problematic, especially if literal rather than figurative notions are relied upon.

Expanding and elaborating on these definitions, we can also rule out some situations that are not always "time capsules," do not always evoke a time capsule experience. This *via negativa* approach can help define a time capsule by critiquing time capsule definitions. In order to address the question of what makes a time capsule a real, literal time capsule, we will posit what *isn't* a time capsule. Consider extreme cases that are not "acceptable" time capsules. Also consider the "anything is a time capsule" attitude. Is any box of *anything* someone closes up deliberately so that someone can open it a "few time periods later" necessarily a time capsule? Secondly, is any found thing or site that vividly, fully "brings back," or reminds someone of any past thing, event, person or place necessarily a time capsule? One can readily say "no" to both of these sweeping generalizations. Many commonplace boxes, discovered sites or objects have been regarded as time capsules because feelings of communion with the past are evoked by the circumstances of their receipt or retrieval. To clarify this rather vague state of affairs, consider how little material content or information can evoke a time capsule experience of a whole past world-period. When only one bit, fragment or item is left from a past period, a mere remnant often must stand for a whole past. There is thus a tension between an ideal time capsule bearing a wide spectrum of detailed content *vs.* the commonly expressed idiom or notion that one fragment, one coin, one little bit of just about anything might evoke or "stand for" a past age. We will address this intriguing question from time to time in this study: Just how little is needed for a "good" time capsule experience? Likewise we will try and isolate a few bad, poor or even "failed" time capsule experiences. We will focus on the degree of possible objectivity in what must necessarily remain a somewhat subjective interpretive experience.

In *positive* terms, though, what does make a phenomena, event, situation or sealed box into a real time capsule? There are several essential attributes to good deposited-targeted time capsules. In general, here are the key features of successful time capsules: "Good" time capsules signify, delineate or symbolically dedicate boundaries. These may be literal geophysical boundary demarcations or solely proclamations of figurative socio-cultural notions (such as "this capsule typifies the spirit of our era"). Successful or powerful time capsules tend to proffer sacred or secular cultural interpretations of peoples' worlds, of their lives. They provide a relation to historical time frames, thus coping with the conundrum of representing a series of mere "time-period snapshots" as eternally preserved images of past worlds. They use techniques of communication and preservation of culturally bound messages and relics to span decades, centuries or millennia. They employ chronological, ritualistically driven remembrance or memorial strategies as a technique and a philosophy of cultural transmission across significant stretches of time. These memorial markers could consist of an anniversary-ritual, a message on a plaque or one in a newspaper. The predesignation of a single target date point in time for a capsule opening quite clearly delineates the modern, secular, "linear-historical" time capsule from the foundation deposit and the cornerstone repository, its historical "twin cousins" (*Centennial Safe*, 1976; Diehm, 1882, pp. 194–200; Viskochil, 1976, pp. 95–104). The mythic-ritual origins of foundation deposit ceremonies ca. 3000 BCE were as fully intended to commemorate and bound the creations of their eras as have been the 1876, 1935–40 and 1938 time capsules of American industrial civilization. Instead of the modern notion of commemoration through retrieval, the ancients held to more primal "consecration as renewal" notions in their dedication deposit rituals, wherein royal descendants were sometimes requested to honor the foundation rite deposit from an earlier reign. Man's experiences with time capsules vary widely and thus can be very broadly defined. Broader definitions of time capsules and time capsule–like experiences include notions of intentional deposit, retrievals (or received cases), pretend collections, interpreted associations with archaeological finds, etc. The term "time capsule" has become a metaphor for many wider experiences than the narrower "history in a can" definition. Hence almost anything or any method of information transfer from the recipient's past to the sender's future can be termed at one time or another as a time capsule. Among generalized definitions are metaphorical characterizations and "ostensive" definitions, some of which have been coined and redubbed many times over by many people in many places. Any time someone has an experience that brings back a period of the past with forceful immediacy, the common adage can be said of such time capsules: "I know one when I see one." Clearly the words "time capsule" have popular recognition, and hence wide promotional-advertising appeal.

There are many narrower, technical definitions of "classic time capsule" requirements. Capsules can be deliberate deposits targeted for future recipients (unlike typical archaeological sites). They are scheduled for retrieval at a specific target date (unlike the "happenstance status" of cornerstone deposits) at the time of their initial sealing-deposit. They might convey a "slice of life" from a past to a (supposedly different) possible future. They might consist of either a sealed container or other sufficiently sequestered package of items or message media. Their contents could range from just a few relics up to whole arrays of artifacts and "encyclopedia-type" stores of knowledge—just about anything. They should be able to pass an ultimate test of a time capsule by conveying over a wide range of time sufficiently evocative past details, *gestalt*, or feel.

The self-addressed "ten-year-span letter" is a distinct type of time capsule. The notion of a wide time range can be relative—for instance, a child's letter from the sixth grade written for that child's own receipt six years later, at twelfth grade graduation. The time spans of such self-correspondence are a significant period of time in a child's developmental context. Schoolchildren's ten-year sealed correspondence to their future selves can be time capsules. Letters can be deliberately addressed to oneself when one is a nine-year-old child. They are then held by a teacher for subsequent mailing to the much different, older 19-year-old student ten years later (Ryan, 1998, pp. 8–9). New Jersey schoolteacher Nancy Johnson began doing this as a yearly class project ca. 1983. The amazed 19-year-olds usually forget that they had written the letters to themselves a decade before, and customarily are awed by the phenomenon of being the recipients of their own intergenerational "dialogue"—or is it a "monologue"? These "personal decade letter" time capsules produced by schoolchildren have the educational value to enhance one's historical notions of time and change over time (Maxim, 1998). These short-term letters seem to work well as time capsule experiences mostly because six or ten years of change in a child's life is a developmental epoch. They are deliberately addressed to and later mailed to a targeted-retrieval date.

The ten-year (or less) self-addressed letter is a third category of deliberately sealed-targeted time capsule. Like its ca. 100-year "centennial" and 1000-plus "millennial" related time capsules, the time span of the ten-year letter capsule correlates with the purpose, size, type and preservational treatment of its vessel. A six- or ten-year time span is probably far too short, too insignificant a deposit period for a time capsule in the institutional life of a university or civic organization to be a "good" time capsule. These "personal decade letter" time capsules were not merely lost or blown away.

There *are* accidental examples of papers literally blown away and later retrieved. They are clearly not "real" time capsules in the deliberate sense of letters in archives or of the ten-year schoolchildren's letters. They are not deliberately deposited with any scheduled target dates. Old photos, long-expired driver's licenses or even birth certificates swept away 33 years before by a tornado can vividly remind us of past times. A birth certificate was lifted up by a June 20, 1957, Omaha, Nebraska, area tornado and landed in a Fargo, North Dakota, yard. That it was subsequently returned 33 years later to its owner is amazing, but this case is not a true time capsule experience in our deliberately targeted sense of the term. The oddness of such an event doesn't necessarily make it a true time capsule by our definition ("Gone with the wind, a certificate returns," 1990, p. A10). These "written on the wind," accidentally sent and found documents are remarkable nonetheless. Deliberate transmission for a target date does dignify deposits, transmittals, etc., with the intentionality of a real time capsule.

There are multitudes of motivations for time capsule senders and receivers. All successful time capsules must evoke in either senders or receivers a real sense of immediacy with a given period of historical-cultural space-time, supplied by a wide variety of significant human details, mundane, grandiose or both. Time capsule sending experiences can evoke very profound emotions in the senders. A time capsule experience can indeed happen at a sending event, even when no retrieval has yet occurred, and people often think profoundly about their own space-time time along with or instead of the future target time. The author's personal experience and discussions confirm that it is common to have thoughts about one's own interpretation of one's own era, what the future targeted era might be like, and what similarities, differences or ambiguities future interpreters might "make" of our time's relics. Imagine that the capsule one seals up is never retrieved, for one reason or another. What "good" or goal have the depositors obtained? The sender has probably had at least one or more reflective episodes about time capsule interpretations and the status of their life and times. Retrievers' or senders' experiences can be described by characteristics such as people's self-reflection on the nature of one's own present cultural patterns, aspirations, practices and beliefs. We can see ourselves from other senders or receivers of capsules. Senders' anticipation as to how future recipients should perceive the transmitted cultural messages. Senders might speculate on how the senders' cultural messages might be perceived by future recipients as incomprehensible, barbaric or in some other very different way than the senders intended. One of the major curiosities about modern time capsule transmission efforts is how they tend to engender multiple cross-referencing back-and-forth between two or more time periods. This curious multiple back and forth reflection is engendered among various pasts, presents and futures those capsule transactions refer us to. Senders can be thinking about the potential cultural conditions of receivers, and vice versa in various ways. Both senders and receivers of time capsules could entertain self-reflections or speculations on how their cultural patterns would be perceived by the other "chronological party" and how possible messages' interpretation might be affected. Time capsule experiences, the time capsule phenomenon, are perhaps the ultimate argument from analogy. Time capsules are, or at least ought to be, evocative of the world that sealed, transmitted and sent them. Time capsule projects are as contingent upon historical interpretation as any other human action. In a sense, deliberate time capsules are subject to the same heightened judgment of posterity as museums, historically preserved sites, monuments, archives, etc. The criterion here is: How well did it interpret that past to this future? A good time capsule explores the meaning of created, organized, preserved, collected, recorded knowledge and items from a specific time. Any supposed significance can be cited or otherwise interpreted in the context of a subsequent culture, time, place or cognitive schema (Jarvis, 1988). Even spontaneous, happenstance gathering plans such as the taking of somewhat worn items to serve as part of "articles of common use" time capsule exhibits are planned, at least in general principle. That is, there was usually such an interpretive goal in mind by the time capsules organizers.

Time capsule transactions and interpretations can be significant models of information transfer model phenomena. Time capsules may carry out very specific information transfer functions. One function is to present messages, records, mementos of one place-time to another (far distant) future time and place, or perhaps to receive experiences from any given past time-place's items in a future setting. An ambitious time capsule's contents may constitute a comprehensive storage of a civilization's knowledge, perhaps even eventually through the eventual applications of a robust electronically based memory technology in which a long term deposit of contents might be synonymous with the totality of a society's recorded data, writing and images. A second function is to afford senders or receivers a self-evaluative opportunity regarding various cultural periods. Time capsule phenomena are potentially one of the highest forms of self-critical evaluation of one's cultural life, in the light of what future interpreters might make of one's age. A third function is service as paradigms of information transfer concept and practices. Such concerns include the organization, transmission, preservation, retrieval and interpretation of information across large spans of time, where recipients may differ in language, culture, species, biological lineage or even astronomical origin from that of the sender. Such information transfer analyses of time capsule phenomena of necessity consider worst-case communication scenarios as well as less daunting contingencies.

In each of these possible major information transfer functions of time capsule transmissions, there is an historical purpose — the goal of communicating information from one time frame to another. Conversely, a "bad" time capsule can be seen in these information transfer terms as one that results in a dropped transaction. It fails in the effort to successfully communicate any significant aspects of a past to a future. Such a transaction can be dropped at either end of the time-span of attempted transmission. The information content prepared for sending is an image of the sender's culture, and is an occasion for self-evaluation by that culture. The organization of that information for future translation and interpretation requires a study of how information is transmitted from one ethno-linguistic framework to another vastly different one. Hence the understanding of information transfer needed here goes beyond the mere evaluation of our own cultural messages. This third information transfer function of time capsules is to present specialists with a "universally" significant paradigm (astronomically as well as linguistically!). A time capsule transaction must address just how to communicate messages in a universal language, suggest universally understood "decoding" of our cultural transmissions, that to the information transfer specialist time capsule phenomena can be seen as communication paradigms of the greatest possible significance. A good time capsule project ought to include elements of both spontaneity and organized presentation in order to convey optimally any slice of life from our present "now" to a future "now." Time capsule projects should have at least some elements of spontaneity in the selection of contents. There is no guarantee that any pre-planned collection or mixed media production will have any predetermined effect, including what spontaneous reactions it may evoke. Many time capsule senders have very definite wishes as to the kinds of interpretation their time capsule's contents will receive in the target-dated future, while other senders might not. An information-transfer model of time capsules can encompass non-terrestrially based examples as well as terrestrially based ones. This definition embraces collections of records and other artifacts representing contemporary life and culture deliberately sealed in a container to be preserved intact for transmission to future recipients. The added space-time capsule proviso is that a capsule's intended recipients may be distant in space-habitat as well as culture-time, and presumably even be a radically different biological or physical form than that of the senders. The space-time capsule typically has no precise target date for its reception. That distinguishes it from the modern terrestrially based time capsule as practiced since 1876.

Time capsules can be considered from several specialized perspectives. Historiographical, museological, archaeological, environmental and space science are approaches to time capsule–like experiences. The terminological approaches to defining time capsule phenomena's characteristics considered here are close to the general schema of information transfer type models. Professionals in various disciplines "do" time capsules and analyze those phenomena from their specialized perspectives. Time capsule phenomena are remarkably inter-, cross-disciplinary topics and it is useful to note concepts about various time capsule functions from these specialist perspectives.

Historiographically, a time capsule is an effort to portray the contemporary present culture of senders as a premeditated historical image (or past) to future recipients of that message-carrying device, presenting one historical period to recipients in future time-periods. Time capsules are often attempts to portray "history as a tale," as a series of objective past periods. A time capsule can contain one or more written histories, even be a sort of historical period presented *en toto*, sometimes as original sources for the history of science and technology. The Chicago Museum of Science's 100-year cornerstone with its assortment of scientific experiments is an example of a mini-laboratory ("Clock ticks twice a year; living cornerstone laid in Chicago," 1953, p. 148). Many mundane cornerstone mementos are small repositories of interest primarily to those affiliated with a local organization, commercial enterprise or civic event. The historical lure of time capsules can interest specialist journals when an article from the title is included in a deposit (Brace, 1938, pp. 311–13; "Capsule for 6939 A. D.: rubber objects preserved for posterity," 1938, p. 52; "This heavy door of shining stainless steel to seal Georgia Crypt until year 8113," 1938, p. 3). Journals dealing with rubber, metal and machinery have featured articles on how these materials are to be preserved for millennia.

There are obvious museological analogies in time capsule practices. Museologically, a time capsule can be a prearranged, "retrospective"-type of sealed-off mini-museum exhibition of the sender's culture to a future recipient's culture. In at least one striking case, an exhibition from an archaeological zone (the 1979 traveling "Pompeii 79 AD" museum show) has been reviewed as "A 'time capsule' from ancient Rome" (Kern, 1979, pp. C1, C13). Let's look here at an example of narrowly defined, true time capsules. Both Westinghouse Time Capsules I (1938) and the Time Capsule II (1965) New York World's Fairs are exhibits of 1938 and 1964 world and U.S. cultures. These pre-planned "retrospective exhibits" are targeted to open on the autumnal Equinox of the Common Era year 6939. There has been speculation about such an opening ceremony ("Journey into time," 1948, pp. 165–68). Although Fair visitors viewed duplicates of capsule and contents, the big attraction at both Westinghouse Corporation

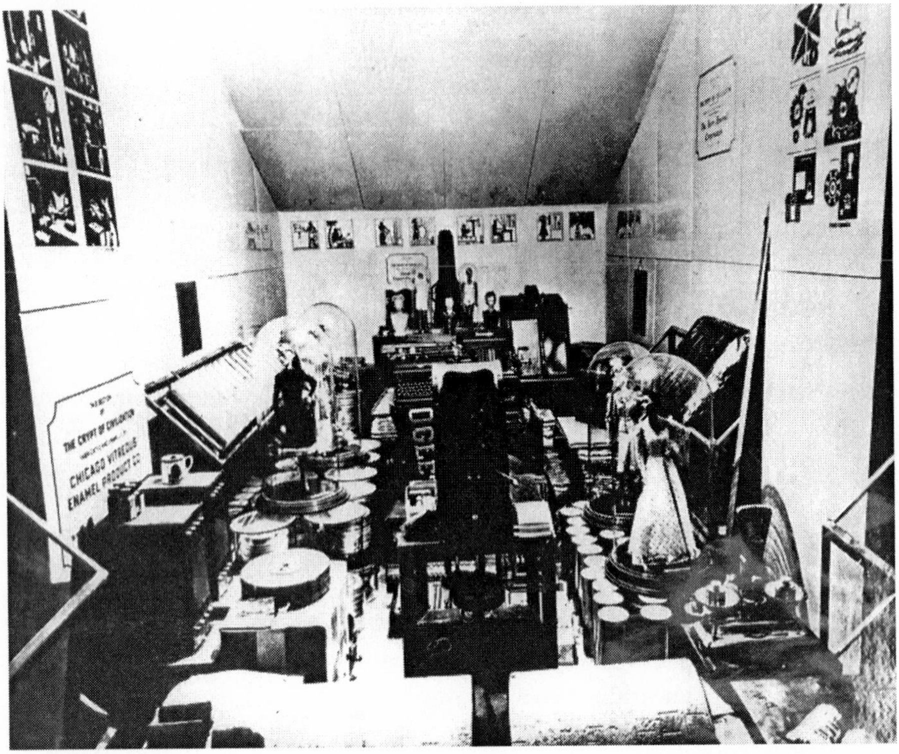

A "proscenium" view of the fully loaded interior of the Crypt of Civilization ca. its May 25, 1940, sealing for 6,173 years. Note the black, neo-pictographic, "history lessons" on the ceramic liner walls, as well as the sheer variety of large objects in this 2000 cubic foot room. (Courtesy Oglethorpe University, Atlanta, GA.)

Exhibits was the Time Capsule itself, an "exhibition" scheduled for the seventieth century. The Oglethorpe University 2000 cubic foot "Crypt of Civilization" time capsule can even more readily be seen as a museum, an exhibition room already packed, installed and sealed for its scheduled AD 8113 exhibition opening. Certain very good museum exhibitions of ancient art evoke time capsule–like experiences in many visitors to them. A new, functional reorganized collection of Classical Greek art and wares in one prominent museum has been described as providing intriguing views into lost past worlds, dissolving time barriers between the museum attendee and the ancient artifact's user (Bowersock, 1999, pp. 33–39). The artifacts are the instruments of information transfer between exhibit-viewer and the item ancient user. The artifacts are time capsules in that sense. The power of museum items' perfectly new appearance seems to magically transport us across the reaches of time, in a marked contrast with the apparent limits of the ruined and worn-by-use artifact to evoke a timelessness effect. That reinstallation's power to re-evoke a sense of various past Attic eras seems due to the pottery wares' functionally realistic era-by-era exhibition table settings, rather than grouping, say, all fish serving platters from several hundred years together. Above the archaeological connectedness and "time capsule" interpretive effectiveness of worn-out artifactual remains, there might well be a separate time capsule efficacy in both worn and pristine artifacts. Setting aside the question of interpreting dimensions of fine art objects vs. everyday items of common use as contents for actual time capsules, we note that there might readily be a multiple interpretative value in the presentation of *both* pristine and worn-down versions of artifacts. One landscape architect noted that one completely furnished and accurately lit residence would better explain any given cultural period than would a thousand books (Steel, 1927, pp. 24–25). In that sense, any antique furnished and preserved building is a museum. As a suddenly unsealed space, such a "time capsule" exhibit would have enormous evocative power. Any number of historically preserved architectural examples can of course be considered time capsules of another era.

The desire to photograph or otherwise capture one's contemporary visage or emotional responses in the everyday world seems almost irresistible. Who wouldn't want to have photographic footage of just about any era or locale in human history? New York City did just that in 1987 with a comprehensive survey of the City via visual film footage (Greer, 1987, pp. A1, C8). Copying a whole town or cultural milieu is a captivating idea. There are contemporary examples of wide time capsule projects that attempt to comprehend the present of a town, both in order to treasure it here-and-now and to present it to the future (NPR, "Jennifer Schmidt reports residents of Walpole, New Hampshire...," August 22, 2000). An interesting applied anthropological approach to measuring a museum exhibit's or historical site's appeal is gauging the degree of "numinosity" associated with it (Cameron & Gatewood, 1998). In a study entitled "Excursions into the un-remembered past: What people want from visits to historical sites," quantitative rating methods were applied to visitors' appraisals to various historic sites. It was an interesting effort to measure the magical aura-historical awe (i.e., "numinosity") evoked by historic venues with such apparent strong links to a distinctive past period or event that they seem to shine with awe-inspiring power ("Religion, study of," 1994–1999; Schilling, 1987, pp. 21–22).

Archaeologically there are three basic different types of "time capsule–like" deposits. One is the deliberate deposit for an indefinite span, a grave or a cornerstone. A second is a deliberate deposit with a definite target date designated by the senders, as with a post–1876 time capsule. Finally there is the case of an accidentally deposited archaeological site with no designated target date for retrieval. Those are often archaeological museum expositions that vividly evoke the immediacy of a past period of time. Numerous varieties of archaeologically related time capsule experiences will be detailed later in the analysis of as-if time capsule–like experiences. Note that Robert Ascher's archaeologically focused article "How to build a time capsule" clearly draws the intentional vs. unintentional distinction (Ascher 1974). It was later formalized in combination with definite target-date vs. indefinite deposit motives into a tripartite taxonomy of time capsule studies (Jarvis, 1988). Anthropologist Clark Wissler had initially characterized the 1938 Westinghouse Time Capsule project as "instant archaeology." Ascher first clearly distinguished the broader conceptual sweep of the archaeological, unintentional, after-the-fact interpreted time capsule–like deposit from the intentional deliberately target-dated time capsule ("Archeologist reverses job: buries relics of today," 1940, p. 222; Ascher, 1974). What accidental, happenstance archaeological deposits don't always do, modern deliberate time capsules can often do in their capacity as "archival" collections. As deposits and repositories, derived from ancient foundation deposit rituals and cornerstone depositories, deliberate modern time capsules have specific, scheduled-in-advance target dates. It is easy for people to imagine that an archaeological site such as a tomb, extinct city or shipwreck is "just like a time capsule." It is thus possible to have a time capsule–like experience when no deliberately deposited time capsule actually exists. This technical distinction can seem to be much too fussy when people are focused on a non–target dated time capsule that is deposited as the repository in a building's foundation, in a cornerstone or on a campus like MIT. What after all is the point of saying: "No! That is not a *real* time capsule, but this *is*"? If our time capsule requirements consist of reasonably clear and distinct ideas, we need no categorical panic about these kindred, fuzzy-set phenomena, with their messy, real world–overlapping boundaries. Imitation here is a sincere form of flattery. For a site, device or repository to be dubbed a time capsule often seems to help evoke contemporary and subsequent time capsule experiences. A pedantic obsession with strict cut-off definitions is unnecessary, and indeed silly when the live stuff of past humanity's existence is the object lesson under consideration. We do not necessarily lose any understanding of the reach of time capsule experiences by acknowledging the broadened scope of what is such an experience. We can include a very wide, liberal range of cases as "time capsules." It is far more important for time capsule practitioners to be clear about their goals, methods and contents in transmitting time

Table 1.1
Types of "Time Capsule" Deposits and Retrievals

	"A Priori" (Intentional Deposit)	***"A Posteriori"*** (*Non*-Intentional Deposit)
Unscheduled Retrieval (happenstance; indefinite span):	1. FOUNDATION DEPOSITS & CORNERSTONES (Mesopotamian deposits; Washington Monument cornerstone) 2. SPACE-TIME CAPSULES (i.e., Voyager 1 and 2 Records)	Pompeii AD 79 and other archaeological sites; sunken ships, such as the RMS *Titanic*, HMS *Pandora* or USS *Yorktown*
Scheduled Retrieval on a Target Date:	1. "PERSONAL DECADE LETTER" TIME CAPSULES: Ten-year span *or less* (Schoolchildren's self addressed correspondence to themselves on the pending occasion of their graduation) 2. "CENTENNIAL" TIME CAPSULES: 100-year span *or less* (The Century Safe; Time Capsule Expo 70 no. 2) 3. "MILLENNIAL" TIME CAPSULES: 1000-year span *or more* (Crypt of Civilization; Westinghouse Time Capsules I & II; time Capsule Expo 70 no. 1)	*(A "sparsely populated" set)* 1. Some retrospective notional contemplation as to what the past *might* have been able to leave for us *if* deposits had been made or archaeology had been found? 2. Archaeological sites deliberately left undisturbed for the time being, reburied and/or have had an informational marker deposited?

capsule deposits than to rule on whether a large variety of actual prior deposited time capsule examples are "real" time capsules.

Time capsules can serve environmental and agricultural purposes. Environmental "antique air" samples and "seed bank" collections can be seen and even planned as deliberate target dated time capsule sampling projects. These mundane areas of preservation can be of value as time capsule technology innovations, of long-term encapsulation. While museums commonly display items in sealed containers, it is a bit unusual to consider the air trapped in old containers as a worthwhile collectable. R. A. Rasmussen became a collector of "antique air," working on the assumption that air sealed away many decades ago provides valuable environmental samples of previous atmospheres ("Professor searching for new angle on fluorocarbon sources," 1976, pp. 1–2). These samples collected in the 1970s are time capsules, benchmarks of atmospheric conditions that got incidentally sealed away for long-term storage. The Bureau of Standards and the Environmental Protection Agency had developed the concept of a long-term deliberate storage facility, a "National Environmental Specimen Bank." Future environmental scientists may have reliable standard environmental samples of past air, water and soil (*The National Environmental Specimen Bank*, 1978). Would-be time capsule builders might consider including a bit of good old-fashioned dirt or water as samples in their (eventually to be) past kinds of environmental time capsules. Another rather antique sample of 101-year-old botanical seed specimens was retrieved in 1980 near Michigan State University. These practices evolved into a ten-year retrieval cycle of various seed packets deposited by W. J. Beal in 1889 ("Botanists dig up weed seeds buried 101 years," 1980, p. 50). He crossbred corn varieties in the late 1890s. The value of bits of ancient "dinosaur" air is yet another case of an environmental time capsule, albeit an *a posteriori* one (Gleick, 1987, pp. D2, D7). The heightened environmental awareness of recent decades has added to our conception of what "slices of life" should be preserved for future analysis. There have even been laments that the preservational fluid in Dead Sea Scroll's sealed jars had lost their odor, something that has been noted as lacking, and (hence?) desirable ("Sniffing through history," 1989, p. E18). The scope of time capsule contents, as well as the technology behind such efforts, can change. Capsules may enable future recipients to routinely "smell the flowers" of our (by then) ancient worlds.

We can universalize the definition of a time capsule by including non–terrestrially located variants. "Space-time capsules" are a special type of indefinitely deposited cornerstone repository. Here we briefly preview this very curious sort of time capsule, without the details of specific cases. More about the history of these space-time capsules later. It is a type not buried anywhere on Earth, in fact not located anywhere at all on the Earth! Time capsule phenomena, terrestrially based earthbound as well as spacefaring "Search for Extraterrestrial Intelligence" type (SETI) projects, present a challenging information transfer scenario. How to maximize communication with recipients who may be of alien language, culture, intelligence and biology? Maybe twentieth and twenty-first century efforts to send vivid, translatable messages to the seventieth century of Earth or tens of thousands of years into interstellar space will be eventually understood. If the details of message content are not comprehended, at least the basic fact of a communication effort has been made on the part of purposeful intelligent senders. The difficulties of ethno-linguistic interpretation are many, even here on Earth amongst us humanoids. The whole discussion of information transfer models raises significant questions about interpreting cultures from any past to any future. Here we merely note the chronological taxonomy of these votive offerings to the great unknown reaches of outer space.

Key Aspects of Functioning Time Capsule Projects

Major problems time capsule projects must solve include the building, selecting, packing, preserving, notifying and interpreting of time capsule "missions." Individual time capsule senders must each build a survivable time capsule vessel, notify future recipients of its existence at a precise location, and select and preserve contents (Pendray, 1939). The construction of a secure time capsule vessel, as well as the preservational technology of its contents, is closely related to the concerns of item selection. Final content selection of items to be contained inside can be very complex. It can involve factors such as sizes, culture depiction-representation and interpreted aspects. Item selection can unfortunately sometimes be controversial, as Carl Sagan learned with the Pioneer Plaque project (Sagan, 1979). Censorship controversies, familiar to scholars, scientists, librarians and publishers, are a possibility when drawing up a time capsule's "shipping manifest" to the future. The challenges of leaving word about the very existence, exact location and possible interpretative guidance regarding a time capsule's contents may be most perplexing. Such dilemmas may surpass in difficulty even the pressing questions about preserving the gift to the future. Time capsule phenomena are excellent thought experiments and excellent empirical field tests of a wide armamentarium of time capsule tools. Time capsule studies employ evidentiary and analytical techniques widely used by communication theorists, archaeologists, archivists, museologists, conservationists and forensics specialists.

Content selection can follow either tried-and-true traditional or explore new uniquely contemporary pathways. It was the selection of available contents, not that of interpretive aids or the utilization of various preservation techniques that was considered the most difficult task of the 1938 Westinghouse Time Capsule Committee. Not even the "delivery" of "invitations" to recipients of the distant future was considered to be as difficult as selecting what artifacts and items of information were to represent the industrial civilization of the late 1930s to the unknown world to come of the year 6939. The selection of contents cannot ultimately be separated from methodological considerations of providing interpretive aids, and selection is a most significant act of interpretation. Undoubtedly limitations of capsule size emphasize the difficulties of artifact and information selection, but even with a 2000 cubic foot Crypt, the Oglethorpe University project still had to carefully select samples of our civilization's artifacts and information. Compared to the cramped seven-and-a-half-foot-long, torpedo-like Westinghouse "Cupaloy" 1938 Time Capsule I, the accommodations of the 1940 Oglethorpe University Crypt of Civilization do seem almost ludicrously spacious. There was room to include a mini-sized windmill for the generation of electricity for the (regular sized) motion picture projector enclosed in the Crypt. A "Language Integrator," a product of the American Mutoscope Co., was placed in the center of the roomy time capsule, but a hand crank powers that device. In the case of the 1938 Westinghouse Time Capsule I for the 1939 New York World's Fair, the instructions for constructing a large microfilm reader or motion picture projector must itself be read on microfilm, resorting to the small enclosed microscope as an aid.

Whatever difficulties compilers of

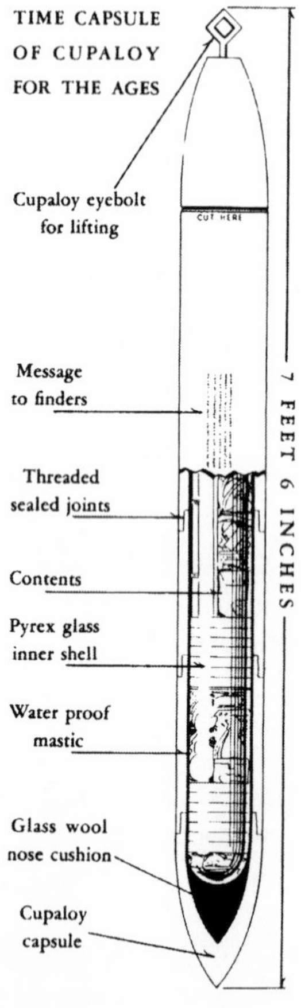

Cross-section view of the original Time Capsule, buried September 23, 1938

Cross-section of the original (Westinghouse) Time Capsule, "buried" September 23, 1938, deposited at the 1939-40 New York World's Fair for 5,001 years (virtually the idealized time capsule archetype). Note the Cupaloy hull's diamond-shaped eyebolt, and the diagram's original labeling. (Courtesy Westinghouse Historical Center, Pittsburgh, PA.)

these millennial encyclopedic time capsules experience in amassing suitable contents to represent their age to the future, it is a virtual certainty that the future retrieval committees will have as their principal problem the interpretation of the contents. (We will assume that something of informative value will be preserved.) Figuring out what an assortment of records meant and what artifacts were used for will be at least as challenging to receivers as were the senders' decisions about including items. Linguistic interpretation, while often daunting enough, is not the only sense in which interpretation can be challenging. Relating the cultural finds of one past to a present, would-be receiver is even today a major challenge to every guide to practically any historical site, park or other set of exhibits. The interpretation of contents and even of the reason(s) why a cultural deposit was targeted to a future culture and period is always a major challenge. This linguistic and cultural interpretive topic is a reoccurring theme in time capsule studies. Topics such as archives, information transfer studies, millennial time capsules, ancient writings and SETI-like space-time capsules constantly touch on the problematic character of the interpretative effort.

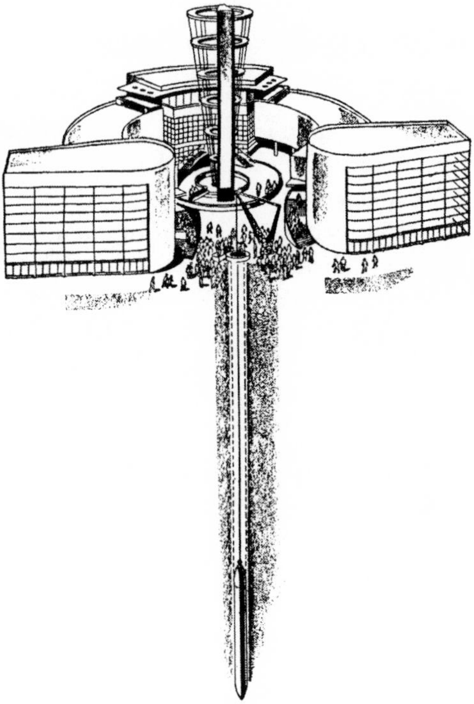

The Westinghouse Time Capsule of Cupaloy, 1938–6939, shown at its deposite site, the Westinghouse Building, New York World's Fair 1939-40. Common brochure image from those days. Obviously not drawn to scale. (Courtesy, Westinghouse Historical Center, Pittsburgh, PA.)

Ways to obtain time capsule "vessels" include store-bought, build-it-yourself and "take-it-off-the-shelf" approaches. It's possible to buy a time capsule, manufacture one "in-house," or just literally take a jar off a shelf for the time capsule vessel. A variety of time capsule vendors and makers advertise from time to time in various magazines, etc. It's possible to buy any size and add further preservational features. One author has described the world of commercial time capsules sellers as providing "packaging" for the future (Gleick, 1999, pp. 253–54). The Smithsonian's Conservation Analytical Laboratory's website posting *Time capsules: Archival protection* lists names, addresses and pricing for various time capsule manufacturers (Smithsonian Institution, 1999). There is a cash cost involved, rather than the labor-intensive build-it-yourself approach. Various small Millennium 2000 inspired "family archive" time capsule kits were available. The Smithsonian vended a *Time Capsule Kit* with an eight-section pamphlet of detailed instructions and a variety of archival type sub-containers (*Smithsonian Kit*, Item 2025, 1999). Other, more modest time capsule kits were vended in the "Turn of the Millennium" period. For example, the Boston Museum of Fine Arts and other organizations featured kits in their gift catalogues (*Family Time Capsule*, 1999, p. 49; *Ark to the Future Time Capsule*, 1999, p. 5). Usually these kits consist of a how to booklet, "memory albums," and various materials to record personal, children's or family mementos. They might just have only a simple molded tin box or plastic container as the outer hull. These sorts of personal time capsule kits resemble the sort of archival records commonly stored by many agencies, albeit with some added degree of "sealing up" which can add to the time capsule aura of the container. Candy "tin" containers and cereal boxes were marketed as time capsule kits in the 1999 period of millennium 2000 pre-celebration (*M & M's Time Capsule Kit*, 1999; *Millenios Time Capsule*, 1999). Apparently one need merely dump in a supply of one's favorite messages and mementos for a few years to produce a rudimentary time capsule. How long such cardboard and plastic time capsules will last is an interesting question, although five years is a long time in a teenager's life. An early example of a kit, long before the Millennium 2000 craze, was an invitation to *Make your own time capsule* (Caney, 1990). The book of instructions included a plastic time capsule container.

If you still want to do it yourself, and have neither the technical capability (nor the urge!) to build anything resembling a sturdy vessel, there is a third way to acquire a time capsule. That approach is to simply fish around for a simple, ready-made, take-it-off-the-shelf container from somewhere around the home or office. A children's 5-year time capsule could be as simple as a jar put on a shelf. The author did this with a mere five-year time capsule for 1997–2002, consisting of a sealed, labeled glass jar of coins, notes and instant photos taken on the spot. The occasion was a youth services program activity at the local public library (Jarvis, 1997). Five years is a long time in the life of a pre-adolescent child, and it will be interesting to be there to open this short-term time capsule transaction. That public library, incidentally, also sports two more substantial time capsules, one sealed for 50 years (1988–AD 2038) and another for 100 years (1988–AD 2088). These two capsules are more substantial both in their packaging and time-spans (Hughes & Jarvis, 1999). The two cylindrical (ca. six inches in diameter and ca. three feet long) time capsules are entitled "April 11, 1988; to the Future Citizens of Pullman — these time capsules contain a gift of Pullman's past created specially for you by the Pullman Centennial Committee, the City of Pullman, and the children and teachers of the Pullman School District." Contents include coins, newspapers, T-shirts, symbolic pins and a city symbol, as well as some dolls. One is a full centennial example to be opened on the bicentennial of the City of Pullman, Washington. (The other, its lesser twin, is sealed for just 50 years.)

Just about any large academic library has a special collections or archives department, where the long-term sequestering and preservation of various written materials is a primary mission. Many items are sealed away in these special areas, sometimes under the terms of a legal deed of gift for a specified number of years. Librarians and archivists aren't strangers to preservation needs, as can be seen from the wide variety of acid-free folder and box products they utilize on a regular basis. Universities, technical schools and institutions with technical facilities might even choose to have one custom-built in house. This was how the Washington State University Time Capsule (1990–AD 2040) was built in a mechanical engineering class's design project wherein students each submitted a proposal (Jarvis, 1990–1991). One could even construct such a state-of-the-art multi-millennial time capsule, complete with an inner pressure hull and segmented compartments. The interior would require acid-free wrappings surrounding an encyclopedic range of exhibits, pressure-sealed with an atmosphere of inert argon gas. Millennia-spanning preservational challenges such as interior degenerative changes, geological processes such as earthquakes, invasive incidents from nearly construction projects, or the prospect of possible sporadic site anti-vandalism security lapses can become rather daunting threats to the integrity of a site. Therefore, such millennia time capsules could well be massive institutional commitments, not to be undertaken lightly.

Preservational technology for time capsules has both classic and avant-garde dimensions. Even with a good time capsule vessel at hand, preservational maxims regarding content selection and packaging are essential. A five-page preservational guide with additional advice about project ideas and content selection was produced as a technical leaflet in 1992. It includes advice on opening, stabilizing and inventorying contents, as well as on pre-sealing and deposit work (Fraser, 1992). One recent set of guidelines is a National Preservation Office leaflet on time capsules (*British Library*, 1999). Yet another is an 11-page *Report* on time capsule preservation techniques published by the Canadian Conservation Institute (Barclay, 1989). A third is posted on the Conservation Analytical Laboratory's website (Smithsonian Institution, 1999). That Smithsonian agency is on the leading edge of the conservator's art (and science) and has taken on the preservation, stabilization and restoration of national icons such as the 1812 "Old Glory" U.S. flag from the Fort McHenry naval bombardment (Wu, 155, 1999, pp. 408–09). Generally, subject index headings such as "Library materials—Conservation and restoration" or "Archival materials—Conservation and restoration" yield good information on preserving the contents of many time capsule contents, especially paper materials (*Preservation of library & archival materials: A manual*, 1999). The Smithsonian's five-year test program on a variety of materials for time capsule preservation was just completed in 2000 (Smithsonian Center for Materials Research and Education, 2000). Test results included determining that some "accelerated use" (aging by heating) yielded an inadequate simulation of the aging processes of actual 200-year-old oil fine art painting compounds. The unknowability of the ultimate needs and uses of future recipients of preserved specimens, such as nineteenth century–collected biological preparations in formaldehyde, etc., is noted (Gorman, 2000, pp. 378–80). Also featured is the U.S. White House Millennium Council's "National Millennium Time Capsule" project, exhibited and stored away by the U.S. National Archives and Records Administration. That capsule is a (U.S. logo) wavy-flag shaped metal alloy repository with contents representing end-of-the-century America. Selections were made by a variety of students and experts. The capsule was exhibited in NARA's Rotunda before the actual sealing of its contents later in 2001. Note both the typical "fungible" deposit date and the not uncommon memorialization of Millennium 2000 with a 100-year only span time capsule ("National Millennium Time Capsule," 2000).

Essentially, everything that is being considered for insertion into a time capsule container should be checked against such preservation checklists. Standards, materials and techniques may well evolve over time. Even the most astutely executed preservational protocols and archival grade materials cannot guarantee protection from *force majeure* (acts of God). Those factors, such as war, civil disorders, vandalism, fire, volcanism, earthquakes, flood, weather and other disasters are potential dangers to time capsules as with other structures. One area of preservational technology that is very applicable to time capsule studies and projects is the mass deacidification of books, print and various library materials (Kellerman,

1999, pp. 170–77). Time capsule entrepreneur James Kusterer has patented a "gaseous diffusion paper deacidification" process specifically applicable to time capsule usage; in fact, the illustration from the brief patent description is apparently of a standard decades-old vendor design "Time Capsules, Inc."–type time capsule (Kusterer & Hind, 1974). Although state-of-the art techniques, materials and designs are important, senders should always bear in mind that their future recipients might well regard our (eventually-to-be) past efforts as primitive. One thousand-year-plus time capsules obviously need more preservational effort than lesser time spanning vessels. Placement choices are an important preservation factor. A vital preservation issue with a time capsule is where and how it is installed. Often a specially prepared outer housing or exterior vault is recommended, especially for millennial-spanning, target-dated vessels. Generally, burial in the ground is not recommended because of water damage possibilities. Time capsules have been placed just about anywhere. In addition to burial options, Earth-based time capsules might be deposited in a foundation, or put into some other section of a structure. They may even be on public display in a lobby area, inside a transparent case. In Syracuse, New York, a time capsule was on display right inside an office building's entranceway, a small aluminum box on a granite cube. The inscribed box informed passersby that it contained predictions about the year 2000, and that it was sealed at a June 14, 1966, commemoration of the company's new insurance service center (Jarvis, 1979). It combines a newer type of content, a list of predictions about the people in the world of the future (the magical year 2000 target date). Its commemorative building function is a 5,000-year-old tradition. The author found this time capsule through an architect who just happened to see it. Apparently, few passersby had taken note of that time capsule over the years, "hidden in plain sight." It's not a bad way to leave word of its existence as well as protect and preserve that deposit as an accessible, but ignored background phenomena. There may be little to back up the legal protection of such "modern" (1876 on) artifacts, written records, media images or sites from vandals or other meddlers over millennia. National historical monument status *might* protect a deposit site as long as there is sufficient legal, linguistic or cultural continuity of authority.

Leaving word is a perennial challenge that can be met by various approaches. The twin Osaka Expo 70 Time Capsules have two special features that may both protect the deposit and publicize its existence (*The official record of Time Capsule Expo 70: A gift to the people of the future from the people of the present day*, 1980; Peters, 1940b, pp. 1–32). We will examine these in detail in our millennial time capsule discussion. The Osaka

Castle Park burial site of these twin capsules is a good example of a context of historical reverence, a commemorative precinct in which the two specimens are buried. The practice of excavating the centennial twin of this twin capsule installation capsule once every hundred years after the year 2000 also serves as a preservational check-up, and also reinforces and develops the traditions concerning this site. The problem of notifying future time capsule recipients of its existence and whereabouts is fundamental. The original Osaka Expo 70 Time Capsule project planners appear to have been initially unaware of the 2000-cubic foot Oglethorpe Crypt in Atlanta, Georgia (*The official record of Time Capsule Expo 70*, 1980). A separation of only 30 years, the language barrier and the absence of the "time capsule" term in the original Crypt name appear to have contributed to their oversight of the Crypt's existence. How then will future recipients of 8113 CE know about the Oglethorpe Crypt and its intended, targeted retrieval date? No one can say for sure, although there have been attempts to maximize the probability that scholars in future millennia retrieve these "miniature museums." The Oglethorpe Crypt project included producing and distributing an announcement distributed to a variety of libraries, archives, monasteries, etc., telling of the basic nature, exact location and target in the area of twentieth century Atlanta (Peters, 1940b, pp. 1–32). Oglethorpe Crypt souvenir metal admission "tickets" were sold then as $1 promotional items:

> CRYPT OF CIVILIZATION In Consideration of Gifts Made By (The Donor) To the "Crypt of Civilization" in the year AD 1939, any descendant of the above-named contributor of the 187th generation, upon presentation of this card, will be admitted to the opening of the Crypt on Thursday, May 28th, AD 8113, Noon 1940 OGLETHORPE UNIVERSITY [Peters, 1940b, pp. 1–32].

Promotional techniques like that might keep alive the knowledge of a time capsule's existence. Six millennia may be too long a time span for any advertising campaign, sign-system or finding aid to convey even the simple, basic message of a capsule's existence. How many (few?) 6,000-year-old messages, 4,000-year-old messages or ancient writing collections do we have to refer to now! The scope of past knowledge and literary output transmitted to our time is clearly very limited. In comparison to the current mass of written and other contemporary knowledge available, the fragmentary character of millennia-old ancient written records appears sparse. The existence of the Oglethorpe University Crypt of Civilization is also recorded on a metal notification plaque's text describing the extent of the deposited contents:

> Near a place once known as Atlanta, Georgia, there was a house of learning known as Oglethorpe University. Its exact location can be determined by a triangulation from Stone Mountain and from Kennedy Mountain prepared by the US Coast and Geodetic Survey in the 20th Century. If the 80th Century scientists will dig at the specified spot they will come upon a crypt of stone 20 × 10 × 10 feet guarded by a door of stainless steel. Within the crypt will be found writings and objects of great value encompassing the best examples of civilization and knowledge known to the world from the time of the death of Christ to the mid–20th century [Peters, 1940b, pp. 1–32; Jacobs, 1945].

One can designate a "timed capsule" site by an engraved plaque, like that on the massive Oglethorpe Crypt door, or by a granite block like the Westinghouse Time Capsules I and II in New York. Time capsules even sit around out in public, although this is probably not a good idea for the long-term missions of millennia time capsules. The MONY Company had a 1966–2000 time capsule on display inside the lobby of a corporate office building doorway in Syracuse, New York (Jarvis, 1979). As its target date drew nearer, someone was bound to take notice of the approaching target date posted on its display case. Although rarely noticed, such public postings can draw sufficient attention to finally accomplish notification goals. That is generally a reliable procedure for a time capsule spanning a short period like 36 years, especially if building security is consistently provided. Time capsules might be cared for "in perpetuity" after depositors have died by including provisions about them in real estate property deeds. Information about a time capsule can then be preserved as long as the record of the deed survived. Restrictions to protect such repositories might be incorporated into the property ownership records. Identification of the exact location, composition, contents and target date of specific time capsules could be clearly listed therein, with specific instructions for custodial care and retrieval techniques. All this could be stipulated in accordance with a locale's legal property practices and record office storage arrangements. Property deed documents could conceivably include the requirement that a plaque or other marker be maintained. That way, messages about a time capsule's existence could be perpetuated, at least throughout the viability of the prevalent legal-political culture. Time capsules are commonly lost (*10 lost time capsules*, 1991; *The 9 most wanted time capsules*, 1999).

Humor is an especially valuable "commodity" to send to the future. It may be a difficult perspective to convey such linguistic and cultural representations (especially over millennium-long time spans) to culturally quite different recipients. One author has observed that in his work *The past is a foreign country* (Lowenthal, 1985; 1998). That is also true of any possible future era. When some electronic mail users encounter a similar cultural-humor problem, they utilize statements such as "(humor intended)" in their messages, or cobble together smile faces and other "emoticons" out of combinations of various ASCII characters. E-mail and historical distancing effects sometimes seem to make broad or low comedy read as dry humor, more like the *New York Times* humor essays of our contemporary writer Russell Baker than, say, the low comedy of the ancient playwright Plautus (Bremmer & Roodenburg, 1997). Consider for example a satire of British political life based on a BBC-TV production series (*Yes, Minister: The diaries of a cabinet minister, Rt. Hon. James Hacker, M. P.*, 1981). This satirical work of fiction is part of the microfilm collection for the BBC Time Capsule (Moncrieff, 1984). Will it be read as satire in 2,000 years? How will that matter to its future interpreters? How broad a satire will it seem to be, and how accurate? Although the chances are perhaps greater that the overall spirit of the work may be interpreted as a satire, it is less likely that many allusions and "send-ups" will be readily comprehended. Some of the potential complexities can be seen in the cultural history of changing humor in antiquity, Medieval Europe and the modern Western world (Bremmer & Roodenburg, 1997).

It is impossible to predetermine with any high degree of probability the comedic (or non-comedic) interpretation of just about any "received" time capsule's contents. Intended or unintended humor may result when a time capsule is sealed or opened or commented on. In fact, some people find it difficult to take any aspects of time capsule studies seriously. Serious students of many popular culture topics report encountering similar attitudes from time to time. This contemporary attitude toward time capsules has its healthy aspects. It does seem almost *de rigueur* that any popular press feature on time capsules ought to be written with a great deal of tongue-in-cheek. The pompousness of some traditional cornerstone or time capsule ceremonies may bring on a reaction of dismissive humor. Maybe the human condition's being "poised on the precipice of eternity" has something to do with the curious mix of humor and awe that people tend to in time capsule experiences and ceremonies. There may be more than a bit of personal existential angst, an awareness of individual biological mortality, when senders or receivers suddenly contemplate centuries and millennia of change via time capsules. Such reminders that a time capsule will survive us can overwhelm the sender. One does not have to be an adherent to some Buddhistic doctrine of impermanence to grasp that people alive in the year 2000 are not likely to be alive in 8113 CE, or

A fanciful depositor's sacrificial angst: Any depositor can experience feelings about what a time capsule might or might not do for them, both in *their* "present" time and in their envisioned future reception of such a capsule. Note the shifting focus of the sacrificial motif from Other to Self. (Courtesy Carol Lay, *Story Minute*: "Time Capsule," 2001.)

even by 2076! Stanley Edgar Hyman and St. Clair McKelway's 1953 *New Yorker* article "Onward and upward with business and science: The Time Capsule" is a humorous review of the 1938 Westinghouse Time Capsule at the 1939-40 New York World's Fair. Its substantial, critical treatment has a droll twist, a leavening of some of the pompous aura surrounding the 1938 Time Capsule of Cupaloy and its 1939-40 New York World's Fair heyday. Consider one satirical e-magazine's take on an "experience" of opening a time capsule. *The Onion* posted a satiric feature about a fictitious time capsule event: "Newly unearthed time capsule just full of useless old crap," 1999). As is the case with good satire, it is right on the mark about a solid, serious point. We really don't know for certain what will interest people who retrieve what is sent to them. Recipients can be disappointed in the meager contents or apparent pointlessness of some time capsule projects or contents. One actual example of such a disappointed group of time capsule openers at the University of Washington is not far off the track of *The Onion*'s satiric piece (Harrington, 1999, p. B2). The "real" University crowd is reported to have met the display of the real, paltry contents with boos, and one spectator called the contents "dumb." Nor can anyone guarantee or lock in desired interpretations of what may well be strange phenomena to future recipients (Elder, 1956).

Various idiosyncratic time capsules demonstrate how real projects can be whimsical too. Not all time capsules are necessarily dull, routine relics in a can. In fact, there are a number of especially idiosyncratic time capsules. Time capsules can commemorate noted individuals with their contents, or even celebrate corporate milestones with an unusual capsule design, such as that of a washing machine corporation ("Maytag celebrates 80th anniversary of its first washing machine with washing machine tub time capsule festivities," 1987). Marilyn Monroe, Winston Churchill, Martin Luther King, the Maytag Corporation, the Canadian Broadcasting Corporation and at least one 1957 Plymouth automobile are identified with unique historical repositories about their namesakes. In the case of the washing machine and the automobile, actual full size machines are buried ("Churchill 'library' in 5 inch time capsule," 1967, p. 182; Grossman, 1987, p. 1; Povich, 1987; Remington, 1954, pp. 16–17; "Time is on Marilyn's side," 1987, p. 11). Comedian Bob Hope deposited a Hollywood memorabilia time capsule with an Oscar award statuette, a letter from Ronald Reagan and various other relics from "Tinsel Town" ("It's hooray for Hollywood," 1987). Reagan not only included another letter in a later time capsule, but clearly found the use of the allusion to a time-encapsulated message an excellent rhetorical device to couch views on future situations ("Reagan-Mondale Presidential debates," 1984). Consider the messages written by

Albert Einstein and others in the 1938 Time Capsule of Cupaloy. These "To Whom It May Concern" letters are written with seventieth century recipients in mind (and 1938 ones too?). Einstein's reads in part:

> Furthermore, people living in different countries kill each other at irregular time intervals, so that also for this reason any one who thinks about the future must live in fear and terror. This is due to the fact that the intelligence and character of the masses are incomparably lower than the intelligence and character of the few who produce something valuable for the community. I trust that posterity will read these statements with a feeling of proud and justified superiority [*The book of record of the Time Capsule of Cupaloy*, 1938].

Leaving word in such a (presumably?) ironic manner is an interesting attempt to convey more than the mere fact of a past presence. Einstein's final line might be seen as an ironic comment on the future's failure to achieve universal, lasting peace. Or it could be read as a naive dreamer's blind faith in a "futurism" of an inevitable, automatic progress. If universal, lasting peace exists in the seventieth century CE, then the naive dreamer, the sarcastic sage, may be hailed as a lofty visionary to whom is attributed the ability to foresee the greatness of a future age. If the killing goes on, but at *regularized* time intervals, then the inhabitants of the seventieth century could conceivably manage to congratulate themselves and Einstein as well! Einstein had left a 1936 letter in a cornerstone with similar sentiments, although with less subtle irony and more bluntness (Dukas & Hoffmann, 1979, p.105). Einstein's 1936 curmudgeonly message for a private time capsule helps clarify the subtler nuances of his 1938 letter's utterances in *The book of record*. Any individual or group can transmit its feelings and works to the future, in a series of time capsules from the same sender over a period of time. Innovative messages to the future might include predictions, declarations of our age's (i.e., the senders' own) aspirations, hopes, fears, etc., about "The Future." Some deposits might seem rather unusual to recipients in the distant future. But which items will seem unusual, and in what ways?

How to conduct time capsule ceremonies and projects. Having looked at how contents might be chosen, and how a vessel might be bought, built or taken off the shelf and used, let's look at ceremonials, rituals and event planning for "send-offs" and openings. Articles stipulating some principles for ceremonials exist. There are innumerable historic precedents of specific capsule repositories to guide us, including the 1938 Westinghouse Time Capsule's various ceremonies. Herbert Mulford's seven classic observations about cornerstone ceremony characteristics are still a good basic guide, even when a more contemporary, secular or unique variation is desired (Mulford, 1950a, pp. 66–67; 1950b, pp. 84–85; 1952, pp. 60–61, 75–80). Two "how-to-do" articles that are brief guides to the practical, ceremonial aspects of cornerstone and time capsule laying are worth consulting when planning a ceremony (Brower, 1972, p. 29; "Foundation stone ceremonies," 1936, pp. 1–85). Both articles are geared to the architectural profession's obvious need for such advice from time to time. Today's time capsule sealing ceremony teams need to value combining a touch of tradition, emphasis on relevant contents (to the sending audience), audience-community participation activities, an evocation of the possible future recipients' time and place, a bit of humor and a shorter (secular or otherwise if wished) ritual without pomposity. By ritual, we merely mean any establishment of a pattern of practices for the ceremonial program, secular in tone or otherwise. It needn't imply any mystical requirements. The bigger the contents and the longer the target span, the more work that should and *will* go into the sealing or sending ceremony. The era of sacral, formal rituals by priest-kings leading processionals with attendant pageantry is now largely a thing of the past, a matter of antiquarian curiosity. However, an appropriate ritual ceremony is something that contemporary time capsule depositors still might consider. The International Time Capsule Society's list of "8 tips" on organizing a time capsule project is instructive of "dos" and "hows" such as scheduling and registering the capsule (*8 tips on how to organize a time capsule*, 1999).

One paradigm case of a major time capsule project was the "Washington State Centennial Time Capsule, 1989–2389." This 400-year, multi-chambered, "incremental" time capsule is deposited in the state capital of Olympia, Washington. Under the leadership of Knute "Skip" Berger, it included coordination of promotional work with schoolchildren's' participation as "Keepers" (Berger, 1990; *Centennial Time Capsule fact sheet*, 1989). The time capsule is to be last opened on Nov. 11, 2389, that state's five-hundredth anniversary. Updates of the time capsule are to occur at 25-year intervals after the 1989 installation, starting in 2014. That program of serial deposits will provide a continuous "chain of remembrance." Each safety deposit box within the larger safe-type capsule is dated with the year scheduled for its intended deposit. The bottom shelf in the time capsule safe has offerings for the 200 ten-year-old children recruited in 1989 to open and take to use in 25 years. This is apparently the first such long-term serial-redeposit time capsule. It gives a tangible motive of retrievable contents to its perpetual generations of keepers. All the while it is accumulating "layers" of time capsule deposits, a process intended to continue over the centuries (Berger, 1990). Such pod concepts provide excellent ways to perpetually accumulate capsule-upon-capsule in one master repository. This pod-cluster-serial approach in positioning of time capsules is reminiscent both of various traditional archival-record-type repositories and of some Millennium 2000 time capsule sites. The "Tropico Time Tunnel, 1966–2966" and the "Washington State Centennial Time Capsule, 1989–2389" can mark and commemorate centennials and millennial anniversaries without having exact target date spans of 100 or 1000 years.

How Do Literal Time Capsules Function as Archival Collections?

If capsules are considered archives, in what ways do they resemble and differ from the technical-professional definitions of various archival materials and collections? Archival collection-oriented aspects of time capsule deposits merit detailed examination. "Archival" record management functions are a key distinctive aspect of time capsules. Archaeologists emphasize the importance of artifacts *in situ* as professionally oriented use-wear interpreters. They tend not to dwell on an important asset that can feature in a time capsule to the future, an appreciation of the importance of archives as a guide to historical interpretation (Ascher, 1974). There is more to the study of the past than just our interpretation of physical artifacts, since a major factor in doing historical interpretation is the contribution of the written record.

Sent and received time capsules can be considered as deliberate archaeology. Messages and relics contained in them are a sort of archive. Archaeologists are performing a role reversal when burying a time capsule deposit. Archivists routinely access, preserve, secure, store, describe and interpret collections of written and other records accumulated for posterity. A key goal of professional record managers— effective long-term archiving of documents— has been characterized as a "time capsule" function. This is another instance of the myriad uses of this apparently indispensable term (Benedon, 1978, p. 109; Barcan, 1955, pp. 218–226). In a 1935 unsolved murder case in the Pend Oreille, Washington, area, a county sheriff initiated his investigative theory as a 1989 graduate student of old archives (Egan, 1992, p. 7). He reportedly experienced the 1935 case files as a "time capsule" from that period. It was a very different era (the Great Depression), when the black marketing of stolen items such as butter, bacon and shoes allegedly led to the apparent murder of one official by another. That investigator allegedly detected from his persistent study of old newspaper and other archival leads evidence of an apparent complex bureaucratic cover-up lasting over 50 years. These usages of the time capsule term for various archival-type records are not really that metaphorical. Old official records, historical collections and archives have literal parallels to customary sealed-up time capsule "contents in a can." "Archives" is used here in a broadly popular, less-technical sense. Record managers' professional procedures do parallel many customary time capsule procedures, requiring professional practices, careful filing arrangements, maintaining and monitoring of storage areas and the following of regular procedures focused on historical preservation and access principles. All of these concerns apply to actual physical container time capsules, and to organizations' records management, traditional archives, special collections and manuscript-type collections also (Benedon, 1978, pp. 108–27; Barcan, 1955, pp. 218–26). The Latin term *recordor*, source of the English word "records," means both to remember the past and to think about something in the future. The records that one hears of in the contents of some time capsules are not necessarily just the narrowly conceived archives that we have discussed. Those commonly dubbed "archives" are more properly, more technically characterized as special or artificial collections. The linking of a future and a past are what matters with these broadly representative collections of items ("*recordor*," 1952, p. 471). "Record management" can be more than office filing drudgery. The sealing away of a non-current group or collection of records scheduled to be made available after a given number of years are a concept familiar to every archivist. In relation to their "time capsule" value is a "50-year rule" with personal recollections and personal mortality, the common fading of personal recollections and ultimately even the death of those in one's demographic cohort. During recent occurrences of 50-year-plus memoirs, reunions and formal celebrations of World War II veterans, one memoir noted the fading of accuracy in one's memory. Over half of the demographic cohort of World War II veterans were deceased at the time of his publication (Kotlowitz, 1997).

Technically, most time capsules' collected contents are more akin to what are known in libraries and archival work as "artificial" or "special" collections, not "archival record groups." That is the strict technical sense of how professional archivists and special collection curators define these terms. Archivists can use these technical distinctions to identify records produced by a person (i.e., "manuscript collections"). Items grouped in a narrow-range collection based on governmental, commercial, educational or other organizations' activities are designated as "archives" (Gracy, 1977, pp. 2–3). "Special collections," also known as "artificial" collections, can be eclectic groups. Most rare book library collections are treated as special collections. Because of its miscellaneous character, special collections may have a general meaning. Many time capsules and their miscellaneous contents could be termed artificial or special collections in that archival lexicon, using the terms "artificial" and "special" to distinguish time capsules from (usually) narrower-scope collections. Time capsule contents can differ radically even from most traditional manuscript, "special-artificial" collections, as well as from archives in the narrow technical sense. Most archival, manuscript or special collections do not contain a massive percentage of three-dimensional artifacts ("realia"). Most archival record groups or even artificial (special) collections do not necessarily present extensive views of an age's life, art and culture. They might not constitute a synoptic recording of a whole civilization. Such record groups may be systematic documentation from an enterprise's, agency's or association's work product. Even broader scope artificial collections (such as special, rare or other narrowly-defined book collections in libraries) and manuscript collections are usually narrower than a millennial encyclopedic time capsule collection's scope. Time capsules such as the 1970 Osaka's Expo 70 no. 1, the 1938 Westinghouse Time Capsule I, or the 1940 Oglethorpe University Crypt of Civilization can be in effect miniature museums with a broad collection of items as well as long-term piles of written "archival" records (Gracy, 1977). Time capsules often exceed the customarily narrower scope of a standard archival collection. It's not impossible that a time capsule consisting of a creative family's personal and genealogical documents might be deemed a "manuscript collection." Overlaps in designations and differences of interpretation characterizing these particular types of collections are always possible.

As technical archival practice, a time capsule is an extended deposit of historical records or other documentation, "sealed" (that is, kept confidential) for a specified time. A time capsule's records are often selected expressly to portray a preconceived view, not unlike many other recollections, records and histories. A time capsule's retrievers might find its contents' historical value differing from a sender's intent. Its records might be narrowly edited and selected, diminishing potential value. Usually projects identified as time capsules differ from standard storage shelf boxes of archival, manuscript or special collection–type historical records. Students at the Moscow, Idaho, Junior High School and the Pullman, Washington, schools helped the Latah County Historical Society prepare a 100-year "Moscow-Pullman Time Capsule" project. It consists of several record boxes stored with other archival materials at the Society's facility (Staszkow, 2000, pp. 1A, 2A). Those record units will not be sealed away. Items can be reviewed on occasions such as school graduations. They may be deliberately added to over time, a practice that differs markedly from most time capsule projects. Cost savings and retrieval-notification issues were considerations in opting for the record box approach to housing the contents. Subtractions from groups of record boxes are theoretically possible over time.

The selection of a time capsule's contents may closely follow the archivist's ethic. Consider the "synchronic" (cross-section from a given time) inclusion of the complete microfilmed contents of a sample of issues of 1938's newsstand publications. They were included in the 1938 Westinghouse Time Capsule (Pendray, 1939). Such *respect du fonds,* basically a reasonable attempt to conserve the original deposited record arrangement, is clearly in accord with the Archivist's Code (Gracy, 1977). Similarly, the inclusion of many whole articles of the *Encyclopedia Britannica* in the 1938 Westinghouse Time Capsule, while not as archivally desirable as is a complete collection of encyclopedias, does offer significant evidence of the interests of the 1938 senders. Archival-type written records and images are potentially of greater historical importance as time capsule contents than are well-preserved material culture items sealed away in capsules for their potential archaeological significance. Deliberately selected time capsules' contents might not always be later seen as all that archaeologically significant. Whether helpful or not in interpreting an era's material artifacts (such as tools, grooming aids, toys or *objets d'art*), it is easier to see that time capsules certainly do have great potential significance in the preservation of civilization's written records, and in their interpretation as well.

Preservation of records should have two major goals. Furnishing an extensive amount of cultural, historical records to future recipients can aid in more adequately interpreting a prior age. Secondly, they should present to future recipients the way the past era interpreted its own culture for itself. Any time capsule that does not attempt something of both is not fulfilling the archival potential inherent in the opportunity of a time capsule occasion. Interpreting ourselves by sending such messages to the future (and thus simultaneously interpreting our world to ourselves at the same time) may be the greatest element in the popular appeal of time capsule phenomena.

While every time capsule may not always provide reliable or comprehensive information on life as lived in a past age, they might be useful not only in preserving archives and other perishable items but also in presenting the aspirations and predictions of one's own age to a future time period. Time capsules may be best at providing to the future the spirit, the conceits and foibles of a bygone era, even if material culture use patterns are readily deduced from archaeological digs. They may communicate that a sender's cultural era did want to send time capsules. That is itself potentially interesting. That is at least a minimal motive behind humankind's perpetual creation of time capsules, to express that primal desire to reach out to the future. This profound need to conduct cultural and information transfers across vast spans of history may well be a primal dynamic. It has become in our own era a refined set of specialized technical practices as well. Even archives and other record sources must be interpreted. One can do so in an endless variety of ways. Archivists, librarians, lawyers and other scholars know that the existence of a copious archival record often fuels hermeneutic efforts, rather than invariably dictating foregone conclusions.

Although time capsules are archival repositories as well as archaeological sites, they differ from typical storage practices in traditional archive, special, manuscript or museum collections. Most archives do not reflect such an extensive view of an age's life, art and culture, since archival record groups usually consist just of the systematic records of one agency or person's work. Even artificial, special collections and manuscript collections may be grouped by one subject, theme or other special purpose (Gracy, 1977). Most such collections of records tend to be far narrower than the scope of a millennial, encyclopedic time capsule collection such as that of Osaka's Expo 70 or the Oglethorpe University Crypt. Only major time capsules attempt this synoptic compilation of knowledge, the multi-millennial encapsulation of a whole "museum" of popular culture and formal knowledge from one age to another. Time capsules are miniature museums and long-term archives.

Archival record storage groups are usually filed, stored, boxed, shelved or sealed away for their intellectual contents and to be preserved from less than appropriate present socio-cultural-physical treatment, conditions and surroundings. Traditional, deliberately deposited time capsules are sealed to preserve their physical contents for the future. These contents usually contain written media relics and other artifacts. The intellectual contents of time capsules are usually publicly known at the time of sealing, although the intellectual climate of future interpretive efforts is unknown at the time of deposit. The systematic, deliberate sealing of relics in elaborate dioramas does bear some similarity to the sealing up of a time capsule. The opening of a museum display case is not usually a grand occasion, even if the museum does not customarily afford continuous display of a case's actual contents. Millennial-span time capsules are more easily set apart from regular archives than are centennial-span time capsules.

Duration, size, and the more grandiose statements of purpose associated with millennial time capsules mark them as a distinctive category of historical record preservation. Time capsule studies are a distinctive "auxiliary science of history" topic area, as are chronology, numismatics, archives or technical archaeology. Time capsules fit into, appropriately enough for such time-traveling devices, a variety of categories. In part that is due to their hybrid status of part archival record and part archaeological deposit. Burial is certainly not essential for a time capsule's collection of contents although isolation from touch and view seem to be the norm. Without such physical isolation from the daily humdrum passage of time, much of the mystery of a time capsule experience can be lost. Time capsule related subjects and topics seem to travel "synchronistically" across academic disciplines, while the actual physical time capsule vessels themselves move or travel diachronically through historical epochs and eras.

How can banks' safety deposit boxes be considered time capsules? Various tales of fiction feature them as almost magical devices that present various treasures or other talismen of fate-altering power appearing from the past. *Zero Effect* (1998) and *Marathon Man* (1976) are two motion pictures where the safety deposit box motif is featured as a dramatic plot device. The prior deposit of some valuable or other in such an enclosed bank-within-a-bank is not only a place to protect something that might be needed later. Rather, it can be a fictional plot device wherein something vital preserved from the past by the sender is later revealed. Recipients may learn deep historical secrets about the sender, or receive great treasures deposited long ago. Safety deposit boxes can be forgotten and lost to their depositors. In Fountain Valley, California, one such depositor received the "new millennium" news that his $250,000 worth of family heirlooms in the bank's safety deposit program had gone missing! The bank cited several moves and mergers for this dropped transaction (Shepherd, 2000, p. 13). In their "times-up" status as abandoned property at least some of the contents of some safety deposit boxes literally become museum pieces. In Texas, the contents of abandoned bank deposit boxes are turned over to museums and historical societies, at least until some relative of the original depositor can establish a valid claim to the items (Garcia, 1991, p. H1).

One good example of what is technically known as a manuscript collection is the Jerome Robbins Collection. Reporters and laypersons simply call these personal collections "archives." These are the personal dance production archives of the renowned ballet choreographer Jerome Robbins, who died in 1998 at the age of 79 (Dunning, 1999). This extensive collection consists of over 100 packing boxes, set sketches, costume sketches, posters and photographs. There are as well more than 30 file drawers with shows and ballet business papers categorized by a range of subject file terms such as "shows," "contracts," and "Exception and the Rule." The *Fiddler on the Roof* archival record series consists of 54 individual folders. Twenty-four sets of journal entries spanning 1971 to 1982 are sealed away and will not be available to the researcher public for 13 to 15 years in accordance with Robbins' deed of gift to the receiving archive. The depository in this case is at the New York Public Library's Performing Arts' Dance Collection, recognized for its a major world dance research materials. Its major audio-visual archive was established in 1964, thanks to Robbins' earlier endowment gift of earnings from the smash hit musical *Fiddler on the Roof.* The records include New York City Ballet material (with Robbins as resident choreographer). The treasures include a 1974 letter to the dancer Fred Astaire, many other personal mementos relating to dance production in our times, and items associated with various celebrity names. In what way is this collection of personal dance archives a "time capsule"? To a degree it is, although it wasn't found in a jar, or a dump, or at a volcanic disaster site. Nor was it deliberately buried or launched to another star system. Time capsule interpretative experiences are relative matters. Robbins' extensive collections over his lifetime are a personal archive with an evocative range. He lived and created vivid visions and it is fun to hear about what he saved and something of what he experienced. Some of his papers are deliberately sealed for a specified number of years. His relics make that world live again — all of which make this Robbins "manuscript" collection a sort of time capsule–like experience. A recent case of the court records of the Alger Hiss 50-year-old Cold War spy case being "unsealed" by judicial order illustrates the related character of classic time capsules and varieties of traditional archival records ("Hiss grand jury archive ordered unsealed," 1999).

Four unique "Centennial" time capsules were sent to the future. These are archival, milestone "centennial" time capsule deposits. "Centennial" here refers to their celebratory time spans of less than 1,000 years, not necessarily just the 100 years of a literal centennial event. One hundred year (or less) time spans are the mode, the typical size of most time capsules targeted for less than 1,000 years. Two cases are really the first true, literal time capsules in the modern target-dated sense. The second two were bigger, deposited after the 1876 era, but had under 1,000-year spans.

The Philadelphia "1876 International Centennial Exposition" gave birth to the first two documented target-dated time capsule projects. The first was New York City publisher Mrs. Charles Diehm's "Century Safe."

The second was the precursor, the core of a later capsule-type project, a 500-photograph memorial exhibit. It was destined to grow into pioneering Chicago photographer Charles D. Mosher's "Memorial Safety Vault" (*Centennial Safe*, 1976; Diehm, 1882, pp. 194–200; Viskochil, 1976, pp. 95–104). Unfortunately, Mosher's "Memorial Safety Vault, 1876–1976" was "interrupted" during its transmission from 1876 to 1976 when it was prematurely opened on August 12, 1908. That was 68 years before its intended Bicentennial target date (Viskochil, 1976, pp. 95–104). Its supposedly secure location was lost when the Chicago City Hall building was razed. Its ca. 10,000 cabinet photographs (portrait-type) and other memorabilia were unsealed and then openly displayed in a museum after the demolition of its host building. The "Century Safe, 1876–1976" survived its final sealing in 1878 to be reopened (as originally target dated) in the U.S. 1976 Bicentennial, and hence became the first successful time capsule when it completed its designated target span. In the checkered past of the invention of the targeted time capsule, it could be argued that Charles D. Mosher's "Memorial Safety Vault, 1876–[1908]–1976" was a first, at least the first to be sealed-deposited, although it did not complete its mission. Mrs. Diehm's "Century Safe, 1876–1976," wasn't actually sealed until 1878. Technically, what Mosher exhibited in Philadelphia in 1876 was merely the beginnings of the contents for his later devised "Vault," while Diehm's "Century Safe" was exhibited as an actual, ready-to-go time capsule device at that 1876 Fair.

The "Vault for the Future," 1956–2056, is an exemplar of the time capsule as a large content, significant sealed Centennial-style archive at George Washington University, Washington, D.C. Its 24 boxes of records are a lot of historical documentation for just a 100 year time capsule ("Vault for the Future," 1956, p. 22)! This large collection of archival records is essentially indistinguishable from various mundane special collections of the sort often sequestered in various libraries and organization's storage until those records are needed for reference or historical research. The Vault's boxes were sealed in a special, buried container for a 100-year period with special ceremony. *Voilà*! Yet another time capsule had been launched into the future, and another information-time-transfer experience had begun. This mundane consignment of 24 storage boxes of historical records was noteworthy because it was a time capsule event.

Filing away archival boxes is not usually an occasion for such celebration. The "Vault" is an object lesson not only of the relation between mundane archive records storage and time capsule storage but also because it has a large amount of contents for a typical centennial type time capsule. The "Vault" is a true, narrowly defined time capsule because it has a target date for its opening, rather than being an indefinitely deposited foundation deposit or cornerstone repository. The occasion of its sealing marked the dedication of its host building. In this narrower technical sense, its boxes of historical contributions are more of a special or artificial collection. They were donated by organizations such as the U.S. Air Force, the U.S. Navy, the U.S. National Council for Aeronautics (precursor of NASA, the U.S. space agency), the U.S. National Bureau of Standards, the American Institute of Electrical Engineering, the American Society of Mechanical Engineering and the American Institute of Mining and Metallurgical Engineering. The June 20, 1956, lowering of the "Vault" vessel into its deposit space dedicated the Tompkins Hall engineering building at George Washington University.

The 1950s were not as grandiose as the 1930s in the production of time capsules. Although there were more cases of time capsules in the late '40s and '50s than in the late '30s, they were not as big as the Oglethorpe Crypt in size or as well publicized as the 1939 World's Fair 1938 Time Capsule. Still, "24 boxes of items" sound like a parcel freight consignment rather than the few tokens which constitute the contents of many cornerstones or centennial, commemorative time capsules. In this instance, the "delivery" will take a century. Twenty governmental agencies and various professional national and local societies picked items for the 24 copper boxes for the Vault. Contents included documents, photographs, reports, strain gauges, ball bearings, gas turbine blades, a gyroscope and ballpoint pens ("Vault for the Future," 1956, p. 22). Customarily, such a century-spanning effort would hold only a smaller collection of mementos. The "Vault for the Future" is unusual in that its wholesale package of extensive information and items is more common in much longer time-spanning, 1,000-year-plus capsules.

The "Tropico Time Tunnel, 1966–2966," is a 900-year deposit that links a prior Centennial civic event and a future Millennial celebration. The Time Tunnel is in a 10,000 cubic foot mine shaft in Rosamond, California. Photographs of the packing events look like a massive rummage sale, with a wide variety of items being placed in long-term storage. For a major-size time capsule, though, it has a shorter time span and less work on preservational packaging techniques. Nor was its full volumetric capacity apparently packed with a maximum amount of contents. In November 1966, the Kern-Antelope Valley Historical Society in Rosamond, California, loaded this non-active gold mine with a wide variety of objects and books. Then a large block of concrete was used to plug the mine entrance, and the Tropico Time Tunnel was off and running for 900 years, until the Kern County millennial celebration in the year 2966. Nine hundred years is a long time for the commemoration of a civil anniversary. It is a relatively short term compared to the major target-date spans of "encyclopedia of civilization" time capsules like the Oglethorpe Crypt of Civilization, the Westinghouse 1938 and 1965 Time Capsules I and II or the Osaka's Expo 70 Time Capsule no. 1. The Tropico Time Tunnel may be a bit sparse in its interpretational presentation efforts, as in its employment of preservational technology. Scenes of its eclectic donations seen in photographs taken during the multi-year packing process look like the offloading of a major shipment of brand new merchandise into a warehouse. Wear patterns on objects can provide valuable historical information that these brand new still packed boxes of furnishings might not be able to supply the future. Although an interesting "pop" commemorative deposit, it doesn't necessarily measure up to the 61 century treasure trove preserved in the Crypt of Civilization at Oglethorpe University. The scope of the Time Tunnel's deposited items does not appear to include a great deal of academic or other written knowledge, as does the Oglethorpe Crypt. Note that this Tropico Time Tunnel has an unusual time span for a time capsule, being deposited for 900 years. That's a rather atypical time span for a time capsule. Time capsules more often seem to have a mode of 100-or-less year minimal time span, or else they exhibit the characteristic of being targeted for at least 1,000 years or more. Due to the sealing date marking the centennial of the founding of Kern County, the Tropico Time Tunnel's 900-year commemorative span does tie in both with centennial celebrations and millennial memorials. It is targeted to be opened on the millennium celebration of that County's founding ("Preserving the present," 1967, p. 27; *Program from the "Tropico Time Tunnel Sealing Ceremonies,"* 1966).

Donated artifacts placed into the Time Tunnel in the multi-year packing period included a motorbike, paper drinking cups, U.S. football game signage, bedsprings, rope and various lamps. Edwards U.S. Air Force Base personnel provided items, including a scale model of the experimental supersonic XB-70, Rocket Propulsion Lab archival documents and related memorabilia and records from various experimental testing projects (Bunker, 1966, p. 3). This 900-year storage project includes enough furnishings for a complete house, with a television set, clock radio, washing machine, motorcycle, mannequins, bird cage, typewriter, Sears-Roebuck shopping catalog, a packed suitcase, vitamin pills, vegetable and flower seeds, pots and pans, a bread toaster, fishing equipment, rifle, bicycle and a Willie Mays World Series autographed baseball. Documentation, records and books deposited included various religious documents, several on the then popular "Is God Dead?" controversy. Written materials inserted included 1966 *Los Angeles Times* issues, assorted other newspapers, magazines, and a library of topical books ("Mine becomes unique time tunnel," 1966).

Those four are good examples of real time capsules. They are deliberately sealed deposits intentionally target-dated for retrieval. The time capsule aspiration is to bridge the cultural-time span in order to reveal something (big or small) from the senders to a future period. As we shall see, not all time capsules really exist as physical vessels. That fact can be at various times an irrelevance, an annoyance, a triviality or just a very interesting kind of experience. Next, we examine various guises of the "as-if," or notional, time capsule.

CHAPTER 2
Notional and Archaeological Time Capsules

Some "Notions" of the Time Capsule

There are all sorts of metaphorical, "time capsule–like" experiences which do not refer to any sort of physical, real container at all, but are commonly called "time capsules." The catalyst for such time capsule experiences need not be a deliberate deposit, or even be a physical object. Various sorts of time capsule phenomena could be characterized as notional, somehow "made-up" time capsule experiences. These various notional types can differ considerably from one another. The expression "time capsule," the function itself, and a variety of time capsule–like experiences are not always limited to literal references about physical containers. It need not refer just to a storage vessel deliberately sealed with items and deposited for a definite retrieval target date. There are several sorts of notional time capsule–like phenomena other than archaeologically induced ones. Instead, "a time capsule" is often used in a metaphorical or other notional sense, perhaps more commonly than it is used to describe real time capsules. In addition to the term's vague metaphorical usage, there are other notional uses of that label, including archaeological site metaphors, fictional literary devices and "as-if-real," thought experiment cases. There are at least four notional senses of the time capsule experience, including the widely used general metaphorical one. Archaeological interpretations are the one form of notional, metaphorical time capsule experiences that are indeed based on tangible, physical remains.

Some time capsules can serve as "trophies," "awarded" to the future by their senders, as this capsule scene from the 1954 Sacramento, California, State Fair suggests. (Courtesy Sacramento Bee Collection, Sacramento, California, Archives and Museum Collection Center, *http://cgi.sacbee.com/ourtown/history/statefair/fairtime1954.jpg*)

These three notional usages of the "time capsule" term are not based on any physical objects: First is the common metaphorical sense of the term, as in the phrase "That house is a perfect 'time capsule' of 'Populuxe' design style." Secondly, there are cases of an "as-if-real" time capsule: "What would you put in a real time capsule, if you were actually going to do one?" category. Thirdly, there is the vast treasury of works that use the physical time capsule motif as a device in literature such as science fiction, historical fiction or satire. Considered merely as a metaphor, "time capsule" can mean virtually any cultural collection of items, or even just one item. Virtually any microcosm of artifacts, images or writings might be characterized as a time capsule of any place, time, social group or situation. Everything from a stuck drawer, a sunken ship, a suddenly buried town, a year's anthology of newsmagazine articles, to an efficiently managed archives' record group has been characterized as a time capsule. The term is now freely used as a metaphor for any apt characterization or evocation of any distinctive time period. The phrase was coined by G. Edward Pendray's project for the 1938 Westinghouse Time Capsule at the 1939-1940 New York World's Fair. "Time capsule" replaced an earlier suggested term, "time bomb" (Jarvis, 1988, p. 338)! The term has become ubiquitous, and is even useful for biographical, nostalgia-oriented cataloguing of specific illustrations of antique ephemera (Biersdorfer, 1998, p. 4; *dMarie Time Capsule*, 1998). The 1938 Westinghouse Time Capsule of Cupaloy was a real physical vessel, not an "as-if" fictional motif or metaphor. Consider what aspects of a situation, microcosm or set of real things call to us as a time capsule of some past time, condition or relic. That "something" would identify exactly what makes that situation a metaphor for a time capsule. Of course, not everything called a time capsule, whether notional or physical, is necessarily a good time capsule. Any sort of time capsule experience needs to be identifiable as a phenomenon wherein someone can be made to feel taken back to a different sort of past time in a palpable, visceral sort of way. That is what is usually thought of as a time capsule experience, whether it's induced by a physical capsule, a notional listing of objects for an as-if-real time capsule or by a fictional literary device.

People can be said to have had a "time-capsule experience" when they indicate that they feel taken back in time — when they have been seized by the past as surely as if they had actually opened a real, deliberately deposited time capsule deposit or vault. That is an okay meaning of the time capsule term, provided that we bear in mind an important point. A mere casual use of the term in an off-handed manner may not be as significant as what people detail in descriptions of their time capsule–like experiences. For example, how does someone describe the sudden evoking of a past world? The inspiration might be a time capsule experience of an "as-if proposal," a spectacularly preserved sunken ship, or a suddenly buried extinct city site. There are limits to the use of these fuzzy time capsule definitions. However, if just about anything old or from the past is always (or often) called a "time capsule," the significance of such a notion can be vastly diminished. Then no *a posteriori* archaeological deposit or imaginary as-if notional case would be considered a time capsule. We will look at the literal and metaphorical role of archaeological sites such as sunken ships and buried cities as time capsules later. For now, our focus is on "as-if-real" and fictional literary types of notional time capsule motifs and references.

How "As-If" and Fictional Time Capsules Work

We can imagine what we might put in a real time capsule and when we would want it opened, *if* we were to do one. If no actual vessel were then sealed up containing items, that would be an "as-if" time capsule project. Such thought experiment–type time capsules can be useful exercises in contemplating not only what would be best to include in a time capsule, but also how our times might be interpreted from those posited contents. These are *a priori*; "posited" but not "deposited" notional cases of time capsules!

These "as-if-real" capsule exercises can be valuable self-reflective exercises regarding our own cultural period in history. *McCall's Magazine* ran a 1976 article positing just such an "as-if" time capsule ("*McCall's* Time Capsule," 1976, pp. 50–51). When seeing that story title in an index, one might assume it would be about an actual capsule. The editors would supposedly just tell the readership how they had actually carried out, or planned to carry out, a capsule project. They would describe a real, physical installation, detail its container's specifications, its contents, sealing ceremony, deposit site-vault, target date for its hoped for retrieval-opening, and any reflective, analytic value to our era. That was a wrong inference in this instance. The story was about what *McCall's* staff would have put into a time capsule, *if* there had been a real physical one. It was a "let's pretend," notional exercise and its time capsule was only an as-if one, a literary conceit. Various celebrity figures suggested the sorts of things they would ideally want to include in such a desiderata type of time capsule. Those included Walter Cronkite's suggestions about selecting mail order catalogues and Sunday newspaper magazine sections for the advertisement contents. At first our reaction was that this article wasn't about a real time capsule, and it's not of course. However, that as-if time capsule exercise has some value. It's the reflective, analytic value to our own era that such an "as-if-real" time capsule can contribute. That is more than just a vague increase in historically oriented consciousness or a tad of journalistic levity. A more recent example is a 1999 *Popular Mechanics* article that asks the readership what they would put in a time capsule ("Time immemorial," 1999, p. 68+). A French mixed media museum show about the 1980s consisted in part of several six or seven foot high transparent containers of typical period objects. Each was called a "time capsule" (Taylor, 1989, pp. 31–33). One reporter used the capsule notion to do a satirical brief in the *Washington Post Magazine* (Cohen, 1986, p. w9). Examples of these as-if, posited time capsule content-interpretive exercises abound. They can serve political rhetorical ends quite well, whether as a notional, pseudo-

1965-era legislative satire or in the 1984 lofty presidential electoral debate (Boller, 1996, pp. 16–17; *Reagan-Mondale Presidential Debate*, 1984). Premeditated exercises in the hypothetical selection of ideal items for a time capsule and concerning speculations about their reception-interpretation are in a sense imaginary. This is in a different sense than how fictional literary motifs or after-the-fact archaeological sites are usually considered "notional" time capsule experiences.

Much of the cognitive effort associated with a real physical time capsule is actually analogous to dreaming up an ideal set of notional-type time capsule contents targeted to some specific time period. Such a set of desiderata is the sort of "phase-one" behavior real capsule projects planners should do. Such "hey kids, let's put on a time capsule!" exercises can convey something of what our world is really like, or what we would like our world to be like. We could just *contemplate*. We might contemplate what would we like our world to be (or seem to be) like to future interpreters. We might also ask what this sort of self-interpretive exercise reveals to us about our own time, place, situation, town, nation or institution. These results might all be attained through an "as-if" time capsule exercise (including the message to the future aspect), and the introspective self-examination effect as well. So these pretend time capsules can have *real* time capsule consequences, and evoke real capsule experiences. That is an interesting facet about time capsule encounters. They tell us more about what is actually going on when people send time capsules or when they receive them, even if the time capsules are make-believe ones. The "*New York Times* Times' Capsule," 2000–3000 AD project was formally launched with a magazine issue featuring preparatory "10 best of" list making essays in 1999. Even without a final phase physical vessel time capsule resulting from these thought pieces on contents-item selection, the essays themselves are interesting metaphorical time capsules in and of themselves. "The best of the Millennium," an April 18, 1999, "Special Millennial Issue" of one week, addressed the topic of what the future will think of "our" Millennium 1000–2000 (*New York Times Magazine*, "Special Millennium Issues," 1999). The editors write that they at first thought of their time capsule as solely an imaginary exercise.

Time capsule notions are common in fiction. One can find time capsule motifs as fictional plot devices in historical fiction and "futuristic" science fiction tales. Time capsule–like experiences have even been satirized in parodies of archaeological method, where possible interpretation of past eras and evidence is presented as bizarrely off the mark. First, it is necessary to define the "as-if-real" time capsule before we can consider the varieties of time capsule phenomena in various kinds of fictional literature.

Our survey here is by no means a complete one. Specifically, we will not extensively examine time machine–travel literature, not compile tales of relativistic time dilation and not systematically list alternative universe motifs. Although all of those cases of speculative fiction can be insightful regarding human motivations and perceptions of time capsule phenomena, considerations of space require their exclusion. It is interesting to consider a metaphorical synonym from the French language rendering of "*La Time Capsule*" with the more picturesque "*machine à voyage dans le temp*" (Rothenstein & Gooding, 1998, #1). One can read this French phrase as the English translation: "machine that travels in time"—in other words a time machine. Time only marches on of course. Always forward goes time's arrow.

The novel *I, Claudius* features a "time capsule" from ancient Rome. *I, Claudius* was written as if it were the Emperor Claudius' secret history of his Julio-Claudian family. Robert Graves practices the literary conceit of having his secret history scroll finally extracted from its preservative-fluid filled jar, 1900 years after the end of Claudius' reign. Graves' notional papyrus scroll "time capsule" seems to be based on an actual ancient Mediterranean preservation methodology used in the antique Mediterranean world's documents, including some Dead Sea Scrolls, various such Hellenistic deposited documents, etc. In the (real world) Dead Sea Scroll instances, sealed pottery jars were used rather than lead (or stone) containers, and cedar oil prevents moths and worms from feasting on precious writings (Wright, 1982, pp. 4–5). *I, Claudius* features an oracular encounter with a prophetess who foretells his unwilling ascendancy to the Roman Imperial throne, as well as the retrieval of Claudius' secret history 19 centuries into the future. The Sibyl ironically observes that in approximately 1900 years, the stammering Claudius' "time encapsulated" written history scroll will clearly "speak" to those future inhabitants (Graves, 1934, pp. 3–13). That is essentially a time capsule concept in all but name, featuring deliberate preparations, preservative technology and even a target date. For example, on the page after the Sibyl's prophecy the character Claudius notes that

> ...I shall treat it with a preservative fluid, seal it up in a lead casket and bury it deep in the ground somewhere for posterity to dig up and read. If my interpretation be correct it will be found again some nineteen hundred years hence [Graves, 1934].

Human beings themselves serve as time capsules in the tales *Looking Backward* and *Sleeper*. Edward Bellamy's utopian novel *Looking Backward: 2000–1887* is about a wealthy young man who (due to the accident of a house fire) spends not just one planned night in a hypnotic sleep but 113 years! He is a sort of Victorian Rip Van Winkle (Bellamy, 1887). The hero of this mawkish romance and Poe-like nightmare experiences the utopian perfection of the Boston of 2000 AD. Meanwhile he muses on the contrasts between the Boston of the years 1887 and 2000. At the end of this utopian tract, the protagonist Julian West resolves to take up the profession of a historian who has lived the past, not merely studied it. This is no premeditated resolve to transmit oneself as an historical message through time. However, the result is, like Pompeii AD 79 site and exhibits, a time capsule experience. Here a metabolically inhibited human can function like a biological-specimen–type time capsule, a concept satirized by Woody Allen in his 1973 film *Sleeper*. Eventually practical techniques of cryogenics or some other metabolic inhibition technology may make it possible to routinely freeze large numbers of people and other species. One day a time capsule might contain a metabolically inert historical reporter who will actually live out the fantasy of looking backward over centuries or millennia. Eventually it may be possible to dispatch such human historical sources to the future, so that beings of future places and times will have in their present historians who actually lived in the distant past, "now" viewed as "history." Gregory Benford's novel *Heart of the Comet* envisions Halley's Comet as a space-bearing colony for a group of twenty-first century Earthlings. They ride within it on its near-century-long elliptical orbit out of the solar system and back again (Benford, 1994). Whether this technological prospect would be viewed as an unmixed blessing is an interesting question. Another space science fiction novel, *Contact*, features a one-person spacecraft launched as an interstellar sarcophagus (Sagan, 1985). Future historians will, however, have their own interpretations of our times, no matter what or how we of the past tell them of our experiences and views! Their own perspectives about the past (our present) may conflict with the "disinformation" from our transmitted time capsule interlopers. Historians can breathe easy, though. No Rip Van Winkle is likely to challenge historiographical principles (in this fashion at least) for a while. "Life in Somebody's Times" tells the tale of a time capsule as an "accessory after the fact." That 1966 short story tells of Harrison Cramer, Ph.D., whose time capsule project gives him the opportunity to covertly deposit the corpses of his murdered wife and her lover alongside some more abstract, formal records of twentieth century civilization (Bloch, 1967, pp. 9–16). One can speculate that the tale drew some of its inspiration from Time Capsule II of the New York World's Fair of 1964-1965, although the burial metaphor is a common one to describe time capsules. In fact, tombs— Egyptian tombs, especially (complete with human specimens)—can serve today's archaeologists as "time capsules." (The future life for which mummies were preserved turned out, of course, to be the life of the archaeologist or museum patron!) At first, one might be inclined to view this tale as just an obscure, macabre variant of fictional time capsule literature. Viewed in the light of the sacrificial origins of building foundation deposit customs, this story may not be quite as marginal as it might at first appear to be. (The time capsule in the story is to be placed in the wall of a new academic building at the local university.) Another modern murder mystery tale incorporating a time capsule theme was an *Alfred Hitchcock Presents* TV episode ("The West Worlock Time Capsule," 1957). Perhaps an audience's realization that a capsule deposit event is a "premature (albeit decent) burial" of a cultural sample might explain the funereal solemnity of some time capsule sealing events. The audience's "hats off" at the October 1940 "Immortal Well" final sealing-off burial of the 1938 Westinghouse Time Capsule I is one example.

The film (and novel) *2001: A Space Odyssey* begins with human technology at the dawn of man, a result of mysterious instructions from an alien space-time Monolith (*2001*, 1968; Clarke, 1999). When people at a lunar science base in the year 2000 discover a Monolith "deliberately buried on the Moon," it is because of the technological heritage initiated by one of these alien devices! The spacecraft Discovery is dispatched on its Jupiter space exploration mission to trace a signal from the lunar monolith. Its sole surviving astronaut undergoes a fundamental transformation in an encounter with (yet another) example of an extra-terrestrial monolith. In *2001*, alien space-time capsule Monoliths actively alter human beings at two points in history. The monoliths are benchmarks of humanity's rite of passage from beast, through technology, to a mysterious penultimate transformation. The alien Monoliths are time capsules molding the alpha origins and omega destiny of human technological and psycho-spiritual existence. One "five million years to Earth" kind of time capsule is in the science fiction–horror film *Quatermass and the Pit* (1967). It features a London subway excavation site where a five million-year-old Martian space ark has been unearthed, its cargo consisting of dormant locust-like beings. The space missile deposit activates its telepathic powers and reveals its demonic-type, mega-hypnotic creature. The scientific wizard Dr. Quatermass saves the day. It was aptly termed a "time capsule" in a TV program listing (*Five Million Years to Earth*, 1984, p. 54). In the novel *Rendezvous with Rama*, a "space ark" is experienced as a dynamically interactive sort of time capsule. Arthur C. Clarke tells the tale of a human encounter with an alien vehicle in the year 2130 (Clarke, 1973). A vast spinning cylinder 40 kilometers in diameter and 100 kilometers in length has traveled into the solar system. Inside, a human survey crew gradually discovers that this huge space vehicle is activating a mini–physical exhibit "ride experience" from the senders' world. The automated space ark, on some unfathomable mission, provides the Earthmen many adventures exploring its artificial environment. "Rama" draws power from the sun and then leaves the solar system, off to the Magellanic Clouds outside the Milky Way. Here, as in *2001*, human civilization experiences a device sent from an alien interstellar civilization. But in *2001*, the space-time capsules interact with humans in a way that makes it clear that the monoliths were intended for such purposes. In *Rendezvous*, the ark-like cylinder uses our solar system as a sort of galactic pit stop. The human encounter with Rama is unilateral. Human efforts do not register on the cosmic scale of Rama's operations. That cosmic road-show time capsule is not necessarily intended just for Earthlings, nor does it reveal all of its mysteries to mere bystanders. *A for Andromeda* tells of mid–twentieth century British radio astronomers who receive a lengthy set of do it yourself instructions broadcast from another galaxy (Hoyle & Elliot, 1962). The three-part message consists of mathematical designs for a computer utility, a program for it and a database to input. In this manner, an alien intelligence from another galaxy transmits a blueprint for an artificial intelligence to Earth. What happens then, only a spoilsport would reveal. The time capsule as algorithm may represent an advanced form of time-capsule technology, which may be valid for speed of light interstellar communication.

Asimov's *Foundation Trilogy* includes an ancient pre-recorded, pre-timed hologramic simulation of a personal appearance in a far distant future. In the first book of Asimov's science fiction trilogy *Foundation*, Hari Seldon, the "psycho historian" founder of an elite Foundation, has arranged to have a "time vault" constructed on the alien world where his Foundation is based (Asimov, 1974). Long after his death, he is thus able to appear via a prerecorded hologram-type technology to give historical and political advice. All of these appearances were to be at times he had previously calculated would be turning points in Foundation history. At radioactively timed intervals, he is able to make a personal-like appearance in order to deliver appropriate speeches recorded before his death. This could be viewed as a form of highly technologized ancestor worship. It can also be seen as a forecast of some possible time capsule prototypes which inhabitants of Earth in 6939 AD may themselves construct. It presents a kind of hologramic video broadcasting from the past.

Robert J. Sawyer's novel *Starplex* is a twenty-first century world where an interplanetary federation confronts the ultimate cosmic questions of immortality, consciousness, space-time travel and the ethics of sentient interactions. This is all brought to the reader via a supra-advanced space base called Starplex. The crew lacks the means to physically move themselves forward the billions of years necessary to solve a pressing communication need with far-future residents. Therefore they prepare a futuristic cubic time capsule with all but one side posing a series of questions, leaving one side open for the answers (Sawyer, 1996, pp. 131+). The time capsule is retrieved as targeted by its depositors-schedulers, eons later. After it is found, the distant future recipients send it back to the original senders via a time machine. Now, however, the blank side is inscribed with an answer from its retrievers. The distant future receivers of the blank capsule side have managed to send back their answers from that far distant future via this expected space-time travel "shortcut" system. The novel's time capsule construction and "site depositing" are both done with verisimilitude, given the ultra-technological phase of the (fictional) Starplex space-faring civilization.

Gregory Benford's "world-line splitting" novel *Timescape* uses a deliberate time capsule device, a very long-term bank safety deposit box, to let the twenty-first century's transmitters of a message back to 1964 know that their message has been received (Benford, 1992). "Time Shards" is one entry in the great time capsule debate between the "How-to" and the "Why not to" exponents. Another Benford story, "Time Shards" sides with anthropologist Robert Ascher and the "Why not to build" school of thought. Such views about archaeological finds as time capsules include various examples of anthropologically oriented reasoning against the value of deliberate time capsules, or at least of the low utility of doing so, if our intent is to really leave a slice of life behind (Ascher, 1974). In Benford's futuristic tale, the Smithsonian Institution has constructed a "Bimillennium Vault" complete with radioactive clocks that will trigger radio broadcasts to the U.S. Trimillennial inhabitants. Meanwhile, one Smithsonian scientist has worked out a method to reconstruct voices and other noises. Those signals were supposedly recorded on ancient clay pots incised with string while being shaped on a potter's wheel. That scientist affirms his suspicion that time capsules (such as his Vault) will be as enigmatic as are the sayings of the Anglo-Saxon voices he retrieves from the subtle groves formed during the shaping of an old clay pot. They comment on the Anglo-Saxon potter who intended to seal up spirits in his pots to pass on to the future. The bemused protagonist-archaeologist notes that the incomprehensible, highly idiomatic, folklore-type incantation of that ancient man is worthless in understanding that past time period. As an interesting historical coincidence, the fictional analytic laboratory is located in the Smithsonian's 1876 Arts & Industries Building. That real-life building is actually the current (year 2002) U.S. repository of many exhibits from the 1876 Philadelphia Centennial Exposition. Not all fictional tales dealing with time capsules take such a "why not to build" line. Science fiction stories of time capsules can expand our awareness of the potential or actual significance of time capsule phenomena.

A time capsule is used as a classic Doomsday testament in the novel *On the Beach*. In that nuclear doomsday world, the last, lingering survivors of radioactive fallout deposit a time capsule at the South Pole. They hope to inform any future intelligent species of the former existence of human civilization (Shute, 1957). They do not, incidentally, include instructions on producing atomic fission! When the world's last surviving humans perish (in Australia), they have left behind a radioactive Earth and a time capsule. That is an example of a terrestrial time capsule deposited for any intelligent species which might evolve (or land) on Earth in the distant future. "History Lesson" is a short story about an Earth-group of technologically primitive survivors of an encroaching ice age who deposit an ancient treasure of odds and ends in a mountain cairn (Clarke, 1959). Venusian archaeologists attempt to interpret the contents of that cairn when the find is taken back to Venus. Clarke's Venusian archaeologists have certain interpretive successes. They learn how to project a film found in the cairn, and they guess that the film is an artistic representation of the lives of Earth people. They fail to understand what is going on in the film. In particular, they do not succeed in understanding the meaning of the last English line printed on the film, which proclaims a cartoon company's imprimatur!

Ethnologically based satires such as that of the "Nacirema," the "Weans," and the "Motel of the Mysteries" are telling "mal-interpretive," fanciful analyses with a moral for time capsule interpreters too. Expositions of time capsule philosophies and techniques can sound quite grand—or is it grandiose? When interpretive arrangements go wrong, they can go *horribly* wrong. As a worst case type of scenario, consider the hilarious consequences pilloried in Horace Miner's ethno-linguistic satirical article "Body Ritual Among the Nacirema" (Miner, 1956, pp. 503–7). The interpretive outcome satirized there is archaeological and ethnographical, rather than a deliberately deposited and targeted capsule project. This satire of interpretive technique is right on the mark. This classic article exposes the underlying ethos of the bizarre "Nacirema body ritual" in pseudo-ethnographic style treatment of typical Nacirema hygienic beliefs and practices as superstitious, alien and injurious. (Hint: "American" is "Nacirema" spelled backwards!) The author cites by way of introduction such required points in the ethnographic canon as to the location, economic basis and legendary origins of the Nacirema. Miner then characterizes the fundamental belief of Nacirema body ritual to be a perception of the human body as ugly and prone to decay. The only way to prevent this fate is seen to be through the practice of body ritual. In his satiric appraisal, some American ethnocentric blinders are (hopefully!) removed by characterizing mundane American bathroom, domestic health care and grooming practices as a set of alien, sadistic, magical, irrational rituals in a 1950s United States. Cultural labels that tend to obfuscate rather than explicate the medical role modeling of the ritual practitioner are exposed to a droll put-down. The spelling of satirized names is either reversed or replaced with an alien-sounding one with pseudo-magical or superstitious connotations. Thus a familiar 1950s U.S. material culture is presented as a strange set of exotic long dead practices. Once the author has initiated this demystification of a culture complex (by an alien-sounding renaming), it is easy for the reader to discover additional symbolic meanings of "Nacirema ritual." The article neutralizes cultural defenses while analyzing a configuration of plausibly bizarre practices and works to convince the reader that "Nacirema latipso" temple-worship is a process of mortification. The actual functional values of the "Nacirema latipso" are perceived to be backward and alienating. It is the reverse, literally and figuratively, of the official credo of the "American hospital." Miner's analysis puts American culture into a sort of conceptual time capsule and takes it out as "Nacirema culture." The result is not only a linguistic garble, but is also an example of cultural misunderstanding—or is it rather a case of penetrating historical hindsight? It is even possible to elaborate on Miner's Nacirema analysis (with medicine chests, etc.), constructing an even more extensive satiric pseudo–cultural system explaining mid–twentieth century North American civilization as a web of superstitious practices, as this author found himself doing after reading Miner's work. Consider, for example, that each Nacirema medicine chest has an attached mirror. One could reason that such "shrines" figure prominently in reinforcing the Nacirema self-image!

Another satire of a long lost ancient world of America is that of the fictional "Weans" (Nathan, 1974). An archaeologist engages in a mock speculation on the cultural practices of the "Weans" 6000 years in the future. He calls the Washington, D.C., site "Pound-Laundry" and wonders what it was that was being washed there (by the ton)! *Motel of the Mysteries* is a broad archaeological-style satire. Relics from a twentieth century Florida motel are mused over from the novelistic vantage point of a distant future (Macaulay, 1979). Note how these various archaeological satires blend into the fictional time capsule category as well. This satirical approach to archaeological-cultural interpretational error is alive and well today. Witness *The Onion*'s satirical positing the literary conceit that there once was an ancient race of "skeleton people." Their skeletal remains are drolly inferred to have been the full biological extent of that ancient people, not just the residual bones of archaeological evidence ("Archaeological dig uncovers ancient race of skeleton people," 1999)!

Obviously in fiction, themes of time capsules can be expanded to cover time capsule experiences afforded by all sorts of objects, occasions, story devices and ancient documents. Some tales feature human beings as paradoxical time travelers. Even in the mundane, humdrum real world, just having a chance to send or open a real time capsule, or even just encountering some object, place or situation from another time, can sometimes evoke a sense of the capsule's past time. Then we leave real time in a sense, and travel back or ahead in time, to some time or place far different than what we conventionally inhabit. We have glimpsed in those archaeological satires the prospect of totally getting it wrong, or perhaps seeing "it" as sheer satire. "It" equals here a valid interpretation of another (past) culture, from a cultural period now past or a different cultural zone in another part of today's world. In those as-if worlds, the "it" of correct interpretation is problematic, because people make up their own time capsules in a sense.

Archaeological Finds and Other Accidental, Metaphorical "Time Capsule Deposits"

Consider how a real, accidental deposit (an archaeological site, etc.) might lead us to imagine an *a posteriori* interpretation dubbed a time capsule–like experience. The *a posteriori* depositional character of archaeologically suggested "time capsule" feelings evoked by shipwreck sites and well-preserved, extinct cities is based on physical sites and artifacts, unlike the other three notional, imaginary kinds of time capsules. When looking at the *a posteriori* character of archaeologically suggested time capsule experiences, we need to consider the feelings that are aroused by such non-deliberately deposited archaeological finds, which include shipwreck sites and dug-up cities. There are basically two different origins of physical, tangible time capsule archaeological find–based experiences. One is the accidental, "archaeological site find" type of experience, when such remains evoke a scene of past lives as an immediate contemporary presence to a present-day beholder. Those are metaphorical usages based on real items and situations. That kind of archaeological time capsule experience is to be distinguished from the archaeology of *a priori* deliberately deposited ritualistic and magical votive deposits (Klinger, 1987, pp. 301–5; Merrifield, 1987). The *a priori* archaeology of time capsule experiences is derived from the deliberate deposit of dedication-foundation consecration items, which are the precursors of the modern deliberately targeted time capsule experience.

Archaeological finds as after-the-fact, *a posteriori* time capsules can be the penultimate metaphorical time capsule–like experience. On the other hand, archaeological interpretation–type time capsule experiences are made-up constructs, notional "as-if," and metaphorical phenomena. The *a posteriori* attributions about remains of the past owe much to the human imagination, no matter how objectively rooted in actual relics or sites. They should not be considered as somehow inferior, quasi- or pseudo-time capsule experiences. They are, rather, just very different, distinctive kinds of such experiences, based as they are on real items and situations. With either the accidental-happenstance (archaeological sites) or the deliberate (foundation dedication, etc.) kinds of deposit, we can see the *a posteriori* time capsule experiences that can result from musings on such finds. Deliberately deposited container-type time capsules bear a strong relation to archaeologically based interpretation in at least two senses: first in examples of accidentally deposited time capsules, and secondly in those cases of the retrieval in one way or another of deliberately deposited time capsules, cornerstones or foundation stones. The language, effects and experiences surrounding these different cases are often very similar. The common "time capsule" name tag affixed to both kinds of interpretive response is a very meaningful one, and not merely an incidental, fuzzy-logic set.

The development of modern scientific archaeological methodologies and theories of interpretation has helped the interpreters of archaeological finds to look back at far different, distant times. Some of those high-technology archaeological experiences can evoke very elemental time capsule–like encounters with past ways, lives and cultural patterns of all sorts. Soil, for example, has been called the premier artistic medium of archaeologists. Often it is the case that reading the trace conditions of even subtly changed soil media is the *best* archaeological message (Lambert, 1997, p. 33). Art objects and structural remnants are not then by any means the sole key archaeologists can use in their interpretative work. Rather it is often the soil conditions and (increasingly) their chemical traces that are the star of the show. Can better archaeological investigations (and thus time capsule–type interpretations) be more readily accomplished through recent advances in chemical archaeological studies? "Chemical archaeology" has been an expansion of the non-dramatic, traditional methodology of soil sifting into the modern technical archaeologist's spectacular applications of the latest scientific archaeology. For example, it is possible to conduct dietary studies via an analysis of various periods of North American Paleo-Indian Woodland Culture inhabitants based on human bone's carbon chemical differentiation (Lambert, 1997, pp. 214– 22). It is even possible to recreate ancient Egyptian beers from traces left of the beverages (Wilford, 1996, p. A5). Also, in addition to chemical traces in bone and even genetic DNA chemical residues as evidence, actual traces of human flesh remains may serve as ways to bring unknown aspects of the past back to life in our own times (Lambert, 1997, pp. 214–57). It would seem that our very soil, the Earth we live on, could be a very powerful time capsule.

Extinct cities and cultures can be experienced as "accidental time capsule" deposits. At least some archaeological sites, finds or exhibits can be experienced or described as accidental time capsules. Here are a few salient cases, beginning with two of the world's most famous extinct ancient cities, Pompeii and Herculaneum from AD 79. "Pompeii AD 79" is an exemplary case of an archaeological site, a culture area of a time period now seen as an accidental, metaphorical time capsule. The 1979 "Pompeii 79 AD" touring museum exhibition was reviewed as "A 'time capsule' from ancient Rome" (Kern, 1979, pp. C1, C13; Ward-Perkins & Claridge, 1978). Such archaeological digs and resultant museum exhibitions can evoke time capsule experiences. The extinct city of Pompeii was of course not deliberately buried by human action and none of the wide range of items there was deliberately deposited as a future relic. That site and its artifacts from the year 79 of our Common Era are not technically a time capsule in our narrow, strict sense of being a "deliberately-deposited-in-a-container-for-target-date-retrieval" kind of phenomenon. There is a very real sense in which these suddenly buried sites are significant time capsule–like phenomena. The whole Pompeii cultural area does manage to represent an experience of, to capture the essence of, a past era. That extinct city's site and assorted excavated artifacts do evoke in a wide variety of observers a "time capsule" experience. A reviewer noted:

> They have put us in touch with the people of Roman Italy in ways that are more "intimate" and personal than would ever have been thought possible with any ancient society. Through the time capsule of ancient Pompeii we can actually penetrate into the private lives of a vanished people in a vanished age [Kern, 1979, pp. C1, C13].

The review describes an essential, ideal set of relics suitable for a time capsule experience:

> It is, in a sense, an inventory of objects of everyday use and contemplation, some new, some more than a century old, some plainly utilitarian, some ravishingly beautiful, which just happened to be present, in that particular moment, when time and history came to a stop.

Obviously it would trivialize the time capsule concept to characterize all examples of archaeological interpretation or all such museum exhibitions as metaphorical time capsule–like experiences. This is not only because of the scope, context and detail of the material culture preserved by Mt. Vesuvius' violent eruption that August AD 79. It is also because of the sudden sealing-up aspects of the destruction. In this case, the "slice of life" metaphor was brutally literal. The Fates (to borrow an ancient Roman perspective) did indeed "destroy those towns in order to save them" for the future. The future in this case includes our era's turn as one phase of that vast expanse of serial futures. We have observed time capsule experiences that traveling museum exhibitions like the 1979 "Pompeii AD 79" show often evoke. This time capsule experience spans 1900 years in a cognitive bridge between modern museumgoers and the ancient volcanic burials of that culture complex. The whole *in situ* set of deposits in these cities, towns and villas in the AD 79 Pompeii, Italy, cultural area can also function like the extracts on exhibit. Pompeii is hardly a unique case in evoking time capsule experiences in today's investigators or site visitors. Other archaeological sites have brought out time capsule feelings in their modern viewers. One example of how this sudden burial instantly preserved everyday life frozen in time is Pompeii's municipal election campaign. Numerous artisan-drawn, officially sanctioned election wall drawings were preserved, as well as extensive vernacular, sometimes vulgar graffiti with their additional perspectives on certain candidates. These Pompeii electioneering examples are perhaps the most famous examples of paleographic wall evidence. Exhibitions of some of the artifacts from this extinct city help keep something of this ancient time capsule region alive (*Rediscovering*, 1990). There are interesting examples of other extinct cities such as Leptis Magna and Sabratha in modern-day Libya (Mathews, 1957). However, such "cities in the sand" were either sacked, abandoned or both. They are less fulsome slices of ancient life. A looted or stripped-down extinct city site is unlikely to have artifacts such as bronze cake baking pans left *in situ*, like those found on a bakery wall in Pompeii (Deiss, 1968, p. 98). Since the shops of the town were not sold off or looted, but rather rapidly buried, the amount of cultural detail is very high. That can be seen in descriptions like "Houses and shops of the Plebs" (Deiss, 1968, pp. 94–99). Extinct cities such as Pompeii and Herculaneum are then distinctly different from merely abandoned town sites. The world suddenly buried 1900 years ago was "returned to the sun" in more recent eras. Ancient Rome has no monopoly on extinct cities, however (Menen, 1973).

Swift Creek Culture's interpretation is based solely on distinctive pottery art impressions preserved for later times. In this light, the Swift Creek Culture's artistic survivals are of particular time capsule–like interest (Williams & Elliott, 1998, pp. 1–11). One anthology based on these artifacts is *A World Engraved: Archaeology of the Swift Creek Culture.* Their pottery art is all we have of this distinctive culture's artistry. Our evidence is a series of physical clay impressions from some wooden paddle engravings at the Swift Creek Site in Georgia. These Paleo-Indian Middle Woodland Mound People's very distinctive pottery design impressions remain only in images originally from canoe paddle wooden carvings. These have been preserved solely in the form of impressions on clay pots (Williams & Elliott, 1998, pp. xv.,1+). Shards of "Swift Creek Complicated Stamped Pottery" are the focus of "Swift Creek Studies." An entire material culture is apparently distinguished from others in the wider archaeological record of that Middle Woodland culture area of the eastern U.S. *only* by these clay impressions. Today's investigators can muse on the possible symbolic meanings of these apparently abstract artistic studies of animal and plant forms. Cultural diffusion among Woodland Hopewell people is evidenced by these Paleoindian designs. A time capsule interpretive moral can be drawn from these clay impressions of apparently unique wood carving designs—namely that the existence of a whole distinctive artistic cultural period has been transmitted from the Swift Creek carvers to our contemporary *fin de siècle* archaeological savants solely by that set of patterns. In a sense, those Swift Creek people live again through their distinctive decorative art. Both the paucity of this archaeological record (in contrast to the full material cultural richness of life in that Paleo-Indian era) and the tantalizing aesthetic complexity and breadth of that glimpsed world are demonstrated in various Swift Creek studies. Of course, no cultural period, no space-time leaves everything, a full-recorded copy of their lifetime, to be interpreted by the future. No one can of course hope to have even a full cargo manifest of an earlier era's material culture as the whole truth about that transmitted epoch. It is even less likely that future would-be interpreters could access to any real extent a fuller armamentarium of any given past's own ephemeral cultural interpretive lore. When we think about how much should suffice or how little could suffice as a cultural-historical legacy of former lives, Swift Creek clay impressions of wood carvings can perhaps serve as a minimum, a floor of significant interpretable relics. Will we "fin de millennium" global inhabitants do even as well as Swift Creek Culture has, even when we deliberately try to commemorate our own culture's existence?

Biological remains are potential sources of time capsule type experiences. Biological specimens have evoked time capsule experiences in their beholders. One is a 37-year-old frozen fish from Lake Erie, and the others are a variety of ancient human flesh remains from the European glaciers, salt mines and peat bogs. These biological specimens are pressed into representing whole ancient worlds, just on the strength of a few accidentally deposited, individual specimens. Finally there is the case of the "Cardiff Giant," the posited "ancient man" who never was anything other than a projection back in time as interpreted by a mid–nineteenth century North American rural culture.

The 1962 "Anthony's Fish" case from Conneaut, Ohio, has been noted as a curious combination of prescience, nostalgia or even sentimentality (Belluck, 1999). Jim Anthony, now a barber, was once a worker in his father's 1950s Ohio fish market. He kept a full blue pike specimen continuously frozen at his residence for 37 years. Mr. Anthony kept stressing to his wife that the value of the frozen specimen continued to increase as its age did. But by 1975 that species was extinct in Lake Erie, due to a combination of habitat changes, pollution and over-fishing. Still, biologists have generally assumed that those blue fish are merely a form of walleye, rather than the presumably extinct species blue pike. The genetic biological question that may be decided eventually by ichthyologists at Cleveland's Case Western Reserve University is whether the DNA in "Anthony's Fish" is identical to those bluish walleye fish found in small lakes. Are there really small genetic pools of blue pike that might be introduced again into Lake Erie? Mr. Anthony apparently felt as if the fish had been integrated into his life, that he has great regard for it. He is very proud it has been named after him (Belluck, 1999). This interesting story fuses themes such as freezer technology, DNA biology, fishery conservation and a kind of modern totemistic, mystic identification with the fate of blue pike. Regardless of the possible re-establishment of the blue pike into Lake Erie, the case of Jim Anthony's frozen fish specimen is biological evidence of a species' DNA that has been a kind of time capsule experience. The experience may not be limited just to Mr. Anthony, but may be one for fish biologists and anyone around Lake Erie too.

"Autoicons," mummies and accidental human flesh remains can sometimes serve as the sole representatives of their times to future worlds;

like Jeremy Bentham's very own self "autoicon" in a glass case at the University of London (Lelyveld, 1986, p. A2). The renowned founder of the Utilitarian school of philosophy (1748–1837) had stipulated that disposition, or rather deployment, upon his demise. Today his skeleton is dressed in his own clothes and sports a waxen reproduction of his full head. Another recent historical case, this time a twentieth century hagiography (i.e., saintly exhibition as a full body relic), is the curious case of V. I. Lenin's Tomb and his embalmed remains in Moscow. This continuous exhibit of human remains is still in the care of a family of embalmers who keep up a modern relic pilgrimage site. It is an ancient custom perpetuated by modern political needs (Verdery, 1999; Zbarsky, 1999). Forensic anthropology of course can be applied to ancient as well as much more recent remains. These traces of dead people's ancient and modern remains continue telling us "stories" about there past lives and deaths (Maples & Browning, 1994).

In addition to the fossil bone record of hominoid paleontology and the renowned mummies prepared over thousands of years in Egypt, there are other flesh remains of ancient peoples. Some of those examples can sometimes evoke time capsule experiences. The Egyptian mummy phenomenon is so well-known, so apt as a survival of the past that only a lengthy discussion here would do the time capsule perspective on it any justice. We will merely note that there is new forensic science–informed work on mummies. The paleopathology of ancient Egyptian mummy deposits can transmit to our times more evidence on the social life and customs before 332 BCE (David, Archbold & Brand, 2000). The world of ancient human remains has also been revealed in *ice*. The 5300 BP ("Before Present") Alpine Iceman's last meal and health record exemplify his era. He was just one man, but he must now stand for his whole epoch. He was about 40 years old when he died, but he is also 5300 years old in a sense. His last meal, his health, even his chronological celebrity as the oldest known flesh remainder of a human being give him the cachet, the aura of a celebrity today. His remains must serve us as the only extant human biological sample, a *de facto* exemplar, of his era. Commentators of course realize that one example of a Late Stone Age man's bio-medical condition and dietary evidence does not equate with a whole bio-cultural period. Such archaeological data is often all that we have to go on in our understanding about a given past period (Wilford, 1999c). Another world of ancient human remains has been revealed in the "Salt Men," ancient Celtic-era humans "salted away" in European mine accidents several millennia ago. These human time travelers from the Alps were found in a Salzburg, Austria, area salt mine, their well-preserved remains still clothed. One was dug out in the year 1573 (Visser, 1986, pp. 56–58). The Celtic Salt Men and their Bronze Age artifacts are classic non-deliberate, archaeological deposits whose retrievals are time capsule experiences to our age (*The Celts*, 1999, pp. 191–94). Several other such remains have been found in recent centuries. The world of ancient human remains has also been revealed in the many Peat Bog People from the Northwestern European Iron Age. Those appear to be an interesting variation on the accidental deposit provenance of "Iceman 5300 BP" and the "Salzburg Salt Man." For the most part, the Bog People sites appear to be deliberate deposits as the result of burial or sacrificial practices. Perhaps they were buried as criminal executions in a sacral justice ritual context (Glob, 1997). There is no absolute distinction between a memorial burial site and a foundation deposit dedication–type site. They can be identical, as in the case of the special hybrid, two-phase foundation deposit ritual practice at an older traditional burial mound in the city of Stalingrad's Mamaev Kurgan site. It is an ancient Tartar burial mound-park at the heart of what is currently named Volgograd. One historian of this battle zone observed that the World War II memorial added there symbolically turned the war dead into sacrificial grave memorials. That Soviet memorial's architects had translated a defending general's "stand-fast" watchwords to the World War II defenders into a literal memorial rendering. The memorial graves became a sacrificial foundation deposit of the stones the Red Army was ordered to fight like. That rebuilt city memorial expresses that sentiment with Stalinist monumentality (Beevor, 1998, p. 173).

At the New York State Historical Society "Farmer's Museum," the "living history" village, which includes authentic-era transplanted buildings, is an exhibit of what was once thought to be an ancient relic. Now it is thought to be really a carnival-type hoax relic of the 1860s (Boning, 1972; Dunn, 1954; Franco, 1990; Kimball, 1966). This "Cardiff Giant" is an exemplar of an ancient man who never was, a false time capsule, a sort of fake diplomat from a bogus past. Its cachet was early nineteenth century rural agrarian America's gullibility, need for ancient-rooted allegory and thirst for entertaining carnival tent spectacles with a veneer of edifying ethical gloss. This nineteenth century hoax fooled many people for quite a while in that pre–geologically conscious age. There is no indication that such a giant man ever lived. The Cardiff Giant only existed in the "once upon a time" world of folklore, in the minds of its nineteenth century U.S. cultural interpreters.

The importance of wearing things out can have great cultural significance for time capsules. Time capsule contents could include spontaneously chosen, broad spectrum, *ad hoc* results of gathered, used goods for the future.

Archaeologist Robert Ascher has pointed out that pristine, deliberated-upon time capsule content could actually mislead future recipients. He says that this could happen not only because of the explicit interpretations included as deliberate messages within time capsules, but also because of the prejudices implicit in the selection and condition of artifacts enclosed. He advocates that time capsule contents be chosen for their indicative wear-mark patterns (Ascher, 1974). For example, the standard practice of placing mostly unused, pristine items in capsules might deprive archaeologists of information inferable from wear patterns left on everyday objects. Exceptions to the pristine deposit habit include a Japanese businessman's notebook placed in the Osaka Expo 70 millennial Time Capsule No. 1 and a string of variety store imitation pearls, rather than a necklace of expensive true pearls. It was reasoned that a selection of expensive pearls might have given a misleading view of a typical Japanese citizen's lifestyle, and specimens of expensive pearls are more likely to be preserved by museums than are the variety store limitation ones. (An archivist can appreciate the value of a used notebook.) When Ascher suggests "how to build a time capsule," he invites two possible options. One could either reject the idea altogether or invite critical suggestions on how to best characterize daily lives through time capsules. Even the most popular culture-oriented, promotional time capsule project has the potential to demonstrate a wide variety of technical preservation and cultural interpretive skills. Since time capsules are mini-museums, it is perhaps unrealistic to expect them to be more pure than their contemporary promotion-conscious "traditional" museum models. Museums and archives are expressions of deeply felt aspirations but also cater to the need to entertain. And popular contents, such "articles of common use" as handbags, hats, dolls and tools, are among the time capsule contents with the most appeal. The selection of personal possessions such as coins and wristwatches can be of more public interest than the title of the encyclopedia chosen to be included or what internal preservation arrangements are made. The emotional appeal of sending typical artifacts and images will inevitably be of more popular interest than the intellectual content of documents enclosed or the construction specifications of the physical capsule. This stress on the importance of time capsule content-interpretation via wear-marks is a very important "archaeological" orientation (Ascher, 1974). Patterns of use on articles of common use can be seen as raw imprints, raw data for a time capsule experience, unmediated by categorical thinking and deliberate formal pre-interpretations of sent contents. Such "tribiological" patterns (marks of use, in plain English) are often invaluable clues to our actual lives, the imprints of our transitory presence on the world scene. In addition to the spontaneous audience participation aspects, used things have been personalized by our use, much as events dated by the calendar bring back memories to us. At the dedication event of a youth club building in the mid–1950s, one youth was asked to donate something out of his pockets to the club's capsule. As a result, several fishhooks, a knife, a length of string, a bottle top, a broken compass and three pennies went into the cornerstone for the clubhouse building (Klein, 1958, pp. 80–81; Remington, 1954, pp. 16–17). Likewise, the sacred character of artifacts such as carved Hopewell Mound builder animal-shaped smoking pipes is deemed likely not only by their sacred burial precinct type site contexts, but also by the striking lack of wear on these grave goods (Fagan, 1998, pp. 184–219).

One should never underestimate the value of used packets of historical information, like dog-eared or marked-up guidebooks and travel brochures. This author's personal copy of the *Official Guide: New York World's Fair 1964/1965* is dog-eared and has blue ink pen dash lines to the left of some sights at that Fair (Time-Life Books, 1964). Coupled with the various brochures found stuffed in it when the bundle was acquired from an antique shop, they can tell the reader-detective quite a bit about someone's Fair journey. That copy does so in a way that a pristine example of that *Official Guide* can't. (One copy, presumably pristine, was included in that Fair's Westinghouse "Time Capsule II" contents.) Not only can we see that this annotated copy had probably been used at the Fair, we can actually trace something of one actual visiting day at the Fair. For example, it would appear from the very selective marking up of the exhibits' entries in the *Official Guide* that not all pavilions and exhibits were prime sites to visit, or at least they were not all equally sought out in a planned way by every fairgoer. The same lessons can be garnered from well-thumbed guidebooks to other world's fairs, of course, including the official one for the 1939 New York World's Fair. Pristine specimens may not have as much evidentiary value as well-worn copies (New York World's Fair [1939-1940], 1939).

The importance of throwing things away can have great cultural significance for archaeological "time capsules"! Refuse disposal analysis is an avenue of archaeological investigation, not only of traditional, pre-industrial cultures but also of our world's industrialized culture as well (Staski & Sutro, 1991). The Garbage Project at the University of Arizona has been excavating landfills in the Tucson area and recording the results as historical archaeological surveys of recent decades in the twentieth century (Rathje & Murphy, 1992). The essence of that archaeological study involves a look at the waste column of what is thrown away. It requires the analysis of the ways such discards had apparently been used, and also of the why and how of the discarding of items. There are a variety of related techniques one can use when sending contents and most especially popular culture contents in a time capsule. Wear patterns can be helpful in the interpretation of the popularity of a certain topic in any printed dictionary, book collection or physical medium of information. Used media artifacts can convey valuable interpretive clues. A well-thumbed magazine can attest to its heavy use. Personally annotated books and notebooks as well as the contents of carry-bags, wallets and pockets can be indicative of their usage. Such selections should ideally be spontaneous, i.e., not chosen in advance by the donor, in order to be good samples. That is "low selectivity." While they won't diminish the responsibilities for future archaeologists, time capsules might save various written records and other, more ephemeral cultural materials, the unique brand of historical evidence that archives put into storage. It is unlikely that most paper and electronic records will automatically survive as long as many Mesopotamian clay tablets have, but some specially prepared records, thoughtfully sealed in time capsule type environments might last for millennia. After our paper-based record systems have disappeared, future archaeologists and historians might erroneously deduce that much of our twentieth century population was virtually illiterate (Cort, 1959, pp. 397–99). That is, unless they access an adequate number of time capsules. That might be the only way in which future ages could realize that our age was so prolific in paper and electronic media, just as were earlier ages in the medium of clay tablets. Archaeological critiques of time capsules (such as Ascher's) neglect archives as important elements of historical interpretation. Such evidence plays a role that archivists are well aware of. An optimistic, "reconstructivist" archaeological perspective might hold that time capsules are at best marginal aids to historical interpretation, and that it is possible to extensively reconstruct past behavior from the *ad hoc* evidence of traditional, non-deliberate archaeological sites (Watson, LeBlanc & Redman, 1984, p. 257).

One curious kind of discard almost qualifies as a votive, building deposit, but not quite! The scene was the old Apollo Theater on 42nd Street in New York City circa 1960, and the occasion was a series of pickpocket thefts of wallets and pocketbooks from audience members between 1959 and 1961 (Lueck, 1996, pp. A1, A13). In the course of the old theater's 1996 demolition, a dozen wallets and several empty liquor bottles were found stuffed in an airshaft behind a wall in the theater. Various old items were found in the concealed criminal evidence, including photo identification cards, photographs, pay stubs, utility bills and even some old fortune cookie statements. The recipients and crime victims were generally delighted to "receive" these memories of theft in their pasts. The sense of loss experienced at the time of these thefts had at least faded over the decades. The suddenly recovered discards enchanted their owners, who received these long lost photos, slips of paper, etc., which recalled to them various memories. This was presumably due just to the sudden, unexpected reappearance of these vernacular deposits. This example falls somewhere between an archaeological happenstance kind of discard deposit and some sort of vernacular building deposit. The protection motive here certainly appears to have been focused on the safety of the thief who used the building and its wall-spaces for his operations! Consider the thought experiment of imagining a retrieval of these wall thief-deposits in 1000 years. The result might be a puzzling deposit activity with an unclear symbolism.

"Toying" with archaeological explanations in miniature is a major interpretive value choice. Figuring out what something meant to someone 5000 years ago is not always easy. Take the matter of terra cotta, "miniature toy-like" figurines for example ("Neolithic figurines: idols or toys?," 1985, pp. 66–67). Earlier twentieth century archaeologists generally thought of all small models of people, animals, utensils, buildings or other structures as ritual objects or supernatural idols, rather than as the mundane miniature toys of children. Obviously, ancient Egyptian servant statues found in tombs are not only models of those ancient lives, but are also ritual objects (Breasted, 1948). In recent decades, some archaeologists have become wary of uncritically assuming a ritual purpose for virtually any apparently "out-of-context" artifact, such as toy-sized miniatures, as automatically being cultic or ritualistic items. Some miniature finds could be readily consigned to a cultic-function category based solely on the premise that various other miniature figurines were clearly ritual objects. By correlating such Neolithic era terra cotta miniature male or female figurines in the context of miniature terra cotta houses, utensils, etc. found nearby the figurines, different interpretations are suggested. Factors such as the crudeness of apparently rapid manufacture, the apparent midden discards of broken specimens, the common factor of domestic dwellings as sites for these finds and the degree of stylistic vs. naturalistic representation are aspects of these de-ritualized analyses. (Votive ritual objects can of course be crudely manufactured too.) This particular area of archaeological interpretive criticism is a cautionary tale in time capsule interpretation. Collaborative, contemporaneous writings can serve as interpretive, clarifying aids as they have in some archaeological analyses, such as in the case of this "sacred miniature or toy?" question. The interpretive fashions of

researchers can change, of course. It could lead to a focus on one form of usage, i.e., the "toy theory," perhaps at the expense of another model, such as a vernacular foundation rite hypothesis. Traditionally vernacular domestic votive sacred practices seem to have been ignored and certainly poorly documented by their contemporaries. Their deposits may even have been covert to most of their contemporary neighbors. In general, the study of one's popular customs has not always been fashionable. We can offer a general caution to eschew vague ritualistic interpretations as theoretical panaceas, favoring instead detailed contextual analyses. There are also two general theses worthy of detailed consideration in the case of Neolithic miniature anthropomorphic, etc., figurines. First, one should not rule out the prospect that at least some of these domestic figurines were employed as foundation rite figurines. Secondly, it is even possible that some might be (ancient Mesopotamian, etc.) counter-tokens used as pre-literate forms of property accounting in some pre–Bronze Age culture areas. Indeed all of these uses might be plausible in one or other of these contexts. Only by detailed analyses of specific site finds in the context of the whole cultural area can the researcher validate any particular explanatory, hypothetical model for a specific case.

A phantom fleet of sunken "time capsules" has been harvested by marine archaeologists. Sunken ships are naturals to be dubbed as time capsules, and there have been many articles about these sorts of marine archaeological expeditions and salvage operations (Ballard, 1989, pp. 622–37; Ballard & Hively, 2000; Garrett, 1985, p. 421; Goddio, 1994, pp. 33–57; Marden, 1985, pp. 423–50). This classic metaphorical comment about sunken ships as time capsules and historical archives editorially prefaced a story on the sunken ship HMS *Pandora* (Marden, 1985, pp. 423–50):

> Fortunately, most nations have come to realize that the world's waters are stocked with untouched time capsules in the form of sunken ships that span almost the entire history of man. As technology picks the lock on Davy Jones's locker, scholars will increasingly turn to the study of this greatest historical archive on earth [Garrett, 1985, p. 421].

Exactly what is it that does make a sunken ship a time capsule? Even sunken ships without any pirate's treasure of precious metals are also treasure of another sort. They serve as archaeological and historical evidence, historical treasures (Delgado, 1996, pp. 40–42). The sunken (1600) Spanish galleon *San Diego* also evoked in the title of an article the "archaeological time capsule" metaphor (Goddio, 1994, pp. 33-37). The author-explorer of the San Diego wreck site uses the time capsule metaphorical term to describe that maritime find (Goddio, 1994, p. 34). The metaphor is apparently so apt that it has become almost *de rigueur* when a sunken ship is found. As bearers of artifacts or as contextual evidence of previous human activity, sunken ships are a historical treasure trove of past socio-economic and cultural practices. Aspects of shipwreck sites that readily lend themselves to ethno-archaeological interpretation include analysis of factors such as ships stores, weaponry, equipment, cargo storage methods and contents and vessels' structural features, as well as wider shipwreck site contexts (Lenihan, 1983, pp. 37–64). All of these clues can be found at one site, often still lying in a definable vessel wreck. A wreck usually remains untouched by human activities since the last crew member movements on board, an accidentally deposited vessel of that era. It is in other words a fine time capsule of the accidentally deposited sort. The ships found wrecked at these sites have been termed self-contained "cultural systems." They are artifacts in themselves and are also carriers of a whole culture complex (Murphy, 1983, pp. 65–89). That the time capsule metaphor comes readily to mind in the context of sunken ships is no idle fancy! Ships, particularly ships at sea, have even been offered up as prime examples of that microcosmic metaphor *par excellence*, the institutional asylum. They were characterized by a preeminent social psychologist as "total institutional" phenomena (Goffman, 1962). Ships at sea, remote islands, hotels, prisons and mental institutions are among the total institutions identified as being complete in their isolation, as total sociocultural value systems. No wonder a sunken ship or an extinct, lost city can readily be compared to a time capsule. Such deposits consist not only of an isolated artifact, vessel or site but also serve as a culture carrier of one world period to another. Boats and ships have long had magical and religious associations with symbolic travels beyond one's ordinary world. There are the well-known examples of Bronze Age Sweden and ancient Egyptian funereal boat-motif practices (Edsman, 1987, pp. 257–62).

Obviously, other sunken ships await discovery (Eiseman & Ridgeway, 1987). Their future retrieval could well provide good happenstance archaeological recovery varieties of time capsule experiences. From a twenty-first century secular perspective, they are seen as not deliberately deposited. At least in the religio-cultural context of the ancient Mediterranean world for thousands of years, all vessels lost by storms could have been considered to be objects of the wrath of the gods. In other words, deliberately sunk, albeit by a posited supernatural agency. So the question of deliberate deposit can be a cultural contextual issue, subject to a considerable degree of variable historical interpretation over different cultural eras. The Ballard marine archaeological expeditions are a remarkable series of time capsule–like retrieval experiences. They are affording our contemporary world excellent examples of shipwreck sites as time capsule–evoking experiences. His Jason Project team's work has included the reacquisition of early twentieth century passenger shipwreck sites, World War II warships (Atlantic and Pacific) and pre-modern Mediterranean shipwrecks along ancient trade routes (Ballard, 1995, p. 27; Ballard & Hively, 2000). Ballard's "hi-tech" approach has three dimensions: preliminary screening of possible search areas, imaging instruments that find the general shipwreck site, and followed then by a submersible video-robot coordinated exploration in detail. This sort of telepresence is used to "tour" lost sunken ships sites with robotic-remote sensing (Arnold & Ballard, 1990, p. 43+). A 2000-year route through time between ancient Carthage to Rome is being systematically retraced. This is a remarkable series of ongoing seasonal expeditions conducted by Dr. Robert Ballard's marine archaeology research team. They are using the U.S. Navy research submarine NR-1 to systematically explore the ancient shipwreck remains along the major Mediterranean trade route between Carthage (in the North African Bay of Tunis) and the City of Rome (Ballard, 1998, pp. 32–40; Wiseman, 1999, pp. 10–12). The *Titanic* and the *Lusitania* were both found and experienced through such telepresence technology. The sunken RMS *Titanic* was found in 1985 and was the first real civilian experience with such a telepresence-based nautical archaeology. Ballard and a colleague provided a description of that expedition's first successful deployment of this undersea technical archaeology (Michel & Ballard, 1994, pp. III.132–III.137). The images from that expedition certainly evoked in many what could be called a time capsule experience (Ballard & Michel, 1985, pp. 696–719). Objects and scenes unseen for many decades were suddenly visible on videos taken deep in the Atlantic. That 1915 torpedoing of the U.S. passenger vessel *Lusitania* was a watershed event between the United States, then a neutral power, and Imperial Germany, then at war with Britain and France (Ballard, Dunmore & Spence, 1996, p. 74). Ballard's group made it come alive again.

The 1998 reacquisition of the USS *Yorktown* has an interesting rededication dimension. The decisive Battle of Midway essentially ended Japanese strategic offensive operations against the U.S. armed forces in the World War II Pacific. On June 3, 1942, U.S. aircraft spotted warships of the Imperial Japanese Combined Fleet moving towards the Midway Islands area. On June 4, the four Japanese aircraft carriers were sunk, and one of the U.S. aircraft carriers was in turn badly damaged in a counterattack. The summer 1998 "Battle of Midway Expedition" was conducted by Dr.

Robert Ballard's marine archaeology research team using a U.S. Navy robot submersible explorer craft (Allen, 1999, pp. 80–93, 100–3). One of the key targets of the expedition was the U.S. Navy aircraft carrier USS *Yorktown*, which had finally been sunk on June 7, 1942. They were able to explore the remains of both Japanese and American sunken warships. Added to Ballard's team for this archaeological mission were four veterans of that World War II battle, two from the Japanese Imperial Navy and two U.S. Navy crewmen. Both Japanese veterans were naval aviation personnel in the 1942 battle. One U.S. veteran was a gunner on the USS *Yorktown*, the other a U.S. Navy airman in that battle. As Ballard's robot submersible probe closed on the wreck site of the *Yorktown* on May 19, 1999, the former U.S. Navy anti-aircraft gunner Bill Surgi was at his imaging monitor station on the expedition's surface command ship. He still had his World War II "tin pot"–type battle helmet from June 4, 1942, when he had to abandon ship when the *Yorktown* explosions had begun. Now in 1998, he was again wearing a World War II U.S. Navy sailor's uniform, including his 1942 Petty Officer First Class insignia of rank. He was 18 years old in 1942. Now in 1998 he had vowed to put the helmet back on only when the Expedition first visually acquired the submerged image of the *Yorktown* site. On May 19, 1998, the expedition imaged the stern of the sunken USS *Yorktown*. It had settled upright onto the Pacific Ocean floor on June 7, 1942, and hadn't disintegrated, as an artistic reconstruction demonstrates (Ballard, 1999, pp. 94–98). Bill Surgi then put his battle helmet back on (Allen, 1999, pp. 84–85). His commemorative reenactment at the moment of rediscovery was a modern sort of symbolic rite that resonates with ancient battlefield dedications and war veteran memorials. A lost moment in time, a period's cultural system, in this case the USS *Yorktown*, was visually reacquired both by professional marine archaeologists and also by several 1942 battle participants. They were able in 1998 to revisit, visually and emotionally, that past scene. Here the World War II veterans were live "experiencers" at both the 1942 deposit and 1998 retrieval times, unlike many time capsule creators. The sinking and the rediscovering of that sunken pocket battleship *Bismarck* is another such complete time capsule experience. Over 45 years later, Dr. Ballard's team entered the picture and was able to visually "reacquire" the sunken World War II vessel (Ballard, 1989, pp. 622–37; Ballard & Archbold, 1991, 85+). Submarines, including German U-boats, have been lost to mines, human errors, machinery malfunctions, just bad luck (surfacing in the middle of several Allied warships, etc.) or coordinated air-sea attack operations (Kemp, 1997). The presumed cause of loss is important in determining the likelihood of retrieving anything of a sunken vessel's hull or contents. For example, it was standard Allied antisubmarine practice to attempt the destruction of all U-boat hulks even after a confirmed sinking. Such heavily blasted shipwreck sites may have less archaeological lure than a vessel lost by a bomb, an accidental sinking or mine. Such heavily devastated shipwrecks may make for especially poor time capsule experiences.

Aeronautical and architectural archaeology can also have sites underwater. Marine archaeological research is not always restricted to the excavation and exploration of sunken ships. Jean-Ives Empereur's marine archaeological team has also discovered the old Hellenistic palace complex area, as well as a Roman sunken ship off the shore of Alexandria ("Archaeology news: Roman shipwreck off Alexandria," 1999, p. 22). Cleopatra's sunken Alexandrine palace has "returned" to rave reviews, at least in archaeology journals (Empereur, 1999a, pp. 36–43; Empereur, 1999b, pp. 62–85; Schuster, 1999, pp. 44–46)! The royal quarter of Hellenistic Alexandria, the Ptolemic palace complex which was once the residence of the semi-legendary yet historical figure of Cleopatra VII, has an excellent set of time capsule ingredients. It is a long-lost palace site thought gone forever, but now found. It is closely affiliated with the story of the semi-legendary Cleopatra herself. It has ancient statues and other relics that have been retrieved after thousands of years. A part of the ancient Hellenistic City of Alexandria founded by none other than Alexander the Great was returned to the light. (In this case, literally — the lights of scuba divers!) The palace site is under shallow harbor water and consists of surviving items sunk into the harbor due to subsidence events such as earthquakes.

There is one further aspect of a time capsule experience that may come to pass at this site, if the plans of the antiquities service there are accomplished. Plans for an underwater tour by glass bottom boat (or by scuba diving) routes for archaeological tourists are envisioned, so that the huge debris field of royal quarter remains could conceivably be viewed *in situ*. There are also instances where marine archaeology is a form of aeronautical archaeology. In the Netherlands, for example, the continuing drainage to create new agricultural land uncovers from time to time crash sites of a variety of downed World War II aircraft. The team identifies a wide variety of crashed remains from most combatants' air forces in that War's European Theater of operations. The Dutch Air Force archaeological team that excavates these sites has to notify family and crewmates of the retrieval of the remains. On one occasion, they had received an inquiry about a long-missing aircraft on the same day that very aircraft's crash site was detected (Daly, 1986, pp. 106–15). The photographs in the article about these Dutch archaeological finds reinforce the notion of time stopped in its tracks. It was an historical period from which personal losses have suddenly been brought vividly back to the attention of crewmates, family members, farmers and the government retrieval teams. In one case, a crew member who had parachuted to safety during the War suddenly re-experienced the recovered personal effects of his downed crewmates and his long-lost aircraft, many decades after he jumped out of it.

"Tunnels of the imagination" can be sources of time capsule type experiences. Tunnels and underground chambers have always had a mythic hold on the human imagination, something akin to the lure of fascination that time capsules can evoke. Tunnels of all sorts can bring forth time capsule–like experiences. Museum treasure vaults, "time tunnels" in played out gold mines, overlooked subway segments and Paleolithic cave art sites are some examples of these time tunnel time capsule phenomena. As always, our goal here is to focus on types of experience for any value as time capsule interpretive phenomena that can evoke via a pattern of details from a past to our receiving present. One such case is a museum storage tunnel in New York City. The Metropolitan Museum of Art in New York City, like many museums, has a huge amount of treasure, which for various reasons is not readily exhibited to the public. Some of these "non-exhibits" may be merely out of cultural fashion, whereas some items just lack room (temporarily or long-term) in which to be shown. Some such stored items are newly acquired, getting conservation care or being prepared for exhibition. One of the Museum's storage areas is just such a massive art treasure trove fashioned from an old tunnel under the adjoining Central Park (McGill, 1987, p. E28). The "Tropico Time Tunnel," on the other hand, is a real time capsule that is also a mine tunnel. It is an example of a true time capsule, one that was deliberately sealed and target dated for reopening. This 10,000 cubic foot Tropico Time Tunnel at Rosamond, California, was scheduled for opening 900 years after it was sealed with cement in 1966 ("Preserving the present," 1967, p. 27; *Tropico Time Tunnel sealing ceremonies*, 1966).

How can we travel back in time riding on New York City's "subways of the imagination"? New York City is a mass not only of skyscrapers and bridges, but of tunnels as well, including a variety of curious, forgotten subway installations. These are not just out-of-the-way, underutilized stations. Rather, these are never-used subway installations! As is the case with written records, the unused is usually the forgotten. Subway sites that have been built and then immediately abandoned are transportation facilities that can evoke interesting time capsule experiences where we can peek into a literal underground world of travel. Perhaps we can somehow "travel" back into portions of unrealized past transportation venues. Riding past unfinished spur line openings on a subway system such as that of New York City has been evoked as a sort of magical journey in time (Aciman, 1999). Roosevelt Avenue's unused 1936-era subway station in New York City is yet another case of such a "time tunnel." The never opened Roosevelt Avenue Station of the IND Queens, New York City, subway line in Jackson Heights is a "chronologically stranded" outpost of transportation archaeology. This still brand new subway station (from 1936!) is a shattered dream, a frozen remnant, and a victim of the economic woes of the Great Depression era. It is used for Transit Department storage and is occasionally toured by local history hobbyists, who on a tour made observations such as "I came to imagine what might have been" and "This is the history that should have been" (Martin, 1996, p. Y19). The Station's walls, which sport finished tile work spelling out the Station's name, have never had commuter crowds. No tracks were ever laid for it. A Second Avenue trackless section also curves off to nowhere, unconnected to any other tunnel. New York City's subway transit system has various other beginning "spurs" of track, never finished or connected to the rest of the transit grid. Alfred Ely Beach's 1870 City Hall pneumatic tube subway station was accidentally rediscovered in 1912. The "future" almost came early to New York City—at least the future of subways. Or rather the future actually came for a little while to one city block for a few years beginning in 1870. After a short period as an amusement ride, it closed, receding into a waiting past. Beach, editor-publisher of *Scientific American* magazine, began carrying out his pneumatic tube tunnel plan in 1868. He secretly expanded it into a nine-foot wide tunnel dug 20 feet down under Broadway, from Murray Street over one (312 foot) block to Warren Street (Burrows & Wallace, 1999, p. 923; Dwyer, 1999, pp. 147–48, 234, 235; Fischler, 1976, pp. 19–27; Hood, 1993, pp. 42–48, 50, 78). In February 1870, the 22-passenger car began to transport a total of 400,000 riders back and forth between the two huge terminals' fans. A ride on the well-appointed subway car cost 25 cents. His rather socially upscale subway platform sported a grand piano, Victorian settees, gas lighting, goldfish tank, a water fountain, Greek-style statuary and frescoed passageways. Despite the resourceful entrepreneurial combination of covert construction and gala inaugural, it came to a dead end. His project had collided with the political power of Boss Tweed's ring, various technical engineering concerns and a lack of sustainable capitalization funding. Beach's subway never made its way to the project goal, Central Park. The subway station was closed, forgotten and only reentered by workmen in 1912, surprised by their breakthrough into the period piece mid–Victorian lounge. (They were tunneling the new Brooklyn Mass Transit line towards Central Park.)

It would be nice to think that Beach's prototype subway section still reposes below City Hall, grand piano and all. Unfortunately, that journey through time must be now made via the subway buff's imagination (Martin, 1996, p. Y19). The Beach tunnel and station became part of the modern New York subway system it presaged by 42 years. One end of Beach's nine-foot diameter subway car was salvaged from its dry rot in the old tunnel and exhibited in the New York City Public Service Commission's offices (Walker, 1970, pp. 87–104).

That technological preview of the future is like one of those perennial, crowd-pleasing World's Fair transportation innovations. The Paris "Metro" was inaugurated on July 19, 1900, in conjunction with the Paris Universal Exposition. That *belle epoque* realm, with its well-known antique gate signage, celebrated its first centennial in 2000. Its 50-mile course has experienced fires (1903), floods (1910), Zeppelin bombing attack (1916), various subterranean intrigues of the Nazi occupation (1940–44) and even more recent hi-tech reconfigurations and design rejections (Grescoe, 2000). One such futuristic World's Fair exhibit-demonstration, the "people mover," conveyor-belt sidewalk "Travelator" was featured transportation at the 1900 Paris Exposition. The 1900 Paris Travelator was an early futuristic transport symbol, followed by such later futuristic World's Fair motifs as the well-known 1962 Monorail, still running at the Seattle Center in the U.S. That 1900 Exposition was held at the site of the Eiffel Tower, left from the 1889 Exposition there. From 1889 to 1930, the Eiffel Tower was the tallest building in the world.

Ice Age European ritual caves have been interpreted as sacred ceremonial precincts. Finally, note the curious status of cave and rock shelter art from western European Paleolithic prehistory (Fagan, 1998). Those Quaternary-era rock wall ritual sites are apparently some sort of deliberate dedication-celebration deposits. Residual pigmented images there have been hypothesized as evidence of periodic "performance art" type rituals at such sites. Their (pre–building plan era) deposits presage the deliberately dedicated deposits later evident in Sumerian-Mesopotamian and Egyptian dynastic architecture. With this series of tunnel explorations, we come to the end of our review of accidentally deposited archaeological time capsules. Along with their various notional, "as-if," time capsule cousins, these archaeological cases constitute the vast world of metaphorical, pretend time capsule–like experiences.

CHAPTER 3

The Time Capsule's Ancient Origins and Modern Transformations

Our historical tour begins in ca. 3000 BCE Mesopotamia and follows dedication deposits through ancient, medieval and modern practices. We'll also explore capsules at the U.S. 1876 International Centennial Exposition in Philadelphia, in the Space and Atomic ages and in the pre–Millennium 2000 decades. Ancient foundation dedication ceremonies were primal archetypal rituals that have changed over time into our modern cornerstone and time capsule practices. We'll examine five millennia of time capsule development. Our 1876–2001 capsule coverage is U.S.–focused.

Deliberate Foundation Deposits and Cornerstone Repositories

Folkloric and archaeological evidence of worldwide votive, dedication deposit practices spans 5000 years. British votive practices include deposits from pre–Roman, Romano-British, medieval and early modern (ca. 1900) periods (Merrifield, 1987). Analysis indicates the depth and universality of dedicatory votive deposit practices and meanings in other world cultural areas. Roman and pre–Roman British "votive deposits of sacrificed animals and fine artifacts on dry land," as well as votive artifacts found in rivers, are known. Skeletal remains of animals correlate with remains of ancient bridge pilings (Merrifield, 1987, pp. 22–57). There are Roman and post–Roman land boundary, wall foundations and gate marking deposits (Merrifield, 1987, p. 119). Distinctive deliberate-style deposits (including animal sacrifices) protected these dedicated precincts. These customs appear to have continued up into the twentieth century in England and elsewhere. They have deep historical roots, and include "Dark age and medieval foundation deposits" (Merrifield, 1987, pp. 116–19) and "Late medieval and post-medieval building deposits" (Merrifield, 1987, pp. 119–21). These later finds commonly consist of votive pots, sometimes filled with peat fire ashes or eggshells. Apparently they were deliberate magical protection burials at thresholds or fireplaces of dwellings. Desiccated chickens, domestic cats and well-worn shoes were secreted under floors, thresholds, inside walls, chimney recesses or roofs from the seventeenth through the nineteenth centuries. A variety of local museums in Southern England feature exhibits on them (Merrifield, 1987, pp. 128–36). Various magical protections were believed to be afforded by an array of "written spells and charms," including building deposits of written incantation squares, "witch-bottles" and maledictory ("curse") leaden tablets (Merrifield, 1987, pp. 137–58). Comparative historians of religions categorize votive deposit offerings as "vows and oaths" (Klinger, 1987, pp. 301–5). These dedication-founding deposits are typical of millennia of votive practices.

Foundation deposits, cornerstone repositories, gravesites and target-dated time capsule deposits are commonly found in sacred precincts. The precursors of modern time capsule experiences are found in ancient foundation deposit practices. Possibly these foundation deposits and practices date back to the Neolithic agricultural settlements of Western Asia ca. 8000 BCE, when clay figurines were deposited in brick walls (Fagan, 1998, p. 96). (Preliterate and indeed any vernacular culture's deposits are less readily tagged as deliberate, often lacking any ceremonial writing explicitly declaring their purpose.) The symbolic import of these ancient deposit customs was refocused in the nineteenth and twentieth centuries. There was a shift away from the immediate, dedicated ceremonial object and its sacred precincts over to a ritual emphasis on the dedication-presentation of the depositors' whole cultural-historical milieu into distant futures. People often assume that the possible targeted future world(s) will be unlike the senders' world. In the ancient past, notions of very different possible futures hadn't been accepted, and the cyclical sameness of past and future had currency. Use of the term "ritual" or "ceremony" need not necessarily posit any solemn sacred, religio-magical context (*Ritual, performance, media*, 1998; Rothenbuhler, 1998, pp. 103–4, 63–64; *Secular ritual*, 1977).

Signs of dedicated precincts at sacred ceremonial sites are found worldwide. Examples of Paleoindian Mississippian Moundbuilder sacred precincts abound. They include Moundville Archaeological Park in Moundville, Alabama; the Kunneman Mound of Cahokia Mounds State Historic Park in East Saint Louis, Illinois; the Fort Ancient, Ohio, area and various Hopewell culture sites. Those earthen structural remains graphically suggest the "intangibility" of vanished ceremonials presumably once carried out within the enclosures of these "ritual bureaucratic centers" (Fagan, 1998, pp. 184–219; Knight & Steponaitis, 1998; Pauketat, Bozell & Dunavan, 1993; Rogers & Smith, 1995; Romain, 2000). Parallels can be drawn with the sacred precinct dimensions of foundation deposit sites of Mesopotamian and other (metallurgical, written-record-keeping) civilizations such as those in ancient Mesopotamia. Comparisons are possible among ancient dedicated precincts, nineteenth and twentieth century worlds fairs and the perpetually (1200-year-plus) rebuilt sacred precincts of the Ise Jingu Shrines site at Ise City, Japan ("Ise Shrine," 1983, pp. 338– 39). Defining points about foundation deposits emphasize more the ritual sites and contexts of such dedication-type deposits rather than focus most heavily on deposited objects. Key factors include site selection, consecration of a survey land area, deposit of the foundation or cornerstone with religious trappings and (originally) sacrifices such as precious metals, coins, good luck foods, people and animals. Dolls, images, animal bones and all sorts of other articles have over time been substituted for blood sacrifices. Dancing, feasts and other celebrations and entertainment are common in building protection-commemoration ceremonies ("Building ceremonies," 1972, p. 169).

Tombs and graves are forms of indefinite votive-deposit offerings, as are cornerstones, foundation stones, prayer-donation offerings and other commemorative deposits. Tomb and grave deposits are sometimes archaeological sites, although most are not deposited with an intended eventual retrieval by excavation. Family burial vaults-crypts are sometimes an exception. Serial-burial sites are still quite distinct from the notion of an archaeological excavation. Witness the (non-aristocratic) burial practices common in the Austrian Empire of Mozart's day, where group pit burial rotations were the norm (*Amadeus*, 1998). Shakespearean England provides a notable instance of communal graveyard burial practices in the guise of the "poor Yorick's skull" scene from the Bard's *Hamlet.* Traditional family vault funeral practices in New Orleans, Louisiana, sometimes feature the consolidation-repositioning of the prior remains to make room for the newest burial. All prior burial remains are grouped further back (Jarvis, 1993a). Still, modern archaeological grave excavation practices are hardly what funeral practitioners throughout the ages have anticipated regarding their ceremonial deposits. Tombs and gravesites are deliberate deposits that are generally not intended for *a posteriori* retrieval. Ossuaries are smaller burial containers for human bones and are a curious kind of grave deposit. These small containers can seem somewhat like time capsules, particularly if they are ancient in origin, like the *New Testament*–priest Caiaphas' ossuary (Specter, 1992, p. 2E). Some archaeological finds of human remains may not have been deliberately buried, although there is a similarity to the physical anthropological-forensic science aspects of all these investigations. One microcosm burial is of the royal court and "state apparatus" of the 2200-year-old empire of China's first ruler, Ch'in Shihuang. His realm gave "China" its name. These 8000 stone burial deposit statues are an accurate microcosm of the military science of the Emperor Chin's realm and appear to individually represent the distinctive facial appearances of the once-living humans they depict. They endure as terra cotta stand-ins for a long dead imperial guard army *(Treasure! Tomb of the Terra Cotta Warriors*, 1999). The unopened tomb of that emperor apparently lies nearby, perhaps in a simulacrum of the imperial palace of his dynasty.

Defining the significance of foundation stones, cornerstone deposits and building ceremonies is a key to the history and function of time capsules. Deliberately deposited cornerstones or other repositories such as modern time capsules are sometimes characterized as deliberate archaeology deliberately left for future retrieval ("Archaeology for the Future now being sealed in Crypts," 1938, pp. 179–80). Obviously, foundation deposits and cornerstone repositories are potential sites or features for archaeological research, just as they can be aspects of architectural history or historical preservation. Many aspects of the history, function and development of foundation and cornerstone deposits as building customs can be traced. Our purpose with these deliberate deposits is to briefly categorize their archaeological value. The origins of the deliberately dedicated deposited time capsule experience can be tracked back at least to the beginnings of ancient Bronze Age civilization, if not to even earlier, pre-metallurgical type cultures ("Building ceremonies," 1972, p. 69; "Cornerstone," 1901–2; Leick, 1988, p. 79). A variety of related practices have been perpetuated over many millennia, continuing into our own age (Hettel, 1952, pp. 209–16). We will be comparing ancient and modern manifestations of these human urges to dedicate sites for various purposes, in order to meaningfully compare past with current practices, and to trace the evolution from the earlier to later forms (Talos, 1987, pp. 395–401). Ancient foundation deposits have been noted in archaeological works which feature brief vignettes of their discovery and presumed ceremony (Parrot, 1955, pp. 30, 78, 106). A wide variety of other building customs are related to cornerstone deposit rituals, including tree-topping ceremonies, roof-tree occasions and flag raisings over structures when they first reach the specified full height (Collins, 1931, pp. 178–82). Technical specialists in fossil fuel materials note that some stone Sumerian dedication tablets and inscribed Assyrian wall bricks are still firmly imbedded in their bituminous pitch (Abraham, 1963, pp. 17, 29).

There are seven age-old characteristics of cornerstone deposits and rituals. A cornerstone is any specially prepared stone placed in a building, for an indefinite period, and considered important for depositors to do a dedication-deposit ceremony. Some may have small chambers for various documents, newspapers, coins or other topical tokens or mementos (Mulford, 1950a, pp. 66–67; 1950b, pp. 84–85; 1952, pp. 60–61, 75–80). A formal ceremony might include a parade or a processional event, followed by a religio-magical invoked sanction (absent in our contemporary contexts), a trench excavation (perhaps now just a token ground-breaking), anointing the spot to appease the building spirits, considering the foundation stone-cornerstone as a seed to "grow" the building (including the insertion of charms, amulets or figurines), leaving valuable gifts such as gold or silver, etc. Finally, Mulford noted the use of inscriptions commemorating the builders, the building and their times. In later eras, documents in containers came to be common in such dedication deposits.

Ancient Mesopotamian foundation deposit practices have been extensively described and explained. The origins of time capsule deposit can be seen in ancient Mesopotamian practices. There are numerous examples of these clay and metal artifact and tablet deposits throughout ancient Mesopotamian history (Ellis, 1968). Old Testament Biblical era cornerstone motifs and practices can be identified as well (M'Clintock & Strong, 1890, pp. 518–19). One whole subset of ancient Sumerian clay media inscriptions consists of door sockets, inscribed bricks and a wide variety of other foundation deposit shapes (Kramer, 1993). These were earlier non-corner, non-repository foundation dedication and votive deposits. When the Mesopotamian city of Mashkan-shapir, founded around 2050 BC, was destroyed ca. 1720 BC, it was not rebuilt. In the late 1980s, an aerial archaeological survey team noticed the clear remains of the city plan. The excavators found about 150 fragments of clay cylinders that had been once been deposited as full cylinders in the city walls. Texts on the cylinders not only identified the city's royal founder but also indicated a city wall construction date of 1843 BC. The cylinders boasted of high laborers' wages. It has been conjectured that these texts were probably inflated propaganda claims (Bower, 1989, p. 198; Stone & Zimansky, 1995, p.118+).

This royal boasting is an interesting early example of a government statistical claim stated for public relations purposes. Extensive investigation of the site does tend to support an interpretation of that city as being a more "consultative" approach to social organization than one might imagine about ancient Mesopotamian societies. Many significant scholarly syntheses of Mesopotamian civilization take note of foundation deposits and their votive type of inscription, and with good reason. Not only are they striking to the modern retriever, they were important as ceremonial writings to their royal depositors (Oppenheim, 1964, pp. 26, 147, 234). Mesopotamian master builders' building inscriptions and foundation deposits boastfully celebrated the achievements of their kingdoms' temples and city walls. These boastful kings were pious preservers and re-depositors of their ancient predecessors' own foundation deposits, sacred traditionalists to the core. It was common to have an earlier royal builder include pleas for future "crediting" by later priest-kings who might rebuild the older "ritual-bureaucratic" walls, city, temple, palace, etc., on the same hallowed site ("Building inscription," 1988, pp. 38–39; "Foundation deposit," 1988, pp. 80–81; Perrot, 1884, pp. 311–22; Woolley & Moorey, 1982, pp. 227–31). Assyrian rulers deposited such "ceremonial writings" in various forms and materials, including clay cones (Donbaz & Grayson, 1984). Sometimes these cones are referred to as "clay nails" or "clay pegs." A treatise on the archaeology of these foundation deposits charts 14 types of these deposits, and associated activities through 15 chronological political periods of Mesopotamian cultures. There are 210 active categories of examples, including site purification, royal participation, human sacrifice, animal sacrifice, pegs, stone tablets, metal tablets, clay tablets, cones, cylinders, prisms, protective figurines, food offerings and offerings of materials (Ellis, 1968, fig. 35). The comparative frequency of each practice is depicted, although not all those cultural periods have yielded evidence of each column category of deposit practice. The archaeological record is unclear on evidence of human sacrifice. Numerous formal dedication objects such as figurines and various clay shapes like nails, spikes, peg shapes, and written cylinders are exhibited in major museums (Van Buren, 1931, Plates I–XX). Those deposits were not necessarily confined to a corner of a building. All four corners of a foundation might instead be singled out for the symbolic planting of an artifact, with or without a container. Mesopotamian brick foundation boxes contained figurines, tablets or other votive deposits. One typical Ur III period pattern contains a basket-bearing, bronze-figurine peg-deposit and an accompanying plano-convex shaped limestone inscribed tablet. These were customarily placed inside bitumen-sealed brick foundation boxes (Ellis, 1968, p. 96, fig. 21).

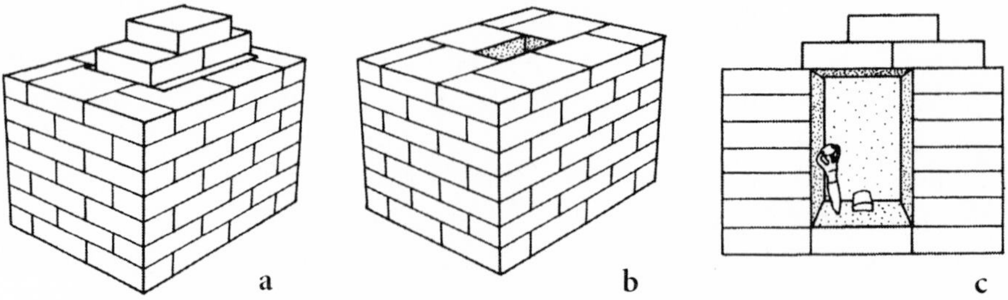

Typical peg deposit "canophoros" (basket-bearing) bronze-figurine and an accompanying plano-convex stone-inscribed tablet in a bitumen-sealed brick foundation box. An idealized schematic of typical Mesopotamian Ur III period deposits, ca. 2100–1800 BCE. (a) Closed top of bitumen-sealed baked brick foundation box-capsule. (b) Opening at top of baked brick box-capsule. (c) Cross-section of the inscribed contents, a plano-convex limestone tablet and a bronze peg figurine. (R. S. Ellis, 1968. *Foundation deposits in ancient Mesopotamia.* Courtesy Yale University Press.)

Ancient foundation deposits were deliberately buried, but they were not deposited with the intent to retrieve them on a given target date. The time span of such a deposit was for the duration of the building it was to commemorate, much as those found in today's buildings' cornerstone deposits. Customarily the consecrated building in question was either a major corporate or public structure such as a temple, royal palace, gate or bridge. Everyday non-special structures such as domestic residences were apparently also formally consecrated with brick-boxed, inscribed figurines, relics or sacred inscriptions (Woolley, 1926, pp. 688–713; Woolley & Moorey, 1982, pp. 227–31). Neo-Babylonian era prophylactic figurines were enshrined in at least some domestic buildings. Apparently already antique (1700-year-old at the time) bricks were reused for those roof-and-walled three-brick shrines. A wide variety of animal and anthropomorphic "apotropaic" sickness-evil charms have been found and described. In some sites, numerous U-shaped, "sentry-box"–style shrines were constructed next to house walls. Such spirit-charm figurines have also been located in buried brick-boxes under domestic thresholds in some other city sites of ca. 600 BCE Mesopotamia (Woolley, 1926, pp. 688–713). As two scholars of the late nineteenth century observed:

> Thus from the beginning to the end of Chaldaean civilization the custom was preserved of consecrating a building by hiding in its substance objects to which a divine type and engraved text gave both a talismanic and a commemorative value (Perrot & Chipiez, 1884, p. 318, figs. 146–50).

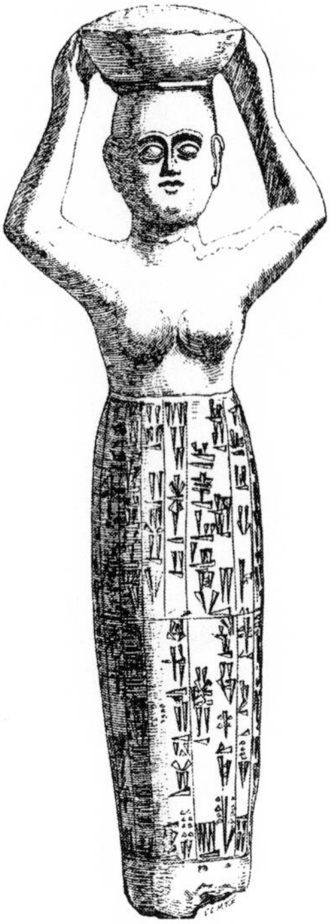

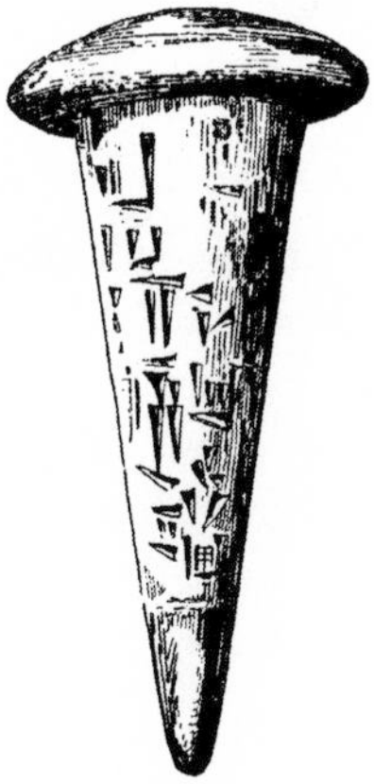

Regarding the festivities of one Mesopotamian palace's foundation dedication, the Assyrian monarch Sargon noted that "The people threw their amulets" (Perrot & Chipiez, 1884, p. 320). This plebian participation was part of a formal foundation deposit ritual, rather than of a vernacular, domestic-building's protection-deposit rite. Some of these very amulets with their small necklace holes are now in the Louvre Museum. Both archival records and artifactual evidence confirm this ancient deposit of hundreds of small figurines, cylinders and cones of terra cotta in the wall and gate areas of Sargon's palace. Nebuchadnezzar, the king of the mid–first millennium BCE New Babylonian period, had terra cotta cylinder seals placed inside *hollowed-out* foundation stones, "foundation boxes" at the angles of new temples. Those messages invoked divine protection for those precincts (Mulford, 1952, pp. 60–61, 75–80; Perrot & Chipiez, 1884, pp. 311–22). Those later Mesopotamian periods' cornerstone-style repository deposits seem in line with contemporaneous Assyrian influences, and may also be seen in Persian and Ptolemic-Hellenistic artifacts. Henry Rawlinson was able to direct his late nineteenth century archaeological dig workers to some of Nebuchadnezzar's foun-

Top, left: Inscribed "canophoros" (basket-carrying) figurine deposit, solid bronze 10.5 inches, Mesopotamia. (Perrot & Chipiez, 1884. _A history of art in Chaldaea & Assyria_, vol. 2.) _Top, right:_ Inscribed cone deposit, terra cotta, six inches, Mesopotamia. (Perrot & Chipiez, 1884. _A history of art in Chaldaea & Assyria_, vol. 1.) _Bottom, left:_ Peg-figurine, "apotropaic-type" deposit, bronze, 8.25 inches, Mesopotamia. (Perrot & Chipiez, 1884. _A history of art in Chaldaea & Assyria_, vol. 1.)

dation deposits. His project was able to retrieve cylinders deposited in the seventh century BCE, based on his experience with ancient building commemoration practices (Mulford, 1950a, pp. 66–67). Another significant series of votive foundation tablet deposits is that of the Assyrian King Esarhaddon, who had inscribed tablets and talismans deposited in foundation areas of important buildings (Ellis, 1968, p. 103). Apparently "prospecting" for royal foundation deposits was (and still is) a ruler's preoccupation throughout the ancient Mesopotamian world. Such pleas and customs resonate today in the current Republic of Iraqi state policy of rebuilding an ancient palace in Babylon (Lewis, 1989, p. A4; Mulford, 1952, pp. 60–61, 75–80). The current Iraqi government apparently continues to deposit bricks at the site of ancient Babylon stamped with the name and date of the current ruler.

There were four basic functions of ancient Mesopotamian foundation deposit practices. Sanctification, protection, commemoration and elaboration are the four types of motivation posited from Mesopotamian foundation deposits (Ellis, 1968). The sanctification and protection of buildings are noted as common motives. Also emphasized is the role of commemorating the ruler and the "elaboration," or enhancing, of the value of the building as motives that seem to predominate in ancient Mesopotamian foundation deposits. Such motivational analyses and inferences from archaeological finds and museum exhibits can be subjective, but it is hard not to see these common motives in ancient foundation deposits, modern cornerstone repositories and time capsule deposits. These larger-ranging and more deeply based expressions of human activity have as a common denominator the broader definition of all such "founding," foundation, buildings' protection, construction or boundary setting practices.

Ancient Egyptian building tradecraft, foundation dedication customs, and modern postscripts are another pre-time capsule tradition. Egyptian foundation deposit rites predate Alexandrine Hellenistic practices (Clarke & Engelbach, 1930, pp. 60–61; Jequier, 1924, pp. 33–60; Petrie, 1938, pp. 46–49). Although Hellenistic practices in Alexandria may have had Dynastic, pre–Hellenistic Egyptian influences, those ancient dynastic Egyptian (pre–Hellenistic) foundation activities seem to have been basically different from later Alexandrine customs and contents. The latter seem to have a line of descent from Persian-Assyrian sources, as we will see later (Rowe & Rees, 1956-1957; Wright, 1982, pp. 18–21). Egyptian building customs and tradecraft appear to be the basic sources of many modern building trade practices. The similarities are really striking, and not solely in building dedication customs. Familiar building trade practices to us today were practiced in ancient Egypt as well. These include: "snapping a line" (actually a *red* chalk line — not a blue one — in Egyptian practice), "blueprints" (not blue, and on papyrus), the use of working site copies sketched onto lime chip "ostraka," and the use of a wide variety of geometric formulae (National Geographic Society, 1951, pp. 158–59). Ancient Egyptian building customs seemed to have included the deposit of miniature tool sets, plaques, and animal sacrifices in the foundations of temples (Clarke, 1930, pp. 60–61; Leick, 1988, p. 79). Many of those foundation deposits were apparently at random. Egyptian illustrations of a temple foundation dedication do strike a contemporary cord. Much the same sort of ritual is done today at a cornerstone-laying celebration. One set of illustrations is a four-frame sequence of a foundation dedication ceremony, complete with ground preparation, supernatural invocations, sand pouring and the (apparently ageless!) practice of a dignitary attending to the level of a foundation building block (Jequier, 1924, fig. 10–13). This is all immediately recognizable in our contemporary world culture. For example, it is almost irresistible to suppose that the tools depicted would likely be special ceremonial versions of those tools. Clarke & Engelbach depict the same four Temple of Edfu's ceremonial scenes that Jequier features (Clarke & Engelbach, 1930, pp. 60–61; Jequier, 1924, pp. 33–60; Rose, 1988; Watterson, 1998). Clarke, however, interprets the sacred pouring, or lustration, as a solely symbolic-blessing lustration with seeds or incense. Jequier states the sand-pouring scene interpretation, which seems more likely since it was apparently both a practical and symbolic foundation-preparation practice of the Dynastic Egyptians. Ancient Egyptian technology, including real and model votive type building dedication tools and items are described (Lucas, 1962). A wide range of Egyptian foundation deposit dedication items have been discovered. These include real-sized tools presumably used in actual first brick-molding events, numerous half-sized symbolic-votive deposit items, tools, finely decorated and inscribed plaquettes and even some of these votive models perhaps retained and treasured by participants as mementos of the momentous occasion (Badawy, 1947).

One of two modern Egyptian postscripts is the relocated Abu Simbel complex and its "contemporary" foundation deposit. In the early 1960s, the whole complex of monumental ancient sacred sites at the ancient Egypt's Pharonic Abu Simbel would be flooded as the Aswan Dam's Lake Nasser filled up. An international team working closely with the Egyptian government moved the monumentally huge Abu Simbel Great and Small Temples, and rescued other architectural monuments and sites in various ways (Gerster, 1963, pp. 587–621; Saeve-Soederbergh, 1987). After an extensive process of disassembling the huge stone figures from their former

These ancient Egyptian scenes of a temple foundation dedication strike a contemporary chord. These rituals are related to our own era's cornerstone dedications. It appears that the ritual's tools included special, ceremonial items. These scenes are from the second through fifth of a series of 14 distinct temple wall reliefs featuring the foundation ceremony, including a procession from the royal palace over to the temple construction site. (De Rochemonteix & Chassinat, 1884–. *Le temple d' Edfou (Vol. X: Memoires publies par les membres de la Mission archaelogique francaise au Caire, Plate XL, b. c. d. e.* Paris.) ***Top left:*** Delineation, "staking-out" of the Temple's precinct grounds; ***top right:*** Groundbreaking and supernatural invocations; ***bottom left:*** The lustration, a consecrating sprinkle, here most probably of poured sand; ***bottom right:*** The (apparently ageless!) practice of the dignitary attending to the level of a foundation block, here a molded brick.

cliff face, the Joint Venture engineers laid the first stone of the reassembled Abu Simbel Great Temple at its new site above flood level on January 4, 1966. Three weeks later, it was time to reinstall the four gods in the Sanctuary. The engineers followed age-old customs of depositing foundation relics under the statues of seated-god-kings. Included were Egypt's National Charter, two Cairo newspapers, various coins, the Koran and an account of the special event (Gerster, 1969, p. 728). The Small Temple had to be cut apart and reassembled. A great deal of discussion over the competing priorities of archaeologically validated verisimilitude, contemporary aesthetic effects and preservational concerns went on throughout all phases of the project. One good example of that process was the compromise decision on how to fill the surfaces of cracks left from its transplantation. Now erosion has been thwarted, the visual appearance is one of clean lines and the interior cracks are obvious future archaeological evidence as to the transplanted status of the installation (Gerster, 1969, p. 744). The Great Temple was apparently carefully oriented to the sun, so that its rays could shine all the way back 180 feet to illuminate its Sanctuary on Rameses' 30-year jubilee (Gerster, 1963, p. 717). Such "archaeologically correct" or at least professionally scrupulous attempts to rebury or to register digging projects of our (to be) ancient excavations is now a regular feature of much archaeological site research and architectural restoration work. Relocated, rededicated obelisks are a second postscript example of modern Egyptian dedication-foundation deposits. The "Cleopatra's Needle Obelisk" was taken in 1878 from Alexandria, Egypt, and then replanted in London. A British foundation deposit box was added, containing photographs of women, a box load of hairpins, a Bible, cigars and a razor (Klein, 1958, pp. 80–81; Remington, 1954, pp. 16–17). Another such Alexandria obelisk was transplanted to Central Park in New York City (Tompkins, 1981, pp. 282–307).

Imperial Persian and Ptolemic Hellenistic foundation dedication tablet inscriptions were major symbolic world-cultural declarations in their day. The ancient building dedication customs of depositing relics in foundations were not limited to Mesopotamia or even Egypt. The Persian King Darius deposited inscribed tablets of solid gold and silver in the four limestone cornerstones of his Persepolis palace 2500 years ago (Mulford, 1952, pp. 60–61, 75–80). These Persian cornerstone-foundation deposit-box and tablet inscription practices later appear in Hellenistic Alexandria. Persian and later Hellenistic Ptolemic foundation-dedication plaque practices are apparent cultural diffusions from Assyrian-Mesopotamian practices (Rowe, & Rees, 1956–1957; Wright, 1982, pp. 18–21). Hellenistic Egyptian items contained in stone foundation boxes seem like Persian Imperial practices. They are markedly different from the non-boxed, non-container Athenian Agora or Egyptian (Old-Middle-New Kingdom) building deposits (Grant, 1990, p. 179). Their line of descent seems to be Persian-Assyrian-Mesopotamian (Ellis, 1968, fig. 21; Rowe & Rees, 1956-1957; Wright, 1982, pp. 18–21). The placement of a deposit within a brick box is traceable back to some Mesopotamian examples (Ellis, 1968, fig. 21). These deposit practices have great popular archaeological interest as conceptual bridges between ancient Mesopotamian foundation deposit rituals and our modern era's cornerstone and time capsule activities (Wright, 1970; 1982). Those resembled Nebuchadnezzar's corner-sited repository (i.e., container-type) foundation deposit "cornerstones." There are clear similarities between the ancient physical deposit rituals of foundation stones and the burial practices of twentieth century time capsule vessels. There is a major difference between the two ranges of dedication phenomena. They differ in the degree to which inscriptions, various ceremonial writings and miscellaneous contents contribute to the character of the foundation deposit. The larger the role or textual lengths of any inscriptions, the more the deposit seems like a modern time capsule. The "inscription content factor" of a container can distinguish an ancient inscribed or contained foundation deposit from a modern time capsule vessel and its distinctive deposits of contents and messages.

The Temple of Sarapis, the Sarapieon, was the crown jewel of the Ptolemies' Hellenistic patron-god in the City of Alexandria. Major archaeological foundation deposit discoveries were made in 1943. From remaining foundation structures in the greater temple area were recovered two sets of ten foundation tablets. These were inscribed with both Greek and Egyptian ceremonial, dedicatory writing on gold, silver, bronze and faience tablets (Empereur, 1999b, pp. 27, 89, 96–97; Frazer, 1972; Rowe & Rees, 1956-1957, pp. 485–520; Stambaugh, 1972, p. 7; Wright, 1982, pp. 18–21). Fortunately the crypt areas of these ancient, treasured time capsules survived the razing of the whole aboveground complex of the Sarapieon in the sectarian violence of 391 CE. The numerous dedicatory plaques, dedication graffiti, statuettes and deposits of coins are part of a complex pattern of extensive dedication foundation deposition in the Sarapieon area and other Hellenistic Alexandrine sites (Rowe & Rees, 1956-1957, pp. 485–520). Foundation deposits play a noteworthy role in the archaeological record of that ancient culture area. Interestingly, these foundation deposit layouts seem to utilize Egyptian-style niches cut into the "living bedrock" of the foundations, although the contents appear Persian-derived (Frazer, 1972). The survival of these dedication plaques in foundation deposits illustrates the high probability of success via a buried metallic document deposit approach to sending long term messages. It underscores the poorer prognosis of such transmissions via cultural collections of books, journals and various other media-formats such as are chronically amassed in the world's great libraries, right out in the open, above ground. When fires or mob action destroys a library, the foundation (and any deposits therein) may survive.

Greco-Roman Mediterranean foundation deposits practices were also commonplace features of their cultures. These are amply documented, as are somewhat later Romano-British examples (Merrifield, 1987, pp. 51–55; Thompson, D. B., 1993). For example the Agora of third and fourth century BC Athens, Greece, was replete with inexpensive special votive pottery, and sacrificial chickens were buried under the flooring of the marketplace's many buildings (Thompson, D. B., 1993). Their use seems to have been rather widespread in that broadly defined cultural era, common enough to have apparently been cheaply manufactured as pottery specimens for these one time votive deposit uses (Grant, 1990, p. 179). One might assume that these practices occurred in earlier centuries as well. The Classical Greek era dedication deposit-protection customs basically predate the Alexandrian Hellenistic period's relics, while the Roman cultural deposit practices continued as basically contemporary with the Hellenistic era's activity. The cornerstone type foundation deposit dedications of Hellenistic Alexandria appear to have been more influenced by Persian deposit fashions, as noted above.

South Asian and East Asian foundation stone and construction rite practices are also variations on this universal global theme. The ancient West Asian and Greek culture periods were not the only traditions with foundation deposit and related signification-dedicatory practices. Moving away from the West Asian cultural sphere, it is possible to identify a variety of Hindu and Chinese culturally rooted dedication deposit rites and objects. The widespread impulse to enact construction and foundation rites includes traditional Hindu foundation ceremonies. Before the foundation stone was put in place, a divinatory rite was customarily conducted (Eliade, 1954, pp. 18–19). There are a variety of Chinese and related South East Asian sacred tablet deposits citations as well (Wright, 1970, pp. 466–68; Wright, 1982, p. 5). These include various Pali sacred texts inscribed on precious metals, as well as approximately 20,000 Chinese Turkestan area Buddhist scrolls secreted in caves apparently against the incursions of non-believing invaders (Wright, 1982, p. 5). These extensive cultural deposits have been rightly characterized as "buried libraries" (Wright, 1982, p. 5). Among the many examples of ancient metallic documents noted in South and East Asia are the Burmese gold leaf Pali Buddhist script specimens.

The ca. 6.5 by 1.25 inches specimens are similar to older Indian palm leaf script examples (Wright, 1982, pp. 467–68). The record of Far East Asian and Middle Eastern ancient metallic documents is extensive (Wright, 1970; 1982). There is a close relationship between the concept of ancient deposits such as foundation dedication relics and the notion of ancient libraries of deposited writings.

European cornerstone, foundation deposit, buildings' customs, construction rites, and other symbolic dedication practices were carried out in Medieval and post–Medieval periods. In Medieval Europe, the familiar cornerstone repository customarily occurs as a part of ecclesiastical deposit practices at western Medieval European Christian churches (Britton, 1836, p. 31; M'Clintock & Strong, 1890, pp. 518–19). It is clear from various such accounts that these building dedication ceremonials were a regular part of church life in the High Middle Ages of Western Europe. There are a variety of records about these Medieval European cornerstone deposit practices. There were a wide number of such rites, customs and deposit practices both as formal and as vernacular occurrences in the later European Middle Ages. Histories of ecclesiastical architecture emphasize buildings, biographies of personages, financial grants and a wide variety of related ceremonials. There are also occasional brief notations of foundation stone dedication ceremonial details. One relates Archbishop John Thoresby's dedication activities at York Cathedral on the (Julian calendar) date of July 29, 1361 (Britton, 1836, p. 31). Later Medieval European builders reportedly placed the names of building fund contributors and other mementos inside the hollowed cornerstones of public buildings (Remington, 1954, pp. 16–17; Salzman, 1952, pp. 82+). The English cornerstone ceremonies noted in one major history of English building traditions (pre–1540) are not indicated as being repositories, containers of relics or stones with small chambers in them. Rather the practices are described simply as cornerstones deposited in buildings. Salzman's work enumerates deposits in fireplaces, windows and walls in addition to deposits in foundations. The historical continuity of dedication, foundation site and other building ceremonial deposits from the pre–Medieval European world is apparent. These ancient practices seemed to have been carried on almost automatically, without much chronicling of details about them at the time (Salzman, 1952, pp. 82+). Another source notes foundation-laying ceremonies in Biblical accounts. Cited as well are dedication rituals at the (AD 1220 England) Salisbury Cathedral and the August 14, 1248, service for the rebuilt Cologne, Germany, Cathedral (Hettel, 1952, pp. 209–16). The Cologne Cathedral foundation deposit was an actual hollowed out repository of various items. Those included an account of the ceremony, consecrated waxen saintly images, coins and some unspecified items apparently typical of the time of deposit. This AD 1248 Cologne foundation deposit ritual and repository's contents have the features of modern indefinitely deposited cornerstone-foundation practices. Other wax-and-string votive forms depicting horse and human portions were found in the fifteenth century Exeter, England, cathedral tomb of Bishop Lacey (Merrifield, 1987, p. 90, fig. 28). All these ecclesiastical commemoration efforts have a wider contextual ceremonial significance of general, traditional consecration practices (Britton, 1836; M'Clintock & Strong, 1890, pp. 518–19). In addition to these formal "cathedral commissioning" foundation ceremonies, there is evidence of more mundane, vernacular, popular, informal practices as well. One later deposit example — an early seventeenth century English child's shoe found behind wooden paneling (in a child's room) — would seem to be just such a building (and building resident's) protection deposit (Boatwright, 1994, p. 18).

Nineteenth and twentieth century "vernacular" building foundation customs were also practiced. Rather than give the limelight to formal cornerstone laying ceremonials at this point, let's examine a few vernacular building trade customs of recent times. These practices survived a variety of cultural transformations in language, religion, society and technological building craft. These traditional practices endured into recent times. Archaeologists of ancient civilizations are not the only researchers to discover building protection deposits, often vernacular, which seem to have magical motivations. British examples of urine-filled (apparently) demon-blocking deposits in the chimneys of fireplaces, shoes placed in walls and burials of various curios under thresholds abound (Merrifield, 1987). These practices seem to have been continued almost reflexively, somewhat in the way people still touch or "knock on wood." The depositors may not affirm a specific belief-system about what they do, but they carry on the practice. It may mean carrying brides over the threshold, or leaving snacks for Santa Claus in anticipation of that folkloristic figure's magical entrance (and exit) via the chimney. Topping off a newly completed structure with a small tree, or flag, or the inscribing of mottos on one's dwelling also express archetypal building dedication-protection practices of humankind's past. One suspects that such practices go back to the origins of building or even to the most rudimentary marking off of human encampments, as a part of such delineation of habitation. Even theme center edifices such as the White House and the Capitol Building in Washington, D.C., harbor evidence of the continuity of this cultural tradition of informal, spontaneous, ancient oral tradition–transmitted folk customs. They can be literal building protection markings. For example, note the reported self-identification of Serbian-ethnic buildings in Kosovo, to avoid sectarian acts of destruction, by marking buildings with the initials of traditional Serbian "rallying cry" slogans (Erlanger, 1999, p. A1). On a more benign note, there is evidence of the persistence (or should we say rather constant manifestation?) of such informal building protection-consecration practices in Britain and in the U.S. One house builder recorded finding a message in a can from the 1850 builder of an American house. It was in a space where only a major renovator of the structure would find it. Likewise, there is the recent practice of leaving lumber crayon–made messages to future craftsman in the houses built in the 1980s as reported by Kidder (1985, p. 140). That author notes the archetypal, mythic-roots of vernacular building dedication impulses. Nothing could be more natural than to leave word of one's creations to those who may one day tend and repair them (Kidder, 1985, p. 140). There are nineteenth century examples of this sort of craft workers' "building signature," such as a British plasterer's written message from the year 1897 (Rothenstein & Gooding, 1998, illus. #30). Nineteenth century African-American ritual deposits under flooring in the Chesapeake Bay area consisted of coins and buttons from the Civil War era ("Hoodoo cache," 2000, p. 21).

It seems that the oral traditional transmission of such vernacular "signification rites" has gone on from generation to generation, handed down as dedication practices by building trades-people and householders. Consider such traditional building customs as the ever present "topping" ceremonies, wherein an evergreen tree (or sometimes, in the U.S., a national flag) is placed atop a structure when the top layer of framework is reached in a building's construction. Where do construction workers learn this? Presumably this is the sort of thing that is passed on by doing, by word of mouth via other construction workers over the years. These practices would seem to be an oral tradition many thousands of years old, at least in its basic thrust if not in every detail of motifs displayed. The notion that such a variety of mythic-symbolic enactments have been transmitted via oral tradition for many hundreds of years might seem farfetched. There are various well-documented examples of hoary, pre-modern British Isle children's folkloristic schoolyard and play-yard ditties, games and chants being documented across thousands of years (Opie, 1977). Presumably, less verbal, more action-oriented building customs have been preserved and propagated across millennia as well, including ribbon-cutting building dedication ceremonials. The vast subject area of building dedications and protection rituals, etc., could itself merit a whole book. Nineteenth and twentieth century construction and building protection rites have been documented in detailed comparative studies of

Dacian (modern Romanian) religious practices and folklore in particular, and in Eastern Europe in general (Eliade, 1972, pp. 162–69+). Presumably these folkloristic stories and rites had precursors in prior ages, although not necessarily in exactly the same patterns as today.

The formal nineteenth century dedication deposit at Promontory Point, Utah, on the afternoon of May 10, 1869, was a noteworthy ritual, the ritual driving of two final rail spikes joining the Union Pacific and Central Pacific Railroads ("East and West: completion of the Great Line spanning the continent," 1869, p.1). The opening prayer, the presentation of the symbolic spikes to be driven in by dignitaries, the speeches by the elite and the overall celebration remind us of ancient Egyptian and Mesopotamian foundation deposit ritual acts. Remember the clay "spike-nails" of Mesopotamian foundation deposits? New York City's Pulitzer Building cornerstone repository-type time capsule was standard, but the storage of its location diagram was unusual. That architectural drawing was itself sealed away in the cornerstone it was supposed to "find" ("Recaptured," 1956, pp. 26–27)! Mementos or relics can be placed inside buildings in various ways, not always in cornerstones or even in foundations of their buildings at all. The physical shape of a capsule can vary widely. There is a rather odd example of a copper grasshopper-shaped architectural ornament that has been positioned atop Boston's Faneuil Hall tower for over 255 years. When it was being repaired in the early 1950s, a rattling noise was heard from inside the hollow insect shape. Inside, a long metal box was found, bearing Boston newspapers dated from 1889, some notes and some cards from city officials of that time. The contents were apparently deposited there in 1889. That was the last time the antique grasshopper had been taken down for refurbishing (Remington, 1954, pp. 16–17). This grasshopper deposit is actually an example of a building elaboration custom, along the lines of other cornerstone repositories and ceremonials. The Allentown, Pennsylvania, School of Nursing, May 13, 1988, was the scene of a cornerstone opening (Lathrop, 1988, p. B13). The cornerstone of the school's building was originally deposited in 1950. The latter occasion was the pending June 11 graduation of the last class of the school's nursing students. After dignitaries opened the cornerstone and displayed contents such as nursing pamphlets, old coins and local newspapers from 1950, the cornerstone repository and its content were put on exhibit in the building's lobby. The plan was to reenter the old artifacts after the June graduates added their own relics during that last, school-closing graduation ceremony.

Cornerstones and the contents of their repositories can become orphaned due to migration or theft. An abandoned East St. Louis, Illinois, synagogue was torn down in 1998, revealing a 1916 copper time capsule about the size of a shoebox. The synagogue's congregation had disbanded in 1961. Local building regulatory authorities had to initiate a search to find descendants of the former congregation ("UP Eye on Illinois: blast from the past," 1998). Yet another indefinitely deposited time capsule was vandalized and broken into, and its content of medals stolen from a city park's World War II monument ("Auburn Vets want new war memorial," 1998, p. B4). Both of these time capsules are really cornerstone repositories, due to their indefinite deposit as part of buildings or monuments. Cornerstones and time capsules can be lost at first, and even damaged during rediscovery. Both of these things happened to the lost cornerstone's capsule of an Ohio Catholic Church (Neary, 1994). The 100-year-old cornerstone time capsule was drilled through after being discovered by the use of a metal detector. One interesting 1983 building dedication ceremonial carried out in France involved the entrenchment of the remains of a building dedication's lunch table remains (Rothenstein & Gooding, 1998, illus. 43).

Washington, D.C., is a foundation deposit treasure trove. The District of Columbia is replete with cornerstone building deposits. The Office of the Architect of the Capitol houses an extensive set of records on the cornerstone laying for numerous Federal buildings in the District of Columbia, including President Kennedy's modification of a tradition begun by Masonic luminary George Washington. Basically, Kennedy apparently disestablished the quasi-official participation of Masonic lodges in the ceremonial business of laying the cornerstones of Federal buildings (Berger & Jarvis, 1999; Hettel, 1952, pp. 209–16; ITCS, 1991). The Washington Monument's cornerstone is a good example of an official secular, civic repository deposited on July 4, 1848. This zinc container in the Washington Monument cornerstone is filled with a copy of the Constitution, George Washington's portrait, samples of money, issues of 75 newspapers and a silk U.S. Flag. It has no deliberately specified target date for retrieval (Klein, 1958, pp. 80–81; Remington, 1954, pp. 16–17; Tompkins, 1981, pp. 321–23, 329–37). The Monument, like the Capital City itself, is a landmark with a foundation deposit of symbolic relics. This deposit commemorates the completion of this Masonic-like obelisk to U.S. Constitutional government and the "Founding Fathers" (Murdock, 1952, pp. 162–65; *To the immortal name and memory of George Washington*, 1984). The Monument is an obelisk, and many memorial stones are imbedded in its structure. A zinc repository was inserted as a cornerstone deposit on July 4, 1848. None other than master Mason and U.S. President George Washington purportedly laid another classic cornerstone deposit at the U.S. Capitol Building.

It has somehow gone missing over the long life of that evolving building (ITCS, 1991). The commemoration of one U.S. president's term of office by another via a cornerstone dedication has been a common practice in Washington, D.C. ("1939: President Roosevelt laid the cornerstone of the Jefferson Memorial in Washington, D.C.," 1939).

Teddy Roosevelt, Harry Truman and George H. W. Bush (1989–1993) has each carried on the White House foundation deposit tradition. During the late 1940s renovation of the U.S. White House, a small marble box was retrieved from under an entrance area. Its contents dating from 1902 building refurbishment included newspaper reports of then–President Theodore Roosevelt's annual State of the Union speech to the Congress, a label from a Maryland rye whiskey bottle and seven Indian head one cent coins (Klein, 1958, pp. 80–81; Remington, 1954, pp. 16–17; "1902 mementos found under White House entrance," 1950, p. 463). President Truman had the marble box and contents reburied in another White House foundation site, adding some newspapers to the renewal deposit. Note the many ancient elements in this twentieth century deposit. There are coins, a message from the "sovereign," evidence of a celebratory toast offering of food and beverages, the box made of special materials, the location of the box as a protective item under an entranceway, the palace mansion structure site, the rebuilding on the site as the occasion of discover, and even the renewal-reburial by the contemporary sovereign. These elements are all features traditional to foundation deposits. Given just the brief bare bones description of items, site and dates, the ancient deposit elements are quite evident. This building commemoration deposit tradition has been carried on in more recent times. George H. W. Bush's 1989–1993 administration deposited a time capsule to commemorate the two hundredth anniversary of the building. It included among other items a winding ring used to service approximately 85 antique clocks there (Knutson, 1996).

The U.S. Capitol Building is a dime-coin "pledge offering" deposit site. In addition to being the home of the 1876-1976 Centennial Safe, the Capitol is home to at least one more recent foundation deposit item. It seems based on an ancient, archetypal urge to dedicate, sacrifice or pledge something at some place designated as somehow special, all to obtain some goal. Call it what you will, but this primordial urge to make votive offerings has its way from time to time. Sometime around 1950, David S. Pryor of Camden, Arkansas, first came to Washington, D.C., as a schoolboy page to U.S. House of Representatives members. He resolved to return as an elected member of that House. He deposited just a single dime (although his ten-cent piece was worth a little more then) and secreted it in a wall crack on the House of Representatives side of that building. He then promised to himself that he wouldn't remove it until he achieved his elected goal, which he did in 1965. He decided not to remove the dime at all, however. Eventually he was elected to the U.S. Senate, on the other side of the Capitol Building. "Pryor's Dime" remains as a donation pledge, a modern civic commemorative example of a personal foundation deposit. The location of the dime coin remained Pryor's secret. His deposit was still in place decades after (Clarity & Weaver, 1985, p. A12).

Ancient Roman and Medieval European founding and cornerstone rituals were drawn on by Masonic societies in recent centuries, as one reading of Washington, D.C., town-planning symbolism explains (Ovason, 2000, pp.74, 76–79+). A distinction is also made there between "chthonic," earth-signifying ancient founding deposits underground and the above-ground, "light-seeking" cornerstone repositories of Medieval Europe and modern times. We can perhaps lay on another layer of symbolic meaning with the notion of our target-dated, future-seeking time capsules. Time capsules can thus be seen as a third modality in the history of dedication deposit practices, buried or not. The Capital City's secret architecture of astrological–Masonic motifs and meanings began with George Washington's 1790's Capitol building's foundation trench dedication rites (Ovason, 2000, pp. 67–89+). There are numerous associations among cornerstone deposits, interconnecting boulevards and key, theme center–type buildings in Washington (Ovason, 2000, pp. 71, 73, 76–79+). Zodiacal decorations, especially Virgo designs, are amply represented in Washington's public buildings. It is tempting to allude here to the 1939 New York World's Fair Trylon and Perisphere theme centerpieces as additional secret symbolic Masonic architectural motifs. The formal chronological rationale for that 1939 Fair was the one hundred fiftieth anniversary of George Washington's ascendancy to the (first) U.S. Presidency, in New York City.

From Ancient Foundation Stone Rituals to Modern Time Capsule and Cornerstone Deposits

Modern time capsule and ancient foundation deposit practices show both obvious similarities and differences in their origins and functions. Even the most ancient foundation deposits included messages to future rulers, so even with these indefinitely deposited foundation relics a future message was sometimes sent, albeit for an indefinite, non-specified, happenstance future-time of receipt. It's an interesting question how and why

Lifting lid of capsules from Cherokee National Female Seminary at NSU, 7 May 1989
placed in cornerstone of Seminary Hall 25 April 1888
right to left: NSU President W. Roger Webb
Cherokee Nation Deputy Chief John Ketcher
Descendants of Seminarians President Betty Sanders Burroughs
Seminarian Pearl Mayes Langston
NSU Alumni Association President R. Lee Fleming

Lifting lid of capsules from Cherokee National Female Seminary at NSU, 7 May 1989, placed in cornerstone of Seminary Hall 25 April 1888. **A representative reception committee conducts the initial ceremonial operations. Dramatizing the life of a building site, the first building's cornerstone ended its solo guardianship after its building's 1887 fire. Note the original professional labeling of these photographs. (Courtesy University Archives, John Vaughn Library, Northeastern State University, Tahlequah, OK.)**

ancient foundation deposit ritual practices have changed and shifted in purpose to more modern "time capsule"–type meanings, functions and ceremonials. Just as the purposes of foundation dedication ceremonies have altered throughout history, so has the range of their contents. A time capsule deposit may for example preserve a memorial name roll of Japanese 1923 earthquake victims for 10,000 years, as does the example that partially inspired Dr. Jacobs' Crypt of Civilization project (Peters, 1940b, pp. 1–32).

Time capsules and cornerstone repositories have a foundation deposit and boundary marker history. Time capsules' forebears, their most obvious antecedents, are the foundation deposits ceremonies of ancient Mesopotamia and dynastic Egypt. Note the striking similarities between cornerstone ceremonies of today and ancient foundation-construction rituals. Cornerstones, cornerstone repositories and cornerstone laying-reopening ceremonies are at least vaguely familiar to many people today. These cornerstone rituals are the direct descendants of ancient practices. They can be traced back at least to the ancient foundation deposit practices of Mesopotamia and Egypt (Clarke & Engelback, 1930, pp. 60–61; "Cornerstone," 1901-2; Leick, 1988, p. 79). How far back in time can we trace precursors of foundation deposit ceremonials? How long have such dedication practices been carried out? By triangulating archaeological, ethnographic and folklore-historical studies of foundation and associated rites, it is possible to glimpse vernacular equivalents of ancient and modern foundation dedication practices. It is possible to postulate similar preliterate cultures' similar sorts of dedication functions (Talos, 1987, pp. 395–401). Ethnographic studies indicate the prevalence of such foundation-type rites into recent times. Ethnographic findings correlate well with folklore, histories and traditional beliefs on protecting domestic housing, dedicating newly constructed bridges, walls and tunnels. Foundation-dedication-construction rituals and beliefs seem to have what historians of religion characterize as "archetypal" status. These beliefs and practices manifest themselves in a variety of perennial and persistent cultural expressions due to deep needs in the human psyche (Eliade, 1954, pp. 18–21; 1972). Obviously, a society without elaborate building technologies or structures might not focus dedicatory practices on building deposits! The historical roots of site-boundary dedication activities seem wider and deeper than solely placing a formal deposit into the foundation of a building. Religious considerations of foundation consecration activity seem to have been (prior to 1900?) deeply, mythically adhered to in the dedication of new structures, whether for religious architectural purposes or for other secular, mundane structures (Davies, 1987, pp. 382–92).

In addition to these enduring traditions of formal culture consecrations, there is also a clear tradition of vernacular, that is, informal superstitions concerning foundation deposits, magic spells, and building customs-superstitions. These are well-documented nineteenth century British and Anglo-American building customs. The documented archaeological evidence of ancient foundation deposits and rites is of formal, priestly and royal official rituals, not necessarily of popular religious culture or any such hypothetical ancient vernacular building practices (Eliade, 1954, pp. 30, 76–77). The keyword terms for such activities can vary. For example, the expression "construction rites" is sometimes used to characterize these diverse practices, although the focus of such dedicatory rites is not always on a building's construction. The dedicatory sphere of such rites and symbolic meanings can go beyond building dedication type functions. One turn-of-the-(nineteenth)-century book has numerous subject-specific chapters on various practices associated with foundation rites, including topics such as "traces of human sacrifice at foundations in ancient times," "human sacrifice at foundations in modern times," "substitution of animals," "substitution of animal and vegetable products," "images," "shadows and specters," "relics," "writings," "circular movements and symbols," "stones," "sacred colors," "pillars and sites," "completion and christening" and "landmarks and boundaries" (Burdick, 1901). This is indeed quite a long list of cultural practices and occasions! That 1901 study was basically literary and folkloric, not archaeological or ethnographical.

Some cornerstones are also target-dated time capsules. Modern cornerstones and ancient foundation stones are deliberate depositions, just like their modern target dated time capsule "cousins." Such cornerstones and foundation stone relic-repositories are *not* targeted to be opened at a specified date in the future, as are modern time capsules. This distinction between intentional and non-intentional deposits, and the assignment (or non-assignment) of a scheduled target date for the retrieval of that deposit, differentiate modern (before-hand) *a priori* time capsules from the happenstance retrieval dates of cornerstone repositories and "space-time capsules." Classic cornerstone repositories (and space-time capsules) have no such retrieval target date assigned by their depositors. *A posteriori* (after the fact retrieval) deposits such as archaeological sites may, as we have seen, evoke a time capsule experience. Like foundation cornerstones and space-time capsules, archaeological sites are not typically prescheduled for any particular retrieval date. Unlike cornerstones and time capsules, archaeological sites were not (with the exception of gravesites) usually deliberately deposited.

Distinctions between traditional cornerstone repository sites and time capsules with given target dates are not always clear-cut to the public or in the mass media. The article reporting on that 1952 Chicago Museum of Science and Industry time capsule ("Clock ticks twice a year; living cornerstone laid in Chicago") was indexed as a "building custom" story, along with other publications on cornerstones. Or a cornerstone repository may be the site of numerous scientific experiments, as in one instance begun in 1952 to be completed at its scheduled opening in 2052. Among the many demonstrations in the "living cornerstone" at Chicago's Museum of Science and Industry is a thermocouple-powered "clock," which was designed to "tick" when the Chicago temperature first reached 85 degrees (Fahrenheit) and then again when a 15 degree temperature is reached in the Chicago, Illinois, winter. This was designed as a long-term weather measuring experiment, recording the seasonal swings in temperature. This is one of those confusing target-dated time capsules deposited within a cornerstone. Although this bundle of scientific experiments is contained in a cornerstone, it is called a time capsule and actually is (a target dated) one. We can't expect the hurry-bury world to always precisely name events, sites, and things for the benefit of subsequent researchers! Popular labels are not likely to conform to the arcane terminological nuances of scholars. In making such subtle distinctions among variants of time capsule phenomena, we classify this Chicago scientific example as a scheduled, centennial memento type of time capsule, and not as a cornerstone repository consigned for an indefinite period in a building foundation. And yet the world sees it as a cornerstone, technical, analytic or scholarly terminology aside. Irrespective of whether there was originally an assigned target date to a deposit like the Chicago Museum scientific instrument foundation box, it has a distinctly modern significance in both contents and the domain it commemorates. Our modern world of technical measurement and scientific inquiry is being celebrated in the form of a traditional deposit practice. A target-dated time capsule at Lehigh University fulfills the traditional impulse to do deposits in the form of an indefinitely inserted building cornerstone repository. It underscores the degree to which true indefinitely deposited cornerstone repositories have been supplanted by the modern target-dated time capsule. It somehow fits our era better for a building dedication deposit to be assigned a future scheduled retrieval date (Borneman, 1990, p. 2). Older cornerstone deposits are retrieved when the building undergoes a renewal or demolition, such as a 63-year-old cornerstone repository at the University of Maryland ("An unexpected find at Maryland College," 1986, p. 58). Another example of an indefinitely deposited cornerstone repository deemed to be a "time capsule" is the 1917 Charleston Massachusetts Armed Services YMCA building deposit, retrieved in 1988 when that social service club and hotel building was demolished (Dickson, 1988, p. 12).

The 1992 "Capsula de Tiempo" tar pit is a curious sort of capsule. That Capsula de Tiempo deliberate dedication deposit exercise was carried out on the closing October 1992 day of the Seville Expo 92 World's

Fair, just outside the formal precincts of the fairgrounds and by an informal group of sponsors (Codrington, 1993, p. 22). An international design journal featured the Capsula de Tiempo project alongside the older, but target-dated 1938 Westinghouse Time Capsule of Cupaloy and the 1940 Oglethorpe Crypt of Civilization time capsules. The Capsula de Tiempo ("Time Capsule") has no apparent target date. Rather it is an indefinitely deposited free-form deposit, informally dedicated and "filled" by a free form, open selection process. This is an example of a modern votive deposit that, although coined by its sponsors as a time capsule, is not a real example of a modern targeted time capsule. The Capsula de Tiempo is a 300-foot-long, ten-inch-wide, six-foot-deep prepared tar pit covered by a mesh-type metal grate. Various small objects were then deposited in a spontaneous collection, merely by dropping them through the grate into the tar. The anonymous organizing group then closed off the Capsula pit. On the Capsula deposit's Expo Island is also a trash pit from a former monastery and the site of an 1800s demolished ceramics factory. This juxtaposition of an indefinitely deposited tar pit time capsule of miscellaneous items and the two prior classic archaeological type *a posteriori* deposit sites poses an interpretive puzzle not only to the future, but for us to guess at now.

"Sanctification," "protection," "commemoration" and "elaboration" are traditional deposit meanings expressed in modern time capsules too. Consider the intended significance of ancient Mesopotamian foundation deposits, including animal sacrifices, clay pegs, stone tablets, terra cotta cones, cylinder seals and figurines (Ellis, 1968). We have seen how such classic motivations as sanctification, protection, commemoration and elaboration function in ancient foundation rites. These clay deposits did not usually contain messages or relics as in the classic cornerstone repositories we see today. The "elaboration," the promotion of a building's overall worth, of its value, has been a desirable trans-cultural motive since the beginning of these practices. While the commemoration of ruler-builders were motives, the magical sanctification and protection of major buildings were also reasons for these ceremonial foundation deposits (Ellis, 1968). Even though modern secular cornerstone and time capsule ceremonies usually do not have all the sacred attributes of ancient foundation stone ceremonies, certain aspects of these ancient customs have been perpetuated. Today it is the ideal of progress that is revered. Today's sent and received time capsule efforts are for the most part civil ceremonies, ones where a sociology of ritual behavior is manifest. Such contemporary, present ritual actions anticipate a future component of ritual action to complement today's actions of sending a time capsule. They often uncannily

The media start-up at a modern "Laying of the Foundation Stone" ceremony for the Atkinson Morley Wing construction site at St. George's Hospital, Tooting, South London, ca. 2 P.M. GMT, Wednesday, March 28, 2001. (Photographs © Dr. Brian Durrans, Keeper, Ethnography Department, the British Museum.)

resemble ancient cornerstone ritual ceremonies, and no wonder. Both ancient cornerstone practices and modern time capsule deposit events have similar dedication and construction ritual motives and techniques, as well as a common cultural history.

"Sanctification" of space, objects and occasions can be one function of modern time capsules. There need be no fundamental difference between sanctifying or consecrating a new construction site of a set of extensive land boundaries, or of a modern time capsule deposit-sealing site. Sanctification is now often a much-reduced motivation, at least in secular rituals. The objective of the consecration is distinct in each case. It may be an ancient foundation deposit, a large tract of land's boundaries, or even of a modern time capsule sealing event. It is distinct from other, basic primordial motivations of the consecrating personages. Even the ritual techniques modern presiding dignitaries tend to use (special metal trowels, special stone, trinkets, etc.) appear very closely related in form, function and objective to ancient dedication props.

"Protection" of space, objects, and occasions associated with ancient or modern deposit rituals is a second possible motivational function. Likewise, ritual motivations and techniques of protection can be extrapolated from archaic foundation deposit rituals focused on a new temple to wider geo-spatial areas, perhaps delineating the land tract boundaries of a new

Top: **This official media dedication ceremony at St. George's Hospital in London was scheduled for a date prior to the eventual placement of the foundation deposit time capsule's installation in the building's structure. *Bottom:* Congratulations all around for the attending dignitaries and Gleeson construction project management. (Photographs © Dr. Brian Durrans, 2001).**

settlement, or even into a temporal extrapolation of ancient practices to cover modern time capsules. Protection here has two distinct although not unlinked meanings. The first is an ancient sacred or magical evoking of a supernatural sanction, by a traditionally theocratic sanctioning priestly-royal authority structure. Those authorities had power to enforce its protective warnings with real-world sanctions. Traditional, ancient evocations of protection were supernatural prayers and practical security measures. The mutually evoked protection was for the buildings and for the foundation deposit items placed therein. The foundation deposit seems to have been regarded as a vital seed of the building, not some mere ornament affixed as an aside. The protection of building and foundation deposit was mutual and unitary. The priestly depositors of foundation dedication items in ancient societies were not oblivious to the needs of what we would call preservation of materials. Even in the archaic, pre–linear-historical civilizations of ancient Mesopotamia, the motive was one of physically preserving representative sacred declarations and other relics of that ancient political class.

"Commemoration" of space, objects and occasions is a third carry-over function from antique foundation deposits to modern capsule repository practices. The ancient commemoration of the reign of a sovereign is another foundation deposit motive with wider spatial and temporal utility in our modern times. Monumental forms like the U.S. Washington Monument obelisk carry such commemorations beyond ancient sacred kingship models from their cultural-architectural precursors. They do retain something of a mythic-cultic ambiance in their architectural deposit symbolism. The folkloristic reverence promulgated by guided tours and guidebooks regarding sites like many of those found in the District of Columbia hammer away at the civic commemoration theme. The modern, deliberately sealed and target-dated time capsule's commemorative mission, that of commemorating an institution, event or even a whole cultural period, is an obvious commemorative goal. Today, in our increasingly secularized and democratically elected political world, the identification of the elected incumbents in government office at the sealing date often seems more of a chronological marking device than a proclamation, a claim of rule over an epoch. The commemoration focus in deposit rituals has shifted from glorification of a ruler to the celebration of a whole cultural era or institutionally significant event.

"Elaboration" of space, objects and special occasions is a fourth function common with modern time capsule deposits as well as with ancient dedication rituals. Ancient foundation ceremonial depositors seemed motivated by a desire to emphasize something special about a major building project. Much the same motivation can be seen in those who use a modern time capsule to jazz-up the publicity activities of a centennial celebration of an institution, business or town. Such activities add something distinctive to a newly constructed or renovated building. Distinctive plaques, gateway structures and other forms of elaboration at the entrances and boundaries of set-aside spaces like parks, private estates or other locales can seem instinctually "right" to us. In visits to other ancient or modern culture areas one can often tell that a site is somehow special, even if all the details of that special cultural context are not discernible.

The St. George's Hospital (London) foundation stone's time capsule interior contains a wide range of medical items, including a cardio-thoracic pacemaker and a chest spreader. (Photograph © Dr. Brian Durrans, 2001).

In today's world culture, the attempted sanctification, commemoration, protection and elaboration of time capsule deposits tends to encompass a whole era. These four dedication categories were identified as motivations inferred from ancient Mesopotamian foundation deposits (Ellis, 1968). Our modern time capsule projects are somewhat differently expressed, in a secular fashion or with expressly designated target dates. The intent of today's senders is similar in origin nonetheless to the ancient dedication-signification motivations of those who once laid down foundation deposits (Jarvis 1988; 1992a; 1992b). We see a multitude of human motivations apparently expressed in time capsule behavior. One anthropological analysis of 20 distinct motivations in three time capsule types resulted in a 60-value tabulation of postulated complexities to time capsule motivations (Durrans, 1992, pp. 51–67). And these are just the permutations of one classification; other schema could readily be devised and the multitude of distinct permutations duly charted! In the case of the Crypt of Civilization, the motive of physically, literally and technologically preserving a representative sample of twentieth century relics and

St. George's Hospital, London. ***Left:*** **The capstone-lid for the stainless steel time capsule container is displayed to the attendees.** ***Right:*** **The Foundation Stone's steel dedication plaque declares the intent to leave a lasting historical record of the hospital's heart and brain medical-surgical specialties. (Photographs © Dr. Brian Durrans, 2001.)**

knowledge is evident in its name. Time capsules can be distinguished from other, less exotic archives and special collections by their more robust, "absolute" and dramatic methods of sealing and sequestration. Documents locked away in archival vaults do not customarily get ceremonial send-offs on the scale of a time capsule or cornerstone repository. Time capsules as special, magical set-aside groups of items do accentuate our awareness of the mystique of collecting (Durrans, 1993).

A paradigm shift from "ancient sacred precincts" to "notional futurescapes" is evident in the evolution of dedication deposit practices in the world cultural landscape of our history. Over the millennia, the deposited objects, attendant ceremonial practices and the sacralized precincts where these rituals and deposits have been carried out have transformed into the

1876–2000 era time capsules. There has been a close relationship of "sacred time" and "sacrifice" in humankind's past foundation and dedication rites (Brereton, 1987, pp. 526–35; Henniger, 1987, pp. 544–57; Sproul, 1987, pp. 535–44; Talos, 1987, pp. 395–401). These notions are all key elements in building ceremonials, foundation dedications and the origins of our own era of time capsule activity. Today's time capsule practices have undergone a multi-millennial functional shift in focus from their primal origins as non–target dated dedication deposits and rites. The ancient ceremonial precinct was typically an architectural landscape in which to celebrate sacred rituals and a place to preserve and delineate with such rituals. Today's cultural landscape of time capsule practices is a more fleeting launch pad than were the foundation deposits in the ancient sacred architectural landscape. Once a time capsule's content has been deposited at a site, the aura of a notional futurescape generated by the primal rite of dedication deposit fades rapidly, remaining only as an ephemeral, unrealized utopian image.

The shift in the last 150 years has been from the original focus on ritually dedicated landscapes and deposits delineating these spaces over into our contemporary world previews of a variety of notional futurescapes. We now tend to focus much more on projecting an envisioned future cultural landscape to which we target our dedicated time capsule projects. This is in contrast to the overwhelming focus of ancient foundation depositors on sanctifying their contemporary sacred precinct boundaries, such as temples or city walls, etc. Among these modern types of dedicated futurescapes are cases of "World's Fairscapes" and even "the New Millennium 2001–3000" examples. Beyond our dawning New Millennium are the possible notional futurescapes of the "Distant Tomorrows" 10,000 Common Era and the year 12,000 CE. Although obviously at least 5000 years old in their building protection ceremonial origins, such ritual dedication deposits may even be seen as having roots in older dedication rituals practices. Our current time capsule practices of target-dating deposits of cultural relics and messages for future retrieval are related to the dedication deposits of former millennia, although significant distinctions between these two sets of practices have evolved. Even in those world's fair temporary creations of briefly realized notional futurescapes, the focus of time capsule deposit rituals is still largely on the distant targeted real, permanent futurescapes in which the deposited time capsules will be retrieved and celebrated.

"Centennial" and "Millennial" Milestones in the History of the Modern Deposited-Targeted Literal Time Capsule: 1876, 1938, 1940, 1976

The "Centennial" time capsule idea was invented for, and first exhibited at the 1876 U.S. International Centennial Philadelphia Exposition. As noted earlier, the honor of constructing the first true, modern time capsule, with both deliberate sealing and scheduled opening dates, goes to Mrs. Charles Diehm. Her 1876 "Century Safe" was exhibited in Philadelphia at the World's Fair that year (Berger, 1975, pp. 161–62; *Centennial Safe*, 1976; Diehm, 1882, pp. 194–200; Maass, 1973). After a two-year transcontinental signature-gathering tour, its inner glass door was finally closed in Statuary Hall of the U.S. Capitol Building on February 22, 1879.

1888 time capsule items at opening ceremony
1847 box to right
Microphone for announcing findings to the group

Opening an 1888 time capsule from Cherokee National Female Seminary, 7 May 1989. University Archivist Vickie Sheffler, center, inventories the contents. The Seminary site was later sold to the State of Oklahoma and renamed the Northeastern State Normal School. (Courtesy University Archives, John Vaughan Library, Northeastern State University, Tahlequah, OK.)

(The date is George Washington's birthday.) It was opened as intended for the 1976 Bicentennial by U.S. President Gerald Ford, a.k.a. Chief Magistrate of the United States, in Statuary Hall. It now reposes in an office in the Capitol Building (Berger, 1975, pp. 161–62; *Centennial Safe*, 1976; Diehm, 1882, pp. 194–200). It had been rechristened as "The *Centennial* Safe." One can see the contents through an inner glass door. Most of those are photographs, autographs of civic personages and prominent civil and military officials (collected between 1876 and 1878), a tea service and a watch. This combination lock, fireproof safe has a purple velvet lining, is 50 inches wide, 40 inches deep and 64 inches high. It is a classic "centennial" time capsule, short in scheduled duration, and sparse in content. It was distinctly commemorative in purpose, rather than being broadly representative of a whole era of civilization. The Century Safe is a notewor-

Preserving NSU Time Capsule at NSU Archives

Preserving Time Capsule at Northeastern State University Archives: **After the Cherokee National Female Seminary building burned in 1887, its cornerstone was placed inside the cornerstone of the *new* building in 1888, along with new deposit materials. Here contents of that larger, 1888-deposited time capsule are being professionally examined under archival-preservational laboratory conditions by Certified Archivist Vicki Sheffler, gloved hands on left. Chronicling nearly a century and a half of higher education, the double cornerstone deposit spanning 1847–1887–1888–1989 was opened in 1989 to tell its story, in what is now called Northeastern State University. (Courtesy University Archives, John Vaughan Library, Northeastern State University, Tahlequah, OK.)**

thy "time capsule" because it appears to be the earliest deliberate, successful deposit targeted for a specified opening target date. It is also of significant size, and was displayed in a major commemorative context, a World's Fair. Mrs. Diehm's original time capsule idea was not basically improved upon until the 1938 Westinghouse Time Capsule was designed for the 1939-40 New York City World's Fair extravaganza. That 1876 Centennial Exposition actually gave birth to two target-dated time capsules projects. The second, Chicago photographer Charles D. Mosher's "Memorial Safety Vault," grew out of a small exhibit he did at that 1876 Fair (Viskochil, 1976, pp. 95–104). Mosher's 1876–1976 vault was prematurely opened in 1908, before Diehm's Century Safe's opening in 1976. Mosher's vault was sealed in 1876, two years before Diehm's safe's final sealing. Charles D. Mosher's Memorial Safety Vault, 1876–1905, was first to be sealed, since Diehm's final sealing wasn't accomplished until 1878 (Viskochil, 1976, pp. 95–104).

The 1876–1976–2076 U.S. Centenaries' time capsules are a series of diachronically linked events. The Century Safe of 1876–1878 was unsealed in 1976, and the U.S. National Archives sealed its 1976 Bicentennial-Tricentennial Time Capsule to be opened in 100 years (*The Reynolds Metals Company Bicentennial Time Capsule*, 1976). The 50 U.S. States, various U.S. territories, the U.S. District of Columbia, the National Archives and the Bicentennial Freedom Train project each received a copy of one of these Bicentennial-to-Tricentennial time capsule boxes manufactured by Reynolds Metals, Inc. (*The Reynolds Metals Company Bicentennial Time Capsule*, 1976). The National Archives has its own NARA copy of a Reynolds Bicentennial Time Capsule. Somebody has custody of another copy of a Reynolds Bicentennial Time Capsule, namely the "Bicentennial Wagon Train Time Capsule," stolen before the scheduled July 4, 1976, when President Ford arrived for the deposit ritual at Valley Forge, Pennsylvania. A 1991 ITCS press release described the perpetrator and the fate of the stolen Capsule as "unsolved mysteries" (*10 lost time capsules*, 1991). About 22 million people had signed a logbook for that stolen capsule. Typical of other U.S. Bicentennial memorial events was a Bicentennial logbook maintained at the Onondaga County Public Library in Syracuse, New York, for the public to comment on the Bicentennial in particular, U.S. history in general or the future of the world (Large & Jarvis, 1999). Ten years later, another interesting U.S. centenary was celebrated, this one in New York City. That July 4, 1986, New York Harbor "Tall Ships" celebration was the triumphal occasion for the fully refurbished Statue of Liberty. That monumental project began solely as the "Torch-bearing Arm" at the 1876 Centennial Exhibition in Philadelphia. The Torch-Arm man-

Top: Mrs. Diehm's gift of a silver and gold inkwell is finally presented to the Future of 1976: Gerald Ford presides as Chief Magistrate of the United States, while George White, Architect of the Capitol, assists, July 1, 1976. ***Bottom:*** Connecting with the past: Note President Ford's obvious delight at receiving this signature book addressed to him as "Chief Magistrate of the U.S." from this first, Victorian-era time capsule, the Century Safe, July 1, 1976. (Both photographs courtesy Gerald R. Ford Library, Ann Arbor, MI.)

aged to be "on hand" for both the Philadelphia Centennial and the New York City Bicentennial celebrations, having spent some fund-raising time stationed on New York City's Fifth Avenue in the 1880s. At various times it has been know as the Liberty Statue or the Bartholdi Statue, after its artist Frederic Auguste Bartholdi. Four months later, the official Centenary of the 1886 original dedication of the completed Statue was celebrated. Part of that ceremony was the formal dedication of a 1986–2096 time capsule deposited in a museum at the base of the Statue, which included copies of the earlier "Liberty Weekend" activities (*Liberty: The French-American statue in art and history*, 1986; Span, 1986, p. D1). These centennial memorial celebrations remain intertwined with the modern time capsule idea, an association that began back at the 1876 U.S. Centennial celebration in Philadelphia, where the Torch Arm was in attendance.

The "Centennial" type of time capsule has undergone two major improvements since the initial 1876 conceptualization. First came the 1956–2056 "Vault for the Future" some 80 years later, with its significant deposit of 24 boxes of scientific, technical and miscellaneous records noted earlier. As we noted earlier, its large archival deposit is not typical of the contents of many garden-variety time capsules targeted for 100 years or less. Later, in 1970, came the second stage in the evolution of centennial-spanning time capsules. Although its major collection of deposited contents is noteworthy, the major claim to fame of the second, junior Osaka, Japan, Expo 70 World's Fair Time Capsule, known as "no. 2," is not dependent on the extent of its contents. Rather it is that capsule's planned serial format. It has a large series of "omega" (i.e. scheduled opening) dates: 2000, then 2100, 2200, 2300; on and on every hundred years after the year 2000, right up to the year 6900 century year. The final sprint of just 70 years will bring this capsule to the final opening year 6970 of our Common Era. This Centennial type time capsule is the twin of the Osaka Expo 70 Time Capsule no. 1, 1970–6970, which is targeted for one unbroken five-millennium span of time.

Another such early commemorative time capsule, deliberately deposited for a scheduled opening, is the McNulta Time Capsule. This small, seven-inch glass bottle repository has souvenirs from an 1879 Civil War reunion ("In Illinois: cigars and bottled history," 1979, pp. 8, 9, 12). Presumably, "time capsule" is a modern label for this deposit. This small quantity of ephemera is noteworthy only because it was deliberately sealed up for a 100-year Civil War commemorative period, not unlike the commemorative associations of the Century Safe. Like cornerstone repositories, short-term commemorative time capsules appear to be definitely

Top: The Colorado Springs, Colorado, "Century Chest, 1901–2001," is opened in the first true, after-midnight moments of the new Millennium, January 1, 2001, at Colorado College, Colorado. (From left to right) David Finley, Wilber Fulker, Andy Morris. See photographs and descriptions at: ***http://www.coloradocollege.edu/library/SpecialCollections/CenturyChest/Appdx.html. Bottom:*** New plaque: The Colorado Springs "Century Chest" awaits the resealing of its antique 1900-era container, April 20, 2001. Note old 1901 instructions on right, newly added 2001 instruction plaque, left. (Both photographs courtesy Special Collections and Archives, the Colorado College Library.)

Top, left: **Contents in archival boxes: Already loaded into the old 1901 Century Chest for another 100 year–spanning "voyage" are various new contents, April 20, 2001. *Top, right:* Resealing Century Chest, close-up of reuse of hot-rivet method: The newly reloaded version of the Colorado Springs, Colorado, "Community Chest" is resealed, April 20, 2001, until 2101. *Bottom:* Don Hanson resealing the Century Chest: A young girl and young boy are among those craning to see the final sealing moments, perhaps pondering its newest target span, April 20, 2101. (All three photographs courtesy Special Collections and Archives, the Colorado College Library.)**

home grown, do-it-yourself folk custom ("vernacular") kind of occurrence often (one is tempted to say *invariably*) associated with local commemorative events. It is not unlikely that the "centennial," ca. 100-year time capsule has been, and will be repeatedly, spontaneously reinvented. The human urge to commemorate anniversaries seems virtually universal. The University of Massachusetts at Amherst has an interesting variant on the centennial-type time capsule theme. It consists of a 10 × 7 × 3-inch copper box filled with 1878 graduation related documents planted under the 1878 Class Tree. Archivists, archaeologists and buildings-grounds staff retrieved it on May 14, 1991, after a college archives search. The records had indicated that the 1878 copper box was deposited under the landmark Class Tree. Retrieval was occasioned by the severe damage suffered by the associated white pine tree during a storm and the tree scheduled removal ("A time capsule helps archivists to look back," 1991, p. 131). Although inspired by post–1876 U.S. Centennial celebrations of the times, this 113-year time capsule was not scheduled for a specific targeted retrieval date. Its depositors had observed that it would someday be of interest. The waterlogged contents required freezing and other sophisticated archival materials preservation stabilization and repair.

"The Field Centennial Time Capsule, 1889–1989" is a good example of a private family time capsule that commemorates a civic event. The 1889 Centennial of George Washington's Presidential Inauguration and its 1989 Bicentennial celebration are effectively the start and end dates of the Field family's heritage time capsule (Field, 1989, pp. 652–60). This story resonates with many time capsule lessons, ranging from the advanced medical and aerospace-type imaging technology used to preview its televised debut, to the classic centennial-memento type of the deposit. The family heritage type of transmission-preservation methodology is an object lesson in how a basic, familial approach to such "historic archiving" can succeed in sending memorabilia "ahead in time" (Field, 1989, pp. 652–60).

The "Millennial" time capsule idea is thought up and realized: 1935, 1938 and 1940. We've noted that G. E. Pendray first coined the "time capsule" term in 1938 for his Westinghouse Time Capsule. That project started as a cut-and-dried idea for a cornerstone deposit ceremony at the Westinghouse Pavilion to be called a "time bomb" before the less lurid "time capsule" tag was finally coined for the project (Hyman & McLelway, 1953, pp. 194+). That irreverent look at the 1938 Time Capsule project is worth reading. Hyman's Time Capsule was in fact the first millennial time capsule to be sealed, in fact as well as name. The idea for the *first* millennial time capsule seems to belong rather to Dr. Thornwell Jacobs and his Crypt of Civilization project, which began to take shape as early as 1935. Pendray's

1938 project was the first to be *sealed*, and hence completed, "realized" as a functioning time capsule. It would be difficult to estimate how many short-term Centennial-type (100 years or less) time capsules are in existence. Just eight "millennial" (targeted for 1000 years or more) time capsules were initially deposited in the years between 1939 and 1982. We will discuss these classic eight millennium-spanning time capsules in detail later in this work. Another rare example is a large content time capsule sealed for *more* than 100 but *less* than 1000 years. But on closer examination it is more akin to a millennial time capsule, due to its dual commemorative rationale of a 1000-year commemorative period determining its 900-year target date. We noted earlier this 1966–2866 "Time Tunnel" at Rosamond, California ("Preserving the present," 1967, p. 27; "Tropico Time Tunnel Sealing Ceremonies," 1966).

The Earth Witnesses the Launching of a New Era of "Space-Time Capsules": 1969–1999

Time capsule "deposits" aren't necessarily confined to sites on (or in) the Earth. Some capsules have been launched into space and are destined for indefinite interstellar journeys, perhaps billions of years in duration (Sagan, 1978). There are "space-time capsules" in Earth orbit, on the Moon and on various spacecraft probe-type time capsules traveling on courses deep into interstellar space (Jarvis, 1988; 1992a; 1992b). The space-time capsule is nearly its own category of time capsule, compared with our definition of deliberately target-dated deposits, time capsules and cornerstones. Non-terrestrially located time capsules (like the Pioneer Plaques and the Voyager Records) are more akin to Mesopotamian foundation deposits than to, say, the Crypt of Civilization. These interstellar "cornerstones" were deliberately designed for ready interpretation if eventually received by very alien beings. It is not assumed that they will be intercepted at any specified place and time. Their plaques and phonographic records are even affixed to space probe vehicles in a manner reminiscent of a building cornerstone. Earthbound, traditional cornerstone repositories are scheduled to be opened only when a building is demolished (or extensively altered). Pioneer Plaque and Voyager Record space-time capsules are intended for retrieval thousands or millions of light years away from their twentieth century solar system, long after their electronic-robot exploratory equipment would have gone to failure. Perhaps they will only be retrieved long after the human species has become extinct or the Earth or solar system has ceased to exist at all, also "gone to failure." Their pulsar maps astronomically date and place these probes, just as the date, place and depositors' names identify traditional building cornerstones (Jarvis, 1988; Sagan, 1978). Such space-time capsules have no precisely spelled-out target year date for their retrieval, although they are definitely targeted for ultimate interstellar interpretation, even if no one knows if these might actually be retrieved. Their larger-sized information storage, the degree of complexity of the data transmission and facets of interpretation-oriented message encoding easily rival the nature of classic millennial terrestrially based time capsules.

The encyclopedic messages of space-time capsules, especially of the Pioneer Plaques and Voyager Records, seem more like modern message-laden time capsules, rather than like building commemoration cornerstone deposits of a few relics. Definite target-dated non-spacefaring time capsules apparently have the capability to communicate the contexts of past lives to very different future recipients. The major space-time capsules appear to be capable of doing that too, so it is desirable for us to acknowledge their unique time capsule character, akin to the informational capacities of modern millennia spanning, terrestrially located capsules. Their large-sized information storage, complexity of data transmitted and interpretive-oriented message-encoding rival that of classic millennial terrestrially based time capsules like the Crypt of Civilization or Westinghouse Time Capsule I. The encyclopedic messages of space-time capsules like the two Pioneer Plaques and the two Voyager Records do sound and feel like message-laden time capsules. There are extensive contents and also complex intellectually based interpretive stratagems employed on these capsule-messages.

LAGEOS and the Apollo 11 Moon landing plaques are modest cases of space-time capsules. Interstellar examples of time capsules tend to overshadow these two less glamorous space-time capsules in orbit around Earth. The LAGEOS (Laser Geodynamic Satellite) Earth Satellite and the Apollo 11 Lunar Lander's Launch Platform left on the Moon each bear a small plaque with a map and micro-sized text ("Apollo 11 goodwill messages," 1969; Sagan, 1978). Both these artifacts were deliberately attached to their respective vehicles with the express purpose of being eventually retrieved by someone in the future who will (perhaps?) interpret these messages. With both of these space-time capsules, there is no announced retrieval date. (NASA anticipates that the LAGEOS satellite and its small plaque will reenter the Earth's atmosphere in approximately 10,000 years if not touched beforehand.) The retrieval date is like that of cornerstone repositories on Earth, indefinitely left to happenstance. Although humans will (presumably) return to the Moon eventually, the Apollo 11 plaque will be our cosmic calling card to any future beings that might discover it. This is perhaps a small distinction, although the deliberate message produced for future retrieval does distinguish the Apollo 11 LEM landing leg plaque from other archeological "trash" left there ("Apollo 11 goodwill messages," 1969). The Apollo 11 message disc has statements from U.S. presidents Eisenhower, Kennedy, Johnson and Nixon, 73 other goodwill messages from various world leaders and the names of various political and technical people affiliated with the program. It is a typical cornerstone type memorial plaque, although in this case each message was reduced 200 times in size to smaller than a pin-head. The LAGEOS plaque likewise distinguishes it from other Earth satellites, objects of "merely" archaeological interest. These deposits of surveying and exploration are like the benchmarks left by geological surveying teams.

The identical Plaques mounted on Pioneer missions 11 and 12 were targeted by classic censorship activities. Designing and selecting messages for time capsules might seem to be a pleasant pastime, a wish fulfilling exercise in preserving something of the varieties of Earth's culture(s). But there can be certain occupational hazards lurking for time capsuleers. Not only can there be a concern about leaving important items out of the sacred souvenir collection, but there may also be controversy about what to include. The nudity controversy around the Pioneer Plaque is a prime example of how seriously some Earthlings take their time capsules. Two engravings on the Pioneer Plaques were nude human male and female figures which drew some protests (Sagan, 1978). There were also protests that the female figure was portrayed as subservient to the male. There were observations (including some contradictory claims among various ethnic groups) that those two figures represented only one-or-another sets of racial characteristics. Sagan's project group concluded that the content choices made for such interstellar deposits were regarded as very important, almost regardless of any probability of alien retrieval. These reactions to perceived gold-anodized "smut" seemed like a sort of interstellar image-projection test, functioning as an evaluation of our behavior. It was thought of as a message that might be received in many millennia, yet interpreted by alien beings in ways familiar to us. Full frontal nudity was excluded from the human biology lesson on the later Voyager Records (although the censor passed a silhouette) as a result of the images on the Pioneer Plaque. That controversy illustrated the major functions of time capsules: to communicate, to self-reflect on what we communicate, to understand how we communicate and (especially) to reflect on what we might be able to communicate.

The book Murmurs of Earth *is an excellent resource for a time capsule sender*. It tells how and why the phonographic records attached to Voyager 1 and 2 were made (Sagan, 1978). Sagan led the team that produced this record of Earth sounds and sights. He also designed the Pioneer 10 and 11 plaques, as well as the LAGEOS plaque described in *Murmurs*. Sagan was an avid designer of space-time capsules, and also compared Earthbound time capsules with their extraterrestrially located counterparts. He did not use the term "space-time capsules" to describe his CETI (Communication with Extraterrestrial Intelligence) space probe messages. Sagan does make a comparison among the 1938 New York World's Fair Time Capsule, his childhood visit to the 1939 Fair, his CETI efforts and an Assyrian foundation plaque inscription in *Murmurs* (Sagan, 1978). The Voyager Record project may be the mother of all space-time capsules. Voyager 1 was launched on August 20, 1977, and Voyager 2 was launched on September 5, 1977. The detailing of Sagan's United Nations misadventures in collecting representative spoken language samples for the Records are obligatory cautionary tales for any time capsule chronicler (Sagan, 1978). Time capsule contents are not merely emotionally neutral relics. They are representatives of our reputation to future ages, and all such representations are potentially controversial. The difficulties in collecting a representative of Earth culture for the Voyager Record were not merely abstractly judgmental or technical in character. Social-political differences turned even a naïve attempt to collect (at the United Nations) a representative sample of Earth's spoken languages into a nearly intractable series of dilemmas. Reading about such difficulties is almost enough to confine a time capsule designer to planting sealed glass jars in backyards! Apparently the selectors for the 1938 Westinghouse Time Capsule were faced with a deluge of commercial representatives, all vying to have their company's products placed in the capsule (Hyman & McLelway, 1953, pp. 194+). Eventually it was decided in the case of the 1938 Westinghouse Time Capsule that only one sample of each generic type of item would be included in the Capsule.

Musical selections and a variety of mixed media alternatives were featured on the two Voyager Records. When and if those phonographic audiovisual discs are played, they will reveal a multi-media show of photos, text, human voices, music, whale songs and other Earth noises. Their "album cover" features pictorial representations of how they can be played with the affixed stylus and a pulsar map like of the Pioneer Plaques (Sagan, 1978). When the Records are played at the desired speed of 216 RPM, the first picture formed is a calibration circle. They contain information on a millennial encyclopedic time capsule scale, rather than the smaller content typical of many cornerstone or centennial memento time capsules. Although its physical size is limited to just one phonographic record, one album cover and one stylus, it encapsulates a massive amount of information. Non–verbally based music and mathematics "languages" and a carefully constructed photographic archive of human traits and practices were used. This mixed media approach to attempted interstellar communication does not rely exclusively on any one-communication format. If the records are played, a wide variety of independent mathematical, visual and oral messages will tell interstellar recipients about 1978 Earth. Music may be the closest thing to an interstellar language (Sagan, 1978). The mixed media format of the Project is the optimization of communication probabilities in a worst case scenario. One form of communication might be misunderstood or a bit of a numerical string of coded be missed by potential recipients, thus breaking the chain of transmission. The Voyager Record project may be one of the finest examples of time encapsulation, especially for its well thought-out photographic archive (Sagan, 1978). Perhaps only a space probe computer programmed for artificial intelligence will beat the Voyager Record of communicability of Earth's way(s) of life. These gold-coated copper phonograph-type records reproduce a variety of visual and audio contents, including 118 pictures of Earth scenes, the Beethoven "Cavatina" from the String Quartet No. 13, opus 130, greetings from the President of the United States, a U.S. Congressional membership list, greetings from the Secretary General of the United Nations, greetings in 54 languages, UN greetings, whale greetings, typical sounds of Earth and a 90-minute musical anthology. The Pioneer and Voyager spacecraft are moving away from our solar system since their planetary imaging phase ended. Although the electronic systems of Pioneer and Voyager will eventually fail, the spacecrafts' apparatus constitute further artifacts for eventual interpretation.

The "Official Halley's Comet Time Capsule, 1986–2061" was an Earth-based time capsule project that celebrated an astronomical anniversary event, the periodic passage of a natural celestial body ("Update: Halley Time Capsule," 1985, p. 2). It was to span the years until 2061, the comet's next return. Contents were to include winning entries from several children's contests and a directory of capsules.

In the late 1990s, the "space-time-capsule movement" made more efforts. In the mid–1990s, Gregory Benford and others began working on a possible time capsule–like message for the Cassini-Hygens probe to Saturn-Titan. In 1997, the "Stardust" comet probe-rendezvous had a sponsored microchip on the spacecraft as a part of the Planetary Society's membership promotional efforts (Benford, 1999, p. 127). The year 1998 turned out to be a watershed for space-time capsule launchings (Benford, 1999, pp. 89–134). One CD-ROM time capsule–type compilation went on a Mars

Pathfinder Mission. Sometimes a capsule has difficulty finding a space travel berth, as with the "MAPEX" scientific package (Benford, 1999, pp. 90–93). This Microelectronics and Photonics Exposure Experiment microdot-sized sample of materials finally got a ride on the Cassini Probe, after false starts and scrubbed missions and projects. A digitized disc CD-ROM compilation of Earthlings' signatures did end up flying on the Cassini Probe vehicle. A JPL postcard campaign gathered personal names for the signature register and a European electronic names-book was put on the Cassini-Hygens bi-modular probe's Hygens lander-vehicle module for Saturn-Titan (Benford, 1999, pp. 90–93+). Although just a stand-alone list of names is trivial from the standpoint of actually transmitting large messages to any alien receivers, the ceremonial commemorative power of the sponsor's promotional effort can be significant. The author's daughter's name was one of many U.S. citizens' names included on the Cassini CD-ROM list (Jarvis A. C., 1996). In addition to the popular appeal among the sender's culture, the presentation of a name list may indicate something of the sender's psychology to any retrievers. The very small, wafer-thin Diamond-Medallion space-time capsule's two-sided etched writing was originally slated for deployment on the Hygens Titan Lander. One side of the 28mm diameter Cassini-Hygens Diamond-Medallion wafer depicts astronomical and spacecraft-history data. The other side displayed symbolic information, including a demonstration of binary arithmetic notation, a left-right stereo photo of a composite, artificially composed scene of a (hopefully) representational group of human beings on a beach, and a ten-micron high list of lab and organizational project related names (Benford, 1999, pp. 121–22). This exemplar of the space-time capsule art didn't fly on that Cassini-Hygens mission to Saturn-Titan. The hiatus was apparently due to contending approaches advocated on transmitting messages through the great interstellar beyond (Benford, 1999, pp. 123–34). A signature bearing digitized disc like that on the Mars Pathfinder was affixed to the (crashed) 1999 Mars Polar Orbiter Mission.

Interstellar radio broadcasts convey time capsule–like messages, and we will also examine them later as types of ancient documents. The ultimate time capsule or foundation deposit may well be a computerized space probe or a complexly coded transmission of electromagnetic radiation. A variety of such complex messages about life, civilization and science-technology could go between Earth and other star systems. It could be two-way if any such non–Earth beings are (or will be) sending or receiving. These schemes would transcend the use of physical containers to transmit messages from our age, using instead only a broadcast medium to attempt a time capsule's mission. When one considers ancient documents as time capsules, such transmissions (and encoded physical records on spacecraft) may well be our ancient documents to a distant future's species. TV broadcasts are of course other time capsules from Earth to outer space (Goldsmith & Owen, 1980, pp. 366+). SETI is alive and well at sending-receiving radio telescope installations (Broad, 1998, p. 1; Sagan, 1978; Sagan, 1973; SETI Institute, 1999; *SETI*, 1990; White, 1990). SETI signals are a form of time capsule "containers" that are solely electromagnetic.

A Short Chronicle of Time Capsule Americana Since 1945

Post–World War II deposits have included numerous indefinitely deposited cornerstone repositories and 100-year or less targeted dated capsules. Other capsules done in this 55-year period have already been noted. Here are some examples selected from countless such capsules. There are also some other interesting examples, unique in form or typical of an era, place or occasion.

There are some examples of time capsules in the 1940s. University of Notre Dame biologists sealed a 200-year target-dated copper box in a stone block cornerstone cavity in 1947 ("Life-form samples sealed for two-century siege," 1947, p. 197). Vitamins, viruses, living organisms, amino acids and selected pharmaceuticals were deposited among those longevity experiments. Samples of soil, clay, lake water and rainwater were also included. Two other time capsules consist of microfilmed archives, various films and relics of journalistic activities from numerous newspapers. They were each sealed for 100-year spans in the *Minneapolis Star and Tribune* (Minnesota) Century Vault (in 1948) and at the Freedom Foundation in Valley Forge, Pennsylvania, during 1949 ("311 microfilmed pages cached for 2048 folk," 1948, p. 39; "100 dailies to be placed in 'capsule,'" 1949, p. 26).

There were some bigger time capsules in the 1950s. The 225-pound cast alloy steel Pershing Square Garage Time Capsule was deposited on April 11, 1952, for 100 years and contained four small boxes of over 200 microfilmed informational items ("From Los Angeles of 1952 to Los Angeles of 2052" 1952, p. 7). It was sited at ground level above the underground garage that was under construction then. Other 1950s-era time capsules cited earlier included the "Vault for the Future" at George Washington University in Washington. Size doesn't always mean success with capsules, however. Two 1953 Washington State territorial centennial time capsules, one of them weighing 4,000 pounds, can't be located. A second supplemental capsule might have been deposited or filed in a closet at the State Capital (*10 lost time capsules*, 1991).

The Sharpstown subdivision in the Houston, Texas, area was founded in 1955 and named after its financier. A time capsule deposit commemorated the opening of that private, 6800-home, upscale housing development. That venture was then billed as the largest such suburban residential site in the world. It was planned as an affluent middle-class American housing division with numerous amenities, including a free residential community membership (social) country club with an Olympic-size swimming pool and golf course. There was a pioneering enclosed-air-conditioned shopping mall. There was also a plush automobile drive-in movie theater. Mr. Sharp's bank failed, but the housing development continued even in the midst of his personal legal-financial difficulties. The location of the March 13, 1955, Sharpstown Time Capsule was moved once prior to its March 2000 opening, away from the site of a new apartment building to the Sharpstown Park, in front of the Park Community Building there. It was opened at 11:00 A.M. on Saturday, March 11, 2000. People traveled from several U.S. states to join various local and state dignitaries at the ceremony, and the contents are being cataloged and the depositors-

Boulder-and-plaque marker at the current deposit site of the March 13, 1955, Sharpstown (TX) Time Capsule, 1955–2001. (Courtesy Fred Jinkins, Houston, TX, *http://www.angelfire.com/tx2/hapyom/page17.html*)

Top: The opening scene, 11:00 A.M., Saturday, March 11, 2000: Sharpstown (TX) Time Capsule, 1955–2001. ***Bottom:*** Opening the Capsule with a "futuristic device," a cordless drill: Sharpstown (TX) Time Capsule, 1955–2001. Many of the contents were somewhat soggy. (Both photographs courtesy Fred Jinkins, Houston, TX, 2001.)

retrievers are being included in a history of the capsule. A new Sharpstown Time Capsule was prepared for the 2000–2025 year period (Jinkins, 2000). This is actually a rather rare example of a time capsule that had been targeted for opening in the year 2000, as well as a more typical example of a New Year 2000 time capsule deposit.

Automobiles are only one unconventional form time capsules can assume. The 1957 Plymouth automobile buried in the Oklahoma Statehouse grounds was planned as part of that year's June 15, 1957, Sesquicentennial commemoration (Berger, 1975, pp. 161–62; Klein, 1958, pp. 80–81). This Belvedere model is a black two-door, hard-top and tail-fin-sporting relic of ostentatious, prosperous Americana. It comes with a five-gallon can of gasoline, hopefully ready to roll out of its deposit site's concrete platform in the year 2007 ("A gift to the future," 1987, pp. 6–7). Its glove compartment is a mini-time capsule containing the typical contents of a woman's purse of the day. It has $2.73 in U.S. coins, a comb, a package of tobacco cigarettes, chewing gum and some cosmetics. Also buried with the car are an Oklahoma flag, newspapers and officials' letters to the future. It is supposed to be exhumed 50 years after its Populuxe design deposit period (Hine, 1986, pp. 101–2). It will be awarded to the person or their heirs who had most closely estimated the 2007 population of Tulsa, Oklahoma. Human burials have also utilized cars— real vehicles or Ghanaian wooden scaled-down model coffin-sized replicas (Rothenstein & Gooding, 1999, illus. 33; "Coffin is a Corvette," 1994, p. A12). Curious sorts of car dedication deposit sites have sprung up, including "Carhenge" in Alliance, Nebraska, where old cars stick out of the ground. Tulsa did another car deposit in 1998 (Warner, 2001). They are a bit like megalithic stone formations from ancient Celtic Europe (Moore, 1992, pp. 52–55). These are not target-dated, unlike the 1957 Plymouth. The moral here is that two deposits can share a common form but serve different ends, and hence can differ greatly in their meaning(s) to the future, irrespective of their external form or inner contents.

Some smaller time capsules were also "sent" from the 1960s. In addition to the 1964-65 Time Capsule II at the New York World's Fair, smaller time capsules were deposited as well. A time capsule deposited in 1960 at the Manhattan offices of the Union of American Hebrew Congregations contained the social predictions of various world political figures about the year 2000 era of its target date (Beyer, 1998, p. 14). Attempts in 1998 to find the repository in order to carry out its move along with the organization's headquarters were unsuccessful. On October 5, 1963, a selection by a group from the American Medical Association of 30 drugs developed in the prior 30-year period were buried in the Bronx, New York. It was targeted for a 100-year time span ("30 leading drugs buried in medical time capsule," 1963, p. 231).

A 1974 Livermore Laboratory time capsule can't be found. It apparently was the size and shape of a typical beer keg. A work crew quietly buried it in order to hide it from possible thievery. Unfortunately, it was apparently also hidden from everyone else as well. Time capsules, unlike tombs, need to be re-discoverable; although like tombs they need to be protected from occasions of vandalism or theft (Shepherd, 1999, p. 21). The New Jersey town of West New York has, or had, a 1948 time capsule which has apparently shared a fate (at least as of 1998) of other time capsule phenomena, that is to say, it is now lost. No instructions or directions appear to have survived, except for a vague oral tradition about the deposit ("In West New York, a time capsule is proving to be an elusive buried treasure," 1998, p. A17). It's not uncommon for universities to have several time capsules on campus. There might even be an unused empty spare in storage, a time capsule with no contents and no target date (Jarvis & Perino, 1986)!

Time capsules continued to be deposited in the 1980s. Faneuil Hall in Boston houses two commemorative-type targeted time capsules, from 1880 and 1930 (Arnold, 1980, pp. 1, 8; "A look at Boston of years gone by," 1980, p. 27). "The Century Box" (1880–1980) and the "Half-Century Box" (1930–80) were both opened at 5:30 P.M. on Wednesday, September 16, 1980, by members of the Ancient and Honorable Artillery Company of Massachusetts in the company of the Mayor of Boston and the Governor of the Commonwealth (State) of Massachusetts. There is also the grasshopper weather vane building deposit, actually a non–target-dated building deposit, which got refurbished in the early 1950s (Remington, 1954, pp. 16–17). A renovated downtown district project in Albany, New York, was done in conjunction with that City's Tricentennial celebrations. It is the site of a 1986 time capsule deposit including a Tricentennial flag, telephone directory and a local history of the City (Wexler, 1986, pp. A1, A8). The Troy Hill Time Capsule was deposited in a bank building in 1986 after a rally and parade, and included a potluck meal for the community. This author was able to participate with the organizer of the events, Tom Marek, in the activities surrounding this time capsule ceremony. That included packing, sealing, a popular address at send-off ceremony and the building deposit of this Pittsburgh, Pennyslvania–area neighborhood time capsule, October 31-November 1, 1987 (Jarvis & Marek, 1987; *Troy Hill Time Capsule: November 1, 1987: November 1, 2037*). Another typical time capsule deposit was the cornerstone ceremony signifying the refurbishment of a 75-year-old Beacon Hill mansion in Boston as a university building (Ledgard, 1981, p. 43). One of the most famous time capsules seems to have

Sealing away of the past of 1987: Troy Hill neighborhood Time Capsule, Pittsburgh, Pennsylvania, November 1, 1987. (Courtesy Tom Marak Collection, 2001, Prospect, Pennsylvania 16052. Time Capsules, Inc., is at: *timecapsulesinc@earthlink.net*)

had a double life, once as a TV fictional time capsule, and once again as a real life time capsule buried by the cast of the TV program. Those are the *M*A*S*H Time Capsules.* In the fictional world of episodic comedy TV, in the February 21, 1983, final season TV episode of *M*A*S*H* the "Hawkeye" and "Margaret" characters deposited a time capsule of wartime items for future recipients ("As time goes by," 1983). Meanwhile, in the real world, cast members actually secretly buried the "M*A*S*H Time Capsule" in January 1983. Its collectable costumes, etc., were buried somewhere in (what was then) part of the TV producer's Hollywood parking lot. Now, it could even be under the property of a hotel since built on part of the lot (*10 lost time capsules,* 1991).

Various Centennial Capsules were done in Washington State. In addition to the 1953 Washington Territorial founding centennial capsule mentioned earlier, there are two other noteworthy Washington State time capsules. All three commemorate various centennial benchmarks dates. The Washington Centennial Time Capsule of 1989, in Olympia, Washington, is an example of a type of ongoing, serial-incremental capsule project. We described this 400-year multi-chambered, multi-dated capsule earlier. It is to be opened for the last time on the State's five hundredth

A special bank floor deposit for 50 years: Capsule yellow lettering further down on the box front notes "Sponsored by the Troy Hill Board of Trade": Troy Hill neighborhood Time Capsule, Pittsburgh, Pennsylvania, November 1, 1987. (Courtesy Tom Marak Collection, 2001, Prospect, Pennsylvania 16052. Time Capsules, Inc., is at: *timecapsulesinc@earthlink.net*)

anniversary, November 11, 2389, and was initially deposited as a celebration of the 1989 Statehood Centennial (Berger, 1990; *Centennial Time Capsule fact sheet*, 1989). The Washington State University Centennial Time Capsule, 1990–2040 is a third example of a centennial capsule. This author participated in the multi-year preparations for this simultaneously 49-year, 50-year and "centennial" time capsule (Jarvis, 1990-1991). It is a centennial-type capsule because it was launched to commemorate the first 100 years since the founding of the then Washington State College of Agriculture and School of Science, Pullman, Washington. It is also called a "50-year time capsule" because its announced commemoration span is for the Class of 1990, who will open it at their AD 2040 reunion. Those future 50-year "Golden Grads" had some opportunities to deposit contents, and two representatives participated in the (1991) sealing. The final sealing ceremony took place on the WSU Founders' Crimson and Gray Day, April 1991, making the capsule in another sense only a 49-year time capsule. All of which is not atypical for a time capsule project at all. Time capsules are commemorative ceremonial devices as well as technical projects. Hence they are often bound by many symbolic and practical scheduling con-

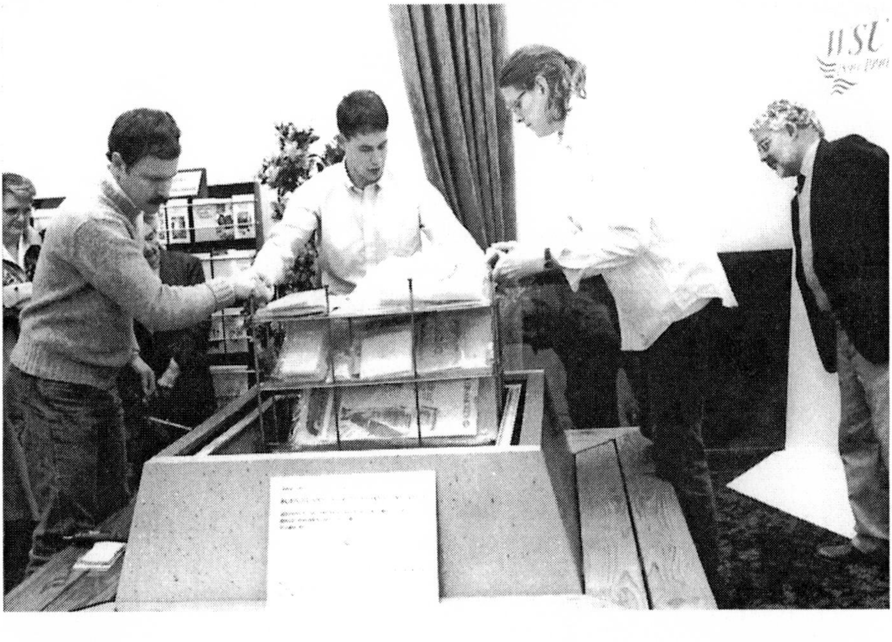

Top: **Washington State University Centennial Time Capsule, 1990–2040. Speaking about capsules: The author (beard, vest, glasses) speaking at the March 28, 1991, sealing ceremony.** ***Bottom:*** **WSU Centennial Time Capsule, 1990–2040: Loading the Capsule, March 28, 1991. (Both photographs courtesy Washington State University Libraries, Manuscripts and Archives; WSU Photo Services, Pullman, Washington.)**

WSU Centennial Time Capsule, 1990–2040. Closing the Capsule: The lid is laid on, March 28, 1991. (Courtesy Washington State University Libraries, Manuscripts and Archives; WSU Photo Services, Pullman, Washington.)

straints. Numerous relics and mementoes of the University were sealed in a group ceremony in which the many members of the participating audience helped screw down the scores of lid fasteners. The capsule was designed and built as an engineering design student project. The capsule was later re-situated in a newly built library building addition in 1992. These sorts of shifting dates and sites can be associated with the same, single time capsule in the course of its "life span."

The "Case of the 10 Famous Missing Time Capsules" is an interesting group of capsule transaction failure experiences. A June 28, 1991, daylong International Time Capsule Society press release "activity" at Oglethorpe University noted ten especially interesting cases of missing time capsules. Since then, two have been found. (The 1954 Washington State Time Capsule was found in the attic of an Olympia, Washington, State capitol building. It appears never to have been buried ["State seeking clues to Capitol time capsule" 2002, July 26, *Seattle Post Intelligencer*].) Eight remain "lost." ITCS members noted, "Time capsules usually are lost due to thievery, secrecy or poor planning" (*10 lost time capsules*, 1991). We have mentioned from this "ten lost" list the *M*A*S*H* TV program cast's capsule, the 1976 Bicentennial Wagon Train Time Capsule, George Washington's laid Capitol Building Cornerstone and the one remaining State of Washington 1950s missing capsule. Perhaps because all time capsules are really addressed to an unknowable future, sometimes their senders deliberately send to their target dates the out-of-the-ordinary, the bizarre, the personal, the newsworthy or just "deviancy-presenting" (a.k.a. "wacky") items. The senders may "lose" them, i.e., become very unsure about any recipients ever finding them. Even if a capsule is (apparently) "sent" successfully, we can't guarantee anything about its eventual reception or interpretation! Capsule contents might seem, or actually be (in their received future), extraordinary. If not totally lost to the future, they might readily be interpreted as bizarre or unfathomable, or even be scorned as worthless and irrelevant junk. Some information or even a whole capsule can be lost in its transmission to the future. The International Time Capsule Society, a group founded at Oglethorpe University in 1990, has carried out documenting and monitoring by registering time capsules, promoting research, carrying out educational efforts, monitoring existing time capsule projects and serving as an informational resource. The ITCS has an extensive online questionnaire to register all sorts of information about the origin, location, contents and type on a wide variety of time capsule projects. During the 1990s, and especially in the ca. 2000 period, thousands upon thousands of time capsule projects have been noted (International Time Capsule Society, <*www. oglethorpe.edu/itcs*>, 1999).

We have seen in this short chronicle of capsule development their beginnings in archaic dedications of sacred, charmed precincts and a stretching, an "elongation" of the original ancient focus on the dedication-protection of that immediate cultural context. The significance of these deposits has shifted into more of a concern with definite spans of time for deposits targeted to definite, distant time periods. Today's definitely targeted dedication deposits also have an increased emphasis on their internal contents. They now often have more of an historic context that features the deposit as emblematic of idealized, futuristic human progress, rather than just a protective commemoration of their environs.

CHAPTER 4

The Golden Age of the Grand Time Capsules: 1935–1982

Millennia-Spanning Time Capsules Have Their Day

Time capsules had their golden age between 1935 and 1982. That mid–twentieth century period originated the most ambitious target-dated time capsules to date. These were capsules designated to span 1000 years or more. They included several 5000-year specimens and even a 6177-year span project. They were also the largest volumetric capsules. Earlier 1000-year-or-more-old time capsule occurrences were really either metaphorical time capsule archaeological sites or were indefinitely deposited foundation stones or cornerstone repositories, not deliberately deposited with targeted retrieval dates. Those deliberately sealed and targeted millennia-spanning time capsules were a zenith, a celebration, in the history of human civilization. In the 1999–2001 "Turn of the Millennium" period, many other 1000-years-or-more projects have of course been spawned, as we shall see later. But the golden years of 1935–82 stand as a unique pioneering era. They were at least eight such innovative time capsules with 1000-year-plus spans created then.

What makes a "millennial" time capsule? Any time capsule targeted to span at least 1000 years can be termed a millennial time capsule (Jarvis, 1988). If a time capsule can be seen (in the loosest sense) as anything or set of things that tries to typify, evoke and vividly recall another time and place, then the millennial spanning examples are potentially the most powerful. That is because of their deliberate sealing for such long time spans.

A target date measured in thousands of years is the next step up from the relatively short spans of "centennial token"–type capsules. Such capsules are ways to bring back to life something of the essence or feel of the pasts of thousands of years ago. These stories are of the four great millennial, encyclopedic time capsules, and the promoter-savants who built some of them. There are three major innovations to the twentieth century 1000-year plus time capsule invention. One is the deposit of such massive treasures of relics and information. Another is the notion of their deposit as multi-millennial midpoint chronological milestones equidistant between posited beginnings and futuristic prospects of fulfillment of civilization. A third is the coining of the "time capsule" term. Millennia-spanning capsules are scarce, just eight cases of target-dated time capsules deposited between 1938 and 1982. Since 1876, untold thousands of shorter-term time capsules have been deliberated sealed for (usually) just 50- or 100-year spans. Millennia-spanning time capsules' contents tend to be vast, "encyclopedic" in scope, to send and help interpret a comprehensive collection of various aspects of civilization to distant millennial recipients. It's natural for senders to think more about the significance of the cultural messages to be transmitted in direct proportion to the contemplated expansion of each communications' range. It just seems to make sense for preservational and cultural interpretive purposes to do a lot of packing for such a long trip into the future. Of course, encyclopedic, comprehensively prepared world cultural repositories do not necessarily require a millennial capsule time span. Generally with time capsules, the scope of deposited contents is directly proportional to the targeted date span, but not always. Encyclopedic content scope and millennial time span do tend to complement one another. The general maxim is that bigger cultural cargoes are directly proportional to longer targeted time spans for capsules. The greater the time span, the larger the contents. If the preservational work for a 5000- or 10,000-year deposit is challenging, why send only a few items? The modern senders of 5000-year capsules naturally seemed especially interested in pondering how such votive offerings would be received.

The New York World's Fair Westinghouse Time Capsule of Cupaloy, 1938–6939, and Oglethorpe University's Crypt of Civilization 1940–8113, Atlanta, Georgia, Opened a Golden Age

Thornwell Jacobs' "62 century long" history project begins! This "modern time capsule" business really began in 1935, with Dr. Thornwell Jacobs

Workers at the Westinghouse East Pittsburgh Plant admire the Time Capsule of Cupaloy's outer hull hanging in air, Westinghouse, Inc., Pittsburgh, Pennsylvania, [July?] 1938. (Courtesy Westinghouse Historical Center, Pittsburgh, PA.)

of Atlanta, Georgia. Oglethorpe University President Jacobs taught a mandatory senior-year "Cosmic History" course, a synoptic syllabus covering natural science and world cultural history. It was significant in the development of the Crypt of Civilization's grand chronological scope and encyclopedic cultural significance (Hudson, 1991, pp. 121–38; 1998, pp. 594–607; Jarvis, 1988; Thomas, 1983, pp. 517–19). The first target-dated "modern" time capsule from the Philadelphia 1876 Centennial Exposition, the Century Safe, was not improved upon until the 1930s advent of these millennium-spanning repositories (*Centennial Safe*, 1976; Diehm, 1882, pp. 194–200; Viskochil, 1976, pp. 95–104). During the May 1935 Oglethorpe University Commencement, Jacobs began discussing with *Scientific American* editor Orson Munn the idea of building a long-term repository of scientific and cultural information. That spawned the first *millennia*-spanning deliberately targeted repository project (Peters, 1940b, pp. 1–32). When he made his November 1936 appeal for support of the project in Munn's magazine, Jacobs' Crypt of Civilization project was really underway (Jacobs, 1936, pp. 260–261). The *Scientific American*'s editor also appealed for its support in that issue ("8113 A.D.," 1936, p. 259). Like Mrs. Diehm and her 1876 *century*-spanning time capsule project, Jacobs did not use the (yet to be coined) term "time capsule." His 61-century-long idea didn't bear fruit until 1938–40, when the Crypt of Civilization was built, packed and finally sealed on May 25, 1940. The historical roots of the Crypt idea stretch back to two major media events of the early 1920s, the Tokyo Earthquake and the Egyptian "King Tut's Tomb" craze. Jacobs' calendric inspiration goes even further back in historical chronology to the year 4241 BC, the earliest recorded calendar date in ancient Egyptian bureaucratic-priestly lore (Duncan, 1998, p. 16). Jacobs did not consciously model this massive historic repository after ancient foundation deposits or even modern cornerstone repositories. His time capsule seems derived from the examples of the contents of the ancient tombs of Egyptian Pharaohs. The Egyptian wall paintings, elaborate miniatures, mannequins, preserved scrolls of various sorts and piles of everyday objects were a suddenly sealed away tableau of a time's future aspirations. Oglethorpe University's Crypt was the first "microcosm" time capsule (Durrans, 1993). Jacobs described his mission in a nationwide NBC Sunday April 23, 1937, radio address (Jacobs, 1945):

> What we propose to do is to provide for future historians an epitome of the life of an old generation — a generation in which we lived. Thus for the first time in the history of a civilized land, future historians will have available a thorough and accurate record preserved for them. Such an epitome should include certain books, encyclo-

The multi-media experience, AD 8113, *à la* Mutoscope (at center): Interior detail, Crypt of Civilization, 1940. (Courtesy Oglethorpe University, Atlanta, GA.)

Top: Fashion figurines in bell jars, antique typewriters, cash registers and sewing machines await the eighty-second century. Interior detail, Crypt of Civilization, 1940. *Bottom:* One of 12 gigantic treated glass container-tubs is already packed with items such as radios, toys and food bowls. Interior detail, Crypt of Civilization, 1940. (Both photographs courtesy Oglethorpe University, Atlanta, GA.)

> pedias, stored in the sealed crypt. Motion picture films would, of course, be included, picturing the world of today and especially the physical features of our cities and countryside.

Actual construction work began on the vault for the Crypt project in August 1937. Like the Century Safe, the Crypt of Civilization would be deliberately sealed and deposited with a specific target date assigned for its opening. Unlike the Century Safe of 1876, the Crypt would be a major storehouse of artifacts and records. It would be sealed not for a mere 98 years, but for nearly 62 centuries, 8113 CE ("This heavy door of shining stainless steel to seal Georgia Crypt until Year 8113," 1938, p. 3). Another attempted repository, Harvey's Pyramid, began at Board Camp, Arkansas. It was never completed because of the death of William Hope Harvey in February 1936 (Berger, 1975, pp. 161–62). The idea of planting a proud cultural-historical record to blossom as tomorrow's antique curiosity seemed to be in the air then.

Start-points, midpoints and target-date-points in the chronology of civilizations are significant millennial time capsule date points. The ancient Egyptian priestly calendar marked a year corresponding to 4241 BCE as its benchmark, zero-start date (Jacobs, 1936). This was 6177 years *before* his own contemporary year of 1936, 6177 years *ahead* into the future gave Jacobs the target date for his Crypt as 8113 CE. In this way, the Crypt of Civilization would be a cultural deposit done from a midpoint in human cultural development when its imagined recipients in 8113 CE would open it. This midpoint, benchmark form of reasoning was later used in fixing the approximate opening target dates of both the 1938 and 1965 Westinghouse New York World's Fair's Time Capsules I and II. The Osaka Expo 70 Time Capsules no. 1 and no. 2 were scheduled on strict 1970+5000=6970 target dating (*The official record of Time Capsule Expo 70: A gift to the people of the future from the people of the present day*, 1980; Pendray, 1939; *The Westinghouse Time Capsule* [1938?]; *The Westinghouse Time Capsules*, [1964?]). In the case of Westinghouse Time Capsule I, a 5001-year deposit-span had been scheduled in 1938. In the case of Westinghouse Time Capsule II, a ca. 4975-year-long deposit-span was targeted, in order to have the two Capsules' opening dates coincide in AD 6939. Dr. Jacobs had just invented the chronological midpoint idea. Namely, that multi-millennia–spanning time capsules should be targeted for opening at a future time which was double the time span since the beginning of the first civilization's identified origins. The exact dates by century, etc., as a cultural benchmark "start date," are obviously a matter open to debate and interpretation. Mere decades and centuries can be relatively unimportant from

New York World's Fair President Grover Whalen adjusts the Time Capsule's internal sealing-up facility, while G. Edward Pendray (with goatee, center left) looks on. Westinghouse Lamp Division Plant, Livingston, New Jersey, September 16, 1938. (Courtesy Westinghouse Historical Center, Pittsburgh, PA.)

the standpoint of time capsule work at any rate, due to the approximate character of demarcating the timeframe of emerging traits of civilization. The basic idea was to frame the senders as transferers of human civilization from its earliest beginnings, into the advances of the twentieth century (our "alpha" deposit start point as midpoint). Then the focus is on the equally distant millennial futurescape "omega" target date hoped for (or feared?) by the senders. This notion of senders at a midpoint in human civilization has gone hand-in-hand with the four longest targeted many-millennia-spanning time capsules of the twentieth century, since any capsule spanning one or two millennia is chronologically out of the running. In the cases of these 5000-year-plus targeted span time capsules from this Golden Era, the midpoint-of-civilization concept applies. In fact, it has seemed natural and obvious ever since Jacobs dreamed up this approach in 1935-36. Jacobs' anchoring the Crypt project in this chronological midpoint idea and his use of 4241 BCE as our "zeta" chronology start point of civilization have produced for us a 1940 time capsule that is deposited and sealed for retrieval after 6177 years. We thus get an omega capsule-opening target date of 8113 CE. This happens to be the longest targeted time span for a deliberately sealed commemorative repository, making the Crypt the world's longest-term time capsule. The subsequent Westinghouse Time Capsules I and II and the Osaka Expo 70 millennial-centennial style twin time capsules have all used the approximate figure of 5000 years back in time for their zeta points. They also used 5000 years into the future as their omega points. Thus the seventieth century could in theory be quite a time for millennial time capsule retrievals from the twentieth century, with three capsules slated for recovery in just a 31-year interval!

The Crypt's interior is revealed! "Only" 1143 years after the two Osaka Expo 70 Time Capsules are targeted for retrieval in 6970 CE, the world is scheduled to receive the Oglethorpe University Crypt of Civilization 1940 CE deposit. It will be necessary for future governments and societies until the eighty-second century to respect the antique conceits of a 6177-year-old target date, established by ancient people in 1936 CE. The 20-foot long, ten-foot wide, ten-foot high chamber is massive for a time capsule (Peters, 1940a, pp. 206–11; Peters, 1940b, pp. 1–32). Its outer walls consist of granite blocks embedded in pitch, surrounding an inner steel hull itself lined with vitreous porcelain enamel. The two-foot-thick stone floor rests on Appalachian granite bedrock. The stone roof is seven feet thick. Jacobs' goal was to assemble a treasury of human achievements that would serve as an academic storehouse of twentieth century art, science and industry for study by an eighty-second century civilization, not just a matter of

Left: **Two Dumont television receivers, and much more, await the eighty-second century. Interior detail, Crypt of Civilization, 1940. *Right:* Jacobs prepares contents during the packing phase of the Crypt of Civilization, 1940. (Both photographs courtesy Oglethorpe University, Atlanta, GA.)**

preparing a cross-section of the 1930s (Hudson, 1991, pp. 121–38; 1998, pp. 594–607; Jarvis, 1988; Thomas, 1983, pp. 517–19). There are many hundreds of common articles in the Crypt. Those include a model electric train set, toy log construction set, an aluminum foil sample, male and female mannequins in glass cases, a pair of binoculars, an Emerson radio receiver, glass refrigerator dish and cover, electric toaster, a still camera, pair of ladies stockings, dentures (upper), plastic flute, glass rolling pin, a quart of beer, lighted makeup mirror, life-size cutaway model of a pregnant woman, phonograph records of music and two early Dumont-manufactured television receivers (*Crypt of Civilization*, [n.d.]; Peters, 1940b). Jacobs continued an ancient tradition by utilizing mannequins in his Crypt project. King Tutankhamen's tomb contained a "dress form" mannequin that may have been for the display of jewelry (Berglas, 1986, p. F19). The Crypt's extensive microfilm collection numbers ca. 640,000 pages. It also holds about 800 books, including *Compton's Encyclopedia*, 200 works of fiction, an extensive set of scale drawings of inventions, many still photographic images (from 1840 on), motion pictures of events since 1898, records of sports and leisure pastimes and also motion pictures of various 1930s-era industrial processes ("Compton's in the Year 8113 A.D.: *Encyclopedia* filmed for Crypt of Civilization," 4 pp., [n.d.]; *Crypt of Civilization*, [n.d.]). Over half a century later, there is still an ongoing fascination with the contents of the Crypt and other such major time capsules. Stories continue to appear listing the Crypt's contents, even partial lists of items, as remarkable curios of our era. These items may be destined to become ancient relics over the millennia ("Lifting the lid on Civilization's shoe box," 1998). A number of the objects in the Crypt are larger items. There is a motion picture projector, a small windmill to generate electricity for the projector, two microfilm readers and a curious device dubbed a "Language Integrator." This Language Integrator, the first prominent object that will be seen when the Crypt is opened, is a hand-cranked 3000-term "Rosetta Stone." When the hand crank of this penny arcade–like device is turned, a metal page will flip up, displaying the picture of an object with its name printed as a caption. At the same time, a recorded voice on a phonograph record will speak the pictured object's name (in English), so that eighty-second century linguists could hear the pronunciation and read the name, and see an image of the object simultaneously. Fused-in color scenes on the enameled surface of the Crypt lining depict vignettes of human cultural history and are accompanied by brief multilingual descriptions, and also a statement of the Crypt's purpose. One curious feature of the Crypt's media contents is the silent film reenactment (by Oglethorpe students in rented historical costumes) of a variety of vignettes from the span of world history. What inhabitants of AD 8113 might make of these curious scenes, all filmed in the Oglethorpe University football stadium, is anyone's guess! A notice printed on acetate-sealed rag paper describes in a number of languages the nature, location and requested opening date of the Crypt. It was supposedly distributed to a wide variety of repositories such as archives, libraries, lamaseries and monasteries.

The Crypt was finally sealed on May 25, 1940. David Sarnoff, founder of the Radio Corporation of America, gave the keynote address at the ceremony. When the Crypt of Civilization was formally sealed on that day, France's "Third Republic" was falling to the armies of Nazi Germany. Dr. Jacobs remarked at the sealing ceremony with unwarranted (yet understandable) pessimism: "The world is now engaged in burying our civilization forever and here in this Crypt we leave it to you." (Brewer, 1940, p.1). An audio recording of Dr. Jacobs' speech at the ceremony was placed into the Crypt at the last minute. Then the stainless steel door was welded closed, leaving the Crypt of Civilization sealed off from the world of 1940, to await its retrieval in the world of 8113 CE. The Crypt of Civilization

Thornwell Jacobs depicted with the realization of his 82d century vision, the Crypt of Civilization. (Courtesy Oglethorpe University, Atlanta, GA.)

time capsule can be seen as a sort of "cosmic bathtub" (complete with an enameled inner coating to its iron walls)! It was actually beat to the finish line by what can be termed a "cosmic thermos bottle." The Westinghouse Time Capsule of Cupaloy's outer packaging consists of a sealed vessel of specially treated glass nestled inside a metal tube. The curious case of Thomas Kimmelwood Peters is especially noteworthy. Jacobs hired T. K. Peters as the Oglethorpe University Archivist to coordinate the Crypt's audio-visual technical testing and processing that would have to be done to prepare samples, records and mementos in the hope that they might remain intact for 6177 years. He was a pioneer in cinema technology and inventor of the first 35mm motion picture camera to use microfilm. Peters had also been a technical advisor on the D. W. Griffith silent film *Birth of a Nation*. That classic motion picture epic had a controversial, racially charged story line. Peters' original ideas about metal film had a practical application in the Crypt project. A man of many talents, Dr. Peters apparently *actually* intended to be at the opening of the Crypt, as he seems to have told a reporter before the May 25, 1940, sealing event. He was a yoga practitioner and apparently a vigorous, thorough believer in personal reincarnation. He apparently claimed to an Atlanta newspaper reporter that he undoubtedly would "come back" in some way or other in time for the eighty-second century Crypt opening in 8113 Peters' apparent expectation about a reincarnation in 8113 seems to have had an interpretive motivation. Peters supposedly indicated that he wished to explain the Crypt site to its retrievers in that remote future and to explain why the depositors had put the Crypt and its contents there in 1940. Peters supposedly declared that he wanted to definitely be there as an interpreter of his 1940 culture.

We all "want to be here" in one way or another. That's why some of us (try to) freeze ourselves alive to be thawed and revived in the era of our choice. That is why people construct crypts, "time bombs," time capsules and cornerstone deposits. Such projects attempt to establish a more vital link between our remote descendents and us. Mr. Peters seemed to be very enthusiastic about *literally* fulfilling his wish to personally "connect" with the future!

The 1938-6939 Westinghouse Time Capsule of Cupaloy debuted as the first sealed millennial time capsule on September 23, 1938. The Time Capsule of Cupaloy, in 1964 designated as "Time Capsule I," was marked for burial in an old ash dump in a swamp on the outskirts of New York City. That ash-landfill, the Corona Dumps, was re-christened Flushing Meadows by New York's mogul-master builder Robert Moses (Hogan, 1939, pp. 76–78; Stern, 1987, p. 730). The old New York of the 1930s was symbolically reborn in Phoenix- or Cinderella-like fashion as a futuristic tableau. That imaginary, notional futurescape, a "world's fairscape," came from a polluted wetland waste site. Today it is known as Flushing Meadows Corona Park, Borough of Queens, City of New York. The 1938 Westinghouse Time Capsule of Cupaloy is seven and a half feet long, and eight and three quarter inches in diameter ("Archeologist reverses job: buries relics of today," 1940, p. 222; *The book of record*, 1938; "Condemns 'despotism' in 'Time Capsule' message," 1938, p. 215; Hyman & McLelway, 1953, pp. 194+; "Journey into time," 1948, pp. 165–68; *The Westinghouse Time Capsule*, [1938?]; *The Westinghouse Time Capsules*, [1964?]). The outer "Cupaloy" alloy skin consisted of 99.4 percent copper, 0.5 percent chromium and 0.1 percent silver, and its various properties were featured in trade magazines such as *Metals and Alloys* (Brace, 1938, pp. 311–13). There is also an inner glass tube that was strengthened by heat treatment and finally heat-sealed shut as a sort of thermos-type bottle filled for 5001 years. Its 800-pound cargo has also been characterized as a "letter" addressed to far distant future recipients ("Scientific events," 1940, pp. 280–81; Youngholm 1940, pp. 301–02).

September 23, 1938, Autumnal Equinox deposit ceremony for Westinghouse Time Capsule of Cupaloy at the construction site of the 1939-40 New York World's Fair, Flushing Meadows, Queens, New York City. (Courtesy Westinghouse Historical Center, Pittsburgh, PA.)

Pendray's group divided the Cupaloy capsule cargo into five categories. Among 35 "Small Articles of Common Use" are an alarm clock, nail file, safety pin, set of alphabet blocks, deck of cards, set of silverware, padlock with keys and a toothbrush. There is also a Lilly Daché brand Paris designer hat from the autumn fashions of 1938. A 15-section "Microfilm essay" serves as an "encyclopedia" of (1930s vintage) twentieth century knowledge and techniques. The microfilm media stores the equivalent of 100 books, 22,000 pages, about 10,000,000 words, and also holds 1000 pictures. A small microscope was enclosed along with instructions for constructing a larger microfilm reader. The microfilm essay also contains instructions on how to build a motion picture projector in order to view the enclosed newsreel film anthology. Microfilm sequences featured aids to translation, views of "where we live and work," examples of art and entertainment and illustrations of various methods of communication. Everything from applied chemistry descriptions to the Sears-Roebuck catalog was gathered here, including numerous articles from the fourteenth edition of the *Encyclopedia Britannica*. There are approximately 75 samples of textiles and materials such as alloys, plastics, coal and cement. There are various miscellaneous items, money, seeds, a Bible, a paper copy of the interpretive aid *The Book of Record* and samples of printing type. (*The book of record of the Time Capsule of Cupaloy*, 1938; Goudy, 1946, pp. 195–96). A "Materials of Our Day" section gathered together fabrics such as an asbestos cloth by Johns-Manville Inc., Rayon samples from DuPont Inc., Celanese Inc. samples, specimens of copper, iron and other metals, and also a sample of aluminum ST 37 Alloy from the Aluminum Company of America. Trade magazines such as *India Rubber World* touted the preservation of their materials in the Time Capsule of Cupaloy ("Capsule for 6939 A. D.: Rubber objects preserved for posterity," 1938, p. 52). "Miscellaneous Items" were samples of U.S. money, seeds and printers' type. Finally, a specially produced "newsreel" featuring characteristic, significant scenes in sound film prepared by RKO-Pathé Pictures, Inc., was provided to give an authentic 1930s experience for the people of the 6930s. Featured are Franklin Delano Roosevelt, billionaire Howard Hughes flying around the world, famed American athlete Jesse Owens running the 100 meters at the 1936 Berlin Olympics, the bombing of Canton, China, in June 1938, and an April 1938 Miami female fashion show. The final sequences are the 1938 preview parade for the 1939-40 New York World's Fair. The 1938 Westinghouse Time Capsule of Cupaloy also contains a wide selection of magazines from a 1938 newsstand rack that might give to the future some of the flavor of that period of the twentieth century. Among the contents of 22,000 pages of microfilm are included small articles of common use, textiles and materials and a microfilm essay. The microfilm essay (really an encyclopedic compendium) includes various books, encyclopedia articles and 37 issues of different magazines. *True Confessions*, October 1938, and *Love Story*, September 3, 1938, share space with *Vogue*, September 1, 1938, and *Amazing Stories*, October 1938. There are also more "serious" periodicals on the Westinghouse Time Capsule of Cupaloy's list of contents. These 1938 Westinghouse Time Capsule microfilms of the contents of a street-side magazine stand are a good example of a broad-spectrum selection process, but are any such range of samples broad enough to convey a full view of contemporary life? Probably no one repository can by itself begin to convey every perspective of contemporary life. A prolific, persistent sealing of capsules, provided content selection and sponsorship is not restrictive, might better achieve that goal (Pendray, 1939; *The Westinghouse Time Capsule*, [1938?]; *The Westinghouse Time Capsules*, [1964?]).

The contents were packed and the capsule actually sealed shut on September 16, 1938. That first sealing event actually occurred at the Westinghouse Lamp Division plant located in Bloomfield, New Jersey, when the inner glass tube was finally heat-sealed there on September 16. One week later, on the autumnal Equinox, September 23, 1938, the capsule was brought to its burial site, smack in front of the Westinghouse pavilion at the New York World's Fair construction site. As a gong solemnly tolled the noon hour, the Time Capsule of Cupaloy was lowered into its steel-tube "time well." The gong was borrowed from a New York area Chinese restaurant, while the basic idea for the time capsule would seem to have come from Jacobs. The 1938 Westinghouse Time Capsule, nestled at the bottom of its Immortal Well, was viewable through a periscope mechanism for the duration of the Fair. At the final closing of the second season, the open "Immortal Well" (also tagged as the "Well of the Future") was filled with various preservatives and packing materials. It was finally sealed off on September 24, 1940 ("5000 year journey," 1940, p. 59; Hyman & McLelway, 1953, pp. 194+; Youngholm, 1940, pp. 301–02). This was the scene of a solemn "heads bowed" dedication deposit ritual. Consider how it is that many different "closing" and "opening" dates can readily be attributed to the same time capsule, as in the case of the 1938 Westinghouse Time Capsule of Cupaloy. The apparent discrepancy between the "1939" in the full title of *The book of record of the Time Capsule of Cupaloy: Deemed capable of resisting the effects of time for five thousand years — preserving an account of universal achievements — embedded in the grounds of the New York World's Fair — 1939* vs. the actual 1938 burial date of the Time Capsule is only an apparent one. The book's title refers to the start date of the World's Fair,

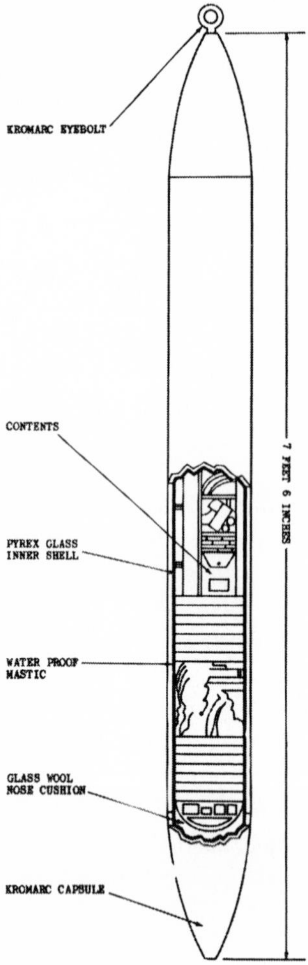

The "Time Capsule" Redux: Cross section of the Westinghouse Time Capsule II, deposited at the 1964-65 New York World's Fair for (nearly) 5,000 years. The contents, hull alloy ("Kromarc") and eyebolt's (round) shape differ from its 1938 progenitor, the Time Capsule of Cupaloy. Note the diagram's original labeling. The shape and target-dated mission to the year 5001 are identical to its 1938 progenitor. (Courtesy Westinghouse Historical Center, Pittsburgh, PA.)

not the capsule's 1938 sealing-deposit date. Nor is it the (1938) imprint date of the book's publication. In the accompanying photograph of the September 23, 1938, burial date, a banner reading "1939" is partially visible. This banner commemorates the *1939* New York World's Fair, the site of which is still under construction in this *1938* photograph. There is a third date closely associated with this 1938 Westinghouse Time Capsule I deposited to commemorate the 1939-40 New York World's Fair. And there is the October 1940 event sealing that "Time Capsule of Cupaloy" in its "Immortal Well." Such time capsule exhibits are (understandably) milked for maximum publicity and ritual, and thus may not have just one single, exact date associated with them. In fact, the retrieval-opening date for the Westinghouse Time Capsule I is synchronized with the target date year 6939, the 5000-year anniversary of its New York World's Fair. The Westinghouse Time Capsule II deposited during the 1964-65 New York World's Fair is apparently also designated to be opened in the year *6939*, rather than say, the year *6938*. The 5001 years being observed are benchmarked to the 1939 NY World's Fair date for both Time Capsules. Since these capsule target-dating matters are not an accounting exercise or an arithmetic drill, these chronological approximations are not necessarily cause for alarm! (Although the fuzziness of all these dates could confuse those trying to track them too closely.) The Century Safe was exhibited in 1876, but was not sealed until 1878. Then it was opened in 1976, which is 98, not 100 years. So exact day-to-day accounting of time capsule spans can be difficult, given the multi-date approximations typical of these activities. Such chronological blurring is common with capsule projects large and small. Many time capsules have a variety of such dates, including official commemorative dates, exhibited-displayed dates, sealing dates, into the well-vault-space dates, burial-fill-up dates, etc., associated with them, as well as a targeted retrieval date.

Priority of the time capsule invention: who was the first inventor of the millennia-spanning time capsule? The 1940 Crypt of Civilization and the 1938 Westinghouse Time Capsule I, the two major time capsules of the 1930s, have a complicated, interwoven provenance (Jacobs, 1945; Jarvis, 1988, pp. 338–40; Jarvis, 1985, pp. 1–4; Peters, 1940b; Peters & Pendray, 1940). T. K. Peters in his (1940b) *Oglethorpe University Bulletin* article credits Pendray as the author of the unsigned science section note from the October 1936 *Literary Digest* ("For 8113 A.D. Oglethorpe University builds a Crypt to preserve culture of 1936," 1936, pp. 19–20). Although Dr. Jacobs, president of Oglethorpe University, first discussed the idea of a major time capsule in 1935, he did not call his project a time capsule. That term was only coined in 1938 by the director of the Westinghouse Time Capsule I Project, George Edward Pendray, as a name for the Westinghouse capsule (Hyman & McLelway, 1953, pp. 194+). Originally the Westinghouse device was referred to as a "time bomb," perhaps an even more curious term than Jacobs' own unique coinage, "The Crypt of Civilization." Of course, the term "capsule" itself was a rather obscure one prior to its being joined with "time" by Pendray's project group. The aptness of the time capsule label has contributed to the notoriety of the Westinghouse Time Capsule I. Another important factor contributing to the fame of that 1938 Westinghouse capsule was its association with the 1939 New York World's Fair. The deposit of the Time Capsule of Cupaloy on the autumnal Equinox September 23, 1938, was a well-publicized event. One week before, its glass inner tubing had been sealed and the chilled metal cap was screwed on (Pendray, 1939; Hyman & McLelway, 1953, pp. 194+; *The Westinghouse Time Capsule*, [1938?]; *The Westinghouse Time Capsules*, [1964?]). As the metal alloy cap warmed, it expanded slightly, snugly locking into place, a method still useful for sealing some time capsules snug. These sealing and deposition events marked the completion of the first major time capsule, the first major collection of an era's information to be deliberately preserved and sealed for long-term retrieval at a specified faraway date. In the case of the Crypt of Civilization, the protection motivation of preserving a representative sample of twentieth century relics and knowledge is especially evident in its name.

The 1938 Westinghouse Time Capsule of Cupaloy was the first deliberately targeted repository to bear the "time capsule" name and the first such major device to be completed. It was not, as we have seen, the first one undertaken. Nor is it the largest capacity installation, or even the longest scheduled duration time capsule. The Oglethorpe Crypt of Civilization has a far greater volumetric capacity than either the two Westinghouse or two Osaka capsules. It still has, as of the end of 2000, a longer span target date than any other time capsule deposit scheduled for a specific opening date. George Edward Pendray, a former president of the American Rocket Society and a New York publicist, knew of Jacobs' Crypt project as early as 1936 (Jarvis, 1985; 1987; 1988). Jacobs had published an appeal for contributors in the November 1936 *Scientific American* and Pendray had publicized Jacobs' Crypt project in a short October 31, 1936, *Literary Digest* article. Although Pendray's Westinghouse project was started nearly a year later than Jacobs' Crypt construction, the Westinghouse Time Capsule was completed. It was sealed and deposited a year and a half before the Crypt of Civilization was finally sealed on May 25, 1940. Jacobs commented on Pendray's apparent borrowing of his original Crypt idea for the Westinghouse Time Capsule project in a September 13, 1938, entry published in his autobiography *Step Down Dr. Jacobs: The Autobiography of an Autocrat* (Jacobs, 1945). Jacobs recounts that while on a business trip to New York City he paid a visit to Pendray. Pendray was then working for the Westinghouse Company on its 1938–6939 Time Capsule project. Jacobs noted that Pendray had formerly been editor of the *Literary Digest* and had announced the beginning of work on the Oglethorpe Crypt of Civilization in that magazine. Jacobs next seems to imply that Pendray then went to Westinghouse with this derived idea for a time deposit type project of his own. That 1938 repository was later dubbed "The Time Capsule." Jacobs indicates that language and ideas from the Crypt project were used in planning and promoting the Westinghouse project. Jacobs indicated that Pendray promised to donate a duplicate Westinghouse capsule for inclusion in the Crypt of Civilization and apparently asked Jacobs for a message so it could be put into the Westinghouse capsule (Jacobs, 1945). No duplicate Westinghouse Time Capsule was put inside the Crypt. Pendray's catalogue of Westinghouse Time Capsule contents doesn't list any such message from Jacobs. Pendray apparently never publicly credited Jacobs' original Crypt repository idea as the basis of the 1938 Westinghouse Time Capsule of Cupaloy (Pendray, 1939; Peters, 1940b, pp. 1–32; Peters & Pendray, 1940). One person from those project days indicated to this author that as late as the mid–1980s, he had never even heard of the Crypt of Civilization, at least until contacted later in the 1980s on a comparative time capsule research study (Jarvis, 1987)! Pendray did arrange for the donation of four Westinghouse films for the Crypt, which were included in its contents (*Crypt of Civilization*, [n.d.]; Peters, 1940b, pp. 1–32).

World's Fairs Are Ideal "Cultural Landscapes" for Time Capsules

There is a significant relationship between the special physical-cultural aspects of sacred precincts and secular playgrounds to some major time capsule sites. Capsule depositions tend not only to make a site somehow special (the "elaboration" noted since Sumerian foundation deposit days), but also to be sited in environs that are otherwise already special. There are interesting contrasts to be noted here between East and West, as well as between earlier modern time capsule deployments and what might be seen as "post-modern styles" in time capsule emplacement. For our purposes in this work, the time capsules deposited before 1941 are what we might term "classical modern." One major example of a repeat of a time capsule vessel type and site which was also a repeat of a World's Fair at that same site is a way to compare those capsules. There are at least two places where a dedicated cultural precinct has also been a major time capsule site. Those two are World's Fair sites that have both become settings for twin deposits on a multi-millennial-spanning scale. These are in New York City and Osaka, Japan. The cultural landscapes of those World's Fairs' precincts are respectively Flushing Meadows Corona Park (in Queens, New York City) and Osaka Castle Prefecture Park in that Japanese city.

What comparisons can we make among the four millennial time capsules found at two World's Fair sites? These deposits of the "modern time capsule movement" have several key functional elements in common. These include the signification of the symbolic dedication of literally delineated boundaries, the spectrum of sacred-secular cultural interpretations, cyclical-linear historical time comparisons, the conundrum of dealing with a series of "period snap-shots," the techniques of communication and preservation of culturally bound messages-relics for the millennia, and the employment of ritualistically driven remembrance as a communication-method. The 1939-40 New York World's Fair and other World's Fairs of the 1930s have been characterized as "Utopia realized," where the technological, technocratic utopian dreams of a future Age of Technocracy were embodied in the precincts of World's Fairs (Segal, 1985, pp. 125–27). The embodiment of this dream of course included the 1938 Westinghouse

Time Capsule I (Kihlstedt, 1986, pp. 97–118). So the reprised New York World's Fair (and the Time Capsule II) in 1964-65 was placed at the site of its grand 1939-40 ancestor. The rhapsodic rhetorical interplay of imaginary or "lost" futurescapes and "worlds of tomorrow" from the bygone yesterdays of the great world's fairs is reminiscent of a sort of ancient future, our "present is tomorrow's ancient past" kind of language (Crowley, 1986). Scholars of world's fairs such as the 1939 ("The World of Tomorrow") and 1940 ("Peace and Freedom") New York World's Fair seasons tend to use imagery stressing that we have already lived through that "world of tomorrow" (Roads, 1998). We noted earlier that the first two target-dated time capsules originated in exhibitions at the 1876 Philadelphia Centennial Exposition (*Centennial Safe*, 1976; Diehm, 1882, pp. 194–200; Viskochil, 1976, pp. 95–104). The U.S. 1876 International Centennial Exposition, Fairmount Park, Philadelphia, was not only a premier world's fair site full of many other futuristic devices emblematic of progress. It was also the scene of Mrs. Charles Diehm's Century Safe, the first time capsule (Dale, 1876; Lynes, 1954; McCabe, 1876; Post, 1976; Westcott, 1876). That first time capsule was itself a "futuristic device emblematic of progress."

Time Capsule II goes to the New York City 1964-65 World's Fair and captures one obscure, culturally transitory, moment for 5000 years. Part of the second New York Flushing Meadows World's Fair was a second Westinghouse Time Capsule. What could be more natural of course than to plant a time capsule at a world's fair? To commemorate the 1964-65 New York World's Fair, the Westinghouse Time Capsule II was buried ten feet *north* of its 1938 twin, and of identical dimensions. Workers began driving the steel casing for Time Capsule II in June 1963 at the World's Fair construction site ("Talk of the town column," 1963, pp. 18–19). Although of identical dimensions, their outer hulls, their contents, and even the character of the Time Capsules' project organizations differed. The 1964-65 project was organized by the Knowledge Availability Center of the University of Pittsburgh, not by a technical department of Westinghouse, Inc. The 1938 capsule weighed ca. 800 pounds and had a Cupaloy copper alloy, while the 465-pound 1965 capsule had a Kromarc steel-based type alloy hull ("Time Capsule II deposited for 5,000 years at Fair," 1965, p. 260). Both have been designated for simultaneous retrieval in AD 6939 (*Time Capsule II*, 1965 *The Westinghouse Time Capsule*, [1938?]; *The Westinghouse Time Capsules*, [1964?]). "Fads forever" might be the motto of the Westinghouse Time Capsule II of the 1964-65 New York City World's Fair ("*American City* magazine article in 5,000 Year Time Capsule," 1965, p. 123; Cohen, 1989; Harrison, 1985, p. C3; "Remains to be seen," 1964,

p. 2; "Talk of the town column," 1965, p. 47). This second of two Westinghouse Time Capsules ("II") was deposited in part to function as a sort of postscript or update of the original 1938 Westinghouse Time Capsule ("I"). The 1964-65 capsule's contents now seem curiously dated themselves. This is true in part because of the specific relics of 1965 era fads and cultural fashions (Harrison, 1985, p. C3; *The Westinghouse Time Capsule*, [1938?]; *The Westinghouse Time Capsules*, [1964?]). Even such a small selection as one randomly chosen flavor of ice cream could conceivably go down in history as the dominant or even sole flavor known "way back then." Time capsules can be rather unwieldy historical repositories because they immortalize the transitory, ephemeral evidence of fads. From a popular culture perspective, capsules are also superb repositories for just that reason. Capsules can trap bits of the past as cultural samples for future remembrance (Jarvis, 1992a).

"Popular culture" has been characterized in a number of definitions of such collections (Cantor, 1997; Cantor & Werthman, 1968; Clarke, 1973, pp. 215–18; Ellis & Highsmith, 1990, pp. 410–13; Geist, 1984; Hoffmann, 1984, pp. vii–9, 16–20; Jarvis, 1988; Jarvis, 1992a). Popular culture collections could include a wide range of written pictorial, sound media, miscellaneous ephemeral and various other materials viewed as especially suited to mass consumption and illustrative of common interests. By focusing on selecting items and interpreting them (and preserving such materials), the very concept of a popular culture collection is expanded. It might include pulp fiction or "lower" titles along with serious, critically acclaimed literature. It is possible to select and preserve a substantial range of popular culture items using perhaps a number of time capsules. Including a wide variety of ephemeral materials in capsules is one way to assist future acquisitions of such items, since their fleeting popularity often leads quickly to the trash heap rather than to systematic preservation. Archivists as well as trash heap archaeologists can thus serve as popular culture curators. Time capsules can be valuable ways to preserve selections of such popular cultural items for reacquisition by future recipients, consisting of both high-formal and popular cultural media-relics. Both the very act of sealing popular item-laden time capsules and the selection of their pop contents can characterize an age or an occasion just as any other capsule process might typify any other group of senders and their sent items. Time capsules can contain more than informational media, such as pictures, writings, and sound recordings. Archival informational media can provide to future interpreters of our past age the ephemeral cultural software of a now bygone culture and time. The study of ancient (or even just pre–twentieth century) popular culture suffers from a lack of sufficient primary materials. The ephemeral character of much popular cultural material, especially paper-based writings and pictures, certainly makes for "succinct" (i.e., sparse!) historical research and simplifies our understanding of past popular cultural patterns. The constant discarding of so much popular cultural-historical data obviously does leave many blanks in any age's montage of past eras' cultural practices.

If even after a few years, things have changed a great deal, just looking at a potential long-span time capsule's proposed content can evoke nostalgia (or wincing?) at the anticipated (mis-?) interpretations in the future. Once-ubiquitous cultural fads, fashions and traits that have fallen into obscurity over the years can sometimes be recalled with a jarring sense of remembered familiarity. Details that have been inadvertently or incidentally included alongside major messages or artifacts from the past can often best evoke a sense of that forgotten past. It was the over-the-counter "patent medicine" iron-supplement commercial advertisement in an old TV news video that really brought back the surrounding popular cultural context for a reunion of President Kennedy's 1962 Cuban Missile Crisis National Security Council "Execom" attendees (Lukas, 1987, p. 22). Sometimes such cultural stowaways can upstage the supposed starring artifacts of a time capsule show. There is a paradox when sealing away a moment in time to represent an era to the distant future — namely, how do we cope with the conundrum of making a 1964-65 snapshot represent or stand for even a decade or century, let alone a millennium or *five* millennia? A 1964 state of the art tuning-fork-type wristwatch was enclosed in Time Capsule II as an example of the latest in technical progress. Now in 2002, it is already a quaint antique item (Gleick, 1999, p. 39). Reading about Time Capsule II and its matching "encore" World's Fair site seems to almost make the significance of some of the many artifacts more fleeting ("Talk of the town column," 1964, pp. 37–39). The intention of the Time Capsule II designers seemed threefold. Representing fads, including a comprehensive collection of written records and images, and illustrating the progress between 1938 and 1964 all seem to be motives reflected in this second take Time Capsule II.

Expo 70 Osaka, Japan, was the scene of 5,000 millennial-centennial twin Time Capsules no. 1 and no. 2. The Osaka Japan Expo 70 Time Capsule project is encyclopedic in scope and has employed state-of-the-art preservational technologies. The capsules contain many world-cultural as well as Japanese-specific cultural exhibits. The Matsushita Electric Industrial Company and Mainichi Newspapers of Japan jointly sponsored this project. A 23-member technical committee was formed to devise appropriate preservation technologies. The selection committee had 27 experts and drew on the advice of a variety of international experts as well as the Japanese people (*The Official Record of Time Capsule Expo 70*, 1980). The layout and contents of the two Osaka Time Capsules are identical twin time capsule burials with spheroid-shaped vessels of a high-grade steel alloy. The Osaka Time Capsules really differ only in their scheduled retrieval dates. One, a classic millennial specimen, is consigned for 5000 years before its opening. The other is a short-term, centennial control in this information transfer experiment. It was initially opened in the summer of 2000 and later resealed. Hereafter it is slated to be reopened, century after century, until finally the 6970 CE target date of its millennial twin also comes due. While one key rationale for this centennial check-up is a "preservation audit" of the capsule's contents, the centennial examination may also perpetuate the memory of the millennial twin capsule targeted for retrieval in the seventieth century. Each of the kettle-shaped Osaka capsules is one meter in internal diameter, with an approximate capacity of 500,000 cubic centimeters, or 500 liters (*The Official Record of Time Capsule Expo 70*, 1980). Each fully loaded copy weighs 2.12 metric tons. The nickel-chrome alloy capsules have 29 internal compartments, and the inert internal atmosphere consists of argon gas. The twin capsules were first exhibited at the Osaka Expo 70 World's Fair site, then finally buried in the precincts of Osaka Castle Park. That locale has no high rise-building foundations that could damage or uproot the capsules in the event of earthquake. The Capsules' contents include a total of 12,098 objects and records (selected from a total of 116,324 original suggestions). There are mementos from the 1945 Hiroshima atomic bombing, articles of common use, records in various media including printed books, newspapers leaflets, stainless steel etchings, microfilm, 16mm motion picture film, picture scrolls, magnetic tape and phonograph records plated with gold. In each capsule there is a plutonium timekeeper device. A maximum-minimum thermometer is separately buried above the capsules to record the annual temperature peak rise-and-fall at changes of seasons. *The Official Record of Time Capsule Expo 70* is yet another time capsule memorial "book of record" printed in 2000 English language copies and 2000 Japanese language copies. It is a catalogue of contents, a set of specification records for the vessels-site and brief history of the project. Detailed technical specification drawings are included in the book's documentation of this state-of-the-art project. The Expo 70 Time Capsule no. 2 was retrieved on schedule in the summer of the year 2000 from its resting place above its millennial twin Time Capsule no. 1 at Osaka Castle Park. The empty capsule's hull went on a brief tour of Japan while its interior compartments and contents were analyzed at the Osaka Matsushita

Technoresearch Laboratories. Its 30-year preservational checkup was a good one. The capsule was repacked, resealed and re-deposited. It is scheduled for retrieval yet again after the first of its series of full 100-year minispans in 2100 CE (Ohmura, 2000).

Sacred precincts can be considered a renewed "ancient Eastern Tradition" of time capsules. This Osaka Japan Expo 70 effort was a masterful creative integration of cultural presentation, preservational technology and cyclical renewal. The second millennium associations of the initial year 2000 CE opening date of Time Capsule no. 2 are an especially intriguing syncretism of Japanese cyclical ritual renewal with stereotypical linear Christian-Western chronological conventions. This is a very Japanese recreation approach. It uses both Western Christian–derived chronological timeline indications and international cultural content elements. That perpetual project site replicates the sacred set of spaces on a cyclical basis. It is also a model of presenting a variety of specific national-cultural heritage and world cultural aspects. Interestingly, the Japanese people have a tradition of sacred shrine precinct replication. For over 1300 years, the Jingu Shrine at Ise City, Mie Prefecture, has been totally rebuilt every 20 years (Popham, 1990, pp. 19–31). The large site consists of a complex of sacred structures including the Inner Shrine ("Naiku") and Outer Shrine ("Geku") complexes at Ise. These are cases of historical reenactment that dovetail with the long-term scheduled Osaka centennial cultural, preservational, ritualistic publicity noted above. Maintaining the Shinto religious character of this "living history" type of the Ise shrine complex has been a paramount cultural priority over many centuries. The sun goddess Amaterasu Omikami is claimed as an ancestor by the Imperial Family and is ritually reinstalled in either the west or east new Inner Shrine every 20 years, in a solemn processional. Toyouke, the goddess of agriculture, is ceremonially re-housed in the Outer Shrine that is located ca. 3.7 miles (or 6 kilometers) from the Inner Shrine. The legendary age of this sacred religious site's structures is ca. 2000 years, and it is held to be Japan's most sacred and ancient Shinto shrine complex. The Shinto rite of *shikinen sengu* every 20 years consists of tearing down the many wooden buildings after identical structures are completely rebuilt at the alternate east-west vacated location, which are then rededicated to the enshrined goddesses. This cycle of building protection, reconstruction and destruction began with the first rebuilding in the year 690 CE, and the sixty-first such rebuilding was finished in 1993. At each of these 20-year events, the Japanese public is permitted to go nearer the Inner Shrine complex in a pre-rededication ritual. The actual building process for these new Japanese cypress wood shrines is itself an eight-year affair. It consists of religious ceremonies, the use of traditional nail-less carpentry and fitting wooden joints with museum-piece type tools. The construction crew consists of approximately 100 local craftspeople who spend anywhere from two to four years on this honored activity. Although written recorded plans exist for every structure, the master carpenters remember and orally explain and manually pass on to new apprentices the expert knowledge of how to do the tear-down and reconstruction with new materials. This rebuilding goes on in a back-and-forth 20-year cycle from the east side of the sacred compound, followed by a rebuilding to the West, etc. (Ise Daijingu, 1979; "Ise Shrine," 1983, pp. 338–39; *Japan Information Network*, 1999; *Jingu, the Grand Shrine of Ise*, 1979; Long Now Foundation, 1999; Kitagawa, 1987, p. 530; Naofusa, 1987, p. 284; Sanger, 1993, p. A4; Shinbunsha, 1965; Suzuki, 1980; Teeuwen, 1996).

The ritual cycles of perpetually rebuilding such shrines are a technical act of construction, a trans-generation educational protocol and a religio-cultural affirmation of sacred values as eternal verities. At the Ise Shrines, all of these acts are promulgated on an indefinitely sustainable basis. That twin-paired process remembrance is an integral act of practical piety, building skills and historic preservation (Sanger, 1993, p. A4). There is of course a tearing-down every 20 years too, all to preserve the traditional functions, forms, essence and meanings of the sacred precinct. The used numinous building materials are distributed to become part of various other "Way of the Kami" ("*Shinto*") shrines. Special forests are also cultivated to provide the wood. The scores of structures of the rebuilt compound are invested by a processional featuring a spirit-bearing mirror of the Sun Goddess. The enduring ceremonial moves to the new site from the old, east to west sites, west to east, back and forth every 20 years. We discussed the development of foundation deposit "time capsules" in relation to ancient precincts' rituals in Mesopotamia, etc. The Jingu Shrines at Ise City are an example of a contemporary yet ancient precinct that is *both* an ancient building protection type of time capsule and a current prototype of constant cycle of reproduction, renewal and demolition. It is a sacred precinct that is maintained on its trip into the future as both a notional futurescape and as an ancient ritual compound. Some such long-term projects in other cultural milieux might focus on a preservation of microfilm or other information-dense media, rather than on historical reconstruction of antique buildings of sacred important. These Jingu Shrines are a striking example of the range of possible historical replication of past cultural features. The Ise Shrine complex is a permanently realized, imagined set of sacred facilities, embodying the "Ise Effect," a linkage between a sacred architectural precinct and a series of successively realized embodiments of a notional futurescape perpetually, permanently re-realized in the physical world. That sacred precinct is a futurescape permanently re-realized every 20 years (*Sources of Japanese tradition*, 1958, pp. 1+). This permanently realizable, or perhaps we should say "permanently renewable sacred precinct as a realized futurescape" is akin to a vision of the year 2000 Millennial Age as a permanently realized notional futurescape. It is possible to envision the historical series of world's fairs since 1851 as another string of temporarily, "provisionally recognized," notional futurescapes. The annual deposit of 4000–5000 new names of the recently deceased (casualties of the 1945 Hiroshima bombing) within the granite cenotaph at the Hiroshima Peace Park is a most interesting (and somber) ceremonial indication of Japanese traditions of cyclical remembrance — memorial name scrolls such as that deposited in a Japanese temple after the Great 1923 Tokyo Earthquake. Jacobs noted that his Crypt of Civilization idea was inspired in part by that name scroll temple deposit for the Tokyo victims. The "1945 Hiroshima Cenotaph" in the Hiroshima Peace Park has more than 125,000 deposited names. A pictorial work on the U.S. nuclear weapons program includes an interesting photograph and caption of that granite coffin where the names of the Hiroshima Bomb dead are deposited. The adding of the list of newly deceased people takes place each Hiroshima Day (August 6) in memory of the 1945 event (Del Tredici, 1987, p. 189, illus. #101). A related sort of perpetually growing memorial is the example of the U.S. Vietnam Memorial "Wall" in Washington, D.C. (*Vietnam Veterans Memorial,* 2000). The ingenious finding aid (and its chronological chart) associated with this cumulative wall-writing memorial are also noteworthy commemoratives.

World's Fair sites have become secular precincts for the celebration of "future mystique" since 1851. We have seen an evolution from archaic, primal ritual-center foundation deposit sites over to secular, futuristically oriented theme park time capsule targeted deposits. As we have noted, capsule deposit practices have developed out of the ancient rituals of temple and palace precinct dedications described earlier (Brereton, 1987, pp. 526–35; Henniger, 1987, pp. 544–57; Sproul, 1987, pp. 535–44; Talos, 1987, pp. 395–401). They have sprung up on the grounds of world's fairs, on the occasion of great celebrations, such as the U.S. Centennial Exposition of 1876 (1876–1976 Century Safe), the 1939-40 New York World's Fair (the 1938 Westinghouse Time Capsule I), and the Osaka Expo 70 1970–6970 CE Time Capsules no. 1 and no. 2). It isn't coincidental that one often finds time capsules associated with world's fair sites and other cultural park type settings. The association of capsules and cultural parks like world's fairs expresses our human interests in protecting and celebrating our cultural heritages. They can also serve to project our own era's aspirations into the distant future. University campuses (such as MIT's), various public parks (such as Flushing Meadows Corona Park or ArtPark in upstate New York) or significant cultural sites (such as Osaka Prefecture Castle Park in Japan) are special locales. These zones are excellent psychological and cultural settings for major time capsule sites. Ever since British Prince Consort Albert's realization of a major international world's fair in the London Crystal Palace Exhibition of 1851, such international expositions were the premier showplaces of high civilization and popular culture, at least up until the second 1940 season of the 1939-40 New York World's Fair. The 1939 opening of New York City 1939-1940 World's Fair was the scene of the first (U.S.) presidential television broadcast, in which Franklin Delano Roosevelt spoke at the opening ceremony. Obviously it is easy to speculate about many factors that may have influenced the decline in the élan of world's fairs. Coming towards the end of the Great Depression of the 1930s, the subsequent World War II, atomic bombs, growth of TV and the ambience of banality in the mass-produced technological utopias have all led many people to regard the 1939-40 New York World's Fair as in fact the last great World's Fair.

The Global Village had its first electronically based online world's fair in 1996. Carl Malamud organized and mounted the "Internet 1996 world exposition," touted as the first Internet-based World's Fair (Malamud, 1996). This project is described in *A World's Fair for the Global Village*. It included numerous groups that mounted exhibits and pavilions. This Internet Fair also featured many online correspondents who "visited" the various exhibits at the Fair (Malamud, 1997). While the Fair was an online effort, it was not "virtual." No one "walked around" in a three-dimensional simulacrum of Fair exhibits. Mounting this project required the organizers to procure expensive advanced equipment of all sorts from a variety of corporate sponsors, work with the many exhibit and pavilion creators, and ponder exactly what it meant to place a world's fair on the World Wide Web. This effort was truly international, extensively featuring Japanese participation. The Fair featured a Public Park, as well as a series of People Pavilions. The first such website termed a "People Pavilion" was one called "Randyland." More than 350,000 visitors had a chance to wander through Randy Walters' linked website home page and make the acquaintance of all its numerous features, all about Mr. Walters (Malamud, 1997, p. 133)! The Fair's Panasonic Pavilion featured an exhibit on the Osaka Japan Expo 70 Time Capsule (Malamud, 1997, p. 266). This Fair's many pavilions, features and interactive events were stored online in a "Central Park," where its 1996-era interactive events can still be visited. In a closing ceremony, Malamud donated a copy of the Fair's CD ROM data storage as a time capsule to the Japanese sponsors of this Exposition. The online character of this major event captures much of the current love of technology, and also echoes the decline in the primacy and vitality of physical world expositions. It concomitantly has the potential to become eventually as obscure and inaccessible as its rapidly obsolescing hardware-software configurations. Physical fair sites are often reduced to a few residuals and theme center remnant features, or even nearly totally dismantled. They may leave only some artifacts, souvenirs and what are called in the Exposition trade "residuals" (some buildings, theme center–type landmarks). The obsolescence of happenings such as the Internet 1996 World Exposition software is not the sort of fading away we associate with traditional physical fairs' layouts. Its "dedicated cultural precinct" is arguably the whole Earth, or at least its digitized electronic networks. The "Global Village" term was coined by Marshall McLuhan (McLuhan, 1964). These obvious associations among world's fairs, time capsules and contemporary online-interactive environments point the way to a future where the three concepts of Global Village, world's fairs and an online environment may become as one.

World's fairs, with their emphasis on experiencing touches and glimpses of the fabulous things and ways of "The Future," once showcased a whole variety of technological wonders to come. And of course the time capsules exhibited at such fairs were among the prime attractions. The Ferris wheel, electric lighting, the first televised presidential speech, the elevator and the traveling walkway (or "Travelator") all became first known to the mass public at world's fairs. These were just some of the numerous technical innovations and popular cultural habits introduced at world's fairs. The Travelator was one of the harbingers of the future of transportation that visitors to the 1900 Paris Exposition Universelle were able to experience (Canto & Falin, 1993, p. 11, illus. #6). Prior to the mass-production of television and saturation advertising about the endless glories of future technical progress, world's fairs were the places to see, and be seen in, the amusement-like parks of "The Future" (Bletter, 1989; Gelernter, 1995). Earlier we entered "subways of the mind" as "tunnels of imagination," seeing that various unfinished New York City subway facilities were caverns frozen in time. One of those permanent world exposition linked technological wonders was of course the Paris Metro, opened on July 19, 1900, in conjunction with the 1900 Exposition there. Unlike many experimental gizmos of world's fairs, the 1900 Paris Metro has continued a practical working existence since its futuristic debut.

In a novelistic kind of coincidence, Great Britain declared war on Nazi Germany effective on Sunday September 3, 1939, at Greenwich noontime, and ca. dawn in New York City. Although the 1939 season of the New York World's Fair ran until October 31, 1939, in a sense the sloganeering vision of progress touted by the Fair ended that Sunday in September. The theme song of the 1939 World's Fair, "Dawn of a New Day," seems in hindsight an ironic reference to the transmutation of the 1939 "The World of Tomorrow" World's Fair into the 1940 season's war-torn theme of "Peace and Freedom" (Gelernter, 1995; Harrison, 1980; Johnson & Bird, 1984; White, 1997, pp. 71–79; Wurts & Appelbaum, 1977). In Flushing Meadows, Queens, New York City, people crowded into the World of Tomorrow exhibition. And the Time Capsule of Cupaloy sat, deep in its Immortal Well, reflecting the utopian images of an increasingly remote 1938.

There was also a smaller 1939-40 World's Fair held at the artificially created Treasure Island in California's San Francisco Bay. Its time capsule was a Redwood chest containing Fair plans (Reinhardt, 1978, p. 38). A parking lot for the Administration Building was later laid down over the site. Beginning with the U.S. participation in World War II, the Treasure Island site functioned as a naval base. Although world's fairs were held again after World War II ended, that grand run of the years 1851 to 1940 had been broken. The life cycle of the first great millennial time capsules is tied to this final 1930s bloom and subsequent decline of world expositions. One can sense in Dr. Jacobs' May 25, 1940, gloomy sealing ceremony's valedictory for the Crypt of Civilization a sort of almost desperate urge to record the existence of 1930s industrial and democratic civilization. One needn't posit any specifically Jungian archetypal, psycho-mythological or mystical interpretation of events in world cultural history when noting the relationship of World War II to both the Cupaloy and Crypt repositories. We merely note that coincidence can have archetypal, culturally synchronized connotations, as well as that of the mere happenstance of two separate events paralleling one another. It is a commonplace that historical events can be fitted into patterns that seem related to one another.

These digital-electronic configurations are of course rather ephemeral phenomena. They operate in less than robust, far less than eternal technological environments. Items like clay tablets, buried chambers or heaps of dead electronics continue to present a variety of cultural messages to possible futures. Mute, dead media of digital-electronics, or even of the unreadable messages of any deposited un-translated records of languages, may merely communicate sheer intent to transmit and signify some degree of past technological skills. It is not at all clear how easily decipherable or interpreted our current online writings, data and graphic images will be in 5000 years or more. With clay tablets, buried chambers and archaeologically significant transformed soil we are (so to speak!) on more solid ground. There is some expectation that some traditional deposits and time capsule phenomena will make it into the distant future. Maybe we are left only with the same preservation imperative that guides historical preservation projects for physical sites and various objects. Perhaps replication and reproduction are better guarantors of permanence than are heroic attempts at monolithic durability. Just as the authors of the 1938 work *The Book of Record* request as treatment for their own cultural legacy, routine translation is perhaps the best universal preservation and interpretive (linguistic and cultural) policy.

World's fairs have been a kind of "living history of the future." Many comparative historical studies have been published about the two centuries worth of great expositions (Allwood, 1977; Benedict, 1983; Findling & Pelle, 1990; Greenhaigh, 1988; Rydell, 1984; Rydell, Findling & Pelle, 2000; Stocking, 1987). The whole world has been declared a world's fair writ large (Rydell, 1984). World fairs and expositions have been characterized as "ephemeral vistas" because these pleasing cultural tableaux have of course not by and large survived their exhibit dates, save for the few residuals at some former world's fairs' sites. They have been analyzed as manifestations of imperialism, of racism, and as demonstrations of the vast expanse and riches of the host's empire. The initial Crystal Palace 1851 era British elitist, industrial utilitarian focus was supplanted by broader appeals to popular entertainment and culture found in French and U.S. events. Technically, modern trans-national expositions really began not with the 1851 London, England, Crystal Palace world's fair, but with a series of post–French Revolutionary exhibitions beginning in Paris in 1797. The 1851 London Crystal Palace inaugurated the modern super-world's fair media event reflecting Great Britain's Imperial world dominance of that time. In this and so many other cultural innovations, the French Revolutionary period was the mother of modern invention. These studies on the various fairs provide a great deal of world's fair atmosphere, as well as a chronological treatment of origins and development of the international expositions movement. Many specialized aspects of world's fairs have been dealt with, including studies on their funding, architecture, status of women, models of racial imperialism and chronologies. Some authors have concluded that the "popular ideological" impact of many of those post–Crystal Palace entertainment-emphasizing world fairs has endured at the expense of the theme of serious enlightenment (Greenhaigh, 1988). These studies have added much to our understanding of the history of technology, architecture, social history and popular culture. The terms

"Exposition," "World's Fair," "Exposition International et Universelle," "Weltausstellung" and now even "Expo" are essentially interchangeable (Maass, 1973).

1973–1982: The "Event Horizon" Closes in on the Last Four Millennium-Span Time Capsules

The four other millennial-span time capsules noted below are significant in different ways from the four major 5000-year or more specimens noted above. Two cases, the MIT 1957 Time Capsule and the ArtPark, New York State 1979 "Rice/Tree/Burial Project" Time Capsule are less ambitious 1000-year capsules. The 1982 BBC Time Capsule seems to have been the last of the "First Golden Age" of millennial time capsules. It was the last terrestrially based, multi-millennia-spanning vessel deliberately sealed in the 1938–82 Golden Age. The fourth millennium-spanning time capsule, a State of India, 1973-6973 deposited encyclopedic-sized capsule was quite prematurely withdrawn from its journey into time just a few years into its 5000-year projected journey.

Two millennium-spanning time capsules (1957, 1979) were each targeted for "only" a one millennium span. These two are deposited for 1000 years. They do not conform to the "encyclopedic content if millennial spanning" rule. Since both are targeted for a 1000-year retrieval, and have relatively non-encyclopedic-scope contents, they are in contrast to the multi-millennial time capsules that tend more to have a comparably large, encyclopedic-type of content. Five encyclopedic-type examples (four of which have already been noted) are multi-millennially targeted and have comprehensively oriented contents to make a representation of specific periods of world civilization.

The "Rice/Tree/Burial Project," ArtPark, New York Time Capsule, 1979–2979 CE is a non-encyclopedic millennium time capsule. This 1000-year span container buried at ArtPark near Buffalo in upstate New York is an exception to the millennial encyclopedic rule ("Art news in brief: time capsule," 1979, p. 11; Denes, 1979). It contains a set of predictions about life in 2979 CE, a number of characterizations of the differences between animals and humans, and the microfilmed publications of its designer, the artist Agnes Denes. But its repository is not as encyclopedic as are the Oglethorpe University 1940 Crypt of Civilization time capsule, the 1938 and 1965 Westinghouse NY World's Fairs' examples, the Osaka Expo 70 Time Capsules or the 1982 BBC Time Capsule.

MIT's 1957–2957 CE Time Capsule is a ten-inch diameter, 24-inch long glass container buried near the Compton Laboratories. Its smaller number of relics contrasts with the more encyclopedic scope of an indefinitely buried foundation deposit that is located under the large "Calder Stabile Sail" on the Campus. Although from the 1950s, the 1957-to-2957 time capsule resembles the ArtPark example noted above. Both are smaller size, shorter-span and lesser content vessels.

A State of India Time Capsule 1973–6973 encyclopedic-sized vessel was quite prematurely dug up just a few years into its 5000-year projected journey. For the 25-year anniversary of India's Independence Day a 280-pound capsule was buried at Delhi's Red Fort celebration. It apparently included an historical narrative of India's independent years to date, as well as audio recordings and portraits of some national figures (Moncrieff, 1984, p. 32). It seems to be "on hold" on its interrupted journey. Inquiries about any possible redeposit have not been answered. Unless that capsule has been opened, it can still be regarded as what we might call a "time capsule in being." The digging-up process does in this instance tend to signify in the popular media or mind an interrupted time capsule experience. It also underscores that time capsules do matter to governments as well as individuals!

The BBC Time Capsule, 1982–3982 CE, was the eighth, last classic, millennia-spanning (terrestrial-based) encyclopedic time capsule. It contains a wide variety of commonly used artifacts, informational media and especially addressed messages (Moncrieff, 1984). Its memorial book lists selections, discusses the rationale of selection processes and provides a thumbnail sketch of some prior time capsules (Moncrieff, 1984, pp. 30-33). Contents included music, photographs, books, miscellaneous papers and documents, television programs (published lists), cassettes, audio discs, newspapers and magazines, commercials and other objects. The books were microfilmed on ca. 10,000 frames, to send as much formal knowledge as possible, to provide some sense of British beliefs, and some indications of life in 1982 (Moncrieff, 1984). In addition to 100 non-fiction works, other titles included Shakespeare and Shaw, serious fiction, ten paperback 1982 best sellers, popular fiction and several romantic novels (titles unannounced so as not to offend the excluded). Magazine coverage also included popular and serious titles, but the BBC Time Capsule was not meant solely to convey the popular or unofficial side of British life in 1982. The Committee's item selections constitute a systematic teaching collection, somewhat like a serious, formal set of items that one might find in museums, libraries or archives. Their official language pick for future universal communication was 1980s English, although a bilingual English-Arabic microfilmed copy of the Koran was included (Moncrieff, 1984,

p. 41). The need to have durable contents deposited for at least 2000 years was considered throughout the item selection process. Other criteria included smallness, cultural representation, and the beauty of those items (Moncrieff, 1984, pp. 43–46). Although church settings were also considered, the ca. 200-kilogram vessel was sealed in a specially prepared vault to deter theft in a burial site at Castle Howard, Yorkshire, England. Potential site areas that were likely to be paved over or government buildings that might be demolished in less than 2000 years were rejected. The selection of the Castle Howard site was based on a geologically "uniformitarian" assessment of those Yorkshire environs, as well as the assumption that the historic Castle site would be of archaeological interest in 2000 years (Moncrieff, 1984, p. 51).

One postscript in this race across time is the end of the Golden Age of time capsules. With millennia-scale time capsules and indefinitely sealed cornerstones, secure site arrangements are geared to optimize practical measures to maximize the probability that a capsule will survive intact. The preservation and security arrangements for century-(or less) scale capsules may seem somewhat unnecessary and even contrived. Wouldn't the standard sealing practices of some archival records and manuscript collections be sufficient security for artifacts and other mementos to be preserved for a "short" period of time such as 100 years? Perhaps, especially with ten-year sealing-up of jars, etc. Both the association of a repository with a building or event and the attraction of sealing (or opening) such as a repository are very important to time capsule and cornerstone practitioners. Time capsule sealing ceremonies are significant beyond the rational goals of securing relics and communicating cultural information to an alien, future time. This is hardly surprising given the ancient origins of time capsule behavior. Also considering the existential leap of sending such cultural messages, it would be most unusual for the transmitters (or receivers) not to feel the awe or thrill of such an imaginative enterprise. At the 1938 ceremony inserting the Westinghouse Time Capsule of Cupaloy into its Immortal Well at the construction site for the 1939 World's Fair, male spectators impulsively removed their hats, while those present at the October 1940 sealing up ceremony solemnly bowed their heads (Youngholm, 1940, pp. 301–2). As in other golden ages, the time capsule builders didn't necessarily realize they were living out one. Nor did they necessarily know that it was over as it faded away and really ended. The era had produced not just the first major millennial time capsules, but also the longest term ones yet finished. It's worth noting that no deliberately targeted time capsules have been yet (2000–02) completed that top the target date-span of 6177 years of the Crypt of Civilization. When people talk of a 10,000-year retrieval targeted time capsule, they seem spurred both by the occasion of our millennium-turning experience, and the coincidences of the significance of 10,000 BP chronology. That's also a time-span readily suggested by the chronological schemes of counting in tens and especially in thousands of years.

The world-wide failure to yet realize any 10,000-year spanning capsule project may be due in part to the lack of past reflection on what we can now see as a sort of millennial time capsule movement. Also, it reflects the lack of a general popular movement, cultural urge or governmental enthusiasm for the celebration of an 8000 BCE (past) spanning forward to a 12,000 CE (future) cultural benchmark. There is no wide consciousness of the significance of celebrating the midpoint of some grand cultural chronology. The Neolithic development of settled agriculture is attributable to the 10,000 BP time period, i.e., the 8,000 BCE major cultural-chronological benchmark. Interestingly enough, a case could be made for the period 10,000 BP (also known as 8000 BC) as an "alpha" set point of origin for Neolithic, settled-village agriculture. We "Turn of the Millennium" humans are currently midway between 8000 BCE (10,000 BP) and 12000 CE (10,000 AP), if we may use "AP" to refer to "After Present" in the standard approximate, rounding to hundreds or thousands fashion. Matching target-date span and scope of contents do remain goals with people working on some capsule projects, concomitantly with the development of interpretive aspects and preservation legerdemain. These factors also play a role in various target date, contents, interpretation and preservation concerns in doing space-time capsules and even in the many garden-variety "turn of the millennia" capsule projects of recent years. Although 8000 or 10,000 years ahead seem daunting enough as a target date, even more distant tomorrows, such as a zeta-baseline date like ca. 800,000 AP, seem impossibly remote for a capsule project target date! Such a date in the past archaeological record of human-tool-using is a plausible time-period to cite as a significant milestone in human endeavor ("Ancient stone tools found in Asia," 2000). Extrapolating it forward in time, as a time capsule project goal, is not!

Postscript: The Preacher and the Rocket-man run the great race of the millennia. A good way to conclude this look at the 1930s Golden Era of grand time capsules is to briefly spotlight once again those two dueling inventors of the time capsule, as we know it. We've seen that that the priority and provenance of the millennial time capsule is complex. But the race is not over, so the priority question is even more complex than its origins might at first indicate. The beginning entrant in the great trans-millennia racing event of the 1935–82 Golden Age was the "Preacher," Dr.

Thornwell Jacobs. He was also a cosmic historian, scholar, professor, historian, poet, novelist, Presbyterian minister, university founder and university president. He was also clearly the millennial time capsule pioneer and inventor of the basic ideas of collecting a historical treasure store, targeting it for millennia, and designating its deposit and retrieval as mid-time points in civilization's progress. He essentially issued the challenge, but he appears not to have been rushing along in the one-sided race being run against him by Pendray. Jacobs did not coin the time capsule term, nor did he finish first with his project's deposit ("For 8113 A.D. Oglethorpe University builds a Crypt to preserve culture of 1936," 1936; Hudson, 1998, pp. 594–607; 1991, pp. 121–38; Hyman & McLelway, 1953, pp. 194+; Jarvis, 1985, pp. 1–4; Jarvis, 1988, pp. 338, 340). The later, but winning, entry in this trans-millennial deposition race was of course made by the "Rocketman," George Edward Pendray, and his 5001-year span 1938–6939 "Time Capsule of Cupaloy" (Hyman & McLelway, 1953, pp. 194+; *The Book of Record*, 1938; Peters & Pendray, 1940). Pendray was a magazine editor, public relations expert and science fiction author. He was also at one time a leader of the American Rocket Society, and later became editor of rocket inventor Dr. Robert Goddard's scientific papers. When Pendray began work as an assistant to the Westinghouse Company president to promote publicity-image activities for the 1939 New York World's Fair, Dr. Jacobs was already methodically developing the Oglethorpe Crypt of Civilization. Pendray and Jacobs were clearly aware of each other's projects before the 1938 Westinghouse project was finished ("For 8113 A.D. Oglethorpe University builds a Crypt to preserve culture of 1936," 1936, pp. 19–20; Peters, 1940b, pp. 1–32; Peters & Pendray, 1940; Thomas, 1983, 1, pp. 517–19). Pendray at first thought of depositing a sealed-up cornerstone for the Westinghouse exhibit building at the Fair, but then came up with a design for a "time bomb," a torpedo-shaped historical repository. When he finally coined the catchy label "Time Capsule" for his glass-lined metal tube, he did much more than just promote a Fair event. The time capsule promotion for that international exposition was successful in distinctively associating Westinghouse with the Fair's "World of Tomorrow" grand theme. Pendray's project had also coined one of the more popular historical metaphors, the time capsule. Today just about anything that makes the past come alive can be, and probably has been called, a time capsule, itself a significant historical legacy.

Jacobs' and Pendray's race to invent, christen and realize the first millennia-spanning time capsule is in a sense a 6100-year-plus race and rivalry. Since neither repository has yet successfully completed its multi-millennial journey, we have no winner yet! If Pendray's Westinghouse Time Capsule of Cupaloy is not retrieved (in 6939 CE?) before Jacobs' Oglethorpe University Crypt of Civilization is opened (targeted to be opened in 8113 CE), then Jacobs' Crypt will be the *first* successful (5000-year-plus, "grand") millennia-spanning time capsule. In 5000, or 6173 years or so, some time capsule recipients might well see which of these two men really came in first! We know now only that both of these unique personalities created today's modern, millennia-spanning, targeted time capsule notions.

CHAPTER 5

Writing Down the Ages: Ancient Writings from Yesterday, Today and Tomorrow as Time Capsule Experiences

Ancient writings can be time capsule–like phenomena and their interpretations can evoke time capsule experiences. These experiences, auras of received writings, can be experienced either as part of, or as separate from, deliberately deposited repository sites. They might be a foundation plaque's ceremonial written message, or even be contained as old writings associated with other deposits. Ancient writings could be deliberately or accidentally deposited. They could have targeted retrieval dates or be indefinitely deposited, just like any other time capsule deposit. A wide range of paleographic (ancient writings) and other older media materials can be distinctive capsule phenomena, literally and figuratively. Books have a long history of appearing in different physical media forms over the ages, yet preserving their distinctive intellectual content (Avrin, 1991; O'Donnell, 1998). Throughout our discussions, interpretation is meant as linguistic and cultural. Interpretive efforts on time capsules may even amount to a full-dress cryptoanalytic exercise, as with the "Bible Code" controversy (Drosnin, 1997; Satinover, 1997; Weldon, 1998). This is a more detailed look at book and writing aspects of information transfer, storage and retrieval over the ages. The history of information retrieval and storage can span everything from ancient records to modern writings, docu-

Cherokee Alphabet.
Sounds represented by vowels.
a as a in father or short as a in rival
e as a in hate or short as e in met
i as i in pique or short as i in pit
o as aw in law or short as o in not
u as oo in fool or short as u in pull
v as u in but, nasalized.
Consonant Sounds.
g nearly as in English, but approaching to k.—d nearly as in English, but approaching to t.—h, k, l, m, n, q, s, t, w, y, as in English.
Syllables beginning with g except ga have sometimes the power of k.—do, du, dv, are sometimes sounded to, tu, tv: and syllables
written with tl, except tla, sometimes vary to dl.

Item Found in 1847
Cornerstone Box
Female Seminary

An item found in a deposit from the former Cherokee National Female Seminary. This 1840s copy of the Cherokee nation's alphabet was one of the antique documents retrieved from the inner, older (1847–87) cornerstone nested inside the 1888-89 cornerstone repository at the First Methodist Church of Tahlequah, Oklahoma. (Courtesy University Archives, John Vaughan Library, Northeastern State University, Tahlequah, OK.)

ments and information retrieval technology (Stockwell, 2001). Ancient writings and modern writings, too, consist of various sorts of records as well as literature and textbooks. Archival records and their management have been, and remain today, central as information for modern life and administration (Cox, 2001).

Items found in 1888 capsule (NSU)

Items Found in Cherokee Female National Seminary's 1888 capsule (NSU). (Courtesy University Archives, John Vaughan Library, Northeastern State University, Tahlequah, OK.)

There are four categories of "ancient writings" to consider. Those include what we have received from the past. (A second is what we have not yet, but might still receive, but has not yet come to light.) A third is what we have left or might soon leave from our day for recipients in some possible, distant tomorrow. Any writings we can manage to leave to our future will be among their ancient documents, provided enough of our paper-based (and electronic-digital) writing and imaging media persist over the millennia (Cort, 1959, pp. 397–99; "Foresees our civilization rated barbaric by future: archaeologist believes clay records of Babylonians will give later scientists more favorable picture," 1938, p. 215). A fourth "ancient document" category is whatever one can imagine in historical fiction or science fiction, of motifs and themes. Imaginary, fictional "ancient writings" can be notional time capsule experiences.

Time Capsule Connections to the Survival of Ancient and Medieval Writings

Surviving ancient records and their archaeological, cultural-linguistic and methodological aspects have time capsule connections. Those antique documents can be perceived in various ways, including their function as cultural-linguistic interpretive varieties of time capsule experiences. Some ancient writings are part of ancient foundation deposits. Some are found as archaeologically retrieved documents. Other old written works are preserved as antiques in surviving library collections. There are many reasons why and how some old writings were lost to our era. The fates of various works of ancient Greek and Latin literature are good cases in point (Reynolds & Wilson, 1974). Some of these communications or transmissions are on the fringe of what might be thought of as ancient writings. Many images and written media items are dubbed "messages from the past." Paleo-Indian California rock art has been termed such a message from the past, as have ancient Jewish bullae, written charm-prayer stamped lockets (Deutsch, 1999; Meighan, 1981). Petroglyphs, rock paintings, numismatically related seals, a wide variety of ancient inscriptions and book-type texts can be understood as time capsules. Ceremonial ancient writings were meant for the ritualistic dedication or protection of buildings. That sort of intended deposit can account for some loss as well (Oppenheim, 1964, pp. 26, 147, 234). These texts, inscriptions, plaques, deposits and various ceremonial writings were of course "deposited," maybe even hidden (rather than just "lost") in their own era of deposit. When we find such a deposit today, *we* say they were once lost and now we have found them. We can dream about what might have been regarding the many ancient works and records that have not been found, not yet received or been transmitted to us. Ancient writings from the past could mean more than just our era's

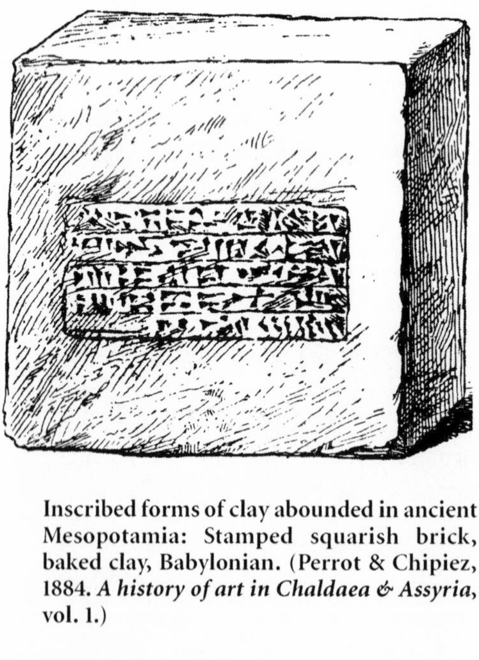

Inscribed forms of clay abounded in ancient Mesopotamia: Stamped squarish brick, baked clay, Babylonian. (Perrot & Chipiez, 1884. *A history of art in Chaldaea & Assyria*, vol. 1.)

Left: **A Mesopotamian cylinder seal. These millennia-old template stone seals can still make their ancient "print-job" images. *Above:* The same Mesopotamian cylinder seal's rolled-out impression, on right. These more recent impressions are "print-job" images from an ancient world. Some such seals actually bear cuneiform writing. (Both photographs courtesy Perrot & Chipiez, 1884. *A history of art in Chaldaea & Assyria*, vol. 2.)**

currently received, known heritage of available ancient writings. We can hope for future acquisitions of more ancient documents. Part of the excitement about the whole topic of ancient writings is in those occasional time capsule–like finds we experience.

The "use it or lose it" principle chronicles the life of lost, found, and saved paleography. The history of the survivals and rediscoveries of ancient documents reads as time capsule phenomena. Considering what ancient written treasures have (or haven't) survived in one way or another, we need a sophisticated approach to preservation and interpretive issues across historical periods. The accidental dry sand preservation of Hellenistic Egyptian papyri underscores the value of wide-scale preservation efforts on all sorts of such writing (Grant, 1990, pp. 141–44). The question for today's time capsule designers is how to systematically store vast treasure troves of literature, encyclopedic treatises, business records and personal correspondence away for many millennia. As with all these interpretive concerns, the best approach to preservational matters is a dual one. Written materials need to be physically preserved from deterioration and protected from human caused destruction. Our considerations about preserving and transmitting capsules' contents to future recipients are applic-

Clay tablet with rolled cylinder seal signage, Mesopotamia. (Perrot & Chipiez, 1884. *A history of art in Chaldaea & Assyria*, vol. 2.)

able to analyses of surviving ancient documents too. One of the older human "written" records extant today is a two-sided limestone tablet with pictographs on both sides. It is from Iraq and is dated ca. 3500 BCE (Highet, 1959, p. 257). Stone buried in dry earth has clearly been a good way to aid the survivability of written and image records, but writings on hard surfaces such as stones, walls and bone are clearly not the only ancient record media which can survive. Papyrus scrolls have survived in a number of physical environments, from both deliberately and accidentally deposited retrieval sites. And there is the realm of ancient metallic documents, often closely associated with the sort of ceremonial writings inscribed on ancient foundation deposit tablets.

What ancient writings were lost? Taking stock of some of the known classical Graeco-Roman written titles that have *not* come down to us (so far) is a sobering exercise. Occasionally something new is found. One instance of such retrieval was termed a "time capsule" find of a complete Greek comedic text (Highet, 1965, p. 270). Another account is that of an Oxford papyrologist working through an Egyptian–Hellenistic Greek papyri dump-heap. He found a scrap of antique Greek writing on a scroll label. It read "Complete Pindar" (Highet, 1965, pp. 262, 273)! The potential is always there for a new big Hellenistic or Roman imperial Greek papyri literary find in Egyptian soil. Pindar's corpus of lyric poetry has apparently survived in only one full work, his *Victory odes*. It was transcribed for our contemporary world solely by means of just *one* early Medieval European manuscript copy (Carne-Ross, 1985; Highet, 1965, p. 271; Pindar, 1997)! Also giving some pause is exactly what contexts and subtle allusions we may be missing even with complete extant ancient texts. Ancient Sumerian writing often used the same syllabic sign to stand for very different word-terms (Knox, 1993, p. 24). The context was the delimiter for Sumerian scribes among the 14 different word meanings of the "*gu*" sign. Today's scholars of Sumerian clay tablets distinguish among these 14 meanings by using numeric subscripts, i.e., "gu_1,"

"gu_2," etc. Processes of modern linguistic translation might be far removed from the ancient contexts of a language's former everyday usage. "Reading between the lines" was literally in demand among the ancients. The extrapolation of absent vowels even in Modern Hebrew is a classic case (Knox, 1993, pp. 25–26). With most of today's alphabetic scripts, the need is just figurative. One era's literary allusions might be destined not to register with a reader from another time. The lesser the corpus of a cultural era's extant literature, the more we may stand to lose when trying to interpret rare examples of long-past publications.

Why were these ancient writings lost? There are many ways to lose writings over time. Written records are not impervious to wars, natural disasters and other violent destructive forces. Censorship takes a toll on the written corpus as ideological or intellectual cultural fashions change. Works become unfashionable, ceasing to be perpetually reproduced. That is just like an electronic file that eventually falls by the wayside of the information highway today, a book dropped from a publisher's backlist or an ancient scroll no longer favored by the copyists. These outcomes have occurred with various ancient Latin and Greek once-extant works. Those surviving papyri specimens and their subsequent copies are modern keys to understanding ancient cultural history (Bagnall, 1995). Once-numerous Latin works sometimes survived in just one single manuscript copy during the Western European Carolingian ninth century AD copyist heyday. Some ancient titles were *that close* to medieval-modern oblivion (Reynolds & Wilson, 1974, p. 90). Vergil's *Aeneid* edged out Ennius' epic poem the *Annals*, which ceased to be hand-copied. Today we would say it "went out of print," off the publishers' backlists (Highet, 1959, p. 262). Today, only some individual "page-length" passages survive, apparently because they were quotable by ancient scholars as archaic style examples. With Aeschylus and Sophocles, only each playwright's seven anthological "best" works were saved. Aeschylus wrote about 80 plays, and Sophocles did over 100. Undoubtedly, these lost works would have sufficient literary or historical value for our own age! Even the most mundane writings of a distant past can yield insights into those inhabitants' worlds, which otherwise we may know little about. Format changes from scroll to codex flat-book occurred, and the way ancient scripts were written changed too. Many significant factors shaped this linguistic evolution, including lower case letter developments, spaces between words and cursive script. These factors made many lesser-valued writings more and more inaccessible in their increasingly antique style. All of these changes could occur without any additional considerations, such as the impact of a language turning into a dead tongue. The aiding of future linguistic translators is a valuable time capsule goal, as embodied in the illustrated "Basic English" guide in the 1938 Time Capsule's memorial work *The Book of Record*. That is only one of the many interpretive and preservational concerns that need to be addressed, based on an examination of the survivability of ancient records to date. Language death, like biological death, is an eternal verity, found in recent times and in ancient history (Crystal, 2000; Dorian, 1981).

Survivability is apparently more likely if a written record is treasured in some way. If it was used, studied or otherwise valued, it would survive by being serially copied. They might even survive via editing processes such as rearrangement, condensation or translations. Overall meanings might substantially shift just by virtue of the rearrangement of the order of the books in an anthology, such as with the Hebrew *Tanak*. Its order was modified into that known as the *Old Testament* by early Christian Church editors. That process was discussed in the study "The *Old Testament*, not *Tanak* or *Hebrew Bible*" (van Buren, 1998, pp. 83–104). Time capsule burial, otherwise depositing or just sequestering a book can be a form of valuation. Another way some written records have survived is through discard or disaster that seals the records away in a fortuitous, preservational way. That can be a *de facto*, happenstance time capsule. When a written record or book has literally become an historical buried treasure (deliberately or accidentally), it could be seen as a time capsule. Although many book lists survive, we are not aware of every scroll or paleographic artifact that has not yet been transmitted to posterity (i.e. found up to now). We might not be the posterity that receives any given item. Ancient items can turn up at any time, in dry Egyptian trash heaps, in Pompeii area volcanic matrices, or even from some library or museum storeroom. Ancient writing categories can range from election billboards, ancient romance novels, whole library collections of treatises, family correspondence, all the way to the deposited votive tablets in sacred or royal structures' foundations. It would be very interesting, for example, to have more and more complete ancient popular texts such as Graeco-Roman romance novels. The Ancients' scroll reading did not consist solely of intellectual works by Plato, Caesar or Cicero. In daily reality popular romances—"trashy novels"—were also read. It is fascinating to read today even just a few fragments from millennia-old novels telling of handsome heroes and damsels in distress (Macallister, 1996; Reardon, 1989; 1991). Tales of shipwrecks, suicides and popular romance-adventure tales are narratives worth studying and enjoying. New, complete textual finds would be very welcome news to today's classical scholars.

There are many unstudied, extant antique records, such as some documents of late Medieval European towns, universities and estates. Some of those legal, governmental, ecclesiastical and manorial records have apparently not been touched since the day their cases were concluded centuries ago. There may be 10 to 20 times as much written parchment material extant from Western Europe after ca. 1100 CE than have survived from the Greco-Roman Classical period (Cantor, 1991, pp. 28–39). Fifteenth century England's inhabitants were separated by three very distinct dialects of late Middle English, in transition to Early Modern "Shakespearean" English (Gies & Gies, 1998, p. 3). North, South, and Midland linguistic variants were so distinctive that North dialect speakers could barely understand South dialect speakers, while the Midland speakers could more readily comprehend both Northern and Southern speech patterns. The "Pastons' Family archive" is a valuable window into the late Medieval lives of a family of English Midlands provincial gentry seen through their domestic correspondence, financial accounts, legal records and other archives (Gies & Gies, 1998). It is these mundane family archives that have made the Pastons notable 500 years later, rather than the family's fifteenth century monumental and ecclesiastical fiscal endowments.

New technologies have improved our ability to copy over and over (and as rapidly lose) our writing, records and images. A ceremonial inscription's focus differs from that of an historical chronicle, religious treatise or other text. While the old standby survivors are still with us, microfilm, electro-magnetically encoded audio-visual and digital computer media have been added to the potential preservational record of paper, papyri, clay and metallic documents. Consider the "as-if" hypothetical case where microfilm became the medium of writing and would thus likely over the years result in any paper books not copied over to the new medium dying out (Highet, 1965, p. 265). Microfilm was once widely viewed as a library-information panacea (Cady, 1990, pp. 374–86). There is a massive literature on the paper codex (i.e. book) vs. digital code sea change now underway in the wired parts of the world. The preservation of digital records is a key concern, equaled in our own era only by concerns over access issues. In the distant future, "all access is preservational" for extant records. Without preservation, the transmission received equals zero, whatever the freewheeling access to a computerized, electronic record was back in the heyday of its initial production. These contemporary microfilm and electronic-computer-digital media observations have ancient-modern comparative value.

Clay, stone and other paleographic media can receive writing experienced as time capsules. A wide variety of paleographic media have received writing over the ages (Thompson, E. M., 1893, pp. 12–47). Paleographic writings have been "received" on bone, clay, stone, cliffs, wall-spaces, metals, wax, wood, leaves, bark, linen, papyrus or parchment mediums. Modern papers, chemically processed films, audio-visual recordings and digitized computer formats are only some of the more recent media that have held humanity's written records and images. Let's begin by looking at clay and stone.

Clay tablets found in the monarch Ashurbanipal's royal library at Nineveh (668–27 BCE) were excavated in 1848. They have been the primary literary source of such ancient classics as the *Epic of Gilgamesh* (Olmert, 1992, pp. 202–03; Jackson, 1974, pp. 4–5). He speaks of collecting works in the then millennia-old Sumerian language (Levarie, 1968, p.1). Pottery shard inscriptions and seal stamp impressions have received writing. There are other ancient cultures' clay writing samples, including examples from the Indus Valley Harrapa civilization of ca. 2800–2600 BCE ("Archaeology news: Early Indus script," 1999, p. 15). Ceremonial writings are also found on Mesopotamian clay cone foundation deposits (Donbaz & Grayson, 1984). Pre-coin and preliterate token-based accounting, clay writing, clay envelopes, all these clay tablet-writing artifacts, accounting tokens, their clay envelopes and (often clay) foundation deposits seem kindred phenomena, at least from our distant perspective. The variety of related clay media "message ensembles" of ancient Mesopotamia is striking, since clay was the note paper of ancient Mesopotamia.

There is an ongoing scholarly debate on the possible (ca. 3500 BCE?) beginnings of the evolution of writing from the use of clay tokens and their sealed-up inscribed clay containers as accounting records systems in ancient Mesopotamia. One thesis is that accounting record-type clay tokens were the precursors of cuneiform writing (Schmandt-Besserant, 1992). According to that analysis, writing may first have arisen from these preliterate practices for accountants to better record amounts of token-counts for animals, produce and other property that those clay containers held. The outer envelope of clay was marked with seal symbols indicating the commodity type and quantity of those tokens sealed within it. Those are the seal markings posited as having evolved into what we can now recognize as a written language. These are developments approximately parallel to the origins of clay foundation deposit ceremonial inscriptions. Positing this origin for writing from Mesopotamian clay container–based accounting practice remains a controversial thesis. A parallel issue is the priority of the writing invention, of Egypt vs. Sumeria ("Ancient tablets show Egyptians may have invented writing," 1998; Schmandt-Besserant, 1992; Wilford, 1999a). The earliest known form of a Proto-Semitic alphabet has been found in limestone inscriptions on the ancient desert road between Thebes and Abydos west of the Nile (Wilford, 1999b, pp. Y1, Y10). These wadi carvings were inscribed ca. 1900–1800 BC, earlier than previously identified Proto-Semitic alphabet inscriptions. This picture is complicated by the plausibility that writing was separately and independently invented in two or more places. Cross-cultural diffusion and instances of exposure to the writing practices of another culture might have inspired a distinctively different form and use of writing in those other settings. Our primary focus in this work is on the significance of the variety of time capsule phenomena in human culture. The curious parallels of clay accounting token-balls, the possible invention of writing and foundation deposits constitute an interesting parallel or at least proximate sets of practices. Perhaps these proto-time capsule–like accounting records could be viewed as having developed into writing? Could time capsule foundation deposit practices be as old as proto-writings and even have a common ancestor? Consider that the sacred royal foundation deposit was a hallmark (even keystone!) of Sumerian building practice. The association is intriguing, albeit not a definitive argument. At any rate, deposits of clay tokens in various ways, forms and functions developed as common practices then.

Ancient Greek pottery remains are another potential ancient (written) source of time capsule experiences, and not only for the artistry of the figures depicted upon many of them. They can provide significant insights into socio-cultural matters of those days afforded by the captioned scenes sometimes featured alongside the figures of mortals, gods and heroes. One example is that of a white background "lekythos" Greek vase from ca. 440 BC which depicts a Muse with lyre seated on Mt. Helicon. The three-line inscription above the seated Muse praises the youth Axiopcithes. The scene is also set by the Muse's iconographically defined image, along with the labeled location and three-line inscription of praise (Boardman, 1973, p. 168). Greek vase inscriptions resemble modern cartoons, with situational-relevant word string statements coming out of the mouths of their human figures. One fifth century vase has the "The Swallow" constellation being noted by three human figures pointing in exclamation to it in the heavens as the harbinger of spring (Duncan, 1998, p. 13; Harrison, 1962, p. 98; Richter, 1936, pp. xxviii–xxxiv). This vase, inscribed "Early Greeks Greet Spring," is one instance of numerous such motto and caption ancient "cartoon dialogues" (Richter, 1936, pp. xxviii–xxxiv). A humorous aside is inscribed out of the mouth of an olive oil merchant (painted on an oil-bearing vase) who is saying that he is going to get rich off the olive oil transaction depicted on the vessel! Inscribed ancient Greek pottery renders all sorts of information about the development of orthography and even social history hints via the types of personal names. These mottoes and captions provide context and (sometimes obscene) insights into those ancient lives (Cook, 1972, pp. 253–60). John Keats, in his "Ode on a Grecian Urn," leaned to a more mystical, mysterious regard of such pottery. That poem posits just that one image of an ancient urn to serve as that poet's "time capsule" (our term). His poem can serve the same function for us (Blackstone, 1959; Wasserman, 1953, pp. 11–12).

Ancient Greek wall writings, official and unofficial, yield time capsule experiences. An imaginary walk downtown and into the Classical Athenian Agora's past reveals a multitude of very real vernacular, informal inscriptions that have been uncovered on pottery fragments (*ostraka*) and graffiti wall surfaces (Lang, 1974, p. 3). These spontaneous and candid writings are important for their insights into the material and their day's popular culture. Those who have inscribed those writings on pot shards and other objects were doing so for their own mundane contemporary purposes, without regard for the our distant posterity's perspectives. Quite a set of time capsule experiences! Deliberately deposited and target-dated repositories have a difficult goal, different than these *a posteriori* instances. These ancient lives' candid transmissions are slices of life communicated from one era's people to another. Wall surface writings from the ancient past aren't all vernacular, profane graffiti. "The Law of Gortyn" is an excellent example of an official wall posting of a fifth century BCE legal code. It is inscribed on stone wall blocks at the Gortyn town site in Crete (Willetts, 1965). The 12 columns of the Code were once arranged as a circular wall with an original diameter of ca. 100 feet, an ancient law court that surrounded the litigants and advocates alike in an architectural legal codification. The Gortyn Code provides us with a massive array of socio-economic, political and cultural detail and can also evoke a good sense of that ca. 480–60 BCE past. Both the general sense of those times and the mass of legal detail preserved there make the Code interesting as a potential time capsule experience. The 1857 discovery of one of the expropriated inscribed stones is a worthy tale of time capsule lore (Willetts, 1965, pp. 13-14). The inch-high letters are written in the *boustrophedon* manner ("as an ox turns in plowing"). This characteristic zigzag type of inscription starts on the right, reads to the left, then reads to the right, then to the left, etc., until it ends on the left. Such writing conventions tend to be completely logical and internally consistent, yet are also disorienting to the uninitiated.

Massive stone Chinese Buddhist scriptural tablets were inscribed in a series that spanned from 605 CE to the year 1644 CE. These ca. 14,300 tablets, chiseled out of stone over a thousand years, were publicly revealed in 1987 (Kouwenhoven, 1996, p. 24). Larger tablets were hauled up to nine mountain caves deposits. Sixteen thousand monks did 16 generations of devoted work to chisel the nearly 35 million characters in Chinese script onto the stone tablets. Some are eight feet by two feet, and some smaller tablets had been secreted in small caves under the Yunju monastery near Zhoukoudian in Beijing Province, China. Aside from the foundation deposit aspects of the smaller tablets buried under the monastery, this project is interesting from a time capsule perspective both because of the very impressive 1000-year span of the preservational effort and of the storage size.

The Dead Sea Scrolls finds are classic examples of deliberate preservation. If any one example demonstrates the value of retrieving deposits of ancient writings, it is that of the various Dead Sea Scrolls' discoveries, of which a great deal has been written. The theological insights from this ancient doctrinal corpus are remarkable, and grist for the mill of comparative religious studies (Shanks, 1992). Those revelations of standard preservative methods for papyrus scrolls throughout various ancient Near Eastern cultural periods appear to have been themselves as remarkable as the textual content. These were fairly standard techniques of preservation, such as cedar oil treatments of scrolls, wrappings in fine cloth and careful sealing of the pottery vessels. These procedures give these documentary "time capsules" a high probability of a successful trip from one time into another very different one (Wright, 1982, pp. 4–5). Interestingly, Robert Graves' historical novel of the Julio-Claudian line of Roman emperors, *I, Claudius*, features papyrus rolls preserved in such a fluid, enclosed in a time capsule–like lead casket (Graves, 1934, pp. 3–13). Gnostic writings from the first centuries AD have been retrieved from such sealed jars. We owe much of our scholarly knowledge of the Gnostic later Roman world's religious variants to the discovery of scroll burials and waste dump retrievals at places such as the Nag Hamaddi sacred text library found in sealed jars (Doresse, 1960; Jonas, 1963; Pagels, 1979). These heterodox writing variants of post–Hellenistic mystery religions and expressions of Judaic and Christian-related "gnosis" religious notions (i.e., esoteric knowledge of spiritual liberation-enlightenment) are fittingly revealed, once secret knowledge from burials, deliberate or otherwise. They have contributed to a kind of quasi–Gnosis in our own day, when their doctrinal world views were suddenly brought to our consciousness when unearthed.

Looking ahead several millennia in the timeline of lost ancient documents to later Egyptian writing samples, there are finds beginning with the fourth century AD which illustrate the early history of the codex. They were the first true, modern book shaped texts. A 1600-year-old codex, the *Cairo Book of Psalms*, was found in a Coptic (Egyptian Christian) coffin burial (Reif, 1988, p. 1). One of the oldest codices, this parchment volume was found under the head of a 12-year-old girl who had been buried south of Cairo about 1600 years ago (Cowell, 1988, p. 11). Two other ancient codex-style bound books (i.e., with covers and sewn pages attached to a spine) are the *Codex Sinaiticus* at the British Museum and the *Codex Vaticanus*. European scholars detected both in the 1840s at St. Catherine's Monastery, Mt. Sinai. The ca. 500-page *Cairo Book of Psalms* may be only the third oldest codex extant, depending on which technical bibliographic details are given priority from experts' checklists. Whatever the exact priority and provenance, that codex is a candidate for time capsule consideration because of its early dates and because it was *deliberately* buried in a grave. The two St. Catherine codices were once housed in the custody of that Mt. Sinai monastery. Their acquisition by European museums is not as much a time capsule experience, at least in comparison to written treasures uncovered from burials. Their sheer survival is time capsule–like, though. Encountering anything so uniquely ancient that was believed "lost" (or at least non-retrievable) can evoke in the researcher a sudden identification with its past age. As an item of what archaeologists refer to as "grave goods," *The Cairo Book of Psalms* discovery is part and parcel with several time capsule–type finds noted in this work, including grave sites, foundation deposits and various paleographic works. Very ancient works have been discovered in the sacred retired document storeroom of a Cairo synagogue's Geniza, put away for safekeeping for ages on end after many years of heavy use (Deul, 1965, pp. 351–81; Kale, 1959). Coptic codices and later medieval codex books have survived in sufficient quantities to fuel extensive study. The physical construction of surviving codices (i.e., true books), as we know them, are artifacts studied today as evidence of the past. They have been said to have an archaeology, as one study, *The Archaeology of Medieval Bookbinding*, puts it (Szirmai, 1999). The beginning of the "Medieval" period noted there is synonymous with the development of the (Coptic) Egyptian Christian codex in the fourth century CE. Matters such as book bindings, book spine construction-labeling and book shelving all have had major developments since the later European Middle Ages (Petroski, 1999).

Vindolanda's wood-sliver "note paper" tablets offer up informative scenes of everyday Roman Imperial frontier life. At the site of modern Chesterholm, excavations of the dumps near the Roman Britain–era frontier fort of Vindolanda yield worn shoes, leather scraps, combs and boxes (a variety of typical detritus), including thrown away letters and notes.

They are currently the oldest known such Roman paleographic evidence (Bahn, 1992, pp. 60–65; Grant, 1990, pp. 129–33). In fact, these are the *only* extant examples of thin wood sliver notes, bent flat for ink writing. One ancient historian had noted their existence, but these were the first to turn up. There is a cursive script on these six- to eight-inch high by two-and-a-half- to three-and-a-half-inch-wide birch (or sometimes alder) wood slivers. Private letters, as well as official military reports, correspondence and governmental accounting records are among these writings. Letters include some shipped to the fort with packs of warm socks. The ca. 1000 wood bark tablets, including a smaller number of wax tablets, offer an excellent example of the archaeology of ancient Roman writing. They make possible the correlation, the mutual confirmation, of this written and other archaeological evidence. The remains of food animal bones and the survival of some mess menus indicate that the frontier forts troops had a substantial meat diet, apparently not a commonplace situation in some other Imperial Roman military posts. Among the many details of everyday life in this military posting are "order of battle" lists indicating that the troop strength was approximately double that which might have been inferred from other non-frontier historical sources (Williams, 1996, pp. 76–78). This mass of deposits at trash dumps consists of both personal writings and official military documentation. These discarded deposits, as well as the miscellaneous, scattered discards in residential rooms and other areas of these military posts, significantly aid the analysis of residues and artifact evidence, themselves archaeologically retrieved records from the site.

Ancient written metallic documents include foundation plaques, tablet-texts, mirrors and coins. There are a wide variety of epigraphic artifacts that are composed of one metal or another, used for a number of purposes. Foundation dedication plaques are notable time capsule–related deposits. The general topic of ancient metallic written documents overlaps the realm of ancient foundation deposits (Ellis, 1968; Wright, 1970; 1982). Some good dedication plaque examples were deposited by the seventh century BC Assyrian King Esarhaddon, among them inscribed votive tablets and talismans in the foundations for future sovereigns to find (Ellis, 1968, p. 103). Not all examples of documents from all culture areas were done as ceremonial foundation deposits. Some sacred texts may have been buried when cultic practices were being suppressed by invaders or by the authorities, and have at any rate ended up as finds at excavation sites (Wright, 1970; 1982). "Foundation and other dedication plaques" are a more accurate description of this class of artifacts. Some were apparently officially posted public announcements and other records. Other paleographic items were lead or tin maledictory "curse tablets," presumably vernacular, folkloric-type practices. The Persian monarch Darius' ruined palace at the Persepolis site has yielded evidence of dedicatory tablets once deposited at each of its four corners, although some appear to have been looted long ago. East Asiatic cultures also used metallic inscriptions (Wright, 1970, pp. 471–72; 1982, p. 5). It is almost impossible (and apparently irresistible) not to have termed in one instance a significant historical treasure a "time capsule" when describing a range of such finds (Wright, 1982, p. 5). Wright cites numerous examples of finds and literature on this scene of metallic written media (Wright, 1970; 1982). A series of bilingual precious metal tablets are from a dedicatory foundation deposit for the Hellenistic Alexandrian Temple Sanctuary of Sarapis (Empereur, 1999b, pp. 27, 89, 96–97; Rowe & Rees, 1956-57, pp. 485–520; Stambaugh, 1972, p. 7). The loss of that temple institution's massive Daughter Library of perhaps 400,000 papyrus scrolls underscores the difficulties in attempting long-term massive cultural transmissions through library, archive and museum collections.

The millennial types of time capsule we have identified clearly commemorate and elaborate their cultural era in a broad sense. Even smaller foundation stone deposits or time capsule boxes are clearly intended to commemorate and elaborate at least some key aspects of their own eras as well. In figurative and literal terms, time capsule boxes and foundation deposits have the attribution of being dubbed cornerstones, key expressions of one's culture, society, institution, place or time. Such deposits and boxes have had such attributions by their senders and by their recipients or other outside interpreters. The symbolic bridge between the similar cultural meanings intended by both ancient foundation and by modern target-dated time capsule deposits, their common spectrum of cultural significance, can be well illustrated by the development of Alexandrine Hellenistic foundation deposit box and tablet practices. After Alexander's conquest of the Persian Darius at the Battle of Issus, his army destroyed the Persian Imperial capital of Persepolis in 331 BC with its corner foundation deposit boxes. One practice passed on from Persepolis through this Hellenistic elite was the deposit of foundation dedication plaques made of various precious materials. They were ceremonially invested in cornerstone-like rock building foundation niches (Wright, 1982, pp. 17–18). Alexandrine foundation plaques were customarily deposits of written ceremonial messages usually sealed into corner enclosures. Although our contemporary archaeological focus is on the exact spots of deposits, the motives of these plaque dedication practices were usually the dedication of the whole sacred-royal environs. The boundaries as well as a key building's structural foundation were to be consecrated. The Ptolemies' Hellenistic foundation plaque practices were clearly lineal descendents of the Assyrian-Persian foundation plaque cultural nexus that shares forms and functions (Wright, 1982, pp. 17–18). We can appreciate the viability of the metallic document approach to sending dedication deposit, "time capsule" ceremonial messages to an indefinite future.

Many other metallic inscriptions were used as ceremonial writing in the form of incantations. These sorts of ancient writings were not mundane work-a-day records, correspondence, chronicles or learned treatises at all. Metallic inscriptions of various sorts were apparently fairly prevalent in Graeco-Roman antiquity, and not rare curiosities. There is a whole realm of curse tablets, voodoo-type dolls, magical items, etc. They were common in the history of ancient Greek and Roman witchcraft and magical practices (Ogden, 1999, pp. 1–90). Clearly, a variety of cultural groups and social strata had carried out these metallic epigraphic practices for a wide variety of purposes: religious-doctrinal, maledictory, burial keepsakes, legal decrees, royal-historical chronicles, important accounting inventories, etc. The practice of inscribing metal plates or tablets has occurred since the earliest days of writing, and there may be thousands of inscriptions extant. Some have probably not been retrieved, are probably still buried, or even already melted down for their metallic content. Examples of non-foundation dedicatory rite metal tablets include Roman Imperial metal mining regulations and various other provincial regulations on several bronze plates as well. These later specimens were discovered at what is currently known as Aljustel, Portugal. Other Orphic doctrinal statements appear as inscriptions on gold plates discovered in Crete and Sicily (Wright, 1970, pp. 462–63). Orphic-Pythagorean golden tablet manuals for an otherworldly journey were deposited to guide the souls of the deceased in Cretan and Southern Italian graves (Zaleski, 1987, p. 18).

Etruscan mirrors' inscriptions are one of the key sources of that language's writing. In the case of the written Etruscan language, extant media of any length is scarce, limited to ca. 10,000 brief inscriptions using Greek alphabetic characters. In fact, inscriptions etched into mirrors found as grave goods and shorter funereal writings constitute much of the evidence for scholarly work. The major time capsule object lessons here are the paucity of the written record and the difficulty of deciphering a lost, dead language. Even if that language is clearly written in a familiar alphabet, there is a great deal of mystery, heightened by the tantalizing familiarity of a script's characters recording a still secret tongue (Hus, 1961, pp. 77–86). The letter-sized Tabula Cortonensis was recently found in the Tuscan town of Cortona. It has added 27 new words to the known vocabulary of today's

Etruscan philologists, several new grammatical constructions and some verb conjugations ("Archaeology news: Etruscan text find," 1999, p. 16). That folded, thin metallic document (only seven of eight parts have been found) is a real estate contract between two families. Such discoveries continue to help philologists tease out snippets of the common discourse of the Etruscan cultural era, in some cases from gold foil tablets (Grant, 1990, pp. 78–80). There are so far less than a dozen extant lengthy Etruscan texts, and there is in particular a dearth of historical chronicles. There are many small inscriptions that are funerary incantations (Bonfante, 1990, pp. 321–78).

Ancient coinage hoards and individual finds are miniature time capsules. They can be capsules not only because treasure troves are often deliberately deposited as buried, or sealed in an underground chamber, often with at least the hope that they will be retrieved at a given time. Because of the visual or other information they may bear, ancient coins can be powerful keys to unlocking past history (Howgego, 1995). Coinage can be a valuable source of archaeological contextual data for correlating chronologies, studying socio-economic patterns, architectural structures and even portrait evidence on obscure rulers and imperial family figures (Grant, 1958, pp. 58–63). The reverses ("tails") of ancient coins can provide unique evidence of architectural design on numerous Graeco-Roman buildings. In many cases, ancient lost Greek art has been copiously illustrated on coinage. Artistic appreciations by the fourth century BCE travelogue writer Pausanias can be correlated with coins' images of scenes which may otherwise have left no physical traces other than his verbal descriptions (Oikonomides, 1964). These coins' images can sometimes take us back to lost world images only they have preserved. Coins and medals of all sorts, ancient and otherwise, have been a mainstay of foundation, cornerstone and time capsule deposits. Many coins are eminently datable, even the majority of ancient specimens which do not contain mint dates. They are durable bearers of images, are related to ancient pre-coin tokens and deposits, and even suggest something of amounting to a "small sacrifice." The sacrifices are financial and symbolic as well, in conjunction with the portrait heads on many obverses. The Alexandrian Sarapieon Temple shows signs of Imperial Roman coin dedication deposits at a time when fire repairs were believed to have been carried out in the second century CE (Rowe & Rees, 1956-57, pp. 485–520). Other archaeological finds in foundation remains indicate coin deposits there as well (Rowe & Rees, 1956-57). All time capsules and kindred deposits are small sacrifices from one age to another, not only these votive coin deposits. Small coins, hopefully not of a value to tempt even the most small-minded deposit robber, definitely make the final cut for inclusion in a modern time capsule's contents. The votive foundation deposit of a coin is certainly an ancient tradition, one documented context being in sixth century BCE Persian Persepolis (Howgego, 1995, p. 4).

"Losing" ancient libraries and trying to find them again can be a time capsule–like experience. The famous "lost" Hellenistic libraries of Alexandria and Pergamon are worthy time capsule experiences. The most famous is that of the research institute complex the Mouseion and its attached "Mother" Library of Hellenistic Egyptian Alexandria (Empereur, 1999b, pp. 96–97; Grant, 1982, pp. 38+; Johnson, 1970, pp. 54–61; Parsons, 1952). History records more than one lost library of Alexandria. The Mouseion and its "Mother" Library constituted what might be thought of as a super research institute. The Temple of Sarapis also had its own distinguished scroll collection, the so-called Daughter Library (Parsons, 1952, pp. 86+). This Temple was the site of the major dedicatory foundation box discussed with metallic document deposits. The Mouseion and its integrated Mother Library facilities appear to have been organized in 10 Halls, each with a significant library collection of its own (Parsons, 1952). It is sobering to contemplate the possible fate of time capsule–type communications across the millennia compared with the dissolution of these large definitive library collections. The fate of the Daughter Library suggests a pessimistic prognosis for such large cultural preservation-transmission attempts for more than a few hundred year–long spans. As for the Mother Library of Alexandria, exact circumstances of the dissolution and destruction of this massive collection of learning have been obscured by the passage of time. Even a series of powerful institutional patrons does not continue forever and a prestigious reputation is no ironclad protection against the ravages of shifting fates. That Library, whatever its true final fate, seems to have been obliterated by one means or another over time, probably in a series of drawn-out episodes. There are several possible scenarios, featuring a multitude of possible depredations (Canfora, 1989; Jackson, 1974, pp. 9–17; Parsons, 1952, pp. 273–432). The bottom line for time capsule studies and such projects is that collections disperse through accidents, deliberate destruction, vandalism or theft. Among the mysteries of this grand Library system is one of its most fabulous collections, the Ships Books. It was constantly being acquired though an interesting sort of tax imposed by the port authority of Hellenistic Alexandria. Each ship making a call at Alexandria was required to hand over any papyrus scroll titles on board for copying by the Library's expert staff. A copy was returned to the source ship and the newly acquired originals went into the Library of Alexandria's vast holdings (Frazer, 1972). Whenever you hear of an ancient Hellenistic or

Roman imperial shipwreck, think of the reading matter that might have been on board, and of the Ships Book copy that might well have once been part of the great Library of Alexandria (Canfora, 1989)! Thumbnail sketches of this remarkable Hellenistic city in its heyday, seemingly on the verge of an almost eerie sort of modernity in lifestyle, technology, foreign trade, information and institutions of learning, clearly reflect its wide-ranging cosmopolitan sensibility (Haas, 1997; Frazer, 1972). It includes descriptions of the study of gases, including the use of automatic steam action devices in temples' statues, Automat coin-driven, vending machine–operated temple doors, and dove figures that rose and fell by means of steam jets and compressed ("BB gun") air guns. Remarkably, steam power was used to drive automobiles in the annual religious parade in Alexandria (Klein, 1967, pp. 153–58). One of the key intellectual tasks in that "world culture" carried out by the Hellenistic scholarly community of the Alexandrian Museum and Library was a systematic standardizing of a variety of Greek texts (Reynolds & Wilson, 1974, pp. 5–15). There has been some interesting reconstruction of the acquisition, cataloguing and accession of these collections of papyri scrolls by their short titles and by individual provenance (Frazer, 1972; Turner, 1968). While specific *libraries* have turned to dust, libraries as cultural institutions continue to survive and develop through a myriad of information media modalities, and in a wide variety of social settings (Lerner, 1998).

It is an important lesson in time capsule–type legacies that the substantial holdings of both the "Daughter Library" of the Sanctuary of Serapis and the "Mother Library" of the Library of Alexandria were not sustainable against the ravages of time and historical change. Meanwhile, discards, or obscurely sequestered items, have preserved much of both ancient literary wisdom and of the humdrum records of daily affairs. These scrolls met various fates. Some were tossed into (dry) trash dumps, buried in volcanic mudflows, buried with family members' remains or secreted in foundation tablet boxes. Others were kept in out-of-the-way places like the Cairo Geniza sacred storeroom or held by obscure institutions, such as St. Catherine's Monastery at the foot of Mt. Sinai (Kale, 1959). Archaeologically retrieved discards, bits of wreckage or obscure minor religious, etc., institutions at the fringes of the great metropolitan institutional centers have been the sources of much ancient treasured writing. The sorry state of the world's archival record does not give a good prognosis for national libraries, centralized repositories or other highly visible "big concept" monuments to the future! The once great library at Pergamon in Asia Minor is another such renowned lost library (Jackson, 1974, pp. 17–18; Johnson, 1970, pp. 61–62). Pergamon has long been associated with the parchment medium for writing. Consider how valuable, how interesting and how informative the preserved contents of a library like the great library at Pergamon would be today!

The Villa dei Papiri is a case of a smaller but famous private patron's villa and library being buried in the August 79 CE eruption of Mount Vesuvius (Deiss, 1968, pp. 4, 8, 47–57). Herculaneum's Villa dei Papiri scrolls are an excellent example of an ancient lost library since found, or at least partially retrieved. In addition to numerous examples of fine bronze sculpture, this fabulous site contains deteriorated, "transformed" (but not irretrievably destroyed) papyri rolls of the Villa's antiquarian library. It seems to have consisted largely of works of various philosophers of the Epicurean school of thought. This library was apparently already something of an antiquarian collection at the time of its AD 79 volcanic mud burial (Reynolds & Wilson, 1974, pp. 32, 177). These papyrus scrolls were heavily, sometimes almost unrecognizably carbonized. Probably at play were water action, heat activity, and hardening of their buried lava-mud matrix (Gallo, 1986, pp. 36–45; Hazzard, 1983, p. 81; Hazzard, 1987, pp. 1, 34; Thompson, J. W., 1940, p. 83; Turner, 1968, p. 18). Carbonized ancient papyri finds have come from other Graeco-Roman sites (Turner, 1968). The first Herculaneum scroll to be successfully unrolled and read was a volume on music by Philodemus (Hazzard, 1983, p. 81). When a few bits were retrieved and unrolled, fragments of uniquely new works by the renowned earlier Greek philosopher Epicurus were revealed ("Epicurus," 1937, pp. 61–162). One thousand eight hundred twenty-six distinct papyrus scroll portions and some marble and bronze statuary were retrieved from this site. The first lumps of scrolls were retrieved from the Villa in 1752 (Thompson, E. W., 1940, p. 83; Gallo, 1986, pp. 36–45). In recent years, computer-aided contrast studies have helped in discerning some scroll lettering (Browne, 1990, p. B6). It has been possible to analyze some comparative stylistic features of Herculaneum papyri vs. Greek finds of various periods in Egypt (Kenyon, 1970, pp. 3–5, 32+).

Poisonous volcanic gases finally ended excavations done between 1750 to 1765. Excavators tunneled vertically down to 27 meters (about 88 feet). Moving around a subterranean series of artificial pathways in the buried remains of the Villa's various chambers, they found scrolls in several places (Hazzard, 1983, p. 81). Scroll retrievals resumed in 1987, a 125-year span time capsule experience on top of the original 1671-year span time capsule retrieval of AD 79 to 1750 (Hazzard, 1987, pp. 1, 34)! Ironically, this papyrological research is on carbonized scrolls damaged in the water and heat of that ancient mud-lava flood. The other work in this field of ancient writing revolves around desertified finds of papyrus rolls preserved in the dryness of Egyptian sands (Grant, 1990, pp. 141–44; Turner, 1968). Only part of the Herculaneum AD 79 scrolls' writing has so far been accessible after physical retrieval, yielding mostly portions of various Epicurean writers, perhaps extracted from just one subject area nook of the Villa's library (Hazzard, 1987, pp. 1, 34). This library was arranged with a table at the center of the room and groups of scrolls housed in distinctive alcoves around the walls of this ancient gentleman's library-study (Thompson J. W., 1940, p. 83). Unfortunately no second *On Comedy* volume of Aristotle's *Poetics* has emerged from the dig's laboratory to take its place with the extant Aristotelian companion work analyzing tragedies. Ancient checklists indicate that Aristotle did pen such a volume analyzing comedic drama, but it remains lost to date (Highet, 1965, p. 268). This Villa's owner at one time had been one Lucius Calpurnius Piso who appears to have been something of a patron of Epicurean philosophy, a sort of pre-modern "foundation-institute-at-home" approach to scholarly sponsorship (Hazzard, 1987, pp. 1, 34). The presence of multiple copies of some volumes authored by Philodemus suggest to some that he had once been the Epicurean scholar in residence at the Villa (Thompson, E. M., 1893, pp. 113–14). While the corpus of Lucretius' Epicurean-based poetic philosophy has survived the ages, very little of the actual *oeuvre* of Epicurus himself has been successfully passed on to our era. In fact, one of the better summaries of Epicurus' own system of principles is the inscribed monument work of an ancient devotee found in present day Turkey. That is an example of epigraphic (i.e., stone or metal) writing. It bests the papyrological medium in preserving detailed tenets of Epicurus' philosophic system (Highet, 1965, p. 272). By "Epicurean" (distinguished as a philosophical school of thought by the use of the capital "E"), we refer to the ancient atomistic, naturalistic Graeco-Roman philosophy of moderation, balance and skepticism toward fear, superstition, atomistic flux and worldly turmoil. Those philosophical ideals were the opposite of behaviors commonly labeled "epicureanism" (distinguished by a lower case "e"). The gluttony, hedonistic license and excess typified by the proverbial maxim "eat, drink, and be merry, for tomorrow we die" are as far removed from Epicurean philosophy as any two value systems can possibly be (Geer, 1964; Nussbaum, 1994, pp. 102–279). The hedonistic licentiousness and vulgarity of this lower-case "epicureanism" in Imperial Rome is satirized in Petronius' *Satyricon*, a "book" that is itself a classic fragmentary survival from the Graeco-Roman Classical world (Petronius Arbiter & Walsh, 1996).

Graeco-Roman waxen tablets are (now) an obscure form of a once common "notepaper," or "legal pad" kind of writing medium. Tablets, usually two or three boards (the *diptych* and *triptych*) of a wooden base covered with wax, were a common writing medium in the Classical Graeco-Roman world. The Pompeii area has yielded some of these (now) rare, once ubiquitous media at the site of the former residence of L. Caecilius Jucundus. In July 1875, various deeds and tax receipts recorded on 127 wax tablets were retrieved there from a domestic records box (Thompson, E. M., 1893, pp. 24–25). Waxen tablets have been uncovered at other European sites besides Herculaneum, where such wooden tablets covered in wax are said to be "legion" (Turner, 1968, p. 39). "Portrait of a Man and Woman" is a rather well known wall image from Pompeii AD 79, depicting a formally dressed husband and wife (*Art: A World History*, 1998, pp. 110–11). He holds a papyrus scroll up to his chin. She holds a stylus under her lower lip with her right hand and a golden-boarded black multi-panel waxen-type tablet in her left. Their identities are in doubt, and so is the intellectual significance alluded to in the painted image's wax tablet. Is the male figure a well-known lawyer, a magistrate or the prosperous baker whose establishment is nearby? Is it a couple with literary aspirations, pretensions and achievements being signaled to their contemporaries? Or is the female figure's wax tablet a household or business accounts management "book"? Five annotated detailed iconographic views are presented in analyzing the wall painting portrait of this couple, and raise these questions in the course of detailed visual analysis. Our time capsule interpretive point here is that we do not know, and may well never know with any greater certainty how to further interpret the intended social significance of these or other sorts of depictions (*Art: A World History*, 1998, pp. 110–11). In recent years, this wall painting (now preserved in the National Museum, Naples) has the attribution "Portrait of a Magistrate and His Wife." This 1 AD–era fresco had formerly been labeled as: "The Baker Paquio Proculo and His Wife" (Dragoni & Fichera, 1997, p. 68). Curiously, the ancient writing media of waxed surfaces re-emerged 1600 years after the Graeco-Roman cultural epoch for an "encore performance" in the form of Thomas Edison's wax cylinder sound recording medium (Hafner, 1999).

Archival and other written records can function synergistically, as complementary aids in finding or interpreting archaeological sites and relics. Acquiring knowledge of ancient lives and more recent bygone ways can involve the interplay between archival written records and archaeological finds–structural remains. There are considerable synergistic possibilities among the use of written records research (scholarship of ancient written records, or of more recent archival records, or even of archival writing among archaeological finds) and archaeological data. The sum total of archaeological reports and the scholarship of papyrus-based ancient written documents can add up to more than either contribution alone. The written record can function as more than a merely ancillary interpretive guide can. Sometimes it can function literally as a finding aid for an archaeological site. In some cases, such as the incantation spell books addressing the anticipated ancient Egyptian afterlife, the finding aid is buried with the "sacred sculpture" of the deceased's mummified body or painted on the tombs inner walls (Hornung, 1999). These works are sometimes haphazardly lumped together and called *The Book of the Dead* (Hornung, 1999). There are actually 15 or more distinct scroll and wall-painted book texts of incantations developed to guide the soul and the mummified body through the otherworldly journey. Reading these once prolific guidebooks, one can see the posited spiritual journey into an afterlife as being aided by these functional user manuals. They formed part of a sort of sacred kit which included the mummified remains, the whole tomb's furniture and profuse wall depictions. The wall copies of these "Books of the Afterlife" are a medium for rendering this ancient wisdom literature of afterlife guide manuals.

Ostraka and papyri discards of 1500 BCE help interpret the lives of the Egyptian New Kingdom artisan class. Another interesting example of acquiring knowledge of ancient lives involves the interplay among grand tomb sites in the Valley of the Kings, archaeological diggings at the site of the ancient village of Deir el Medina and the various writings found in that village's dump. In Deir el Medina, the skilled artisans of the Pharonic New Kingdom tombs lived and sometimes did their work. Nineteenth and twentieth century finds of papyrus rolls and ostraka in the village and its dump include sales documents, reports, correspondence and written records. These ostraka consist of potsherds and limestone flakes, the ancient Egyptian equivalent of cheap note paper. Ostraka are better known as the ballot medium used in the classical Athenian city-state for votes such as referenda on banishment. (From the recording of such votes on a pottery shard, an *ostracon*, comes the modern English loan word "ostracism.") In large part because of these documentary finds, a great deal is known about the second BCE millennium life of this royal artist-village's working class. These written sources tell us more than what the tombs, the archaeologically investigated town site or the (non-written) artifact remains reveal in and of themselves (Lesko, 1994, pp. 7–8). For instance, it is clear from documentation retrieved at the village dump that laundry was done off-site by paid workers, rather unusual in typical villages of that period. It seems that the freelance use of at least some specialized tomb-grade artistic materials and tools was allowed the village craftspeople as a job perk in order to earn an extra bit of income (Lesko, 1994). Our composite picture of that ancient village is a clearer one with archival sources to complement non-media archaeological analyses.

The "Water Board" archives of Alexandria's cisterns have been a valuable source in not only interpreting what ancient Alexandria looked like, but in finding numerous such underground water tunnels. The archives in this instance consist of records of more recent vintage from nineteenth century municipal hydraulic engineering studies (Empereur, 1999b, pp. 124–44). Here, as in some sunken ship–related archives, the records are not ancient sources, although the water board's excellent survey contains recorded archaeological data. We have noted that the Great Serapeum of Hellenistic Alexandria is an archaeological site that has been jointly described from the distinctive perspectives of both archaeology and philology. Those investigations illustrate the great value of such a dual-disciplinary contribution, of the synoptic synergy of analyzing respectively the written and archaeological records. Investigating topics such as foundation deposit plaques, metallic writing, ancient papyrology and numismatics shows the possible contributions of such synergistic relationships in historical research. The archaeological excavations and archival-philological analyses of such Alexandrian Hellenistic Egyptian sites as that of the Great Serapeum are models of such scholarly synergy (Rowe & Rees, 1956-57, pp. 485–520). The two reports of Rowe and Rees in "A Contribution to the Archaeology of the Western Desert: IV. The Great Serapeum of Alexandria" both illustrate the value of synergistic collaboration between scholars of ancient written records and the excavators' documented archaeological investigations. The whole of this archaeological report and the scholarly analysis of ancient written documents are greater than the sum of both individual studies. Archaeologist Rowe is the author of "Pt. I: The Archaeological Evidence" (pp. 485–512). Rees, the philologist of Classical Greek, is the author of "Pt. II: The Literary and Other Evidence" (pp. 513–20).

Homeric Epic served as a sort of "modern finding aid" for the sites of the ancient layers of Troy. Another interesting example of acquiring knowledge of ancient lives via the use of ancient writings and classical geographic naming is that of Heinrich Schliemann. He apparently acted on Frank Calvert's original explorations and analysis at the then Ottoman Turkish site of Hisarlik. The excavations at what was once the classical Greek City of Ilion (later the Romans' Ilium) revealed the site of Homeric Troy. These ancient written clues from the Homeric *Iliad* are clearly not the whole story in that complex tale of discovery. Our focus here is on that practical aspect of ancient records as contemporary finding aids to archaeological discovery and historical interpretation (Allen, 1999, pp. 35–47). This is a complex case of controversial priority and credit for that fabulous late nineteenth century archaeological discovery. It has taken on the aura of a latter-day archaeological mystery story. Another sterling example is the use of shipping archives as finding aids or interpretive guides. The sites of some old sunken ships have been deciphered with the aid of antique maritime records. The virtual "fleet" of sunken ships featured in *National Geographic* and *Archaeology* magazines are sometimes found with the aid of various archival written sources, or at least subsequently interpreted with the aid of such written records. Even if a sunken ship can be seen as a complete cultural microcosm or complex on its own, written documentary explanation is often relied on to provide an independent interpretive context for marine archaeological investigation (Lenihan, 1983, pp. 37–64).

Conquistador Francisco Pizzaro's belated forensic autopsy in 1984 was correlated with historical accounts of that figure's assassination in the year 1541. In this case, the forensic biological anthropological skeletal record fit with the written historical record of sword thrusts and bone wounds. This is a very interesting instance of the matching up of sixteenth century archivally based descriptions and of the late twentieth century forensic anthropological skeletal analysis (Maples & Browning, 1994, pp. 3, 207–08+). There is no shortcut here to sound and rigorous archaeological method, just as there is also no substitute for interpretive record-based methods. Our small paleographical sampling of some salient retrievals of ancient writings and documentary records should adequately underscore the value of time capsule–like deposits in preserving and acquiring the historical treasures of a past era's records. We need all the archival sources we can receive in order to best integrate our analyses with archaeological finds.

Today and Tomorrow: Nineteenth and Twentieth Century Examples of Attempted Communications to Future Millennia

Our modern times have developed an "epigraphy" of sound and photographic image media. In relation to ancient Graeco-Roman waxen tablet media, we noted Thomas Edison's use of wax cylinders. Earlier in the nineteenth century, the inventor Leon Scott reputedly traced a graphic-type "phono-autograph" of U.S. President Abraham Lincoln's voice at the White

House in 1863. He invented a machine that scratched sound patterns by using a drum covered with sheets of soot-black paper. That nineteenth century device generated no audible signal. Instead, just a paper-graphed record was generated as a chart of the traced voice. It is intriguing to imagine finding such a graph and recapturing Lincoln's spoken voice with today's technology. Apparently, only two such "auto-phonographs" are extant, one at the Smithsonian and the other in the collection of the sound technology historian Allen Koenigsberg. The Lincoln tracing, if ever done, hasn't turned up in any archive or attic (Hafner, 1999).

"Mutoscopes" and metal film reels are time capsule gadgets intended to serve as audio-visual aides to inter-millennial communication. The Crypt of Civilization's mini-windmill power generator was enclosed in that time capsule largely to provide power to run the metal film reel projector inside it. In the case of the 1938 Westinghouse Time Capsule I for the 1939 New York World's Fair, only the instructions are enclosed for constructing a large microfilm reader and motion picture projector. In order to read on microfilm, there is also a small microscope provided as an immediate imaging aid for the microfilm. T. K. Peters had invented the metal film reel stock years before its employment as an audio-visual system in the Crypt of Civilization. The presumed durability of the metallic film made it a logical choice for the Crypt (Peters, 1940a; 1940b). The American Mutoscope Co.'s "Language Integrator Mutoscope" is a peep-show kind of hand-cranked machine like those from old amusement arcades. The Crypt's version has a series of images with the English language name of that object printed under each image. An audio recording sounds out the name of each labeled object in series as the crank action is turned (Koningsberg, 1987, p. 229).

Is preservational microfilming a "magical medium"? Microfilming has in the history of libraries and archives been held up as a magical savior of past records, the bedrock of the "library of the future" (Cady, 1990, pp. 374-86). Microfilming, including the 1980s fashion of computer-output-microfilm backups for 1980s-era online library catalogues, seems to be an established perennial favorite stratagem for information storage. Archival grade preservation microfilming is a tool for preserving records 500 years or more. Silver film media are exemplars of our ca. 2001-era preservational microfilming technology. Our turn of the millennia preservational material of choice is archival-grade silver gelatin microfilm stock that is carefully stored, monitored and only used as master archival templates ("Silver-gelatin film," 1996). The robust track record of a 200-year life expectancy of silver film has led microfilm preservationists to posit a LE-500 (500 years "life" expectancy). Accelerated use studies of materials and structures of all kinds clearly rely on reasoning from analogy that a certain kind of definitely measured shorter term wear-stress factor is proportional to the effects of some problematic longer term wear-stress factor. A vessel, or its internal atmosphere, or some of its contents, or the written impressions on a record's medium will probably fail at some predictable rate and in predictable ways and phases. The failure rate and phase of transmutation could even be inferred to be zero, or of no practical significance. Such technical inferences from analogies about a material's survivability or immutability from one set of conditions to another generally lack any *absolute* assurance of reliability. Silver gelatin–based microfilm preservation is a web of mutually dependant material preservation techniques and staff service-operational protocols. It is not merely a matter of sealing silver-filmed media into a pristine can. Other factors: The careful imaging onto LE-500 silver gelatin film stock thin-coated with poly-sulfates, or gold (alloyable with the silver base), acid free storage containers, controlled storage area air environments, carefully ongoing monitoring for degenerative changes, reproduction via new preservational film stock as needed, and exclusive use of service copies. Only the second-generation "service copies" get heavy wear in any actual use by researchers. These rigorous procedures are needed for the 500-year-plus preservation microfilm archiving of library and other media materials. The general principles underlying these practices are ideal best practice for any millennia-targeted time capsule installation. Preservational technologies and procedures such as careful packaging, environmental controls, quality monitoring and perpetual reprography of master and use copies are highly desirable in the operations of any archival repository. In the case of silver film preservational microfilming, there is a historically validated preservational data set on the survivability and legibility of images over 500 year plus time spans. That is an excellent technical baseline from which we can infer the survivability of silver film images and writings on that medium ("Silver-gelatin film," 1996). Technical handbooks on the preservation of library materials as part of our cultural heritage illustrate some of the common (i.e., less than millennium) time span hazards paper, books, library materials, etc., face in terms of preservation and conservation. Preservational archiving manuals give specific advice on special materials such as photographs, motion pictures, sound recordings and videotape (Swartzburg, 1995). Careful practice is necessary for longer-term time capsule and non-capsule preservation, but even state-of-the-art library-archival preservation practices are not necessarily sufficient by themselves for multimillennia span preservation efforts.

Is the attempt to preserve an archive from some Millennium 2000 type digital library yet another "magical medium"? Digital archives are more vulnerable than are paper ones. Software and hardware for their computers become obsolete rapidly. The magnetic disk and tape storage media on which digitized information are written will "go to failure" over the decades and centuries (Hafner, 1999, pp. D1, D5). It would appear that our post-modern libraries of digitized information might face the preservational fate of ancient papyri libraries. That is, unless technical means and socio-cultural practices enable time capsule–like survival of our written records, so they may someday be someone's future ancient surviving written records. Stewart Brand is one author who has built a compelling case for "Ending the Digital Dark Age" (Brand, 1999, pp. 81–92). There are other preeminent writers on information technology who have underscored this pessimistic preservational outlook on the digital, electromagnetic, computationally based critique of the survivability of our contemporary digital record (McKenna, 1996). Brand's citations include one somewhat acerbic critic who cites the idea of a five-year limit to digital shelf life (Brand, 1999; Rothenberg, 1995, p. 42). Long-term cultural transmission of our human words can be envisioned as a series of successive incarnations, with successive media being deemed avatars of writing, ranging from ancient scroll media to the contemporary cyberspace medium (O'Donnell, 1998). It has been noted that contemporary file formats obsolesce rapidly. Their physical media also have shorter life spans and electro-magnetic based formats seem to go to failure within a five- to ten-year period. Pristine CD-ROMs can maintain their data integrity for 5–15 years. Reading devises (proper computers, etc.) for electronic media are a problem, leading to scrambled lost databases and images (Brand, 1998-99). Constant recopying of digital media sources is one preservational strategy. Error correction programs, and "checksum" validations of text-data are becoming increasingly necessary to raise the level of quality assurance to prevent a single digital bit error garbling a mass of digital information storage (Wallich, 1999, p. 50). Hunter systematically addresses the pressing issue of the long-term preservation of digital information. He delves into its archival operational, physical media, and digital formatting aspects. Rothenberg seeks a way to ensure the longevity of digital documents, to find a viable technical foundation for digital preservation, to avoid "technological quicksand." Pondering these thorny problems of digital preservation and various methodologies to deal with these puzzles, he concludes that perpetual "software emulation" is the most viable alternative (Hunter, 2000, pp. 42–44; Rothenberg, 1995, pp. 42–47; 1999). The protocols, operating procedures of checking, monitoring and re-checking endlessly are presented as analogous with the needs for preservational microfilming maintenance. One

British anthropologist has observed that the electronic historical media and data of recent decades have not always fared so well (Durrans, 2000a). Ironically, a pre–1995 survey by the British Design Council's "Project 2045" survey of time capsule deposits in Great Britain is currently inaccessible due to computer disk and equipment readability problems with their "antique" configuration (Durrans, 2000a; Durrans, 1995; Pivaro, 1995, pp. 1–9). Likewise there is an apparent loss of data from the "BBC Domesday" survey project of Britain in the 1970s. Efforts are being made to utilize the resources of some "antique" computing machinery in a small museum to read the BBC data. In another time capsule example from the United Kingdom, a 1970s dual deposit by the then very popular BBC children program *Blue Peter* was retrieved two years ago. Recording tape wrapped in plastic came out of steel boxes soaking wet (Durrans, 2000a). Electronic-digital media face old storage hazards as well as their own specters of material-failure and technological obsolescence.

A new micro-etching process onto silicon discs may be the way to preserve written-imaged-analog-imaged records of our world period (Brand, 1998-99). Norsam Technologies, a New Mexico–based contractor, sells archival preservation services aiming to last for several thousand of years. They attempt that by engraving scanned images into nano-scaled records on two-inch metal discs and then retrieving them. This may be one of the more sweeping time spans for written (and other) images extrapolating from accelerated use-based failure-analysis methodologies (Norsam Technologies, *HD-ROSETTA ion beam system provides eye-readable permanent information and images on a 2" metal disk,* 1999; Norsam Technologies, *MEMS & micromachining devices and systems based on surface, bulk and/or focused ion beam micromachining processes,* 1999). That technology produces analog, font-script type English, etc., writing or images, not any ASCII, digitized computer language coding. Such micro-messages can be scanned into digital computer media formats. The imaging capacity of a "HD-ROSETTA" ion beam engraved disc can range from 1,000 up to 100,000 images arranged in xy coordinates of 4096 pixels by 4096. These etchings can be read by a 1999 era, off-the-shelf high illumination ca. 1000x microscope. It is possible to hook up an OCR–type scan for downloading to a computing system in any digital format. These costly systems are not backyard commonplace tools. A typical Norsam Technologies scale for a scanned historical document's storage size can be 100 nanometers. These are not computer media digitized images, but rather actual analog images at greatly reduced size. Because they can be digitally scanned via Optical Character Recognition and be uploaded into a variety of digital computing media, their information transfer value is high.

Our archives, libraries, and museums can be seen as time capsules, as building today's ancient libraries for future times. Selection and preservation of a wide variety of popular cultural materials is one of the primary concerns of librarians and archivists of various collections of writings, images and numeric data, including popular cultural collections. This is a way that time capsules might aid future generations of researchers, curators, archivists and librarians by providing actual items. Such capsule contents might be able to convey as well the surrounding cultural significance, or at least the senders' stated "for-the-record" interpretations of formal knowledge compendia and of popular cultural items. Consider how restricted most of our ephemeral popular cultural material is. Compare the amount of popular ephemera available from, say, the year 1700, or even later, when compared to the prolific presence of twentieth-first century materials that surrounds us in every way right now. While today's material is produced in great quantity, modern print and film technologies are not very durable. Time capsules have the potential to be every person's archive to leave for the future, without the mediation of high culture's critics, thus avoiding loss of future cultural resources either by deliberate discard or by preservational technical failures. There are several questions to address here: What has been going into time capsules, large and small, official and unofficial, and what should go into them? What is likely to be thought about the capsules themselves, their senders and their contents, most especially the priceless, ephemeral, popular cultural primary materials included in them? And finally, how can senders maximize the interpretive, or hermeneutic, options of retrievers?

Popular culture aspects of time capsule vessels and ceremonies have been characterized as being at least as important as those contents. And contents are linked to such overall characteristics of time capsules as sending dates, intended span of the information transfer (which can limit preservation attempts) and the character of send-off ceremonials, which are themselves, in turn, often based on ancient foundation dedication-deposit traditions (Jarvis, 1988, pp. 347–48; 1992a; 1992b). Libraries of books and journals, as well as bibliographic catalogue lists, are suitable contents for time capsules. Here we just mentioned the idea of leaving whole libraries and large-sized bibliographies and book catalogues to the future. When people weigh various libraries' and museums' preservation efforts, they might consider what historical treasures of ancient writings have survived from the past in one way or another. Future historians would eagerly seek any ancient memoir. One personal memoir on American life between the World Wars is a good example of the sort of narrative diarists all ages would do well to emulate. *I remember distinctly: A family album of the American people* discusses everything from common views on politics to

This was placed here on the
fourth of June, 1897
Jubilee Year. by the
Plasterers working on
the Job. Hoping when this
is Found that the
Plasterers Association
may be still Flourishing
Please let us know in
the Other World when
~~got~~ You get this, so
as we can drink
Your Health.

Signed. W. Gallop
F. Wilkins
H. Sainsbury
J. Chester
A. Pickernell
Secretary

DISTRICT COMMITTEE'S ACCOUNT.

INCOME.

Ldgs.	No. of members in July	Aug.	Sep.	Organising Soc.'s dues. £ s. d.	3d levy £ s. d.	Federation dues. 2d. p qtr. p mbr. £ s. d.	District dues 1d. p qtr. p mbr. £ s. d.	Totals. £ s. d.
1	154	152	154	4 0 1¼	17 5 0	1 4 0	0 12 10	23 1 11½
2	84	85	85	2 4 3	3 9 6			5 13 9
3	100	106	100	2 14 6	2 13 6½	0 16 8	0 8 4	6 13 0¼
4	143	146	137	2 18 0¼	6 3 1	0 9 0	0 11 9	10 1 10½
5	96	99	101	2 13 0	9 0 9	0 15 10		12 9 7
6	*	58	60	1 11 10½	3 10 0		0 4 10	5 6 8½
7	*	107	*	2 2 7½	3 1 0	0 9 2	0 8 11	6 1 8½
8	110	111	115	2 10 3	0 4 3	0 16 8	0 9 3	4 0 5
9	139	141	141	3 5 3	11 17 9	0 19 11	0 11 9	16 14 8
10	180	182	185	4 15 10	15 10 0	1 9 0	0 15 0	22 9 10
11	91	*	91	1 10 4½	4 14 3			6 4 7½
12	94	90	96	2 6 0	7 4 6		0 7 6	9 18 0
13	59	63	64	0 14 6	1 13 3	0 3 8		2 11 5
14	210	198	196	4 16 6	3 14 6		0 13 0	9 4 0
15	118	122	124	2 19 1½	13 8 3	0 19 8	0 10 2	17 17 2½
16	52	52	60	1 4 10½	4 15 9	0 7 6	0 4 4	6 12 3½
17	96	102	105	0 18 1	3 17 9	0 7 6	0 8 4	5 11 8
18	92	82	88	1 16 0	1 9 0	0 13 6	0 6 8	4 5 2
19	20	*		0 10 3	0 2 6	0 3 0	0 1 6	0 17 3
20	45	49	55	1 5 2	4 2 4		0 4 5	[illegible]
21	82	87	88	0 17 5	5 8 0	0 13 4	0 8 8	[illegible]
22	27	28	27					
23	29	29	22	1 1 8	2 7 0			3 8 8
24	*	40	36	0 11 8	0 8 9		0 3 1	1 3 6
25†	24	27	31	0 7 10	0 11 0	0 2 6		1 1 4
26†	n.l.	15	22	0 1 10				0 1 10
27†	"		26					
31	20	21	21	0 10 8	2 1 6	0 5 0	0 1 3	2 18 5
Metropolitan Soc. ...				6 13 11				6 13 11
Totals ...				£57 1 7½	£128 13 2½	£10 15 11	£7 9 7	£204 0 4

	£ s. d.
Johnson and Turner Appeal from No. 16	0 1 0
" " " " 24	0 6 9
District Committee Dues for June Quarter from No. 19	0 1 8
" " " " " 14	0 5 0
From Metropolitan Society, proportionate share of printing "Proposed Bye-Laws" and "Analysis of Voting"	1 5 5
From Met. Society, Amount paid to their Bros. during Spencer dispute	0 15 0
Balance from last Quarter	30 [illegible]
Total ..	£237 11 2½

n.l. New Lodge. * No Number given in Monthly Report. † Lodges which have not been established 6 months pay no District dues.

EXPENDITURE.

	£ s. d.	£ s. d.
Organising Secretary's Salary from July 3rd to October 1st (13 weeks)	27 6 0	
Travelling Expenses and Postage of Org. Sec.	5 13 8½	32 19 8½
7 Sub-Committee meetings held July 20, 22, 29, Aug. 23, Sept. 6, 20, 22	1 4 0	
Conferences with Met. Soc. Bros. Scott, Battin Collins, Cole	0 [illegible] 0	
" " Smale	0 6 0	
Deputation to Executive Council, Bros. Scott, Smale, Anderson	[illegible] 6 0	3 2 0
200 Balance Sheets, June Quarter ...	[illegible] 0	
2 Reams Official Levy Sheets ...	[illegible] 0	
" " Heading Sheets for crspdnce.	[illegible] 5 6	
300 Copies "Proposed Bye-Laws"	1 2 6	
50 Copies Analysis of Voting on "Proposed Bye-Laws"	[illegible] 8 6	
Window & Hand Bills, Opening of Ealing Ldg.	[illegible] 6 0	
" " " Kingston "	0 11 0	7 6 0
To London Building Trades' Federation ...		8 0 0
Band " " Demonstration		3 10 0
Sashes for District and Organising Secretaries		1 [illegible]
Rent of Committee Room		0 16 6
Secretary's Salary		2 10 0
Stationery		0 2 11½
Carriage of Parcels		0 9 9
Postage of Receipts, Summonses & other matter		1 13 7
Audit		0 5 6
To Bro. W. Edwards, No. 9, Turner dispute...	[illegible] 8 0	
" J. Bailey, 12, Johnson " ...	1 [illegible] 6	
" J. Maundry, 12, " " ...	[illegible] 6	
" H. Anderson, 12, " " ...	0 15 6	
" T. Raynor, 15, " " ...	0 11 8½	
" J. Barton, Metropolitan Society ...	1 4 5½	5 8 8
To Org. Sec. to pay men at Spencer dispute ...	16 15 6	
" " " Anstey " ...	4 9 3	
" " " Grover " ...	3 12 0	
" " " Rooke " ...	18 0 0	42 16 0
Total ...		£109 13 11
Total Expenditure ...		109 13 11
Balance in hands of Secretary ...		127 17 3½
As per Income ...		£237 11 2½

Examined and found correct,

W. HOLMAN, Senior Auditor (No. 2.)
J. WARR, Junior Auditor (No. 3.)
H. PARISH, Secretary.

*** FORWARDED TOO LATE FOR AUDIT.

Lodges.	O. S. Dues. £ s. d.	Levy. £ s. d.	Fed. £ s. d.	D. Com. Dues. £ s. d.
11	0 17 11	3 10 6	0 15 8	0 7 7
13	0 13 5	3 1 0	0 2 2	0 5 0
2				0 7 1
21		0 17 6		

An 1892 National Assocation of Operative Plasterers trade union accounts sheet for the London District Committee, found behind a Tate Gallery wall in 1985. It was a commemoration of the 1897 building refurbishment at the time of Queen Victoria's Jubilee. (Courtesy Tate Gallery Archive, TGA 971.50.)

the use of buttons prior to the invention of clothing zippers (Rogers & Allen, 1947). It gives a sense of what it was like to have lived in that past. It may not be as quite a high priority, but the identity of an author can also be a form of historical puzzle worth solving, or pondering. Literary sleuthing can reveal that literary mysteries can surround recent centuries' writings as well as the provenances of ancient documents. Was the nineteenth century doggerel-based poem *A Visit from St. Nicholas* (a.k.a. *The*

Opposite: **An 1897 National Association of Operative Plasterers handwritten message, found behind a Tate Gallery wall in 1985, commemorated the building refurbishment during Queen Victoria's fiftieth year as British Sovereign. (Courtesy Tate Gallery Archive, TGA 971.50.)**

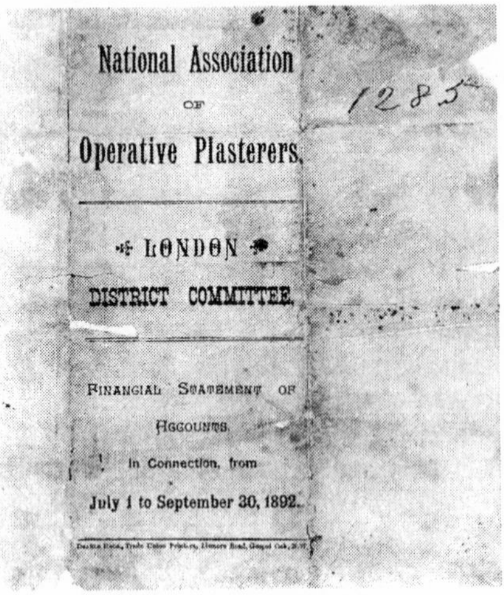
National Association
OF
Operative Plasterers.
LONDON
DISTRICT COMMITTEE.
FINANCIAL STATEMENT OF
ACCOUNTS
In Connection, from
July 1 to September 30, 1892.

An 1892 National Association of Operative Plasterers accounts book label, deposited in 1897 and found behind a Tate Gallery wall in 1985. (Courtesy Tate Gallery Archive, TGA 971.50.)

Night Before Christmas) composed by Clement Clarke Moore as customarily credited, or by Henry Livingston, as his family has long maintained (Foster, 2000; Kirkpatrick, 2000)?

The book of record of the Time Capsule of Cupaloy: Deemed capable of resisting the effects of time for 5000 years — preserving an account of universal achievements — embedded in the grounds of the New York World's Fair — 1939, 1938. The Time Capsule included this memorial volume as a herald of our age and an interpretive aid for the "instant archaeology" of the Capsule. The title alone could fulfill an interpretive mission if its bibliographic citation survives in some library, bookseller or museum's catalogue. Copies custodians are requested to translate copies into all evolving new languages. The "Basic English" primer feature of the work may be a Rosetta Stone–type key to aid future retrievers. In addition to a paper-bound copy, a microfilm format copy was also sealed inside. The other 3649 print copies were distributed to notables, historical repositories and libraries worldwide. It is a finding and interpretive aid recording the Time Capsule's latitude, longitude, and targeted excavation date on the autumnal Equinox, AD 6939. It's a translation guide to 1930s American English, providing interpretations of senders' customs and letters from Robert Millikan, Thomas Mann and Albert Einstein. Somewhat paradoxically, the original dissemination of these 3650 presentation copies did not include sale of any on the regular commercial mass markets of book publishing or on the World's Fair memorabilia market then. This scarcity does enhance its current value. A deliberate dissemination of this title beyond the archives, libraries, monasteries and other repositories via a strategy of commercial sales may have more assuredly "left word" for the people of AD 6939. One linguistic feature that is simultaneously desirable, useful but potentially too limiting was the condensation of our period's sprawling Late Modern English vocabulary into a primer chapter done in "Basic English." That is a vocabulary of a mere 850 words, like C. K. Ogden's ("Languages of the world: English:

Basic English," 1963, p. 34). It is advisable to alternate such "basic" languages' passages with fuller, richer linguistic usages in order to avoid "dumbing down" messages to possible futures. Einstein's letter has two interesting historical features. It is printed both in English and German, providing a bilingual sample from the twentieth century. And it is also apparently satirical, along the lines of his 1936 cornerstone deposit note. The 1938 letter from Einstein is not his only time encapsulated message to a distant future. Einstein wrote on durable rag paper a brief statement to the effect that unless the future recipients were more peaceful, rational or devoted to justice, they could go to "the devil" (Dukas & Hoffmann, 1979, p. 105)! It is even signed with a bit of "I once existed" vein of self-deprecating humor as well. The tenor of his 1938 *The Book of Record* letter is drier in its irony than his more private earlier 1936 letter.

This "instant" rare book was printed in a limited collector's edition of 3650 copies, including 176 copies printed on special handmade, watermarked "Rosapina" paper by Thomas N. Fairbanks Co., New York City. The remaining 3474 copies were printed on "Permanent Ivory Wove" 100-lb. rag paper specially made by Fred W. Main at the Hurlbut Paper Co., South Lee, Massachusetts. The end of the final (unnumbered) page 51 distinguishes each copy's paper stock. Some 1650 of the 3650 copies were bound in royal blue cloth buckram, "library board," with the short title gold stamped on it. Two thousand copies apparently have a handmade paperback-style binding, the short title stamped in aluminum metal. The Time Capsule's copy is a paper with an aluminum-stamped cover. Type font design and print job type matrix were partially set by F. W. Goudy. A small sample of Village No. 2 typeface was also included in the Capsule (Pendray, 1939). Frederick W. Goudy's work might survive as an example of the fine art of typographical book print design (Goudy, 1946, pp. 195–96). That 1946 *catalogue raisonné* of this renowned typeface designer's art includes an entry on the "Village No. 2" typeface for the work *The Book of Record of the Time Capsule of Cupaloy.* Syracuse University's copy has a Goudy book ("Cutter") registration number, not a Westinghouse one, indicating that it was primarily treasured as an example of Goudy's Village Press typography. The "Vocabulary of High-frequency English" portion of *The Book of Record* was Monotype set in Gill sans-serif typeface. "The story of the Time Capsule" described *The Book of Record*'s design and contents (Pendray, 1939). It was also published by Westinghouse Co. as *The Story of the Time Capsule* (pp. 5–8 discuss *The Book of Record).* Stanley Edgar Hyman and S. C. McKelway's 1953 *New Yorker* article "Onward and upward with business and science" irreverently looks over the project, featuring numerous excerpts from *The Book of Record*, and relates valuable details. A one sheet ("leaf") *Time Capsule II* was shipped to known 1938 holders of copies of *The Book of Record* after the October 16, 1965, final deposit of the Westinghouse Time Capsule of Kromarc (*Time Capsule II*, 1965). That page might have erroneously been "tipped in" to some copies of the 1939 book *The Story of the Time Capsule*, as happened with a Syracuse University Libraries' copy (Jarvis, 1978).

There are some good examples of the secure archival deposits of today's treasured records in time capsule–like placements. Sites like these are suggestive of at least partial time capsule installations, along the lines of ones pictured in science fiction. The Belfer Audio Laboratory & Archive of Syracuse University Libraries, Syracuse, New York, is an interesting example of a partially but deeply earth-recessed cultural repository and research facility. The Audio Lab & Archive moved into its new facility in 1982. Within a short period of its founding by Walter L. Welch, Curator, 1963–91, it has become one of the three biggest such repositories within the U.S. More libraries and cultural repositories should ideally be at least earth sheltered to assist in mundane preservation as well to afford a degree of long-term survivability (*http://libwww.syr.edu/information/belfer/index.html*, 1999).

"The Crypt of Civilization, 1940–8113 AD" time capsule at Oglethorpe University in Atlanta, Georgia, not only has the capacity to have included within its "time cargo" many paper print book and journal issues, but numerous canisters of microfilmed written records as well (*Crypt of Civilization* n. d.; Peters, 1940b). The media housed within include several metallic written materials, including the metal flip name-of-object cards of the hand-cranked Mutoscope, the metallic motion picture filmstrips invented by T. K. Peters. Even the hot set type used to print the front page of an Atlanta, Georgia, newspaper from that very morning was included. That front-page type matrix announces the sealing later that day of the Crypt of Civilization, and sits front and center of its contents (Peters, 1940a; 1940b). That newspaper's set typeface matrix can be seen in front of the peep-show type Mutoscope in a classic sealing day photograph of the contents. That item is a nice preservational touch, made possible not only by careful planning but also by the available 2000 cubic foot volumetric of the Crypt. Somewhat like the Mount Pony facility discussed below, the Crypt is partially recessed into a basement level nestled into stone walls. Although covered in rock slabs, the Crypt is not necessarily as securely situated as one might imagine. An installation cut entirely into rock and accessible only through a short tunnel would seem more secure. Sealing the tunnel entrance to such a chamber with large blocks of stone completely covered in a rough-looking stone "disguise" would probably raise the preservational-security confidence factor even more.

The U.S. National Archives and Record Administration Building in Washington, D.C., houses among its many archives and historical record groups documents such as the 1776 Declaration of Independence of the 13 former colonies in North America, the 1789 U.S. Constitution, and its first Ten Amendments forming the 1789 Bill of Rights. These have been protected since 1952 by a time capsule–like device by which the Declaration is lowered nightly into a safe-like vault that could also be used in a sudden daytime emergency. This sort of protection is reminiscent of the care of some ancient sacred documents being deliberately protected by their creators. The new preservational arrangements unveiled in early 1999 will enable the full Constitution to be simultaneously displayed. All three documents have an argon-inert atmospheric encasement within treated light-shielding glass, and are now provided a less vibration-prone protective encasement at night. The former Richmond, Virginia, Federal Reserve Bank bomb vault at Mount Pony, Culpeper, Virginia, originally handled all electronic fund-transfers for the U.S. banking system. It was once designated as a key "continuity of government" site. It is designed to shield against radioactive fallout from an atomic weapons attack, with one-foot thick steel reinforced concrete walls, lead-lined shutters to drop down over the semi-recessed facility's windows, and burial in two to four feet of earth. Today it is a new Library of Congress audio-visual collection archival storage site (Schwartz, 1998, pp. 213, 317). Facilities for these audio-visual media formats may contribute to what has been called the "archaeology of the cinema" (Ceram, 1965).

Among the business and other records management-storage companies with an underground storage site is Iron Mountain/National Underground Storage, Inc., which has a major secured facility in an old limestone mine 220 feet underground in northwestern Pennsylvania (Iron Mountain, Inc., website, 1999). The miles of storage facilities support more than a thousand staff members who store, manage and reproduce a variety of paper and other media format documents and images. Another example of an underground record storage facility is far from any mountains, but utilizes old salt mine shafts under the Kansas prairie. The Underground Vaults and Storage Company, Hutchinson, Kansas, rents out depots in an old salt mine located there (Visser, 1986, pp. 58–60). It lies 650 feet (200 meters) underground and is stocked with relics, memorabilia, media materials, file records of some commercial companies, commercial trade secret food formulae, a preserved food supply, sleeping cots and various survival items. An archive of the working scripts from the producer of such golden age of TV comedy program series as *Your Show of Shows* and other Sid Caesar classics was recently retrieved from a forgotten, shut-away storage closet of the Manhattan performing arts facility City Center. The 47 boxes of paper scripts include programs worked on by such veterans as Mel Brooks, Carl Reiner and Neil Simon (Collins, 2000). The article title described the find of antique documents in a painted-over closet area by noting a "Mother lode of TV comedy is found in forgotten closet." This example is an archival manuscript collection that is also akin to accidental buried Hellenistic Egyptian papyri that are *a posteriori* time capsule experiences.

The bottom line is that large-scale multi-millennial survival of the bulk of any age's written records and imaged media is of a low order of probability, if not an outright dim prospect. This goes for our era's configured digital or electromagnetic audio-visual items as well. That does not mean much of value can't last for thousands of years, especially if the contents are relentlessly reproduced in new media, formats and configurations. We need not absolutely rule out metallic micro- or nano-based large-scale storage. Sealed-away vaults and time capsules would seem to stand better chances of eventual survival for multi-millennial spans of retrieval than do any library archive or socio-cultural record keeping arrangements, such as the ca. 2001 World Wide Web, British Library, etc. Corporate record vault services and companies do maintain certain corporate, governmental and organizations' records in buried facilities, and rightly so. Consider the impressive genealogical ("mountain of names") record facility in a Utah mountain (Shoumatoff, 1985). That huge mass of record groups will undoubtedly be of some historical value. It does seem curious that our age lags behind in employing widespread measures to systematically store in high-grade preservational settings collections and other records of its formal and popular cultural life and history. We must strive to "time encapsulate" our era's writings if they are ever to be available as ancient writings for future millennia of humankind.

Imaginary Communications: Historical Fiction, Science Fictional Futures and Interstellar Messages

The realms of imaginary or imaginable communications outlined here are a bit different than the ancient writings we have considered so far. Imaginary writings from our pasts are assumed as a device of literary fiction. They have never been real, haven't happened yet. Whereas future-to-future or future-to-interstellar civilized species communications might eventually occur. They might happen more or less as imagined. Let's consider here not only imaginary writing as in works of fictional literature from our past, or even just fanciful tales that never were, but also fictional examples of imaginary communications from distant future to distant future. How do such cases create time capsule–like experiences? We will consider our own imagined communications to interstellar recipients in CETI efforts, "Lincos" and leaked audio-visual radio-television programs or other telecommunications transmissions. Semiotics, the science of communicating by signs, has been employed most notably in pondering nuclear waste dump warning signs that can convey danger to people millennia in the futures (Sebeok, 1984).

Imaginary written records from a fictional past occur in some historical novels. The relation of "imaginary libraries" and "imaginary books" to time capsule experiences is worth noting at this point. Just as an imaginary time capsule list of contents or kind of interpretive aid or method of materials' preservation can have a real influence upon a visionary's perspective, so can imaginary libraries and books motivate the "imaginer" to consider a different kind of world or time. And any list of desiderata, any wish list of books or list of just about anything else, can function to inspire both future efforts to re-interpret our world (Borges, 1998, pp. 112–18; Thompson, L. S., 1975, pp. 304–10). In our discussion of fictional ancient documents, we shouldn't totally neglect time capsule phenomena such as tales of imaginary ancient Biblical-era papyri. Daniel Easterman's potboiler spy novel *The Judas Testament* posits a twentieth century espionage struggle over a recently discovered papyrus scroll apparently written by Jesus from Nazareth. One of the plot elements is the potential impact of an ancient papyrus volume on a well-organized modern belief system. The protagonist is a professor of ancient documents and the reader has the fun of "discovering" an ancient imaginary document. It is also interesting to see papyrologists as fictional characters at the center of a struggle over world views. In real scholarly life, such paleographers do study and sometimes discover new world views from the ancient past, or alter our perceptions about the way a specific past was like (Easterman, 1994). Robert Graves' historical novel of the Julio-Claudian line of Roman emperors *I, Claudius* prominently features the literary conceit that the Emperor Claudius mused about burying a time capsule–like lead casket containing a secret history of his imperial family for discovery 1900 years later. It alludes to its sealing in a jar with a preservative fluid used to protect its papyri (Graves, 1934, pp. 3–13). The fictional Claudius observes that documents survive mostly by chance, explains that he writes in Greek to insure readability in the far-distant future after the Sibylline prophecy of Rome's fall is fulfilled. Cedar oil was used in the Mediterranean world of

Graeco-Roman times to preserve papyrus scrolls deposited in sealed jars, caskets, etc.

Imaginary written records from one fictional future to another more distant future are found in today's science fiction literature. The novel *Memoirs Found in a Bathtub* is yet another take on fictional "ancient" documents, in a sort of far-distant future "dis-continuity of government" facility's bomb shelter. The tale is set long, long after the surface of the Earth has been devastated by war, and long after any sense of coherent life, organizational or otherwise (Lem, 1973). The standard bureaucratic method of attending to paperwork in Lem's underground world is for all working documents to be circulated *ad infinitum* throughout the office bureaucracy. Anyone may pick and choose what to do with the item in that world of total workplace empowerment. Another science fiction classic, *A Canticle for Leibowitz*, has twin themes. Its vision of Earthly nuclear disaster-after-disaster is tempered by the responses of organized monastic learning's survival and striving over the ages (Miller, 1959). The futuristic, post– atomic war land of Britain is a theme of the novel *Riddley Walker*. There the title's protagonist communicates in a world at once regressively primitive and yet curiously tormented by the grandeur of a past that is not quite destroyed. The verisimilitude of the author's imagined future is evoked in part by its exclusive use of what we will call here a "Post–Late Modern English" dialect. The "English" used seems almost as remote from today's Turn of the Millennia 2000 era English as is Chaucer's Middle English (Hoban, 1980). In relation to time capsule studies and our current world's efforts to preserve life, knowledge and inquiry, these science fictional worlds are exemplars of such possibilities, successes or failures. They fire our imagination with imaginary books, libraries, languages and futuristic cultural periods. We are transported to places and times where the persistence or even absence of fictional ancient records makes a difference. One noteworthy science fiction example of ancient libraries and collections (albeit electronic) of written records of a distant future includes the electronic readout hieroglyphic-scroll library of the (now extinct) telepathically enhanced, super-enlightened Krell species. As depicted in the film (and novel) *Forbidden Planet*, set in the year AD 2390, the Krell have long since mysteriously died out (*Forbidden Planet*, 1956; Stuart, 1956). The character Dr. Morbius explains to the United Federation of Planets' cruiser crew how his massive IQ boost (via the psychological technology of the "Krell Laboratories") enabled him to gradually decipher some of the Krell's written knowledge. The mind-boosting "Educator" machinery, the online library and the massive fusion power facility are all presented as perfectly functional even after the ancient destruction of Krell technological civilization over 200,000 years before. In the novelistic treatment, there are further information technology features that don't appear in the film. One is the philologist character Dr. Morbius commenting that just one theorem in particular from the Krell online library enabled him to decipher that super-species' huge "logical" alphabet, not the film's "page of theorems." Two other portions of the tale feature notional documents, imaginary writings that are featured in a purported 2600 AD dated preface and the postscript just in that novel.

The fictional character A. G. Yakimara is presented as the author of the notional historical reference work *This Third Millennium — A Condensed Textbook for Students* (Stuart, 1956). In this imaginary (microfilmed!) textbook, another set of "ancient-future" documents are discussed. Those are the Krell technology-based "cerebro-micro-wave" ("ancient" metallic media) mind recordings which the characters Dr. Morbius and one of the space cruisers' officers are depicted as utilizing. These notional metallic-electronic records are depicted as having been only deciphered 60 years later, i.e., in the AD 2450 of the *Forbidden Planet* story.

In Asimov's realm of *The Foundation Trilogy*, microfilm book-chips are projected onto a university office wall on the megalopolis-covered planet of Trantor. That fictional Foundation's huge notional Encyclopedia Galactica project sited on the fictional planet Terminus is a major narrative aid, a sort of bibliographic character (Asimov, 1974). Notional quotations from this Encyclopedia Galactica begin the first novel and help set the stage for Asimov's Foundation-ruled Empire. The literary conceit is of a thousand-year series of such *Encyclopedia* editions with a fictional citation from that imaginary reference work. The fictitious citation is purportedly from the 116th edition which was supposedly published in the year 1020 of the Foundation Empire rendered "1020 F. E." In that universe of fictional chronologies, encyclopedias and "psycho-historians," knowledge and scientific mastery of galactic cultural history span millennia. Savants in that fictional world publish an encyclopedic volume every ten years, generation after generation, endlessly updating older works in turn. Such continuity of cultural legacy and the preservation of past knowledge systems are a deep-seated dream of humankind. That may help explain the vast popularity that this trilogy has earned. The satirical science fiction short story "*Ms.* Found in a Libry" [sic] more than adequately pillories the contortions of written record keepers in a hi-tech nano-storage world. In that realm, intensive processes of abbreviation (such as that of the term "Library" into "Libry") and the unceasing miniaturization-optimization of record storage media results in lost records (Draper, 1963, pp. 52–58).

Signposts up ahead! We tour some "atomic time capsules" in America.

The goal is a noble one. Multi-millennial communication efforts that today's nuclear waste dump depositors could utilize to communicate to a world several millennia hence something of the potential dangers of atomic waste products inherited by them. That topic could have some bearing on the long-term communication needs of space-time capsule projects and other multi-millennial efforts. Essentially the deliberate creation of a (to be) ancient form of writing is being contemplated. In addition to the SETI literature we will examine, there is one government-sponsored study of long-term nuclear waste repositories that is especially relevant to these sorts of time capsule notification-protection concerns. The U.S. government contracted study *Communication measures to bridge ten millennia* developed some intriguing, unusual possibilities (Sebeok, 1984). The duration of hazards at nuclear waste sites, measured in ten thousand year periods, is a problem for future millennia of people. One proposed solution is a result of a semiotic analysis, and proposes to use deliberately crafted legendary tales and specially promoted ceremonials to communicate vital environmental information to coming generations. The task of preventing loss or distortion of information is to be carried out by an "atomic priesthood" that supervises the translation of the message into the sign systems valid at each time. Deliberately transmitted taboos, superstitions and "archetypal" warning icons would be artificially created. Although the creation of such an atomic priesthood may seem bizarre, this is an important study in multi-millennial, trans-cultural communication. Time capsule sites are in need of both long-term sanctions for protection and enduring traditions to commemorate their locations. The need of long-term traditions to protect and remember time capsules had been met through folkloristic building customs of foundation stone and cornerstone ceremonies.

Three basic kinds of interstellar communication efforts (CETI) are possible non-physical space-time capsules. Consider three sorts of electromagnetic-based language time capsule transmissions from our planet Earth into interstellar space. First of all are our own imaginary communication attempts to any available interstellar recipients in our Communication with Extraterrestrial Intelligence effort (CETI), or Search for Extraterrestrial Intelligence (SETI) as it is called today. Second are the studies in formulating and using logically deductive languages, such as Lincos. Lastly is a consideration of the ongoing, non-deliberately leaked audio-visual radio and radio-television program broadcasts. These three sets of "imaginable communications" are potentially ancient language interstellar time capsules from our era on this Earth. In *Contact*, both the film and the novel on which it is based, logical alphabets, television transmission and the overall technologies employed in SETI work are illustrated (*Contact*, 1998; Sagan, 1985).

"CETI-grams" are a sort of broadcast by numbers, an xy-coordinate-based pictogram. CETI-grams (as we shall term these cosmic telegrams) are a kind of space age pictogram from (if received) what might eventually be regarded as ancient sources—namely our twentieth and twenty-first century contemporary Earth period. The search for interstellar languages from intelligent species, termed SETI, has a close counterpart in Communication with Extraterrestrial Intelligence projects, or CETI (Broad, 1998, p. 1; Sagan, 1973; 1978; SETI Institute, 1999; *SETI*, 1990; White, 1990). Compare the communication problems raised by terrestrial millennial time capsules with the difficulties found in CETI projects. Techniques such as those used in classic interstellar space broadcast tutorials are useful on Earth. In fact, the binary type of coded pictogram broadcast from Arecibo, Puerto Rico, to the Messier B Star Cluster in 1974 was used for one of the messages included in Time Capsule II at the 1964-65 New York World's Fair. This binary code, written out as a string of zeros and ones, serves as a worst-case contingency for communication with the possibly alien recipients of AD 6939, regardless of planetary origin (*The Westinghouse Time Capsules*, 1938; [1964?]). Unlike the 1964-65 New York World's Fair use of this binary pictogram code in a written message, the Arecibo radio telescope broadcast had to use a dot-dash type variation in signals. That Arecibo message consisted of 1679 binary signals. Factored into two prime numbers, the result is 73 groups of 23 characters (Sagan, 1973). The resulting visual depiction of these binary signals in a grid pattern is something like a crossword puzzle without any letters in it. The pictograms visible on this grid are of planets about our sun, the chemical elements of our life forms, etc. SETI experts have long considered the prospect of broadcasting instructions about computer, algorithm and database construction as possible ways to communicate our technical and cultural civilization (Sagan, 1973; 1978). It is not impossible that various technical civilizations among the universe's myriad galaxies might miss one another in the vastness of space-time. In a worst case scenario, one civilization or species might perish long before the other receives a message, or even before sufficiently powerful signals could be widely propagated between them (Sagan, 1973; 1978; *SETI*, 1990; White, 1990).

Say it in Lincos? Lincos is an attempt to develop an artificial, logical, mathematical, universal language suitable for broadcast across interstellar space-time. It is expounded in Hans Freudenthal's book *Lincos; Design of a Language for Cosmic Intercourse* (Freudenthal, 1960). Based on his studies in logic and in the foundations of mathematics, it uses elementary notions of the arithmetic operations— add, subtract, multiply and divide— as the building blocks of an artificial language. Lincos is a real-life parallel of the fictional "Krell" species' massive "logical alphabet" in *Forbidden Planet*, with its decipherable alien logical theorems (Stuart, 1956). The real-life Lincos logical language is used to make emotive statements. But, as Carl Sagan pointed out, even if this form of mathematically based language is broadcast, missing one part of the transmission would leave a recipient very puzzled (Sagan. 1973; 1978). That is a real Achilles Heel for digital information in general. One of the advantages of the prime number, binary-coded, xy-axis CETI-grams (when they are pictographically rendered) is that each image can be independently interpreted without a step-by-step decoding of separate links. A disadvantage of such binary pictograms, and of engraved plaques, is that so little information can be conveyed. Binary pictograms and metal plaques might be little more than mementoes, dedication plaques from one alien intelligence to another. Another drawback to metal plaques, broadcast binary pictograms and mathematically based grammars is that they convey only a one-dimensional image of the human species, literally and figuratively. It would be better to send interstellar space-time capsules that were more varied in expression, carrying much more information that could be separately interpreted.

Standard audio-visual Earth radio-television program transmissions of our (eventually) ancient language and (immediately!) alien time capsule broadcasts have been underway for about 100 years. At first these signals were in binary Morse Code, then also as audio-radio broadcasts, and later (since the mid–1930s) as powerful TV broadcasting (Goldsmith & Owen, 1980, pp. 366+). Decipherment or the mere signal intelligence of capturing electromagnetic wave modulation light years away from their Earth origins might be daunting or even impossible. There is also a question whether any beings will exist to eventually receive our deliberate and non-deliberate signals. Radio-television audio-visual program transmissions might be somewhat more comprehensible to interstellar recipients because of the series of images and coordination of audio-visuals in TV broadcasts. Just as ancient business and legal records have provided us insights into past lives here on Earth, commercial and governmental telecommunication signals might conceivably yield some valuable clues of Earthly cultural life to any hypothetical alien intelligence receiving them.

Reading cryptic messages into a "Bible Code"? A spate of intriguing books on the neo–Cabalistic "Bible Code" conjectures are excellent representations that may tell future recipients something about our era's notions of scientific knowledge. That controversy illustrates a number of linguistic, cultural and cryptographic complexities in sending messages from one era to another. One critical analysis of the Bible Code controversies demonstrates how one very distinctly antique text can be read as having contemporary acrostic-type name linkages (Weldon, 1998). Cryptoanalytic-type analyses of the methods and outcomes of the Bible Code controversial procedures demonstrate how various texts can be read, "read-in-to," decrypted or permutated to yield contemporary acrostic-type names, prophetic phrases and linkages of all sorts (Drosnin, 1997; Satinover, 1997; Weldon, 1998, pp. 47–55). This cryptoanalytic approach is an additional kind of interpretation, in addition to linguistic and cultural interpretation. Examples are given of (non–Biblical) textual analysis via "equidistant letter sequence" (ELS) methods to "breakout such decodes." One critic of Bible Code methodologies cites 13 references to an envisioned assassination of various late twentieth century political figures found encoded in Herman Melville's nineteenth century novel *Moby Dick*. There are even thematically appropriate pronouncements "hidden" at various ELS throughout the United Nations document set *The Law of the Sea* (Weldon, 1998, pp. 47–55)! Even without computer data processing algorithms a variety of linguistic or historical (overt and covert) meanings can be attributed to antique or contemporary publications. Although distinct, they are often interrelated when interpreting the past, and especially its written records. The multiplicity of methodologies for critical textual analyses is illustrated by works such as *Decoding the Bible Code: Can We Trust the Message?* It employs an interesting variety of distinctly articulated theological-doctrinal, philological and socio-politically critiques of Bible Code theories. Strictly secular statistical and cryptological analyses are articulated as well as theological rebuttals (Weldon, 1998). The multiplicity of possible linguistic interpretations might be even more of a challenge than the indecipherability of an ancient metal tablet from 1000 BC or a clay ceremonial writing cylinder from 3000 BCE. A Lincos data package, a CETI-type pictogram or even a TV episodic "sitcom" program can all be beamed over the millennia from Earth toward a potentially very alien recipient, very different from us Earthlings of ca. AD 2001 (Sagan, 1973; 1978; *SETI*, 1990; White, 1990). It's interesting how the topics of confidential communications, data encryption, codes, ciphers, computing, decoding of ancient languages and quantum physics are interwoven as themes from these various disciplines (Singh, 1999).

Ancient writings of all eras and formats can be time capsules in all sorts of ways. Humankind deeply wants capsule experiences expressing one time period to another. The notion of ancient writings communicating across the ages is destined to remain a compelling time capsule medium.

CHAPTER 6
Keeping Time in a Perpetual Futurescape

The 1999–2001 Turn of the Millennia craze was a time of time capsules. The two phenomena are deeply intertwined in the popular consciousness and resulted in millennial musings of all sorts, including a blizzard of time capsule activities (Jarvis, Hudson & ITCS, 1998-1999).

Bi-millennial 2000 Global Events

"Happy New Millennium"? At the dawn of our new Millennium, there was a widespread urge to ruminate about our world today and how its future might be. The *National Geographic* thought piece "Making Sense of the Millennium" (Swerdlow, 1998, pp. 2–32) asked where our world is now and where it is going; the question has been pondered in a wide array of publications and discussions. Many people wanted to make some sense out of these millennial phenomena. There seems to be a tendency to multiply a thousand-fold one's natural inclination to reflect on New Year's Eve themes at the end of any year's calendar. Will any such intensified contemplative effect continue to be substantial over the decades? Will the three New Year Eves of 1998, 1999 and 2000 continue to have any sort of suc-

Opposite, top: Concrete outer shell for Time Capsule from Tahlequah* (OK) *First United Methodist Church sealed 12 June 1932 to be opened in the year 2000. Opened 11 June 2000: **Ready for examination in 2000. *Opposite, bottom: Tahlequah* (OK) *First United Methodist Church inner copper time capsule opened 11 June 2000; has since been refilled with new materials and resealed:* Repository and contents are under examination here in 2000. (Both photographs courtesy First United Methodist Church, Tahlequah, OK; Vickie Sheffler, photographer.)**

Concrete outer shell for Time Capsule from Tahlequah First United Methodist Church
sealed 12 June 1932 to be opened in the year 2000
opened 11 June 2000

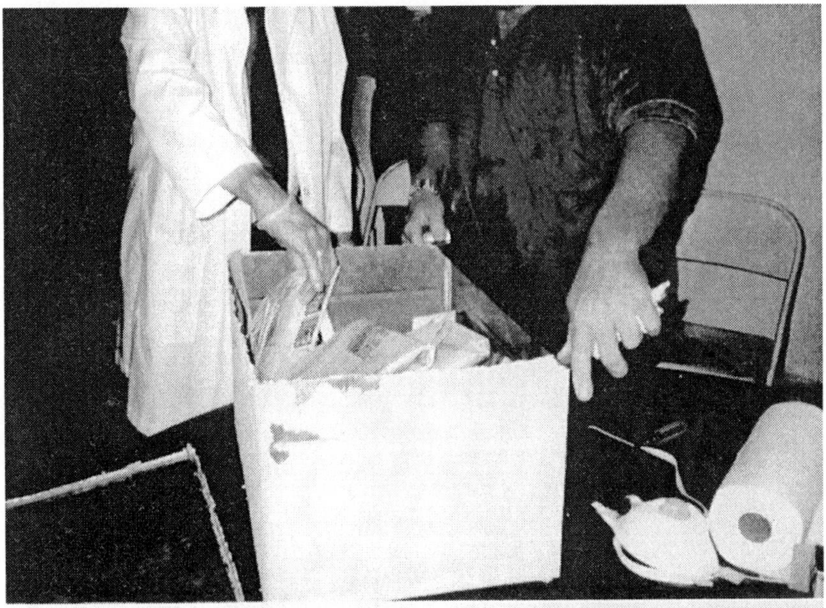

Tahlequah First United Methodist Church inner copper time capsule
opened 11 June 2000; has since been refilled with new materials and resealed.

cessive multiplicative impact on our chronological consciousness? Not only was the "Turn of the Millennium 2000" heavily billed as a theme travel destination, it was an obvious stimulus on time capsule activity. After the hype of its initiation, perhaps the New Millennium of the years 2001–3000 might continue to seem a unique time period, a perpetual notional futurescape now realized permanently. Perhaps we will now think of humankind continuing to live in an actual, permanently inhabited cultural landscape of tomorrow today, a 2000-era futurescape. Or perhaps the New Millennium was after all just hyperbole, an after-effect of a pent-up anticipation and calendar-linked novelty. Perhaps then the new 2000-era had far more futuristic aura and meaning in 1999, 2000 and 2001 than it might in the year 2005, or 2012. Perhaps we will see one way or the other, as the 2001–2010 decade goes on. Clearly there was a great deal of New Millennium 2000 hyperbole, but the question is whether there is more than just hype in the phenomenon. Whatever the case, this calendar transition seemed to be of considerable popular cultural significance in the 1999–2001 period. Likewise, time capsule depositors also tend to experience an anticipation of a capsule's target date's imagined futurescape. Millennium celebrations and time capsule depositing are appropriately paired activities because of this shared sense of a participation mystique regarding pending futurescapes. For those who deposit time capsules of 50–75 or more year spans, of course the "participation" can only be assumed to be a vicarious, anticipatory kind of experience.

The new Millennium was heavily promoted as a premier travel destination, a celebratory space-time target of great import. There were countless Millennial events scheduled in many places around the globe. Examples include such festivals as the Expo 2000 World's Fair in Hanover, Germany, the 2000 Summer Olympics in Sydney, Australia, and the first opening of the shorter termed copy "no. 2" of the Osaka Expo 70 twin Time Capsules in Japan. Such travel opportunities are one millennial outcome sought by many in search of futuristic milestones, rather than a landscape of doomsdays or social utopias. The sentiment seems as prosaic, albeit warm and friendly, as "Have a Happy New Millennium!" rather than merely "Happy New Year!" as a mundane, less dramatic welcoming of a new era (Hoffman, 1999). The titles of typical celebratory Millennium articles can capture the ambivalent motivations in such "end of the millennium" popular attitudes: "Time and again: counting the years to make sense out of life," reflects just such a deeper archetypal need. The benediction in that popular print also echoed the conventional wish for good fortune found in such holiday greetings (Hoffman, 1999). In Gisborne, New Zealand, a first-of-the-new-Millennium musical concert was held right next to a 1000-

kilometer Millennium Wall along the coast ("Lifeline column: New-Age Eve," 1999, p. D1). The *New York Times* Travel Section of Sunday, December 27, 1998, was a millennial travelogue listing various millennial celebration destinations throughout the world ("Big party. Big headache?," 1998).

The Millennium year 2000 celebrations celebrated in Great Britain were a good example of the Millennium as a travel venue. Plans ranged from a mass deposit of commercially available time capsules by individual purchasers to the grand celebration slated for the Greenwich zero degree longitude Prime Meridian site. That Greenwich Mean Time site signals a sort of millennial "ground zero" aura, perhaps resonating with the three zeros of the year 2000 (*Time Zone 2000*, [1998?]; Maddox, 1998). Those "Time Zone 2000" time capsules were vended with the notion that all deposits would be registered. Those now constitute an array of time capsule deposits, marking some imaginary finish line for a human calendar countdown to the future. New Year's Eve 1999 also marked the inaugural of the Millennium Dome, the site of a continuing exposition as a protracted World's Fair–like event (Maddox, 1998; Hoge, 1999, p. 13+). The Millennium Dome, at a cost of over $1.2 billion, covers about 20 acres, is two-thirds of a mile in circumference and 165 feet high. It also has a Teflon-coated glass fiber roof. It can handle 37,000 people, with a central 12,500-seat arena. Grouped around that are some 14 "lifestyle zones" where interactive technology exhibits on topics like mind, a multi-faith spirit zone, rest and recreation. In the body zone, people move around inside a huge human shaped structure that is bigger than the Statue of Liberty (*Britain building Millennium Dome*, 1998). There was also a 50-year time capsule prepared by a BBC-1 children's program for the Dome's center. It is a 50-kilogram, five-meter burial targeted for the year 2050 (*British Museum* staff, 1999).

An attempted criminal mastermind heist of a $500 million dollar diamond display occurred in November 2000 at the Millennium Dome. The story of this failed rip-off featured bulldozer-driving and bomb throwing gangsters ambushed by waiting police ("Crashing into the Millennium Dome on a bulldozer and throwing smoke bombs...," 2000)! It would have been a world's record robbery. In several previous instances in this work, such as the movie theater's pickpocket wall deposits, and in the forensic anthropology of the physical remains of Latin America historical figures like Pizzaro, we compared a crime scene to a time capsule. Certainly activities such as preserving a crime scene, maintaining a chain of evidence, reconstruction or reenactment of a crime (scene) are familiar "encapsulating" notions to our contemporary TV viewing public. Returning to the scene of the crime is such a hoary cliché, it verges on the archetypal. In the case of "The Great Millennium Dome Diamond Heist," the scene of the crime came to the scene of the Turn of the Millennium! It is possible to consider crime scenes, their forensic work-ups and their legal "Exhibits A, B, C" as time capsule analogs. Such scenes can be cognitively framed as time capsule precincts, contents, rituals or deposit experiences. Earlier, we have viewed forensic, biological anthropologic studies of twentieth century homicide victims and even of the prehistoric archaeology of human remains as time capsules of one sort or another. We noted accident scenes such as that of the Iceman, Celtic Salt Men or Danish Bog People to be "as-if" time capsule experiences. We have also viewed the true crime venues of forensic specialists' "scenes from," or the equivalent of, time capsule contents and experiences. The operational research analysis approach to reconstructing the nexus of cause and effect in recent period military-industrial accidents of friendly fire shootings of U.S. Army helicopters (by U.S. Air Force jet fighters) reminds us how the interpretation of a lethal accident scene can be akin to a time capsule interpretive experience (Snook, 2000). Case studies of organizational behavior and leadership management of accident investigations can not only be a military science study of friendly fire incidents or an engineering science of transportation accident reconstruction. They can be, like the crime scene studies they also resemble, time capsule experiences. They can take us back into the past, using reconstruction of contexts and causes to understand what an "incident" (accident or crime) scene once was like in times gone by. The Millennium Dome has "happened" twice as a destination, first as millennium celebration 2000 history, then as a (crime scene) farce.

As a Millennium 2000 postscript, what really happened? Reporting from hindsight, how did the Turn of the Millennium 2000 work out? The world, our Earth, did not end. Post Soviet-era terrorism fears apparently blended with Y2K computer bug numerological foreboding. The "Y2K Fear" of 1999-2000 emerged as a sort of Nemesis or *doppelganger* for the prospective 2000 year Millennium traveler ("For travelers, Y2K starts now," 1999; "Seattle's New Year's Eve celebration canceled," 1999). Computer bug and potential terrorists had merged into some sort of blurred, synergistic menace. People tended to stay home, rather than fulfill the heralded Millennium as a premier travel destination. We seem to have entered and remained in a sort of permanent futureland. It is a notional (i.e., imaginary) futurescape whose frame of reference of forever starting anew is daily underscored by those three zero digits on each date. We have entered a decade and a century for which we have no ready, easy designation, unlike the 1990s, 1980s, etc. The author tends to say (and even sometimes write) the twenty-first century's first decade's years as "2-K-1, 2-K-2, 2-K-50" for the years 2001, 2002 and 2050, respectively. This short-cut has *not* yet caught on! The world of Millennium 2000–3000 might continue to be considered as an enduring sense of a permanent world of the future. Will this New Millennium futurescape be unlike the provisional futuristic theme park–like world's fair grounds, which were declared over in just a few seasons of futuristic pretend? It remains to be seen how superficially, or how profoundly, the post-modern global villagers' futurism is maintained as a belief system. Obviously, millennia-old habits of many old twentieth century cultural attitudes and human ways will remain much the same in 2000, 2001, etc. The Y2K Glitch-Fear period of rumormongering took on the character of a sort of Global Village urban legend. The numerological fear of the three zeros in the New Millennial Year 2000 date was equated in the popular mass consciousness as a sort of secular, technocratic apocalypse. That feeling may linger and color our Global Village–type cogitation about our future. Will the future always be "right now," from now on? Since 1876, that desire to evoke visions of the future has been a lure of time capsules, a source of their popular appeal. Deposits have traditionally protected and dedicated building thresholds and other entrances over the eons. Perhaps our time capsule deposits and other dedication ceremonies over the Turn of Millennium 2000 have added to our collective sense of protection on the threshold of this entrance into the third Millennium future's cultural landscape?

The "Y2K Fear" was an example of a modern natural-technically-based Apocalyptic prophecy or Doomsday scenario. It is interesting to read works that chronicle past apocalyptic ideas and fears about the end of our cosmos. However secular they are in spirit or clothed in computing machinery lingo, the 1999 era Y2K Fear deeply resembles our ancestral, magical-religious fears of worldly apocalypse (Weber, 1999). The "Y2K Fear" was that some or maybe much computing machinery might fail. There was a deep concern that there would be a wide computing machinery failure to adequately distinguish the year 2000 from "zero-zero" (a blank) or even from the year 1900 because of a two-digit-only limitation in some computer coding. This is a uniquely modern, naturalistic-secular (i.e., non-supernatural or religious) kind of (potential) technological apocalypse. The projected prospect failure can be seen both as a human-invented disaster and as a number-bound outcome, with emotive overtones of a numerological occult, mystical Doomsday kind of fate. No magical thinking or religious, millennialist belief system is required to experience this end-time kind of angst, which has all sorts of commonplace manifestations. Concerns range from those about accidental wars to all sorts of civil disorder or deprivation due to a feared crash of the developed techno-structure of the "North" half of the globe.

We seemed to have concentrated all of our irrational, superstitious dread on the Western, Gregorian AD–BC, secularized numerically continuous dating system (Matz, 1995). The Y2K Fear may be the greatest urban rumor or Global Village legend yet. Model year 2000 motor vehicles newly registered in the State of Maine during 1999 were magically redesignated "horseless carriages" due to a computer bug in the State's new car registration software ("Y2K glitch identifies new cars as 'horse-less carriages,'" 1999, p. 5). The "Y2K Fear" seems to have functioned as some sort of *rite de passage* which the (electronic-digital) Global Village experienced in our transition into the year 2000 and the subsequent New Millennium. Our world's experience of the Y2K Fear, that anxiety focused on the prospect of mass computer disaster, can be seen as having been a rite of passage into this New Millennium time reference. It was a fear of a cultural landscape overwhelmed with zeros. It lacks any reassuring defining features, being rather a pseudo-numerological, desacralized fear of techno-structural collapse. This literal and figurative concern about an atavistic rollback to the year 1900 is a sort of post-modern technological replacement for ancient religio-magical apocalyptic anxieties. We have (perhaps?) passed completely through this initiation rite into our permanently realized notional future culture landscape, or at least we have moved away from that "Great Y2K Fear."

The Gregorian Great Leap Forward is a series of time transfer messages. The Gregorian reforms are a series of successive approximations, arithmetically rounding off the calendar year to just 365.2425 days over each 400 year period ("The calendar," 1996, pp. 584–85; O'Neil, 1975, pp. 10–11; Wald, 1998, p. C3). This maintains our Earth rotation's 365 day–based timekeeping in reasonably close alignment with its annual elliptical Solar orbit. A technical chronological rule in the 1582 Gregorian Calendar reform (i.e., *only* century years evenly divisible by 400 need a Leap Day) determined the presence of a year 2000 Leap Day and its absence for the year 3000. Essentially a 1418-year-old message was sent to timekeepers of the millennial year 3000 (when it was "scheduled" or decreed in 1582) to be the first skipped "Leap Millennial Year." That ancient time capsule–like message includes the instruction that the year 3000 will not have a February 29 Leap Day.

The start of 2001 was of course another real new Millennium, the actual one according to the dictates of technical chronology. At zero longitude, the Greenwich Meridian, Britain's Millennium Dome failed as a perpetual futurescape. The BBC reported its closure on January 2, 2001 (Higham, 2001). It closed much like any other provisional world's fair futurescape. It had been a notional fairscape for just a season, amid the fiscal deficits and lack of permanent functional purpose typical of its close cultural cousin, the World's Fair. No word yet on the next (commercial?) fate of the Dome (or its "Blue Peter" time capsule, noted above). Although there clearly weren't as many news stories, thought pieces and news articles about New Year's Day 2001 as the dawn of the year 2000 garnered, the sense of being on the threshold of the future endured. One December 31 article intoned that "The Future is coming faster" in a "A virtual space odyssey," and featured an illustration of a 1946 view of the very antique "ENIAC" computer at the University of Pennsylvania (Johnson, 2000). Newspaper year-end roundup stories from New York City to Lewiston, Idaho, also had diverse takes on the significance, if any, of the imagined future of 2001 ("'Real' new Millennium approaches," 2000; "Some cracks in the foundation," 2000).

Doomsday Schema vs. Alternative Themes

A variety of cognitive schemas ("frameworks") relate to time capsule target date musings and to futurist studies in general. Some such views are nihilistic, others utopian, and some neither of the above. In addition to Doomsday, dystopian and other nihilistic visions (a "bunker mentality," etc.), a variety of positive, naturalistic, humanistic themes can be used as organizing principles in comprehending time capsules and futurist studies. Utopian visions can also be proffered, of course, sometimes (unconsciously?) projecting perfection and progress forever and ever. Regardless of the positive-negative spin one imparts to a capsule's targeted series of possible futures, a process of naturally occurring oblivion will ensue to much of humankind's various spiritual and material creations. Things will pass in and out of existence over the ages and will most likely change in many ways over many millennia. No nihilist-doomsday doctrine need be embraced to assume the alteration of the human world in history. Nonetheless, time capsule senders-receivers and futurologists may well project their distinctive attitudes on their futuristic canvas.

Doomsday themes abounded at the turn of our millennia. There have been thousands of works written on the end of the world theme (McIver, 1999). Our limited purpose here is the same as with the many other diverse topics and disciplines taken up throughout our work here. Our goal is not to systematically survey them, but rather to demonstrate their general relevance to the study of time capsules. We must stress here that natural changes in the ordinary passage of time can bring about massive change without positing a Doomsday end to any period of world culture or social context. It is not necessary for example to anticipate an artificial, i.e., human-caused, atomic or other environmental oblivion as a theme associated with millennia-spanning time capsule sealing. We do not require a metaphysical or theological thunderclap to mark the keeping of some millennial calendar observance. That does not mean that world cultural conditions will not undergo change over the passage of millennia, or even just feel differently in a new century or millennium (Dowling, 1987). Such teaching aids as a Doomsday Clock are not necessarily heralds of absolute fatalism. The "Doomsday Clock" rhetorical device of *The Bulletin of Atomic Scientists* was done up as a giant mockup model (in 1995). It really has been a good example of a notional, as-if chronological teaching aid rather than a piece of hardware, chronometer or actual clock. Nor is it an inevitable symbol of unavoidable Apocalypse, although the organization's occasional press releases do sound a pessimistic warning note whenever they decree a change in the clock setting. A recent example is that of the June 11, 1998, press release "resetting" the clock from 14 minutes away from Doomsday-Midnight to a mere nine minutes before "zero hour." Started in June 1947 with a decreed setting of just seven minutes to midnight, today's Internet Doomsday Clock is an interesting precursor of the various Doomsday heralds one sees now on the Internet and other media (*History of the Doomsday Clock*, 1995; *Nine Minutes to Midnight*, 1998). In that cautionary vision, the closeness of one possible future is viewed as a prospect of an atomic war Doomsday.

The atomic bunkers and missile tunnels of Cold War America can be seen as Millennial votive offerings, futuristic dystopias frozen in time. Nuclear power in both its electricity generating and weapons systems forms has powerful time capsule and futurist associations for humankind. Communication over millennia, destruction of billions of people and the survival of military and political elites have all been envisioned as offerings to be made to weaponized atomic power. As to how to verify the operational status of aging nuclear weapons stockpiles without conducting sample tests, critiques of accelerated use simulations are paramount. The two time capsule–related themes of atomic repository stewardship-storage and accelerated use–simulation analogies are closely linked in this case (Glantz, 2000). We have contemplated various communication efforts to transmit over a ten-millennium span. Humankind is also attempting to communicate across indefinite reaches of space-time. These efforts have some obvious similarities, given the proposed length of time and probably culture gaps (Sebeok, 1984). A wide variety of different perspectives on such multi-millennial attempts are needed to maximize any communication across the eons. One detailed plan has been realized in a ten-millennium communication project, the Waste Isolation Pilot Plant in New Mexico. That is where recent expert thinking about the ten millennia nuclear waste warning conundrum has been focused (Benford, 1999). Benford describes a visit by his advisory group to this underground salt bed tunnel system. The Waste Isolation Pilot Plant in New Mexico ("WIPP") is now open for business as a Third Millennium hi-tech repository (Brooke, 1999, pp. 1, 17). Any such long-term storage bunker can not only provide preservational technology tips for literal time capsule projects, but also can stir our chronological imagination about structures and installations that might endure for millennia to come. They can serve as aids in doing both literal capsule projects and our imaginary visions of notional examples. Incidentally, this salt bed geology site has also been the source of some interesting, controversial microbial studies. A group of scientists claim to have extracted primal, "archaea" type bacterial specimens that may be 250 million years old (Travis, 1999, p. 373). The scientific jury is still out on this archaic-like spore vs. present-day contamination debate. It would be very interesting if this 10,000 AP ("After Present") nuclear-waste repository would also turn out to be the site of archaic bacteria preserved there from 250 million years BP (or "Before Present"). Such an interpretation of this site recalls the midpoint-in-time notions that played such a key role in the 5000-year-plus millennia-spanning time capsules noted earlier. However, a "mere" 10,000 years ahead in time are only a minute fraction of the 250 million year spans of the bacteria that may reside there. Therefore a broader, more humbling perspective on the brevity of humanity's atomic waste deposits emerges. These recent deposits of the atomic age are just a minute increment in the ancient span of life on Earth, against the hypothesized quarter-billion year origins of microbial life.

The American Century broadcast its visions of "Atomica Americana" to the future in a proliferation of commemorative, curio and atomic landmark time capsules in the 1945–90 period. The Cold War legacy of Atomica Americana that we see in the aspirations of time capsule senders poses three possible questions. What atomic warfare historical sites remain as monuments to an era now passing from world history? What influence did the Cold War and Atomic Era America have on literal, target-dated time capsule deposit vessels from 1945 to 1992? Lastly, what trans-millennial communication theories and practices have come out of the activities of that era, including warnings of the dangers of atomic waste products down the millennia? These themes are related not only to what we have left for posterity to ponder, but how those "ponderables" might be preserved. These are relevant questions to consider about long-term communication needs of space-time capsules and other such multi-millennia-spanning efforts. There are futurist perspectives on visiting U.S. "atomic tourism" relics and various "banking on destruction" government bunker sites. There are of course a vast number of historic atomic weapon–related sites in the United States, and elsewhere in the world too, that remain as monuments to that short epoch in world history. Test sites, weapons systems deployment sites and continuity of government sites of all sorts seem to be planted everywhere, once one begins to look for them (Schwartz, 1998). We are considering these U.S. relics of the Cold War as time capsule–like treasures. They are deliberate deposits and monuments that reveal historical contexts and contents to us in our new post–Cold War era. A website entitled "The Bureau of Atomic Tourism" covers "Atomic Museums" and "Sites of Atomic Explosions" (*The Bureau of Atomic Tourism*, 1999). Among the atomic museums are the National Atomic Museum and the Titan Missile Museum, billed as "The World's Only Public Underground Missile Complex." The featured sites of atomic explosions include Trinity Site, the Nevada Test Site, Hiroshima and Nagasaki. Test sites and production sites of atomic weapons are still very much with us. These decommissioned installations and former test sites in the states of Nevada, New Mexico, and in U.S. Territorial Pacific Ocean sites remain as very long-term atomic weapon exhibits. Production sites in such places as Oak Ridge, Tennessee, Hanford, Washington, and numerous less notable locales abound, standing as monuments to the atomic–Cold War past and as safety and communications challenges for millennia to come. Many U.S. Air Force Atlas F and Titan II liquid fuel intercontinental ballistic missile silo bases are for sale, as a sort of Cold War surplus votive offering to the future. One of these "Halls of the Titans" is perhaps the most spectacular of such monumental relics of the atomic–Cold War era (*The Titan Missile Museum*, 1999). This one huge Titan II base, one of a cluster of 18 situated around Tucson, Arizona, has been turned into a massive museum. Apparently it is the only such silo still containing a Titan II missile hull. The liquid fuels and fusion warhead of the 110-foot high missile are gone. Note that in contemporary U.S. culture, such retrospective musings over the memorials and remnants of the world's atomic and Cold War eras tend to be expressions of a spirit of sober social satire, rather than being any grandiose, grotesque celebration of destructive, aggressive power. That is indeed the spirit of criticism presented in our views of these atomic travel venues, museums, satiric writings and electronic guides.

"Banking on destruction" could be the epitaph of a variety of continuity of government sites in the United States that are monuments to the Cold War–atomic era. The United States government, like several other Cold War–era nuclear weapon nation-states, had developed extensive continuity of government relocation-operational plans and special command control shelter facilities (Schwartz, 1998, pp. 309–25). Many of those key continuity of government facilities are featured in the Brookings Institution study *Atomic Audit*. That major work claims to be the first systematic study of U.S. atomic weapons, nuclear propulsion and nuclear generation of electric power ever conducted. These special U.S. installations include a Federal Reserve Bank bunker stocked with pallets of circulated $5 U.S. bills (to preserve or restore a money economy in the ruins), a huge U.S. national-security emergency Congressional meeting-housing facility (at Greenbriar, West Virginia), a U.S. government administrative underground complex (at Mount Weather, Virginia) and an Alternate National Command Center for presidential-military personnel (at Raven Rock, Pennsylvania). These emergency command centers are reminders of what an atomic residence would be like in any post-nuclear World War III environment.

Time capsules needn't be regarded as a kind of "surrogate survivalist" offering. Story devices like the fictional Antarctic time capsule of Nevil Shute's novel of atomic oblivion *On the Beach* feature time capsules as general warnings about ancestral folly. The oblivion of today's culture will most likely occur naturally, even gradually, just as our languages become dead, transformed tongues. In five to ten millennia, it is unlikely that any significant built-up structures from our age will be extant, regardless of the status of our political world, environmental activities or of the impacts of human technology. For example, bear in mind the fifteenth century England linguistic scene and its three very distinct dialects of later Middle English in their slow transition into Early Modern "Shakespearean" English (Gies & Gies, 1998, p. 3). Undoubtedly, no one then would have noticed these incremental changes, yet the linguistic world was changing. Our other cultural practices also often slowly transform into other sorts of behavior patterns, becoming eventually quite alien to the distinctive cultural practices and cognitive patterns of our own time. Depending on the durability of established social orders, the dynamics of materials' preservation, etc., it is likely that any whole, original or complete artifacts or functional informational media from our times would be at best very fragmentary. Speculation on such distant futurescapes almost invariably cause prophets to lapse into a conditional tense. Thornwell Jacobs, having just completed the Crypt project in May 1940, mused about the possible world of 8113 AD:

> The only structures on earth which are certainly as many as 5,000 years old are the oldest Pyramids of Egypt. They could hardly be classed as component parts of a city although they were in the environs of ancient Memphis. They are more of the general order of an artificial Stone Mountain. It is to be assumed that the forces of time will operate in the future as in the past. We may, therefore, confidently say that when the Crypt is opened in 8113 nothing hitherto constructed by man will remain on the North American continent remotely as it is today unless, as I said above, it is rebuilt and replaced because of its historic interest (Jacobs, 1942, pp. 1–2; 1945).

(Incidentally, Dr. Jacobs was referring to a literal physiographic terrain feature called Stone Mountain, the natural surficial geological formation that is prominent in the landscape just north of Atlanta, Georgia.)

The Modern Target-Dated Time Capsule Deposit Has a Futurological, Futurescape Visionary Context

Time capsule projects, like other expressions of human civilization, use technological capabilities to communicate the realities of one age to another. But we make capsules in our image, or rather to present an image favored by the project sponsors. If and when computer hardware eventually becomes capable of operational survival for millennia, artificially intelligent time capsules may then be possible. One can realistically envision computerized "expert systems" as time traveling ambassadors, provided physical durability and rapid system obsolescence issues are put aside. Puny processors that have fallen apart in their time vaults would make poor ambassadors! Then the means and the end, the form and the content of a time capsule would be a realizable futuristic technological vision. Problems of linguistic translation and perhaps even some aspects of cultural interpretation will then be solvable. No technological fix, however, can compel or guarantee a specific interpretation of our own cultures or messages by a later age. Such cybernetic time capsules could be either Earth-based or spacefaring. The current state-of-the-art in time capsules, however, is still typified by both the Osaka Expo 70 Time Capsules and the Voyager 1 and Voyager 2 interstellar Records. The likelihood is that the Pioneer Plaques and Voyager Records will travel through space for many millions of years, perhaps forever, unless they are somehow, someday retrieved. Thornwell Jacobs, the father of the modern time capsule, was fully aware of the probable low survivability of civilization's built-up areas over the millennia. As noted in 1988:

> Here on Earth our cities, skyscrapers, archives and museums may disappear, but buried time capsules and foundation deposits might survive the decay, destruction, and placement of our current technical civilization, to provide archival as well as archeological evidence from our era, to make our civilizations live again in an alien, distant future age, to pay our "archeological debt" to the future [Jarvis, 1988].

The future has quite a history, as a series of ideas that is. Our notions about possible futures have a cultural history of their own. The now venerable interdisciplinary field of Future Studies, or "Futurology," has a well-developed literature (Beckwith, 1984). Books such as *The 500 year delta: What happens after what comes next* signal that futurist studies are alive and well (Taylor, 1997). Anthropologists also can, and do, study the future as the exotic and mysterious place it is, or might be. Some apply ethnological concepts to social, futurist forecasting, such as in the work *Cultures of the future* (Maruyama & Harkins, 1973). That sort of perspective has been utilized to work out what cultural patterns might be like off our Earth, in what has been termed a "cultural futurology" or an "extraterrestrial anthropology" (Maruyama & Harkins, 1975). Trying to anticipate what we send from a passing world period to a possible future will be of value to future interpreters of our culture and life. It is only to be expected that time capsule researchers will continue to imagine at least some aspects of future days and worlds (Ascher, 1974, pp. 241–53; Durrans, 1992, pp. 51–67; 1993, pp. 50–59; Hudson, 1998, pp. 594–607; Jarvis, 1988; 1992a; 1992b). Another work, *The History of the future: Images of the 21st century*, narrates a fictional "history" that is largely drawn from works of science fiction and tableaux posited at various world's fairs (Canto & Faliu, 1993). Another study of the history of the future also weaves the history and criticism of the future in science fiction literature and in popular culture (*Histories of the future: Studies in fact, fantasy and science fiction*, 2000). Sometimes, for example, the 1960s are referred to as having been the Space Age. And of course the future is sometimes thought of as some sort of almost heavenly, Utopian, ideal pristine place, a well-known image in our nineteenth, twentieth, and new twenty-first century. For example, a work about the progressively accelerating wave of intellectual property rights and technology advancement sports the title *Owning the future* (Schulman, 1999). The title suggests that the future is up for grabs. It might also suggest to some that such a pristine, yet untrammeled time period should not be sullied by personal or organizational dominant property ownership. Of course, an attitude that the future is to be a time of wonderful opportunity could also be inferred from that title, at least to some interpreters who envision owning a market share or controlling economic aspects of the future. We can see how the notions of a shining, beckoning technological and economically rosy future played themselves out in the popular prints and world's fairs of the 1930s. Time capsule senders sometimes anticipate disparate outcomes in possible futurescapes, such as primitivism, desolation, technocratic sterility or relative comfort. However, it is still common for time capsule senders to wish that *their* sent relics, messages and views be part of the future. In an imaginative sense, time capsule senders want to "own" at least part of the future, whatever they say it might be.

Another interesting take on futurological visions can be found in Isaac Asimov's 1986 commentary on Jean Marc Cote's fanciful 1899 card illustrations of aspects of life in the year 2000. Asimov frequently seems to take Cote's whimsy just a tad too literally. His commentary sometimes implies that we should critique those apparent whimsies as literal predictions, ones which may be right on target or way off the mark (Asimov, 1986). Cote's illustrations are replete with images such as airborne police officers hovering around and schoolchildren being "downloaded" (as we would say today) the contents of ground-up books via wire sets to the head! The cards were, according to Asimov, produced under the manufacturing auspices of a novelty and toy manufacturer, presumably as a promotional novelty. In an interesting example of popular cultural provenance, many of these same series of cartoon-illustrated year 2000 cards also appear in a 1993 work. Those are featured along with a variety of similar-theme chocolate bar novelty cards from 1912. They depict a technofuture of the year 2012 (Canto & Falin, 1993, illus. #4–5, 10).

Humankind has journeyed from its past sacred precinct deposit behavior into futurescapes such as our new Millennium 2000 era "permanent" future. We noted earlier various archetypal, common meanings in both ancient and modern commemorative-consecration deposit ceremonials. The Ise Effect is a sort of bridge between an ancient sacred dedicated precinct and today's temporal renewal ritual sites. The modern time capsule deposit and target-dating practices have been ways to envision and evoke notional futurescapes of imagined futures and distant tomorrows. Clearly the modern time capsule's dedication role has evolved in a transformation from its origins in the consecrations of ancient sacred sites. (See Table 6.1.) Those deposit practices have come to take the form of a content-laden time capsule as a votive gift to some future cultural landscape. The close links between boundary delineation–consecration ceremonials and symbolic-world-creation belief-cultic systems are found in both formal and folk religious motifs and practices. These chronological themes are perennials in archaeological, folkloristic and ethnological stud-

Table 6.1
Sacred Site Dedications, Notional Futurescapes and Time Capsule Experiences

The origins and development of either provisional or perpetual "notional futurescapes" begin in the ancient cultural matrices of dedicated architectural landscapes. The following is in roughly chronological order.

Sacred ancient precinct-dedication traditions and cornerstone custom survivals: Beginning with Mesopotamian and Egyptian examples, founding dedication deposits delineate "theme centers" or boundaries of an architectural landscape. The tradition of deliberate deposit of building, founding and other commemorative relics, ceremonial writings, etc., for indefinite time spans continues in our cornerstone repository rituals to this day. Although subsequent deposits might result from later dedications at a previously utilized site, most ancient foundation deposits and current cornerstone practices do not feature perpetual renewal as a continuous, deliberate policy. Such one-shot examples remain commonplace.

Sacred ancient precinct dedications currently sustained by viable, ongoing renewal traditions: The Ise Shrine complex effect is an example of how perpetual re-dedication and renewal of deposits, structures and boundaries of a cultural-architectural landscape can make possible a realized series of ongoing notional futurescapes. Such perpetually sustained renewals are rare.

World's Fair architectural landscapes as temporary, ephemeral notional futurescapes: Beginning modestly at the end of the eighteenth century in revolutionary Paris, France, and then continuing into our twenty-first century Expos, the World's Fair movement gathered strength through notable expositions in 1851, 1876, 1893, 1939 and 1970. Temporary glimpses and imaginary visions of possible futures in effect created the effect of a series of temporary notional futurescapes in our Global Village culture, each lasting one or two exhibition seasons. World's Fairs, beginning with the 1876 Philadelphia Centennial Exposition, have become associated with literal target dated time capsules projects.

Modern target-dated time capsule vessels as ways for senders and any receivers to (temporarily?) imagine notional (imaginary) futurescapes: The display of the Century Safe at the Philadelphia Centennial Exhibition of 1876 began the deliberately deposited, target-dated modern time capsule. It became a way for senders, as well as any completed or contemplated receivers, to envision a variety of possible future cultural worlds as a target date. Periods of large-sized time capsule depositing have included the years 1938–82 and the ca. year 2000 era. Episodes of serial redeposit at time capsule sites and anniversaries (i.e., U.S. Centennial and Bicentennial deposits) and even of the redeposit of the same time capsule vessel (i.e., the Osaka Japan Expo 70 Time Capsule no. 2's 1970–2000–2100, etc., to 6900–6970 CE retrieval or re-sending schedule).

The new millennium 2000–3000 CE as a possible permanently realized perpetual notional futurescape: The period around the year 2000-2001 is certainly a temporarily realized millennial notional futurescape of (at least) the electronic sectors of our Global Village. Only time will tell if (and to what extent) this new millennium will continue to be perceived as a notional futurescape in future decades or even centuries.

(continued on page 236)

TABLE 6.1 (*continued*)

Distant tomorrows (such as new millennia 3000–4000 CE, 10,000–11,000 CE, 12000–13,000 CE) as possible perpetually realized notional futurescapes: Now that our Global Village's techno-culture has gone through the secular *rite de passage* of the Y2K fear alert, perhaps only notional futurescape visions of the Millennia of 3000 CE and beyond will have sufficient, significant imaginary attraction to give our era's inhabitants a "Future Thrill."

All of these posited versions of notional futurescapes might be conceived as temporarily realized only notional futurescapes, not just the ephemeral world's fairscapes, but any time capsule target-dated possible future or the futurescape of any distant tomorrows. Nor is it clear whether the new era of Millennium 2000 might continue to service as a perpetual futurescape, or whether the new Millennium cultural futurescape might readily be seen as having been only temporary or provisional.

ies of ancient religions and sacred sites around the world (Eliade, 1954, pp. 9–11; Fagan, 1998, pp. 143+). Eliade's generalized conceptual framework clearly has value in charting some basics of East-West cultural-chronological distinctions. Related conceptions of vertical-horizontal: time-to-space: Japan-Western Worlds, etc., can also be found in discussions such as Nishida Kitaro's classic exposition "The problem of Japanese culture" reprinted in *Sources of Japanese tradition*, 1958, pp. 857–72. Such dichotomous conceptual frameworks are not confined to either the Eastern or Western Hemisphere. Kitaro's 1938 take on the persistent time sense polarity was "vertical-horizontal" rather than the "cyclical-linear" phraseology expounded by Eliade. "Vertical" (West, secular, etc.) translates well the depth aspect associated with cyclical ceremonials too, but perhaps not as explicitly. Civilizations such as those in ancient Mesopotamia maintained beliefs and practices focused on enhancing the distinctive value of temples and city walls as symbolic worlds set off from other locales (Brereton, 1987, pp. 526–35; Henniger, 1987, pp. 544–57; Sproul, 1987, pp. 535– 44; Talos, 1987, pp. 395–401). We might say that archaic sacred places were more cyclically celebrated than the peripheries of their ritual centers. Other examples of ancient sacred precincts are the ritual centers built up in the eastern United States by the Paleoindian Mississippian mound-builders for their societies' ceremonials (Fagan, 1998, pp. 184–219; Knight & Steponaitis, 1998; Pauketat, Bozell & Dunavan, 1993; Rogers & Smith, 1995). One famous scholarly instance of mythopoetic study is the priesthood of Nemi discussed by James G. Frazer at the beginning of his noted study *The golden bough: A study in magic and religion*. The priesthood's incumbent was a fugitive murderer who had sought sanctuary there at Diana's sacred grove at Nemi in Italia. That could be accomplished by killing the previous murderer that patrolled the sacred precinct. Eventually, yet another fugitive murderer came along and continued the tradition of sanctuary *ad seriatim* (Frazer, 1922, pp. 1–7+). This striking tale is one example of the perpetual renewal of the guardianship of a sacred precinct through endless renewal! It is also a serial murder crime scene, and harkens back (or is it forward?) to modern crime scenes and the dedicated precincts and time capsule associations noted above.

The continuing desacralization in the nineteenth and twentieth centuries of these archaic, cyclical archetypal forms of consecration has resulted in today's more secular, modern linear-historical commemoration style in historical thought and mass consciousness, and in time capsule dedication practices too. Notions of time have shifted from a more sacred-cyclical focus to include linear-secular-historical perspectives. Basic archetypal consecrated foundation-cornerstone deposits eventually evolved newer forms of expression in the (terrestrial) time capsule deposit and even the space-time capsule. It is true that to a degree the original kinds of sacred, cyclical ceremonial consecration deposit behavior continues to be practiced in modern times, with variations. It is also true that those traditional beliefs and practices have been substantially demystified, desacralized, especially over the last 150 years. We can see this especially as all sorts of popular dedication depository practices of today's schoolchildren and ordinary citizens. A cornerstone ceremony or time capsule dedication ritual need not necessarily imply a religious, supernatural or magical practice. Terms such as "ritual" or "ceremony" do not necessarily assume even a solemn context for the activities (*Ritual, performance, media*, 1998; Rothenbuhler, 1998, pp.103–04, 63–64; *Secular ritual*, 1977). Sociologically, then, a wide variety of non-magical, rule-driven group enactments can be termed rituals too.

It is at least possible to try to re-sacralize, to recharge the numinosity of a vertical, cyclical depth time-sense, especially in conjunction with seasonal ritual experiences. For example, guidelines for the renewal of rituals of traditional seasonal observances are presented in *The Winter Solstice: The sacred traditions of Christmas*. It brings to life not only the mythic dynamics underlying that season, it can return the reader to an emotionally connected sense of a primal, sacred, archetypal timeframe for that winter season. We can be guided "back" or "out" of our contemporary desacralized, technologized cultural landscape (Matthews & Matthews, 1998). The cultural past of the Winter Solstice is awakened in our consciousness and that underlying, previous world-view is evoked and made alive to us.

Let's consider some basic dynamics of notional futurescapes. There seem to be at least five ways to notionally posit such futurescapes. These include the use of a target-dated time capsule (or by means of an indefinitely dated cornerstone repository) venue:

- A systematic program of repeated commemorative renewal might regulate the physical preservation of a sacred precinct site's cultural symbolic significance, such as with the Ise Effect. Those precincts could thus be perpetual sacred architectural landscapes.
- Time capsule deposits imply project definite target dates-eras, while cornerstone deposits with their indefinite receipt-dates posit different futureworlds' potential retrieval dates.
- World's Fairscapes can serve as embodied visions of experimental cultural landscapes, notional futurescapes. But these notional worlds' fairscapes will usually last just one or two summertime seasons, but they may leave some residual site structures and boundaries. The relics of Seattle Center, Seattle, Washington — its Space Needle theme center and its futuristic Monorail train from the 1962 Century of Progress World's Fair — are examples of such residuals.
- "Futurological" imaginary, speculative musings in science fiction or the prognostications of (perhaps) more prosaic futurologists can provide the contemporary citizenry with visions of possible notional futurescapes of temporary, provisional or even perpetual duration.
- A fifth sort of perpetual, notional futurescape may be our current 2000 CE–3000 CE Millennial Era. Our New Millennium 2000 era might be seen by some affluent electronic Global Village sectors of Earth's inhabitants as the *first* permanently realized perpetual, notional futurescape. Of course the sense of permanent present futurescape may just be a fad, a chronological, futurist conceit. Perhaps the sense of living in a permanently present futurist landscape of cultural possibilities will diminish. We early twenty-first century inhabitants may be left by 2003 or 2004 with just a fading memory of a provisional, temporary, now dissolved or dim set of memories, dreams, Y2K fears and hopeful sense of perpetual new possibilities in our times.

What then has shifted, been lost or been gained? Where and how is this paradigm shift taking us into that series of notional futurescapes of our Global Village's possible distant domorrows? We have identified some contemporary forms of notional futurescapes such as "World's Fairscapes," the "New Millennium 2000" and finally the possible notional futurescapes of distant tomorrows such as the eras 10,000 CE and 12,000 CE. What has shifted? Our sense of dedicated precincts has shifted from a cultural-perspective of a primal sacred precinct solely rooted in past times, into idealized images of the future, into which we can send time capsules and their various explicit content and implicit contextual messages. What has been lost? Nothing has been *irretrievably* lost to our world culture by that cultural paradigm shift. At least in terms of Mircea Eliade's conceptions of Western linear progression in a secular, technological civilization, the primal symbolic grounding of our time capsule rituals can be termed as shallowly buried in the linear, technologized human psyche. The deeper psychological-symbolic associations have been rendered at least partially unconscious to us in the course of the linear chronological plot of our world's historical progress. The very progress of time's arrow is exemplified by the deliberately deposited, target-dated time capsule. What has been gained? A tangible sense of a series of target-datable possible futures, the notional futurescapes of our imagination has been gained, perhaps *irreversibly* so! Where is this paradigm shift continuing to project our imagination? What are the prospects within the perpetual notional futurescape of our current New Millennium 2000 and of the Global Village's futurescapes of distant tomorrows?

How is it doing so? Since the development of the World's Fair movement in the nineteenth century Industrial Revolution, humankind's world civilization has been "traveling" through secular, linear space-time. The concurrently developed modern time capsule (1876–2001, etc.) is an exemplar, a working model of this linear time travel of projected cultural ideals. Now humankind's world cultural development has traveled through a series of brief World's Fair–type futurescapes, into a sort of perpetual World's Fair in this New Millennium 2000–3000 CE. The Global Village presaged by Marshall McLuhan has (at least partially) now been realized in our New Millennium's electronically wired zones of habitation. This New Millennium era is world culture's first notional futurescape to last more than the one or two years of a World's Fair's ephemeral World's Fairscape. In a sense we have recently realized a permanent or perpetually realized notional futurescape, namely Millennium 2000. Perhaps we finally inhabit "the Future"—perpetually, that is! In pragmatic, everyday experiential terms of chronological reference, slightly higher year dates such as 2020, 2030, etc., may not have anything like the impact of the year 3000 CE. After all, we have surpassed the year 2000. Perhaps in a few years,

2000-plus year date designations may not feel that impressive. We may then see just how permanently realized our Millennium 2000 notional futurescape is! The concept of a variety of notional futurescapes and a series of perpetually realized such futurescapes is comparable to the broad use of a set of "cultural landscape" ideas found in contemporary anthropological analysis. A variety of cognitive styles characterizing symbolic-cultural definitions of human worlds have been outlined. Examples of analyses include conceptual landscapes in ancient Egypt, ideational landscapes in Mayan culture areas, the Inca cognition of landscape, the centering of ancestral worship mound-sites in Paleoindian America, East Asian Buddhist landscapes and various mythic landscapes in Iron Age Britain, etc. (Ashmore & Knapp *et al.*, 1999). A number of those contributors elaborate these and other diverse examples of such constructed archaeological landscapes. Time capsule–like experiential landscapes are closely related to various cultural landscapes. Examples of such dedicated, exalted, visionary realms include ancient sacred precinct landscapes, world's fairscapes and a variety of notional futuristic, or target-dated futurescapes. These sacred or notional cultural landscapes are comparable to anthropological contributors' conceptual formulations about various archaeological landscapes.

Our modern target-dated time capsules vessels have been a way to meditate upon and also to take us to notional futurescapes such as time capsule target dates. In the twentieth century, capsules sometimes served as powerful aids to imagining the futurescapes of distant tomorrows. Although we have literally reached (as of the year 2000) one such distant future, many other such possible distant futures remain to dream about. For example, future cultural target periods such as those of 10,000 CE or 12,000 CE remain as the inspiration of fantastical, futurological dreams and aspirations for today's time capsule senders. Time capsules are still one way we can envision our primal origins, current endeavors and possible futures. They are perhaps the best way to measure our significance, positive and negative, over the millennia. They are ways to project our fears, dreads and other less-than-optimistic concerns by sealing them up in a time capsule and sending them away into their possible futures. Likewise when we retrieve a time capsule, we can realize an instantly created presence of a "futurescape connection" with the past depositors' imagination about their future, our present. On the receiving target date end of a time capsule's retrieval, anyone's year or era might feel like the capsule senders' futurescape. To recycle a time capsule is to further multiply our comprehension of humankind's chronology. The observance of such year 2000 time capsule events as the Symposium on "Time Capsules in the Modern

World" (in Osaka, Japan) and the recycling-rededication of the Osaka Time Capsule no. 2 marked the year 2000. Those were just two examples of humankind's regrounding of a cyclical sense of time with a more linear version of historical chronological time. A series of successive capsule target dates can themselves be seen as a series of temporary notional futurescapes. The Osaka Expo Time Capsule no. 2's long series of scheduled re-openings in the years 2000, 2100, 2200, to the year 6000 CE and finally in 6970 CE is another fusion of cyclical and linear time conventions. Those retrievals and re-deposits are even slated to occur at the Osaka Castle Prefecture Park, itself a sacred, historic park precinct. Furthermore, the Osaka Expo 70 Time Capsules no. 1 and no. 2 were initially exhibited at the Osaka Expo 70 World's Fair site, yet another futurescape association that these two time vessels have.

A Sample of Year 2000 Spawned Time Capsule Projects

The year 2000 "Turn of the Millennium" was an impetus for a myriad of time capsule and capsule-like projects and efforts, large and small. Some were centenary-type spanning capsules, while others were 1000-plus-spanning "millennial" projects. In particular, there are now clearly far more millennial span designated time capsules, due to the 1999-2000-2001 Turn of the Millennia catalyst. Compare that to the mere eight millennium–spanning time capsule projects documented between 1938 and 1982. In fact, the true numbers of this millennium time capsule binge may not even be divined. Due to the Millennial event hoopla, a 1000-year-span time capsule seemed quite the natural thing to deposit. Here are a few samples, focusing on millennium-spanning projects. ITCS time capsule consultants indicate that in 1998 and 1999, the International Time Capsule Society received well over a dozen queries a day. These queries have been from people who want to do their own time capsules and even business people interested in selling their empty time capsule containers (Jarvis, Hudson & ITCS, 1998-99). Requests for newspaper interviews abounded too. Numerous consultants, including the other co-founders of the ITCS, and this author gave a variety of people advice during the heightened time capsule interest of the new Millennial period.

"The (British) Millennium Time Capsule, 2001-2201" is one of the many interesting Millennium examples of deliberately deposited and target-dated time capsules occasioned by the ca. 2000 year Millennial craze. This mega-project site consists of a large stockpile of corporate, organizational and individual "pods" to be sealed for just a 200-year period beginning in 2001. The project designers have opted for a commemorative focus and hence shorter time span. Since the number of one's descendents tend to multiply geometrically over millennia as a population biological function, the prospect of bequeathing one's cultural messages and curios to some readily single personal descendent is a remote one. People are invited to ship an actual tailor-made time capsule pod back to the Millennium Time Capsule project after they fill their own container with specimens of their own choice. Businesses, organization, families and individuals may "e-mail the future," transmitting messages to their descendants in 200 years. These e-mails will be converted to a "preservationally friendly" form and sealed up in smaller time capsule modules or pods as well. Anyone contributing an actual pod will receive a legal certificate granting them legal title to the pod and its contents. The organizers of this enterprise hope to assemble from this composite mass of deposits what will amount to a very full record of British life and culture. The technical details of this project's design are as impressive as its broad cultural and participatory scope, including the protective concrete support structure internally insulated and conditioned to minimize temperature and humidity-caused deterioration. Each inserted pod is constructed of polypropylene with an inner atmosphere of inert argon gas. Attention is also being given to the particular characteristics of internal packaging materials and the make-up of the inventory of items in the collective contents, including resistance to acid-induced decay (Durrans, 1998; Millennium Time Capsule, 1999).

The New Zealand "Millennium TimeVault" and its mini–time capsule pods are another mass pod repository of time capsules in an English-speaking island nation-state in New Zealand, half a world away from Britain's Greenwich Mean Time Meridian. New Zealand's "Millennium TimeVault" contains three options for groups of individual time capsule pods. Options for purchasing 50-year, 100-year, and 1000-year pods were offered each person or group sponsoring a time capsule deposit. These "short-term" capsules cost ca. $180 in New Zealand dollars. Each mini-capsule pod was a crush-resistant cylinder individually sealed for the storage of various written records as well as compact discs, photographs, magnetic audio-visual tapes, etc. Standard document storage expertise was employed to consult on proper transport, storage procedures and facilities. A "Year 2000 Commemorative Medallion" was designed as both a millennial commemorative medallion and as functional receipts for the shipment of time capsules and their cargo. These medallions were intended to function as family heirlooms, leaving word until the specified retrieval date. The medallion design features are intended to clearly convey its purpose, each uniquely designated by an eight-digit alpha numeric identifying the inheritors' specific time capsule with the storage Vault. Two thousand spaces were reserved for "1000 Year Capsules" and were priced at, of course, $2000 (New Zealand) per capsule. These thousand-year capsules are high-impact resistant and the size of a medium suitcase. The "Millennium TimeVault" was designed not only to be sealed with an inert gas, but also to be water- and air-tight (New Zealand Millennial Vault & Time Capsules, 1999). The "Experimenta Media Arts Time Capsule," Melbourne, Australia, is a project by Experimenta Media Arts, an organization that exhibits and promotes various media arts to investigate new conceptual and aesthetic contexts. Their website lists various organizational promotional events associated with their millennial time capsule projects (Ball, Macarow, Nancarrow & Whiting, 1999; Jarvis, 1999c). The Antipode of the Northern Hemisphere also has its share of cultural islands targeting the future!

The "Long Now Foundation Clock and Library Projects" are very interesting "10K Year" efforts. Led by a number of San Francisco, California–based visionaries, they are to have a functioning millennial Clock and a long-term Library resource to parallel the Clock effort (Brand, 1999). The patent-pending Clock invention by Daniel Hillis is billed as "the world's slowest computer," designed to tick just twice a day, and to chime once every thousand years. The Long Now Ten Thousand–Year Library collections scope and content was still in the discussion-planning phase in mid–2000. It is envisioned as including various works (or a whole collection) intended as a start-up guide for a future culture (Brand, 1999, pp. 94-103). The author of the Gaia Hypothesis has proposed something similar (Lovelock, 1998, pp. 832–33). One possible part of such a Library's collection is the "How We Did It" segment. Some other collecting ideas are more standard, the "Best," the "Most Candid" (diaries, pop culture?), the "Most Historically Minded" disciplines (paleontology, archaeology, etc.) and the notion of a Research Library (Brand, 1999, pp. 94–103). (These labels are ours.) This ambitious set of twin projects can be viewed as an instance of technologists functioning as preservationists and prophets (Oravec, 1999 *ms.*). Many time capsule senders are a bit of both, of course. America Online Inc.'s "AOL Member 1000 Year Time Capsule" project was launched on May 10, 1999, and was a limited term input available to the Internet provider–search engine–library company's subscribers. It was an invitation to contribute what they thought was important to provide for a time capsule to last 1000 years ("Coming soon: the AOL Time Capsule," 1999; Jarvis, 1999b). This was an online-diary-plus-images sort of time capsule, along the lines of the notional cases sketched earlier. It is now stored in a print medium format off-line.

The "Biological and Environmental Specimen Time Capsule 2001" (or "BESTCapsule 2001") is a 1000-year series of deposits planned for burial 65 feet into the Antarctic ice pack (Jarvis, Hudson & ITCS, 1998-1999; Kamiizumi, 1998). The project's original goal was to begin its drilling down 65 feet into the Antarctic ice pack at 00 hours 01 minutes on January 1, 2001. As of the end of 2000, that deposit date was rolled back. There is now some rethinking of the project, according to various anthropologists. An international scientific team had conceived of depositing several thin torpedo-like ceramic or perhaps steel vessels for a target date of 1,000 years. The proposed containers are ca. six and a half feet long, have a diameter of ten inches and can hold nearly 100,000 specimens apiece. Other copies of this Antarctic deposit could be stored in a variety of various cryogenic labs above ground around the Earth. The intended contents were to include the traditional seeds and other samples of seawater, rainwater, air, soils, various spores, reproductive-type cells, human mother's milk and DNA specimens. Choices would have to be made out of millions of samples. These time capsule containers are targeted at scientists in the year 3001 with the hope that these materials could be useful in environmental and biological research. These deposited items are intended to be a sort of reference work or database for the future. One leader of the project group, Takeharu Etoh, projects a steady minus 60 Celsius temperature and substantial isolation from human or geological disruption. (The project team has its eye on the Moon as a future environmental time capsule site since minus 230 Celsius readings are present there.) Scientists and engineers at Kinki University in Higashi Osaka City, Japan, who are organizing the project, held a workshop in November 1998 with representatives from biological specimen banks in Germany, the United States of America and the Federal Republic of Germany; initial planning had begun in 1993. Some historians and anthropologists who study, analyze and advise about time capsules also presented papers, including one on ethnological motivational aspects of time capsule phenomena such as the BESTCapsule 2001 project team (Durrans, 1998). There have been financing obstacles (ca. $10 million U.S. dollars) and also legal-ethic issues (raised by the team itself) surrounding the biological bans of the Antarctica Treaty.

The *New York Times*' Millennium "Times Capsule" 2000–3000 project was (of course) widely heralded by the *Times*, by way of the *New York Times Magazine* and the paper's various web pages. There were a total of six 1999 "Special Millennium Issues" of the *New York Times Magazine* including the initial issue on "The Best of the Millennium," April 18, 1999. It featured the subtitle "The best: ideas, stories, and inventions of the last thousand years." The *Times*' "Times Capsule" project invited comment and suggestions on its year 2000 to year 3000 effort when a time capsule was deposited at the American Museum of Natural History in March 2000. The editorial staff had originally proposed it as just a notional exercise (*New York Times Magazine*, "Special Millennium Issues," especially in the sixth, December 1999, special issue "The Times' Capsule: Will they get it?," 1999). That special issue featured the vessel and its contents. Of course, a "mere" 1000-year time capsule span can be something of a missed opportunity to have done instead a 5000-, 8000-, or even a 10,000-year time capsule. A great many such objects will probably survive 1000 years without the benefit of a time capsule. The many very good 25-50-100 year Centennial-type commemorative time capsules are great for celebrating events, but the really different world periods of our possible futures are many thousands of years away from our own times. The *New York Times* Capsule winning design was by the Spanish architect Santiago Calatrava, and will contain numerous items for 1000 years at the American Museum of Natural History in New York City, adjacent to Central Park. Based on origami-type designs, it can be opened in individual segments, each hermetically sealed with inert argon gas and special thermal packaging as well. The capsule can contains 50 cubic feet of storage space, is five feet high, weighs two tons and is made of $66,000 worth of stainless steel. The capsule was at the Museum in the exhibition "Capturing Time: The New York Times Capsule." It was held from December 1999 until March 2000, prior to being sealed and deposited there until the year 3000 ("Spare times: attractions: museums and sites," 1999). In addition to the then empty Times Capsule were many of the contents already selected for it. The exhibition featured many of the ca. 50 proposed time capsule designs submitted in a *New York Times*'–sponsored competition. Inside are the six Millennium issues of the *New York Times Magazine*, recorded both on acid-free archival paper and stored as well in Norsam, Inc.'s registered process of micro-engraved nickel format, basically a microscope-scannable disc ca. 2 inches in diameter ("Design is ṣelected for *New York Times* Capsule," 1999; *HD-ROSETTA ion beam system*, 1999; *MEMS & micromachining devices and systems*, 1999). "HD-ROSETTA" media technology is engineered for long-term survival. However, not every hi-tech talisman, such as spacesuits, will magically survive degenerative changes over time. Hi-tech Space Age type motifs (and artifacts) can sometimes seem to be invincible, as eternal. The merely celestial is not rendered preservationally perfect for ever and ever, unfortunately. In the case of some 30-year-old U.S. Moon suits, the degenerative changes of rubber, etc., layers are the proverbial feet of clay, according to "Mighty Moon suits are falling apart" (Leary, 2000, pp. 1–2).

A Symposium was held on the topic of "Time Capsules in the Modern World" at Osaka, Japan, in September 2000. It was held at the National Museum of Ethnology there, on the site of the 1970 Expo fairgrounds (*Time Capsules in the Modern World Symposium*, 2000). The international Symposium was held in conjunction with the recently retrieved Osaka Expo Time Capsule no. 2, and a public program was held in conjunction with those events. A technical report on the condition of the capsule and its contents was featured among the Japanese and English language Symposium papers (Ohmura, 2000). That capsule had just undergone the first of its opening-resealing century-by-century series.

"Small" time capsules are alive and well at the turn of this Millennium! A typical garden variety, mundane yet quite serviceable time capsule project was done by the senior class at Rhodes College in Memphis, Tennessee, in conjunction with the one hundred fiftieth anniversary of that college in 1998 ("Seniors put their past 6-feet under," 1998, p. A8). It was targeted for a 50-year time span. One classic life and death of a building cornerstone–type time capsule experience in Edmonds, Washington, involved opening of the 1928 City Hall building's cornerstone repository when that structure's demolition began. The subsequent dedication of a replacement structure included a new 1998 indefinitely deposited cornerstone repository ("Edmonds to open, bury time capsules," 1998, p. B 2). We saw earlier that a second Sharpstown, Texas, Time Capsule was sealed in March 2000 in conjunction with the opening of the first Sharpstown, Texas, Time Capsule, 1955–2000 (Jinkins, 2000; Hendricks, 2000). And of course as the 1999-2000-2001 turn of the millennium has rolled around, time capsules are literally everywhere, a phenomenon that we will address later. If the reader doubts how ubiquitous the modern time capsule is, the documentary film *Time Capsule: Message in a Bottle* will perhaps be convincing (O'Connell, 1999). It is the first full-length documentary exclusively featuring the subject of time capsules.

Messages to the Millennia

When the party is over, what next? Once a time capsule has been retrieved and opened, a World's Fair season has ended, an archaeological site or building has been restored or otherwise modified or a new Millennium has been entered, it seems only fitting to mark that occasion. Somehow we feel the need to commemorate and record what has been experienced or changed. Sometimes with former World's Fair sites, residuals remain, as civic playgrounds and improvements. These residuals sometimes remain as monuments to the world of aspiration, achievement or entertainment that once occurred at that place. The Eiffel Tower (1889) and Seattle Center's theme center Space Needle (1962) are two examples of former exposition sites that retain something of their élan as fair sites. Another site of two New York World's Fairs and of the two time capsules associated with them (the 1938 Westinghouse Time Capsule I and the 1964 Westinghouse Time Capsule II) is the "Unisphere" site at Flushing Meadows Corona Park, Queens Borough, New York City. At the new, higher than Aswan Dam–level site of the ancient Egyptian Abu Simel colossal statues and shrine, the restoration-archaeological team in early 1966 did a foundation deposit. The commemorative coins, *The Koran*, Egypt's *National Charter* and contemporary newspapers should indicate the time period when this historic structural monument was moved from one physical site to another (Gerster, 1969, p. 728). We have repeatedly stressed the exemplar status of the Japanese Ise Shrines 1200-year rebuilding throughout this study.

A "time tour" reveals several grand capsules scheduled for reopening in the seventieth and eighty-second centuries. Here are some ideas about what it would be, or might be like, to open four great multi-millennial time capsules. Since the seventieth century (6900s!) is scheduled to be rather crowded with the twentieth century's millennial time capsule target dates (three), it might be fun to imagine what could be the interpretive experience people might have opening these time capsules then. For example in 6939 CE, Westinghouse Time Capsule I is to be reopened on the autumnal Equinox, Flushing Meadows, New York, as is the 1965 Westinghouse Time Capsule II, providing a dual view into 1938 and 1965 CE life. Just 31 years later in the year 6970 CE, Osaka Expo 70 Time Capsule no. 1 at the Osaka Prefecture Castle Grounds, Osaka, Japan, is targeted to be opened. Its centennial twin, Osaka Time Capsule no. 2, is also targeted to be reopened, just 70 years after its last centennial-period re-opening in 6900 CE. This series of five major openings in the Common Era years of 6900, 6939 and 6970, if obeyed by the inhabitants of Earth, would then be a unique historical opportunity. Of course, other time capsules could be deployed for target dates then or at other significant clusters. Given the unique cluster of omega points in the 6900s, it might be a good idea to target more millennia range time capsules for that century. In 8113 CE, the "Crypt of Civilization Time Capsule" is targeted for reopening at Oglethorpe University, Atlanta, Georgia. We can talk about what it might be like to get into the spirit of opening up any of those three time capsules and interpreting what we would find. With the "Crypt of Civilization Time Capsule" scheduled 8113 CE re-opening, one might be able to really "get into the experience" literally. It does after all have a 2000 cubic foot interior!

Will the great (as well as more prosaic) time capsules be remote imaged before their requested opening dates by non-invasive technical sneak-and-peek previews? Archaeologists are heavily involved in remote sensing and relatively non-invasive micro-fiber-optic, remote controlled viewing of the interior spaces of archaeological sites. Can time capsules be far behind? Probably not, which is unfortunate in two senses. Anything that diminishes the mystique of a time capsule's sort of secret space is a bad idea, at least in this author's view. And at least the fiber optical devices currently being deployed are invasive, albeit relatively "non-"! Low energy, perhaps passive reception-only instrumentation, might alter the terms of the technique-objection, although not the mystique-deflating one. Arthur C. Clarke at various times has envisioned an eventual usage of the natural back-scatter, background radar length electromagnetic wave energy as a way to passively detect and image objects, for example. The technologists have five or six millennia of remote sensing developmental prospects to sneak a peek inside a time capsule, and they just might do that. Archaeologically tasked radar arrays are commonplace in such cultural surveys, as are periscope-type probes (to screen Etruscan tombs, for example). Italian scientists have used miniature, sterilized video equipment to "enter" the marble tomb of Fredrick II the Holy Roman Emperor from 1220 until 1250 ("Scientists probe tomb of emperor," 1998). The sarcophagus was opened for nearly one month during a refurbishment of the cathedral in Palermo and the tomb's interior was probed; the family's foundation was never consulted about the invasive procedure.

Time capsules are in a sense technological fixes. They are ways in which we convey our human interests to the future. Over the years, people have used whatever occasions and technologies were available to do that: monuments, graves, cornerstones, Westinghouse Time Capsules, Pioneer Plaques and Voyager Records. In our own time, the terrestrial burial of a time capsule at an exhibition of industrial progress has been supplanted by the post-industrial achievement of space travel and the prospect of interstellar SETI via space-time capsules. Getting back toward the narrower focus type of deliberate deposit-and-targeted time capsules, we can just barely see the tip of new formulations of time capsule phenomena, time capsules as robust, perpetually reprographic electronic configurations, as space-time capsule projects, as complex socio-technical autorenewing institutional arrangements. We have, among other tasks, looked here in this work at some of the early harbingers of the dawning new age of time capsule projects, systems and studies. Perhaps such technological feats as massive computer information storage into increasingly tiny spaces will put the world, or at least its written records and audio-visual imaging, into a small box (Gelernter, 1991). It is possible to see in the historical development of deliberately deposited time capsule phenomena a human refocus of the symbolic import of such deposits somewhat away from the immediately dedicated object (and its wider location). The emphasis over time has shifted over to that of making a presentation of the depositors' cultural and historical place and time into a very distinctive future, much unlike the senders' world. Concomitantly, the development of modern scientific archaeological methodologies and interpretive theories has also led the interpreter of archaeological finds into a very similar ability to look back at distant, distinctly differing cultural pasts.

We can speculate on possible associations among holograms, "monads" and the functioning of time capsule–like remembrances. For example, consider the hologram phenomenon of breaking one hologram plate image into many fragments of varying perspectives of the same image. The phenomenon can be seen as a metaphor of the multiplicity of perspectives of cultural interpretation. The phenomenon can also be viewed as an organizational technique, a method to convey many perspectives on many worlds by "projecting" vital slices of whole time periods forward in time. Metaphorically, time capsules can be like the (seventeenth century European rationalist) philosopher Leibniz's "monads." He envisioned monads as mini-world units, each with a slice or perspective on all other such world units. Perhaps there is a parallel between the notion of a monad and that of a "good" time capsule. To transmit a good time capsule experience, "the Sent" must be similar enough to the larger world it is sent from and different enough to "the Receiver" to seem a vital part of another world. It should be a past world-time that can be suddenly evoked as present and accounted for. Also, perhaps there is more than a passing coincidence of the time capsule experience to a hologramically based cognitive science schema and theory of human memory? Perhaps that is why such a small thing as a sent time capsule or even a single found item can be received as evoking a whole past, distant feel of a world in a future human brain (Pinker, 1997)? Such explorations in the intersecting fields of cognitive neuroscience, neuropsychology, evolutionary biology and psychology currently have a somewhat speculative dimension — the perspective that at least one's subjective time capsule experiences are as much about the workings of minds as they are about sealed containers of items. Such philosophical psychological considerations are valuable, intellectually fascinating and even pedagogically laudable. But the goals of time capsule phenomena can be achieved without intricate technological fixes and sacred or secular ceremonials. Sometimes the essence of time capsule phenomena can be sensed in a single memento, talisman, book, artifact, film or other relic which reproduces the experience of a (until then presumably) lost world of place and time. On other occasions, a time capsule transaction can be evoked with a whole realm of things and contexts presented as a tableau of a past. Technology is necessary but not sufficient to make an enduring time capsule. Technique alone, however, cannot guarantee a good time capsule experience. Without the feeling, seeing, touching, experiencing of such a transmitted slice of the past, even the most elegant technology, the most thoughtful package of goods or the best of intentions are unlikely to be a good time capsule experience to sender, critic or distant receiver. A time capsule in the deepest sense needs to be alive or have been a part of life in order to bring anything or any era back to life.

What are the prospects in humankind's quest for digitized-computerized time capsules? In the aftermath of the twentieth century's Space and Atomic ages, it is worth reflecting on the origins of time capsule deposits in ancient foundation deposit ceremonies of Egypt and Mesopotamia. Outer space radio transmissions, spacecraft probes and digital computer emulation are among the hi-tech approaches to time capsule–like propagation of past world cultures to future recipients. Beyond our current Earth-based and space-launched time capsule projects, these ancient practices would appear to have a cybernetic future, as does (apparently) every other aspect of human civilization. Twenty-first century extra-terrestrially based space-time capsules, for example, could be "cybernetic" in one of two ways. Space-time capsules could contain artificially intelligent devices programmed to conduct SETI, with databases loaded with records of an (by then) ancient terrestrial civilization. This interactive capability of twenty-first century space-time probes is in contrast to the passive interstellar two Pioneers and two Voyagers space travelers. (Voyager I & II, along with their twin records, are "celebrating" their first quarter century of space travel. They are probably within a few years of crossing the heliosphere, the solar wind particle field at the electromagnetic edge of our Solar System [Wilford, J. N., August 13, 2002, "Voyagers Reap a Bounty of Discovery and Beauty," *New York Times on the Web*: <www.nytimes.com>].) When these four planetary probes eventually begin the final interstellar phase of their travels, the exploratory electrons on board will no longer be working. These interstellar space-time capsules are passive objects, just like their earthbound counterparts. One form of a possible space-time capsule has been widely discussed by SETI specialists, and was the subject of Fred Hoyle's novel *A for Andromeda*, noted earlier as an "ancient future" kind of time capsule–like communication experience (Hoyle & Elliot, 1962). Is it conceivable that an interstellar broadcast of specially coded information can be a kind of space-time capsule (not unlike a Pioneer Plaque or a Voyager Record)? If so, then an interstellar broadcast could consist of not just a kind of scientific encyclopedia but rather of instructions for the construction and programming of a computer. In this way, a cybernetic space-time capsule could travel at the velocity of light rather than the slower speeds of space vehicle probes.

Another approach is just to send a physical, automated cybernetic space probe into interstellar space. Such cybernetic technology could eventually be also used in terrestrially based time capsules and cornerstones. The task of notifying future recipients of a time capsule's existence, location and contents, and of supplying a prearranged interpretation of such a legacy, could be assisted by a cybernetically interactive time capsule. Such a project could not only present an interactive presentation of a time capsule of messages and records, perhaps it would have (or approximate) an actual dialogue between a cybernetic emissary and the interstellar civilization that might retrieve it. By programming an artificial intelligence to speak to future recipients on our behalf, human civilization would have fashioned time capsules of great durability and information capacity. However, each age, and each transmitting-receiving species, could cast its own interpretation on such mementoes, no matter how detailed the canned interpretation provided by others. Such a computerized space-time capsule technology could also be used to equip a terrestrially based time capsule with an internal, self-announcing, self-interpretive capability. Then time capsule interpretation would enter a new stage, where the recipient's interpretive dialogue with the past would be a more literal dialogue between recipient and sender. And, since the recipients would (one hopes) have their own cybernetic interpreters, senders and receivers would conduct a dialogue between machines. But no machine, no matter how artificially intelligent, will remove the necessity, or human curiosity, to interpret the past in one's own way.

In our studies of ancient writings as possible time capsule experiences, purely digital iterated-forms of emulations-encapsulations were noted as clearly compatible sorts of time capsule–type experiences and potentially very valuable concepts in long-term information-transfer projects. Such emulation and encapsulation strategies seem well thought out, long-term archival-operational and media-preservation of information in digital format. Perpetual, rigorous, ongoing software emulation coupled with a strict encapsulating of digital information is advocated as the most plausible, most efficacious digital preservation option (Hunter, 2000, pp.

42–44; Rothenberg, 1995, pp. 42–47; 1999). Earlier we cautioned against any naive embrace of a "magical medium" kind of solution to our era's digital media's survival chances. Any notion that non-paper digitized media easily serves as a reliable archival source for future ancient electronic libraries needs a strict, critical, ongoing review. One hopes that these digital emulation proposals will not be uncritically relied on as magical media or procedural techniques. From our "all things time capsule" perspective, this would mean that digital emulation of records, images, data sets and algorithmic coding sequences might well indicate to us the way to the most durable time capsule. It may be possible that the most comprehensive such long-term cultural record and microcosm repositories might be best realized as systematic, endless iterations of digital-computerized emulations over successive human generations. Instead of Marshall McLuhan's "internalizing the old medium as an art form," these new infinitely superseding, supra-preserving computing domains could be used to successively "nest" every cultural record internalized as an archival record form. Digital emulation-preservation on a comprehensive repository scale faces many basic challenges, such as:

- Conceiving how one can get all of this *into* the digital storage system.
- Conceiving how one can get all of this *out of* the digital storage system.
- Maintaining these long strings of computer coded emulations, as they are entered inward to, and also go outward from, digital storage system domains.
- Wisely monitoring processes such as initial selectivity, ongoing costs, tunnel visions, changing values and tendencies to discard in carrying out any such digital archive or other information storage projects.

The essence of the correlation problem is managing the elusive goal of getting sufficient essential contents into a time capsule vessel. This is a version of the classic puzzle of how to have a microcosm part (such as a time capsule) function as a valid representation of any whole such cultural period in some mere capsule contents. The underscored protocols, the well-delineated operating procedures of checking, monitoring and endless re-checking in Rothenberg and Hunter's writings are clearly analogous with the needs of other preservationists, such as in preservational microfilming maintenance. The overarching long-term vigilance required includes practices such as adherence to well-defined technical standards of environmental-storage, copying-access procedures and an incessant quality review program. These requirements seem equally high for both silver microfilming facilities and for digital-electronic media emulation configurations ("Silver-gelatin film," etc., 1996; Swartzburg, 1995). The preserved entities and artifacts do differ in many ways. The Norsam Technologies, Inc. "HD-Rosetta" micro-etching metal disc technologies noted earlier are a third possible long-term preservational technology useful for time capsule considerations. Simultaneous utilization of these three approaches might aid the long-term time capsule–like survivability of ancient documents. Interestingly, both the silver film preservation microfilming and the laser-etched micro-discs are contemporary sorts of modern metallic documents, descendants of those metallic writings of the ancient world we have described earlier.

What are the ultimate tests of a time capsule? We are coming to the end of our 5000-year historical tour of time capsule experience and interpretation. The span of our study has been no less than the totality of human recollection and imagination, past, present and future. The scope of time capsule history encompasses our present day, all our possible futures and many of humankind's past epochs. We began this "time travel" with an examination of ancient foundation deposit customs; we end with a vision of twenty-first century interstellar cybernetic exploration. Time capsule phenomena are not just isolated obscure practices left over from a superstitious past, although they are that too! Time capsules, whether in the form of foundation deposits, cans in the ground or interstellar messages, are relics of our civilization. They can tell a great deal about our civilization, both to all of us and to future beings and times. They are secular equivalents of traditionally sacred treasures, of cultural offerings now dedicated to the future. They might eventually be the occasion and stimulus of the evoking and retelling of significant tales of the sender's ancient culture. The customs, beliefs, libraries, artifacts and buildings of our Turn of the Millennium 2000 period may disappear or be unrecognizably altered by any number of progressive, regressive or other transmutations. Time capsules and foundation deposits might survive the decay, destruction or transitions of humankind's current cultural or technical civilization on Earth. So, what should one try to provide via the contents placed inside these time treasuries? Perhaps we can provide everyday slices of life as well as archival and archaeological evidence from our era, to make our civilizations live again in an alien, distant future age. We can try to pay what has been called our "archaeological debt" to successive futures (Jacobs, 1942, pp. 1–2; 1945). So our sense of wonder about the future (or even our need to tell the future about the quality of our "antique air") can lead us to produce meticulous long-term storage containers or cybernetically sophisticated "electronic diplomats" to present our achievements to future beings.

Communicating with other times, places and beings can be attempted in many ways, not all of them being high technology or big budget. The bottom line on these diachronic information transfers is that the time capsule transaction should work from sending age to receiving future. A strong test of a time capsule deposit is how well the capsule carries on a continuous loop of observance-expression-preservation-communication-observance, etc. This chain of dedication practices, the motivational mix behind time capsule deposit phenomena, reflect humankind's compulsion. We have an archetypal urge to dedicate, commemorate and recall a variety of pasts for any number of possible futures. Time capsule deposits are a focused way we express that aspiration.

We seal these time capsules not so much to ward off ancient demons or fears. We do so to deliver a small measure of our lives to posterity, whether that is thought to be an imaginary time of shining peace and progress, or to an age as imperfect, confused and potentially lethal as our own. Still, we seal away some of the same things that the ancients did when they dedicated their major building complexes with cornerstones, images, special messages, coins and seeds. We sacrifice a little from our times in order to protect our cultural memory for the future. We have seen how these experiences unfold, how they do the work of dedicating times and places, and we now end our cultural history tour of "end times," Turn of Millennium 2000, dedication deposit rituals and the 2000-era time capsule art. Just as individual time capsules can cast their spell across time, from one era into another, the time capsule notion has itself grown over the last 5000 years, casting its spell across the millennia.

CHAPTER 7

Epilogue: Our Ideal Time Capsule

Having held forth at length on various time capsule specimens and experiences, here are some considerations for good time capsule installations.

Specifying

Our own "Ideal Time Capsule, 2001–12,001 CE" would strive to realize the best of what we know about good time capsule vessels and experiences. It would contain a full set of cultural-technical information drawn from the whole of human world culture (and of all known technological and natural history). The "Ideal Time Capsule, 2001–12,001 CE" would also portray the minutiae, gestalt and feel of our capsule's historical foreground in this New Millennium 2000 period. A multitude of personal testimonials, comments, and observations would be included in various media. More formal, objective cultural and historical data would be enclosed as well. A capsule devised by a committee, nation-state, region or organization would inevitably include contents characteristic of the sponsoring entity. Individual sponsors should ideally make room for groups' varieties of experience and groups make room for individualistic expression as well.

It would have a 10,000-year target span date. Our Global Village's years are now commonly chronicled in terms of decades, centuries and millennia. It seems logical to launch a time capsule project specifically for 10,000 years, the next factor-of-ten beyond just one millennium. To date, no such 10,000-year target-dated time capsule project has been realized, and it is time for humankind to actually build one. The Long Now Foundation proposed in 1999 another target date. Their thinking is to use the Tenth Millennial Year 10,000 for their 8,000-year-span Clock and Library project ideas. That would be a celebration of the Ten Millennium chronological notion, but not by literally aiming for a 10,000-year span time capsule span from our ca. "Year 2001" start date. There is quite often a functional correlation of time capsule time spans, sizes, sites and preservational complexities. Considerations of sites, size, content and preservational complexity should ideally increase in proportion to the time span between the deposit date and the anticipated target date of any time capsule. We have seen this with some of the multi-millennial grand "golden age" time capsules featured earlier. Putting a jar on a shelf for ten years or a copper box in a cornerstone built for only 50–100 years just won't do for a 2000 or 5000 or 10,000-year span time capsule's load. And why bother to send just a few trinkets or messages to a distant tomorrow millennia from now? Many external and internal specifics relate to factors such as site planning, time-span target dating, and the specific time capsule mission of a capsule project. A ten-millennia "Before Present" chronological milestone is probably a zero-baseline of civilization's beginning. From such an approximate beginning period of Neolithic proto-civilization, we can mark any current time capsule depositing era's *alpha* time point. Our contemporary era's *alpha*-start date can thus be readily bracketed as a midway time point between *zeta* zero cultural beginnings and *omega*, end-goal for futuristic target-dates thus spotlighting it on the historical stage as midway between the beginnings of proto-civilization and an idealized, futuristic endpoint landscape of civilization's apotheosis.

So a 10,000-year time capsule should not only be secure, but also exist in multiple copies and various formats distributed at disparate sites. Copies of the time capsule content should be redundantly stored in several locations and in several formats at each deposit. Thus an ideal project would require a wide number of multiple forms of redundant deposits and messages with at least two sites that are widely separated geographically. Of the minimum two secure physical deposit sites, at least one (or more) secure, inaccessible and one nearer a interpretive visitors center might maximize ongoing knowledge about the project. There should be at a minimum a secure, inaccessible site to enhance preservation and also a site near an interpretative center. This would also maximize ongoing awareness of the project. Obviously, we are asking for the Moon, figuratively speaking. But literally having a third such time capsule "copy-site" on the Earth's Moon would be a good idea too. And while we are on the topic of pie in the sky, transmitting the full audio-visual scan of our Ideal Time Capsule's contents as an interstellar beamed transmission stream would be a fourth redundant storage of content that would also illustrate the modalities of time capsule phenomena.

Serially deposited time capsule pods should ideally be added to the various Earth and Moon time capsule sites every decade or century until the year 12,001 CE. These capsules' repository sites should ideally receive incremental-cumulative deposit modules or pods for two reasons: First, the new deposits could not only chronicle the events, media and views of each decade, but also embody any state-of-the-art upgrades to preservational-interpretive features. This Ideal Time Capsule project would emphasize both a continued popular awareness of physical capsule sites and installations redundantly secured in several backup varieties of physical and digital modalities and copies. It would probably cost a fortune! In other words,"We have seen the future, and it is expensive" (author's maxim)! The *second* reason would be the ritual remembrance occasioned by such serial deposit ceremonies.

Preservation Redux?

A variety of electronic media and physically deployed copies of a time capsule's contents could boost the possibility of successful survival and transmission of the time capsule pod repositories' messages to the future. Every conceivable combination of multiple locations, multiple-pod sites, multiple media deployment and any other venues should maximize the redundancy of the whole venture. A digital electronic Internet-type copy or version of our time capsule repository's pods could be a fourth format for our Ideal Time Capsule's messages, writings and images. That would be in addition to acid free paper, polysulfate coated silver halide microfilm and the Norsam Technologies, Inc., type of "HD-Rosetta" micro-etched metal disc formats of a time capsule's content. The electronic access versions of the contents could reside on computing machinery platforms placed at two or more geologically separated sites. One of those would probably be best stationed at the visitor center for maximum interpretive and ceremonial appeal. As with all things to do with time capsules, security and promotion are in creative tension. One electronic platform at least should be accessible by the lowest possible number of personnel. Rothenberg's (1999) proposal to execute a perpetual series of digital emulations of electronic archives seems an obvious necessity for the eternal perpetuation of such records. A third electromagnetic venue is both more traditional and more *avant garde* at the same time: namely, an electromagnetic radio wave broadcast of an audio-video–formatted version that would reproduce a capsule's contents. This would include full written text and still images, as well as live-action video signals. This is just the "SETI *Encyclopedia Galactica*" idea that has often been alluded to both by astronomers such as Carl Sagan and science fiction writers such as Isaac Asimov. This vision of a "compleat" encyclopedia of an advanced civilization's understanding of the cosmos can be applied in principle to measure time capsules' comprehensiveness and comprehensibility. The SETI– type radio wave transmission format is another electronic form of time capsule content and a *fifth* format or mode for a time capsule. The mass expansion of the online electronic era since the late 1980s has added a new dimension to a classic type of site redundancy planning, including time capsule deposit site planning. Reproducing contents in accessible electronic-digital as well as the two-site physical media composition would provide such repositories with elements of both mystery and transparency. The author had posted recommendations along these lines to the Long Now Foundation web site discussion board (Jarvis, 1999a).

We should bear in mind a few basic preservational technology issues analyzed earlier in this work to specify the ideal specific preservational solutions for the perfect time capsule installation. *Four* distinct information media formats require rigorous preservational auditing to optimize their survival. Library-archival paper materials (such as books, journals and written records) require acid free paper and carefully balanced temperature-moisture-lighting facilities. Preservational grade *microfilm* ("silver film") stock, electronic-based *digital* computing media, and some form of *micro-printed* solid tablet-like medium, preferably onto a ceramic or synthetic-rock type of material, are four media formats which need to be considered in consignments for time capsules.

Ceramic artifacts as informational media have a particular aesthetic allure to both sender and potential receivers, along with their obvious durability and pedagogical utility. The 1940–8113 CE spanning Crypt of Civilization utilized some pictographs imprinted into its steel hull's ceramic lining, courtesy of the Chicago Vitreous Enamel Co. Although museumgoers can admire ancient sun-dried and baked-clay brick, etc., ensembles from Mesopotamian venues, our own age is not without the artistic technique to craft vivid, striking, durable images on ceramic tiles. They could be incorporated into time capsule "installations" that might tell even cartoon-style illustrative narratives for future recipients, perhaps complete with balloon dialogues. American art tiles demonstrate the artistic variety suitable to signify images for long-term deposit in some sort of time capsule site (Karlson, 1998, pp. 76, 91, 95, 109). Their beauty and the linguistic-cultural contents could endure for as many millennia as a site's security could permit.

Inside

Working on the assumption that the longer the time span, the more significant the contents ought to be, this imaginary "Ideal Time Capsule, 2001–12,001 CE" project should be as comprehensive as possible in its world cultural contents. While it is certainly unrealistic (and probably unnecessary) to detail every aspect of a comprehensive world-cultural content list envisioned for such a major time capsule, it would be quite helpful and interesting to delineate the basic parameters of such an "historical cargo-manifest." The informational media content could consist of at least five categories: a general declaration of intent and purpose, some generalized attempt to interpret multi-linguistically and multi-culturally the full spectrum of the Capsule, a full contents list (of media and non-media items), a massive, mega-encyclopedic compendium attempting to cover, preserve and present the whole range of human knowledge and practice in the world and of the world. This includes our understanding of the natural universe, and a significant sample of a variety of actual physical items, devices and artifacts. It would contain all sorts of things, as much to show the variety as to cover everything of our world.

Evoking sensory experiences from bygone worlds would be an interesting kind of time capsule content puzzle. If we could readily evoke realistic sights, smells, even tastes of all of the world's ancient cuisines, we would do so. Although the visuals seem to be doable with today's media technology, this goal could be quite an olfactory, gustatory challenge. As Fernand Braudel noted, having the ability to experience the olfactory aspects of a cuisine appears to be an excellent way to evoke vital aspects of a whole civilization (Braudel, 1981, p. 61). Earlier we had cited the assertion that an era's fully furnished house would ideally represent that past to a future time period. Such a house with a flavorful kitchen might be the optimum historical interpretive site!

We need to avoid creating a gargantuan conundrum. We shouldn't mindlessly pile up unwieldy blocks of items and data when attempting to represent our world period in a capsule. We must avoid absurdities such as trying to copy one's whole world on a ponderous 1:1 scale, like the absurdist map scene depicted in Jorge Luis Borges' "Museum: On exactitude in science" (Borges, 1998, p. 329). In that fable, the (now decaying) map once overlaid the whole country (Aizenberg, 1990; Bell-Villada, 1981). The mythical country is essentially covered by a tattered awning map! Even worse could be trying to minutely copy each time period's world on some attempted very large scale. The dilemma with any representational schema is how to represent the whole without growing into its fully identical twin in size, content or function. Just how big does something, a load of contents, a file, a time capsule or a museum, have to be to accurately evoke the essence of another world in sufficient contextual detail? This is easy to envision when the archiving facility is able to repeatedly go back and rescan through the to-be-represented world and abstract slices of it, like a news network doing video studies of human life on Earth. It happens regularly, and we are beamed the visual digests by satellite everyday. But what if we want to preserve a wide-ranging archive with a full scope of world contexts for 1000 or 10,000 years? How little can be enough of everything to essentially evoke all that matters? Ask these questions when doing your time capsules and you will probably hit on good compromise solutions. Of course people in Pompeii early on August 24, 79 CE, were probably just trying to save people and a few valuables. That whole world of Pompeii was of course destroyed then, but partially saved in terms of our times. Pliny the Elder, Admiral of the western Roman fleet at nearby Miseum, was trying to save a few acquaintances when he perished. No one was trying to "save" the entire city, and certainly not for a future museum exhibition 1900 years later! And yet the city was "saved" for 1900 years in a very different sense. We have a very rich archaeological record, a preserved residue of that extinct city. One does not know what "time capsules" our best actions will preserve vs. what will result from natural processes on our left behind discards and residues.

One hopes to be able to capture the *Fingerspitzengefühl*, or "fingertip feel," of one's own immediate "history" for the future to receive, just as one hopes to receive such a vivid, whole pattern of past lives and time periods. We noted the power of a museum item's perfectly new appearance to transport us across the reaches of time, the ability of buried extinct cites to act like a sort of time machine that takes people back into an earlier world. We have noted the value of worn or wear-patterned finds to archaeologists and time capsule transmitters. Being able to evoke a wide spectrum of feelings about past worlds should be the achievement of a good time capsule, especially a large-content one.

We should have the goal of accumulating time capsule upon time capsule upon endless time capsule: accretions of prior deliberately sealed and target-dated time capsules. Each deliberately targeted time capsule can be something like the world units envisioned in Leibniz's *Monadology*, where that seventeenth century continental rationalist philosopher posits that our world consists of innumerable "monads." Consider this metaphor of each mini-universe reflecting or manifesting a perspective on all others, and it is possible to conceive of a series of ten millennia targeted time capsules each containing a synopsis of one another. Then consider the prospect that each time capsule complex or facility would contain the full contents of all other older time capsules.

We would be building a comprehensive collection for any possible future's "ancient library." We have discussed the topic of preserving and thus transmitting writings from one era to another. Here we entertain a grandiose project in the preservation of civilizations' records, creating a vast repository of its vast writings and imaging on virtually every subject. Here we are finally considering what Ideal Time Capsule library and book information contents we should try to leave from our time for the distant future. Even more fundamentally, *how* we should try to do so. It is basically easy, and possible to attempt to save virtually everything written for some distant Future's study. How to do so may be more complex. Matters of linguistic and basic cultural contextual interpretation may be more challenging to us all, provided that something has first been transmitted!

In terms of content, of item selection, obviously a wide variety of encyclopedic works, magazines and comprehensive books, as well as a vast array of primary sources of all kinds should ideally be stored, preserved and reproduced. Two recent books out of thousands are *The American Century* and *The Way of the World* (Cantor, 1997; Fromkin, 1999). Works of this sort can be of great value in a major time capsule, especially if every conceivable author's viewpoint is represented in the collection of works included in the time capsule's "library." Perpetual reprography of written media, images and data are essential for a maximum of civilized development. Vergil's *Aeneid* had edged out Ennius' epic poem the *Annals*, when Ennius' work ceased to be reproduced (Highet, 1959, p. 262). It became lost to history as its older copies succumbed to the reuse, deliberate destruction and degenerative changes of its ink-papyrus media. When such works were no longer fashionable, they ceased to be "perpetually reproduced." Similarly, ten-year-old electronic files have fallen victim to the old format trap that we discussed earlier. If punctually and dutifully copied and converted, ca. 2001 electronic formats, software application versions or word-processed files would have to go through more than 100 major conversions to survive just 1,000 years. The obsolescence of its hardware platform, the going-to-failure of its hardware or software, or the physical durability of its installed suite are all possible weak points for a time capsule deposit. The Tower of Babel may be replaced by "The Iterations of

Babel." This may be the fate of an electronically formatted written work or visual image that is not taken out of the electronic reprographic cycle and converted to silver film preservation grade microfilm protocols or acid free-and-durable ink document media. The perpetual reproduction of masses of written records, image-rich frames or numeric data arrays will need to be pressed into the widest variety of media copies if the content is to stand any chance of survival. Obviously a lot won't, due to economics, concepts of utility, changes in taste or plain old short-sightedness. Any physical medium might go to failure due to its own make-up, or be lost through outside, human actions. Salt or limestone mines or dense ferromagnetic mountain underground sites would be desirable. Our earlier discussions of commercial archives, nuclear waste storage or archaeological finds of ancient salt miners are relevant.

Communicating

Leaving word, notification and the interpretive effort are key features of an ideal time capsule project. The notification of potential recipients in the year 12,001 of our notional ten millennia time capsule is probably best maximized by the use of several approaches— plaques on site, records distributed widely around the world, commemorative everyday "rituals" every ten to 100 years, and an alarm clock–type device. In regard to efforts to provide interpretive aids for future retrieval, the use of a full spectrum of options is desirable, especially since matters of cost are irrelevant in our imaginary project. Cybernetic, automatic announcement devices could in theory be deployed, or a multiplicity of written and imaged media and examples.

Commemorative techniques can be based on an Ise Effect associated with time capsule pod repository accumulations and celebrations. A second benefit of a serial deposit of decade-by-decade pods— a Time Capsule Symposium each decade and a wide deployment of the time capsule pod's messages and images— would be to maximize the institutional memory of humankind as to the existence of these capsule examples. The continued use of such sites and practices would succeed in leaving word across the millennia. This regular schedule of celebrations around the Ideal Time Capsule project will then serve as a way to promote the renewal of a time capsule's interpretive and notification capability on a regular, ritualized basis. These reoccurring celebrations would be at once a preservational audit, interpretive exercise and the occasion for the deposit of a new time capsule pod each decade. Essentially we should attempt to generate some contemporary analog of the Ise Effect discussed earlier. That effect could be approximated by accumulation of new time capsule pods, rather than a literal rebuilding of a time capsule pod repository.

This remotely possible future of multiple sited time capsule pod repositories, each with a 10,000-year target span for the initial deposits and with its associated institute of time capsule studies, decade-by-decade symposia, etc., would be costly. No social institution or technical installation has perpetuated itself or even just endured for anything like a 10,000 year span. We imagine our ideal time capsule installations would perpetually continue as secure deposits, tended or abandoned, displayed or hidden. It is worth considering this notional Ideal Time Capsule, 2001–12,001, for all the thought provoking self-reflection and technical assessments it can engender. That is true even if never realized in either a distant future retrieval or a ceremonial deposit event now.

Bibliography

The Interdisciplinary "Time Capsule Studies" Field

The first wide scholarly study of the variety of time capsule phenomena was a 25-page article (Jarvis, 1988). Most prior writings on time capsules were just brief popular press pieces or short books about a single capsule or a few other examples. There were also a few articles on the history of modern cornerstones and ancient foundation stone dedication ceremonials. *The New Yorker* had notes on the 1938 and 1964 Westinghouse Time Capsules.

Commemorative books and articles focused on a single time capsule sometimes briefly mention other capsules and provide useful details on their featured capsule. An example is the "Complete List of Contents," etc., in Pendray's 1939 article "The story of the Time Capsule." One (pre–1988) scholarly anthropology article analyzed artifact-wear and discard patterns and took an archaeological approach to dump deposit sites not originally intended for retrieval (Ascher, 1974). There was also a definitive two-page reference book entry on various time capsules (Berger, 1975, pp. 161–62). Not much research or analysis on general dynamics or comparative cases is published.

Work has been done on anthropological aspects of time capsules (Durrans, 1990; 1992, pp. 51–67; 1993, pp. 50–59). Synoptic, systematic studies on time capsule phenomena include Durrans' work and Jarvis, 1988; 1992a; 1992b. These few interdisciplinary time capsule studies are something new in world intellectual culture. Studies focusing closely on cornerstones, foundation deposits and (metallic) foundation plaques do date further back (Ellis, 1968; Mulford, 1950a; 1950b; 1952; Van Buren, 1931; 1952a; 1952b; Wright, 1970; 1982).

The study of time capsules is a research field in its own right, an auxiliary science of history. It is kindred to fields such as archival studies, technical archaeology, numismatics, diplomatics (seals), technical chronology, collective bibliography, general philosophies and histories of civilization. Documented records of these topics are filed in libraries under a broad "auxiliary sciences of history" classification of these types of technical historical publications (Library of Congress, 1975, p. 4).

Time Capsules, Cornerstones and Foundation Deposits: Terminology and Scope

Noting Time Capsules' Dates

We interchangeably use "CE" and "BCE" year labels with their "AD" or "BC" equivalents, unless someone's usage was quoted (CE="Common Era"=AD, while BCE="Before Common Era"=BC). BCE and CE use year counting identical to AD and BC conventions, but the "Common Era" labeling has more contemporary, multicultural, and neutral connotations. On occasion, "BP" or "AP" ("Before Present" and "After Present") may be also employed. Many other calendar schemas are available to humankind. We usually label those Common Era years chronologically near to our own ca. 2001 era as 1776, 1938, 2076, etc., without any CE, AD, etc. labels. These are recent or "local" dates, i.e., ones we are familiar with. Dates like "8113" or "2979" seem just like any one of many sorts of numeric data points. Since those dates seem far removed from our timeframes of reference, we give them their "*AD* 8113" or "2979 *CE*" labeling.

Time capsule sealing-depositing or receiving-opening years are often cited in this work as "1938–6939 CE" or "1940–AD 8113." We suggested the use of the term "*alpha* date" to indicate the "starting" deposit date of a time capsule and of "*omega* date" for the "ending" or re-opening date of a capsule, if it has one assigned. Some time capsules are of course deposited for an undetermined period of time, perhaps for infinity. If a capsule has no stipulated retrieval date, there is the distinct possibility that its custodians may one day be tempted to open it prematurely, before contents have acquired a maximum or even optimal antiquarian significance. Multiple depositing dates can sometimes be attributed to the same capsule. The Westinghouse Time Capsule I's inner glass tube was first heat-sealed at the Westinghouse Lamp Division plant, Bloomfield, New Jersey, on September 16, 1938. It was then deposited in an "Immortal Well," essentially a glorified pipe deep in the ground, a week later (September 23). It was exhibited at the 1939-40 New York World's Fair and finally "sent" in a well-sealing ritual in October 1940. It is targeted for retrieval in 6939 CE and is commonly called a "5,000-year" time capsule rather than a "5001-year" capsule. It's not uncommon for a time capsule to be finally deposited or even sealed sometime after its official ceremonial send-off date.

Multi-millennial midpoint date spans and timelines are significant in devising some time capsules' target dates. As we noted earlier, some multi-millennia–spanning capsules have target dates marking their sealing year as a culturally important chronological midpoint in world civilization. The deposit date comes mid way between the approximate origins of civilized activity and the fabulous, futuristic target date of the capsule in the march of civilization. In addition to the "depositing date=*alpha*" and the "targeted-opening date=*omega*" designations, multi-millennia–spanning time capsule timelines may utilize a third chronological milestone. We have dubbed this designation "*zeta*=baseline date of civilization," i.e., the earliest beginnings of civilized activity. Such an approximate zero-start zeta date is convenient whenever "midpoint of civilization" notions are associated with 5000 year or more time capsule spans.

"Time Capsules": A Subject Scope Note

The ephemeral character of time capsule news and the often-metaphorical usage of the "time capsule" term are obstacles to acquiring adequate citations on actual, literal, physical specimens. The vast majority of citations retrieved by the online keyword term searches of magazine and newspaper indices for time capsule(s) tend to be these metaphorical uses of the term. Many "time capsule" stories are about sunken ships, extinct cities, fabulous tombs or other *de facto, a posteriori* time capsule archaeological sites. Articles on time capsules tend to be either brief newspaper or magazine notes on one particular time capsule event. Many of these popular articles are repetitious, briefly noting the same four or five famous oldtime capsules. Occasionally a short descriptive feature article appears on major specimens, a few novel oddities, and some topical local capsule of some sort. Time capsules are rarely the subject of a scholarly or scientific analysis. The Wilson Company's *Art Index* and *Reader's Guide to Periodical Literature* are widely accessible (public library, online) sources of historical citations on building customs, cornerstones and time capsules in periodical literature. Two "how-to" articles that are brief guides to the practical, ceremonial aspects of cornerstone/time capsule laying are noteworthy: Brower, 1972; Foundation stone ceremonies, 1936.

Cornerstone Repositories and Foundation Deposits

We have not exhaustively surveyed modern non-repository building cornerstones, i.e., those examples without a repository chamber. This is because of their vast number and also due to their low correlation with today's content-laden repositories. Ancient foundation deposits were often discussed even if they weren't repository vessels with interiors and contents because of their seminal historical relation to contemporary cornerstone dedication and time capsule practices. The terms "cornerstone" and "time capsule" are often used interchangeably. If specimens or publications about them are not indexed as time capsules, they may appear under "cornerstone" ceremony or "building custom" terms. It would probably be better for such cornerstone repositories to be indexed as time capsules as well as under the entry "building customs." They are clearly something of both. At any rate, the public and the popular prints loosely use these terms interchangeably, regardless of the presence or absence of any given target date. Cornerstone examples might be found under "time capsules" or "foundation" ("-deposit" or "-stone") index entries. Researchers should also try search terms such as "building customs," "dedication customs," "deposits," "deposition" or "votive deposits." Those can yield relevant citations in books, journals, the popular press and indexing sources. Note especially Herbert Mulford's three definitive articles on cornerstone-foundation stones, deposits, history and ritual (Mulford, 1950a; 1950b; 1952). R. S. Ellis' definitive 1968 treatise *Mesopotamian foundation deposits* is a key archaeological work.

Key Sources

In addition to the general sources listed in each chapter's parenthetical citations, the following is a short list of key bibliographic entries on time capsule studies selected from *General Sources*. An asterisk (*) indicates *technical preservation* sources:

*Barclay, B. (1989, November 2). *Notes on time capsules. Report.* Ottawa: Canadian Conservation Institute/Institute canadien de conservation. Conservation Services *Report.* Updated November 2, 1989. Dr. Barclay is Senior Conservator, Historical Objects.

Berger, K. O. (1975). Time capsules in America. In D. Wallechensky (Ed.). *The people's almanac* (pp. 161–62). NY: Doubleday. This concise entry accurately describes several famous time capsules.

_____. (1990, March). *The story of the Washington Centennial Time Capsule of 1989.* This eight-page report of Project Director Knute "Skip" Olsson Berger summarizes, lists contents and includes a schematic drawing. The safety deposit set of containers are to be serially filed in the strongbox safe-type capsule until 2389. Berger, a journalist, was one of several co-founders of the International Time Capsule Society. See also: *Centennial Time Capsule fact sheet* (1989). Washington Centennial Commission Documentary Report, compiled by Maura Craig, March 15, 1990; Egan, Timothy. (1989, October 10). The art of burying a Century alive. *New York Times* [p.?]; With help from a cadre of kids, Knute Berger devises a time capsule that time won't forget. (1990, April 2). *People Magazine*, [p.?].

The book of record of the Time Capsule of Cupaloy: Deemed capable of resisting the effects of time for five thousand years — preserving an account of universal achievements — embedded in the grounds of the New York World's Fair — 1939. (1938). NY: Westinghouse Electric and Manufacturing, Inc. The Time Capsule as compliment to archaeological data is on (pp. 5, 6–7). The Einstein letter is on (pp. 48–49).

**British Library's National Preservation Office Leaflet: Time Capsules.* (1999). (Rev. ed.)

Brower, M. A. (1972, January 9). How to dedicate a building. *American Institute of Architects Journal, 57*, 29.

Durrans, B. (1992). Posterity and paradox: some uses of time capsules. S. Wallman (Ed.), *Contemporary futures: Perspectives from social anthropology* (ASA Monographs Series # 30, pp. 51–67). London & NY: Routledge. Anthropological aspects of time capsules in relation to social, futurist forecasting are analyzed. See also: Durrans, B. (1990, April 2–5). The dialectics of time capsules [Unpublished paper, *Ms.* copy]. *Anthropology and the Future Conference.* ASA Edinburgh, Scotland. Dr. Durrans is Keeper of the Ethnography Department, The British Museum.

_____. (1993). A box of tricks: collecting as magic. *Social History in Museums, 20*, 50–59.

Eliade, M. (1954). *The myth of the eternal return: or, Cosmos and history.* Princeton UP. (This classic has also been published as *Cosmos and history.*) A key history of religions study on the archetypal functions of time, history and renewal in archaic and modern societies. Hindu construction-foundation examples are on (pp. 18–19). Construction rites in general, including foundation rites, are discussed on (pp. 18–21, 30, 76–77). Boundary delineation consecration and symbolic world creation are covered on (pp. 9–11).

Ellis, R. S. (1968). *Foundation deposits in ancient Mesopotamia.* Yale UP. Fig. 35 and p. 103 discuss Esarhaddon's deposits. Numerous examples and analyses throughout this comprehensive work.

Foundation stone ceremonies. (1936, November 21). *Journal of the Royal Institute of British Architects, 44*, 1–85.

*Fraser, H. (1992). *The time capsule: Repository of the past or romantic notion?* (AASLH Technical Leaflet no. 182). Nashville, TN: American Association for State and Local History. A supplement to the 1992 volume of AASLH *History News.*

*Gorman, J. (2000). Making stuff last: Chemistry and materials science step up to preserve history, old and new. *Science News, 158, 24*, 378–380. Includes the one-page box: Gorman, J. (2000). Locking away tomorrow's history. *Science News, 158, 24*, 379. It features the "National Millennium Time Capsule," 2001–2101.

Hettel, J. N. (1952, 18 November). The cornerstone: its significance and ceremony. *Journal of the American Institute of Architects*, pp. 209–216.

*Hunter, G. S. (2000). *Preserving digital information: A how-to-do-it manual.* NY: Neal-Schuman. 2000. Hunter cites Rothenberg on (pp. 42–44, etc.).

Hyman, S. E. & McLelway, S. C. (1953, December 5). Onward and upward with business and science. *New Yorker, 29*, 194, 196–206, 209–16, 219. This somewhat irreverent article on the 1938 Westinghouse Time Capsule I includes some interview material from G. E. Pendray. It traces the genesis of the Time Capsule project, the coinage of the term "Time Capsule" and features excerpts from the 1938 *The book of record of the Time Capsule of Cupaloy.*

Jacobs, T. (1942, September 27). What will the world be like in 8113 AD: when the Crypt of Civilization is opened? *Atlanta Journal Magazine*, pp. 1–2.

_____. (1945). *Step down, Dr. Jacobs: The autobiography of an autocrat.* Atlanta, GA: Westminster. This autobiography by former Oglethorpe University President Thornwell Jacobs has a few brief diary entries about the Crypt project and reproduces on pp. 880–992 a number of articles and speeches about the Crypt, including T. K. Peters' January 1940 *Oglethorpe U. Bulletin* article and Jacobs' articles from the 1936 *Scientific American* and the 1942 *Atlanta Journal.* Transcripts of radio broadcasts and 1938 dedication and 1940 Crypt sealing ceremony speeches by Jacobs are reproduced.

Jarvis, W. E. (1988, January). Time capsules. In *Encyclopedia of library and information science* (Vol. 43, *Suppl. 8*, pp. 331–555). NY: Marcel Dekker. First major article approaching time capsule phenomena from the perspectives of a variety of auxiliary sciences of history, including archival, archaeological, ethnological and popular cultural aspects. The history and dynamics of deliberately deposited target-dated vessels and other categories of time capsule phenomena are compared.

_____. (1992a). The time capsule as a way for the future to acquire popular culture items. *The Acquisitions Librarian, 8*, 33–45. Reprinted monographically in B. Katz (Ed.). (1992). *Popular culture and acquisitions* (pp. 33–45). Binghamton, NY: Haworth.

_____. (1992b, summer). Modern time capsules—repositories of civilization. *Libraries and Culture, 127, 3*, 279–295.

Kline, J. (1958, May). Time capsules and what they hold. *The American Mercury*, pp. 80–82.

Merrifield, R. (1987). *The archaeology of ritual and magic.* London: Batsford. A key analytic survey of the vast topic of votive offering deposits and rituals. Many British examples since Roman times.

Mulford, H. B. (1950a). Research on cornerstones. *Wilson Library Bulletin, 26*, 66–67.

_____. (1950b, February 11). Noah also laid cornerstones. *School and Society, 1834*, 84–85.

_____. (1952, June). Adventures with cornerstones. *Hobbies—The Magazine for Collectors*, pp. 60–61, 75–80.

O'Connell, K. (Director). (1999). *Time capsule: Message in a bottle* [Film]. 53 minutes. Zia Films, Seattle, WA. <*www.bigfoot.com/~timecapsule*> The first full-length documentary exclusively featuring the subject of time capsules.

Pendray, G. E. (1939). The story of the Time Capsule. *Smithsonian Institution Annual Report.* This article was also published monographically under the corporate authorship of the Westinghouse Inc. as: *The story of the Time Capsule.* (1939). Pittsburgh, PA: Westinghouse Electric and Manufacturing, Inc.

*Peters, T. K. (1940a). The preservation of history in the Crypt of Civilization. *Journal of the Society of Motion Picture Engineers, 44,* 206–211. Peters describes audio-visual media preservational aspects and also some autobiographical background as the Crypt technical archivist.

_____. (1940b, January). The story of the Crypt of Civilization. *Oglethorpe U. Bulletin, 25,* 1–32.

**Preservation of library & archival materials: A manual* (3rd ed.). (1999). S. Ogdon (Ed.) Andover, MA: Northeast Document Conservation Center.

Preserving our history in a tomb. (1938, December). *Popular Science*, pp. 110–113. Well illustrated with time capsule scenes and gadgets.

Remington, F. (1954, May). Filing cabinets for posterity. *Think*, pp. 16–17. A typical, useful but very brief set of descriptions of various classic and odder time capsules.

*Rothenberg, J. (1995, January). Ensuring the longevity of digital documents. *Scientific American, 272, 1,* 42. Five-year digital shelf life discussed.

*_____. (1999). *Avoiding technological quicksand: Finding a viable technical foundation for digital preservation.* Washington, D.C.: Council on Library and Information Resources: <*text/html http://www.clir.org/pubs/reports/rothenberg/contents.html*> This RAND, Inc., expert's report analyzes various extant and proposed digital preservation methodology to cope with the key long-term preservational issues. He concludes that extensive annotations, fully digitized encapsulation, and complete, successive software emulation of digital documentary-contexts are the most cogent preservational approaches.

Rothenstein, J. & Gooding, M. (1998). *The Redstone diary 1999: Messages to a future.* London: Redstone P. This appointment diary is itself an anthological missive to possible futures, full of colorful illustrations of time capsule–type phenomena, and concludes with a 16-page "Supplement" illustrating, explaining and defining time capsule containers, effects and advice.

*Silver-gelatin film, etc. [Index entries]. (1996). In L. L. Fox (Ed.) *Preservation microfilming: A guide for librarians and archivists* (2nd ed.). For ARL. Chicago: ALA.

**Smithsonian New Millennium Time Capsule Kit.* (1999). Smithsonian Institution. Washington, D.C. Sale item #2025.

*Smithsonian Center for Materials Research and Education. (2000). <*www.si.edu/scmre/timecaps.html*> Smithsonian Institution. Washington, D.C.

**Time capsules: Archival protection.* (1999). <*http://www.simsc.si.edu/cal/timecaps*> Smithsonian Institution. Conservation Analytical Laboratory. Washington, D.C.

Time Capsules in the Modern World Symposium. (September 2000). Osaka, Japan: National Museum of Ethnology. [Unpublished papers and subsequent Symposium discussions.] Thirteen abstracts in Japanese and eight in English.

Van Buren, E. D. (1931). *Foundation figurines and offerings.* Berlin: Hans Schoetz, G. M. B. H., Verlagsbuchhandlung. Photographs of 40 such Mesopotamian figurines and offerings are provided at the end of this (English) text in Plates I–XX. See also Van Buren's: (1952a). Foundation rites for a new temple. *Orientalia, N. S., 21,* 293–306; (1952b). The building of a temple-tower. *Revue d' assyriologie orientale, 46,* 65–74.

Wright, H. C. (1970, summer). Metallic documents of antiquity. *Brigham Young U. Studies, 10, 4,* 18, 21, 457–477.

_____. (1982, December). Ancient burials of metallic foundation documents in stone boxes. *U. of Illinois SLIS Occasional Papers, 157,* 4–5, 17–18.

Chronology and Calendars at Our Turn of the Millennia: A Short Bibliographic Essay

There are a variety of related chronological topics pertaining to the recent "Turn of the Millennium" craze. The interrelations among the topics of popular and technical chronology are considerable, including calendar studies, clocks, the "Y2K Fear" (a modern, natural-technical Apocalyptic dread!), the history of ideas on Futurism, notions of Progress, dreams of Utopias, anti–Utopias, humanistic-naturalistic celebratory attitudes and various miscellaneous Millennial fixations. All of these ideas, rituals and areas of study are creations of what might be called Chronological Humanity. Here are a few to consider.

The linear sequential sense of time is a set of deliberate conventions. We humans know much of what we know because we know what time it is. That is how much of humanity's daily experience and formal knowledge is organized. The linear and cyclical frameworks of time are human-created frameworks that can be analyzed as topics of comparative religious and general cultural study (Eliade, 1954). We Earthlings are no longer even on Earth-based Solar time. Now our chronometrical framework of Universal Standard Coordinated Time is an atomic measured time mode based on the quantum oscillations of Cesium-based nuclei (Duncan, 1998). One satirical piece touts a fictional MIT announcement of a new conceptual discovery, "time"! This new protocol is praised as providing for the sequencing of (previously) separated events for the first time, instead of having all things occur simultaneously. This novel fourth dimensional capability is praised as a brand new conceptual tool, one appropriate for announcement at a scientific news conference. Time concepts are as-if conventions that are invented protocols related to cause-effect corollaries and "time's arrow" reversibility paradoxes. In a general psychological, cognitive schematic sense, humankind constantly reframes its experiences with various cultural interpretations (Goffman, 1974). This set of conventions are cleverly outlined in *The Onion*'s satirical "news brief" ("New 'time' to keep everything from happening at once," 2000).

Counting time in tens, hundreds and thousands has clearly led to a magical-like aura around discussions of millennial dates. The philosophical views on the year 2000's Millennial "omega" end-point range through a spectrum including Utopian, anti–Utopian, religious, naturalistic, numerological-occult, numerological-skeptical, mere calendar-adjusting and just about everything else (Gould, 1997; O'Neil, 1975; Stearns, 1996; Zerubavel, 1981). *Calendar* features an excellent bibliographic source section and has introductory pages with a "calendar index" of key human calendar-related events. There is also a "Year 2000 will be" page with 11 comparative calendar dates from other traditions, as well as an appended "Time line: a chronology of events: the Calendar." That whole Millennium 2000 hubbub was not just about the numeric content of three zeros just incidentally appearing in a particular year-date. A good visual sense of how bracketed our secular technological perspectives are by this approximately 20,000-year past-to-future time span can be gained by examining the National Geographic Society's 1998 map *Millennium in maps: Physical Earth.* The *Physical Earth* map charts the history of tectonic flow as well as providing several featured timeline inserts on the map. The map features a logarithmic, geometric historic-geologic time scale of "Before Present"-to-1000 year; then to 10,000, then 100,000; then to one million, etc., etc., years (National Geographic Society, 1998).

The scheduling of an observance of a special Leap Day in the Year 2000 was a 418-year communication project. That was a potential Millennial Year 2000 problem. The prospect of an *erroneous* observance of a Leap Day in the Year 3000 looms ahead, as a sort of Y3K potential problem. The Year 2000 is evenly divisible by 400, while the Year 3000 is not. That is the Millennial Leap Day test. Some computing machinery, software configurations and even non-computer chronometers might in theory have *mistakenly* registered the year 2000 as not being "Leap Day Year," (or "Millennium Leap Year"?), and erroneously omitted a February 29, 2000, date for the Year. (Few issued calendars actually omitted the required Leap Day.) Considering how to leave word about the existence of time capsule deposits and how to read their contents is a key difficulty when successfully transmitting a message or instruction to a distant future. Looking at how obscure time keeping conventions such as the Gregorian Calendar Reforms have been successfully communicated from 1582 to our world of the year 2000, the effectiveness of such long-term cultural transmissions is cause for hope. The year 2000 was "scheduled" to be a Leap Day Year (with a

February 29, 2000) quite a while ahead of time, when the Catholic Pope Gregory 13th proclaimed his calendar reform in the year 1582. The year 1600 was also decreed to be a Leap Day Year. The coming centennial years 1700, 1800 and 1900 were decreed *not* to be (what we will call) "Leap Day Century Years." That was one of several rounding measures to keep the ritual-paper calendar synchronized with the seasonal changes on Earth. Essentially this was done to align the ongoing calendar days of Earth's axial rotation with the solar year of the Earth's rotation around Sol. Arithmetically, the goal of these approximations is to keep the 365 date year calendar in close enough alignment with the (still approximately!) 365.25636042 (Earth axis rotation) day-length "sidereal," solar year. The solar year is of course one revolution of the Earth around our Sol (O'Neil, 1975).

The *first* rounding measure decreed was a one-time catch-up "Leap Season" by skipping ten days, going right from October 4, 1582, to October 15, 1582. Other one-time catch-up periods were utilized later when countries such as Sweden and England used (what we will call) a "Leap Season" to catch up the calendar to the progression of the seasons in the 1700s. The *second* rounding measure was one that we all know today. Every year that is evenly divisible by four that is not a century year is to be a "Leap Day Year," with a February 29 date. The *third* rounding rule was that only century years evenly divisible by 400 would be "Leap Day Years," i.e., have *no* February 29 that year. This is something humanity has to remember to observe once every 200 years, a rather difficult thing for human culture to do! A *fourth* possible future corrective rounding measure could really tax the collective cultural institutional memory we call historical recollection, since very little calendrical calculation is done in thousand-year units. That further ("neo–Gregorian"?) rounding measure will be required in ca. three millennia. Marking future time dates in this way was and is quite a message transmission feat, a time capsule type of phenomenon.

There is a vast literature of chronology, history of time and millennial themes. The literature on chronology and calendars seems as vast as the physical universe in which we project such concepts. It's possible to see the mythic dimensions of geological time concepts and to view the numerical significance of various millennial notions as equally arbitrary (Gould, 1987; 1997). Archaeo-astronomer Anthony Aveni has done a major comparative study of ancient Megalithic Great Britain's Stonehenge ritual complex, Mayan calendrics and Inca calendar keeping. These cases are sandwiched in between the conceptual frameworks of the origins of sky-time–keeping and of modern chronometrical developments (Aveni, 1997). Students of millennial chronology converge from a wide variety of disciplines. It's striking how many different disciplinary perspectives can lead to calendar and chronological studies, "traveling" from archival, astronomical, archaeological, folkloric, sociological, geological, computing, etc., perspectives into the same-shared zone of time studies. All those perspectives track the ways we keep, or try to keep, our socio-cultural time in a world of cosmic time-related processes (Richards, 1999; Waugh, 2000; Zerubavel, 1981). The Millennium Year 2000 was the occasion for a forest of activities or publications with a variety of views regarding calendars, clocks, other time-keeping methods and chronological concepts (Stearns, 1996, pp. 35–490). There are many studies on "technical chronology" and the history of calendars (O'Neil, 1975). One excellent work is *Calendar* (Duncan, 1998). Another work lists bibliographic sources on the European history of "historiometry" and the "quantification of reality." It covers ca. the years 1250 CE to 1600 CE, outlining that particular form of Western European linear-historical cognition (Crosby, 1997, pp. 75–93). Books of world chronology tables are excellent candidates for deposit in a time capsule, as well as useful sources in chronological studies. Classic historical tables include: Grun, 1991; Imhoff, 1998; Mellersh & Williams, 1999; Richards, 1999; Steinberg, 1991; Wetterau, 1990. The complex cultural development of human number manipulation demonstrates its high symbolic and indeed mystical aspects (Ifrah, 2000). We have commented on the numerological symbolism of three zeros in the "Great Y2K Fear." Numbers in dates, zeros in dates and the cultural systems of notations of numbers in commerce, science or chronology are symbolic and complex (Ifrah, 2000). Three zeros can add up to a lot, including a fear of zero, "The Void"!

References on Chronology and Related Topics

Aveni, A. F. (1997). *Stairways to the stars: Skywatching in three great ancient cultures.* NY: Wiley.

Crosby, A. W. (1997). Time. *The measure of reality: Quantification and Western society, 1250–1600* (pp. 75–93). Cambridge, England; NY: Cambridge UP.

Duncan, D. E. (1998). *Calendar: Humanities' epic struggle to determine a true and accurate year* (p. 16). NY: Avon Books.

Goffman, E. (1962). *Asylums: Essays on the social situation of mental patients and other inmates.* Chicago: Aldine.

Gould, S. J. (1997). *Time's arrow, time's cycle: Myth and metaphor in the discovery of time.* Harvard UP.

_____. (1997). *Questioning the millennium: A rationalist's guide to a precisely arbitrary countdown.* NY: Harmony Books.

Grun, B. (1991). *The timetables of history: A horizontal linkage of people and events, based on Werner Stein's Kulturfahrplan* (3rd Rev. ed.). NY: Simon & Schuster.

Ifrah, G. (2000). *The universal history of numbers: From prehistory to the invention of the computer.* NY: Wiley.

Imhoff, S., et al. (1998). *Timelines of world history.* Surrey, England: CLB; NY: Distributed in the U.S. by Quadrillion.

Mellersh, H. E. L. & Williams, N. (1999). *Chronology of world history* (4 vols.). Santa Barbara, CA: ABC-CLIO. Vol. 1. *The ancient and medieval world, prehistory–AD 1491.* Vol. 2. *The expanding world, 1492–1775.* Vol. 3. *The changing world, 1776–1900.* Vol. 4. *The modern world, 1901–1998.*

National Geographic Society. (1998, May). *Millennium in maps: Physical Earth.* The *Physical Earth* side of this *Millennium in maps* charts the history of tectonic flow, providing various timeline "boxes."

New "time" to keep everything from happening at once (2000, 14 April). *The Onion: America's Finest News Source.* Website: *<http://www.theonion.com/onion3614/index.html>*

O'Neil, W. M. (1975). *Time and the calendars.* Sydney, Australia: Sydney UP. An excellent concise tour of the history of calendar studies and chronologies.

Richards, E. G. (1999). *Mapping time: The calendar and its history.* NY: Oxford.

Stearns, P. N. (1996). Refining the calendar. *Millennium III, Century XXI: A retrospective on the future* (pp. 35–49). Boulder, CO: Westview. A balanced overview of many millennial-driven themes.

Steinberg, S. H. (1991). *Historical tables, 58 BC–AD 1990* (12th ed.). J. Paxton (Ed.). NY: Garland.

Wald, M. L. (1998, February 9). Leap Day 2000 might pose big problems for some computers' software. *New York Times,* p. C3.

Waugh, A. (2000). *Time: Its origin, its enigma, its history.* NY: Carroll & Graf. A history of ideas about time.

Wetterau, B. (1990). *The New York Public Library book of chronologies.* NY: Prentice Hall.

Zerubavel, E. (1981). The calendar (pp. 70–100). Sacred time and profane time (pp. 101–37). *Hidden rhythms: Schedules and calendars in social life.* U. of Chicago P. Approaches standard chronological calendrical issues from a sociological time perspective and treats Mircea Eliade's classic timeline-time cycle dichotomy from a unified social scientific perspective.

General Sources

Abraham, H. (1963). *Historical review and natural raw materials* (Vol. 1, pp. 17, 29). *Asphalts and allied substances: Their occurrence, modes of production, uses in the arts, and methods of testing* (6th ed., 5 vols.). Princeton, NJ: Van Nostrand.

Aciman, A. (1999, January 8). My Manhattan: next stop: subway's past [Leisure/Weekend]. *New York Times on the Web: <www.nytimes.com/>*

Aizenberg, E. (Ed.) (1990). *Borges and his successors: The Borgesian impact on literature and the arts.* Columbia: U. of Missouri P.

Allen, S. H. (1999). *Finding the walls of Troy: Frank Calvert and Heinrich Schliemann at Hisarlik.* Berkley: U. of California P. "*Ilion*" or "*Ilium*" as the site of

Homeric Troy on (pp. 35–47). Details deductive processes, etc. on this, controversial tale of the discovery.

Allen, T. B. (1999, April). Ghosts and survivors return to the Battle of Midway. *National Geographic, 195, 4*, 80–93, 100–103.

Allwood, J. (1977). *The great expositions.* London: Cassell & Collier Macmillan. Definitive chronological treatment.

Amadeus [film]. (1998). Warner Home Video.

American City Magazine article in 5000 year Time Capsule. (1965, February). *The American City*, p. 123.

Ancient stone tools found in Asia. (2000, March 2). *Associated Press via New York Times on the Web: <www.nytimes.com>*

Ancient tablets show Egyptians may have invented writing. (1998, December 15). *Associated Press via New York Times on the Web: <www.nytimes.com/>*

Anonymous master: portrait of a man and woman. (1998). *Art: A world history* (pp. 110–11). London: DK Publishing.

Apollo 11 goodwill messages. (1969, July 13). *NASA-News-Release-69-83F.*

Archaeological dig uncovers ancient race of skeleton people. (1999, December 8). *The Onion: America's Finest News Source. <http://www.theonion.com/onion3545/ancient_race.html>*

Archaeology for the Future now being sealed in Crypts. (1938, September 17). *Science News Letter,* pp. 179–180.

Archaeology news: Early Indus script. (1999, September/October). *Archaeology, 52,* 5, 15.

_____: Etruscan text find. (1999, September/October). *Archaeology, 52,* 5, 16.

_____: Roman shipwreck off Alexandria. (1999, May/June). *Archaeology, 52,* 3, 22.

Archeologist reverses job: buries relics of today. (1940, October 5). *Science News Letter,* p. 222.

Ark to the Future Time Capsule [Time Capsule Container Advertisement]. (1999, December). National Public Radio catalog. *Wireless,* p. 5.

Arnold, D. (1980, September 18). Captain Forbes had a noble vision. *The Boston Globe* [Newspaper], pp. 1, 8. Thanks to consultant Allen Large, Redmond, WA.

Arnold, R. J., & Ballard, R. D. (1990, June). The miracle of telepresence: technology meets show & tell. *Sea Technology, 31,* 6, 43+. Photonic telepresence technology expounded.

Art news in brief: time capsule. (1979, August 20). *Post-Standard* [Newspaper]. (Syracuse, NY), p. 11.

As time goes by. (1983, February 21). *M*A*S*H* [Episodic TV Program Series]. D. Wilcox & T. Mumford, Writers. Director, B. Metcalfe. <*"http://www.mash4077.co.uk/guides/season11.html"*> Website summary: "Hawkeye and Margaret encapsulate the breadth of their wartime experience when they bury souvenirs as a reminder for future generations."

Ascher, R. (1974). How to build a time capsule. *Journal of Popular Culture, 8,* 241–253.

Ashmore, W., & Knapp, A. B., et al (Eds) (1999). *Archaeologies of landscape: Contemporary perspectives.* Malden, MA: Blackwells. Various contributors' concepts of "conceptual," "mythic," "ideational," "ancestral" and "cognition" as categories of "landscapes" are presented.

Asimov, I. (1974). *The foundation: Three classics of science fiction.* NY: Avon. Contains the three volumes *Foundation, Foundation and empire* and *Second foundation.*

_____. (1986). Jean Marc Cote (Illus.) *Futuredays: A Nineteenth Century vision of the year 2000.* NY: Henry Holt.

Auburn Vets want new war memorial: $50,000 needed to replace wrecked monument. (1998, May 25). *Seattle Post-Intelligencer* [Newspaper]. (WA), p. B4.

Avrin, L. (1991). *Scribes, script, and books: The book arts from antiquity to the Renaissance.* Chicago: ALA.

Badawy, A. (1947). A collection of foundation deposits of foundation-deposits of Tuthmosis III. *Annales du Service des antiquites de l' Egypte, XLVII,* 145–156.

Bahn, P. G. (1992, January/February). Letters from a Roman garrison. *Archaeology, 45, 1,* 60–65.

Ball, S., Macarow, K., Nancarrow, J., & Whiting, L. (1999). *Experimenta Media Arts Time Capsule* [Personal information]. Various e-mail discussions between the author and Whiting *et al.* Experimenta Media Arts (*<http://www.experimenta.org>*) includes L. Whiting, K. Macarow (Artistic Director), J. Nancarrow (Development Manager/Executive Producer) and S. Ball (Project Coordinator). Experimenta's Time Capsule project is sponsored and funded by the City of Melbourne, Cinemedia, Arts Victoria, and the Australian Film Commission.

Ballard, R. D. (1989, November). The *Bismarck* found. *National Geographic, 176, 5,* 622–638.

_____. (1995). Explorations—my quest for adventure and discovery under the sea. *TLS, The Times Literary Supplement, 4819,* 27.

_____. (1998, April). Roman shipwrecks—probing the depths of the Mediterranean Sea, a nuclear submarine locates the remains of trading vessels that sank west of Sicily 2,000 years ago. *National Geographic, 193, 4,* 32–40.

_____. (1999, April). Finding the *Yorktown. National Geographic, 195, 4,* 94–98.

_____, & Archibald, R. (1991, spring). Discovery of the *Bismarck*: Germany's greatest battleship surrenders her secrets. *The Public Historian, 13, 2,* 85+.

_____, & Hively, W. (2000). *The eternal darkness: A personal history of deep-sea exploration.* Princeton UP.

_____, & Michel, J. L. (1985, December). How we found *Titanic. National Geographic, 186,* 6, 696–719.

_____, Spencer D., & Christie, J. (1996). Exploring the *Lusitania. The American Neptune, 56,* 74+.

Barcan, A. (1955). Records management in the "paperwork age." *Business History Review, 29, 3,* 218–226.

Barclay, B. (1989, November 2). *Notes on time capsules. Report.* Ottawa: Canadian Conservation Institute/Institute canadien de conservation. Conservation Services *Report.* Updated November 2, 1989. Dr. Barclay is Senior Conservator, Historical Objects.

Beckwith, B. P. (1984). *Ideas about the future: A history of futurism, 1794–1982.* Palo Alto, CA: Beckwith.

Beevor, A. (1998). *Stalingrad* (p. 173). NY: Penguin Putnam.

Bell-Villada, G. H. (1981). *Borges and his fiction: A guide to his mind and art.* Chapel Hill: U. of North Carolina P.

Bellamy, E. (1887). *Looking Backward: 2000–1887.* NY: Regent P.

Belluck, P. (1999, March 15). In angler's freezer since '62, fish may refute "extinction." *New York Times on the Web: <www.nytimes.com/>*

Benedict, B. (1983). *The anthropology of world's fairs: San Francisco's Panama Pacific International Exposition of 1915.* Berkeley, CA: Lowie Museum of Anthropology. Scolar P.

Benedon, W. (1978). Records management. *Encyclopedia of library and information science* (Vol. 25, pp. 108–27). NY: Marcel Dekker. "Time capsule" allusion (p. 109).

Benford, G. (1986). Time shards [Short story]. In *In alien flesh* (pp. 33–43). NY: T. Doherty Associates; Distribution: St. Martin's. "Afterward" [1 p.] covers the ancient background potters' wheel noises acoustical engineers have been able to detect. See also (Woodbridge, 1969).

_____. (1992). *Heart of the comet* [Novel]. NY: Bantam.

_____. (1992). *Timescape* [Novel]. NY: Bantam.

_____. (1999). *Deep time: How humanity communicates across millennia.* NY: Avon. A wide-ranging work. Pt. 1: Ten thousand years of solitude (pp. 31–85) dealing with nuclear waste projects such the U.S. Waste Isolation Pilot Project. Pt. 2: Vaults in a vacuum (pp. 89–134) focusing on efforts to transmit messages to potential extraterrestrial civilizations. Pt. 3: The library of life (pp. 135–68). Pt. 4: Stewards of the Earth: the world as message (pp. 169–201).

Berger, K. O. (1975). Time capsules in America. D. Wallechensky (Ed.) In *The people's almanac* (pp. 161–62). NY: Doubleday.

_____. (1990, March). *The story of the Washington Centennial Time Capsule of 1989.* This eight-page Report of Project Director Knute "Skip" Olsson Berger summarizes, lists contents and includes a schematic drawing. The safety deposit set of containers are to be serially filed in the strongbox safe-type Capsule until 2389. Berger, a journalist, was one of several co-founders of the International Time Capsule Society. See also: *Centennial Time Capsule fact sheet* (1989). Washington Centennial Commission Documentary Report, compiled by M. Craig, March 15, 1990; Egan, Timothy. (1989, October 10). The art of burying a Century alive. *New York Times* [p.?]; With help from a cadre of kids, Knute Berger devises a time capsule that time won't forget. (1990, April 2). *People Magazine* [p. ?].

_____, & Jarvis, W. E. (1999). [Personal information]. E-mail discussion of Berger's earlier visit to the Office of the Architect of the Capitol, U.S. Capitol Building, Washington, D.C. Berger observed that President John F. Kennedy appears to have changed (in the early 1960s) the U.S. Masonic societies' ca. 170-year semi-official participation in laying the cornerstones of U.S. Federal buildings.

Berglas, L. A. (1986, May 4). What's new in mannequins: Tracking an Era by its clotheshorses; greeting mannequins on the stairs; from Pharaoh's tomb to Fifth Avenue. *New York Times,* p. F19.

Beyer, L. (1998, July 27). Where, o where, did they put the future? *Time, 152, 4,* 14.

Biersdorfer, J. D. (1998, June 4). Chose some "good old days" and see how they really were. *New York Times,* p. 4.

Big party. Big headache? [Travel Section]. (1998, December 27). *New York Times on the Web: <www.nytimes.com>* Issue lists various millennial celebration destinations.

Blackstone, B. (1959). *The consecrated urn: An interpretation of Keats in terms of growth and form.* London: Longmans.

Bletter, R. H. (Ed.) et al. (1989). *Remembering the future: The New York World's Fair from 1939–1964.* NY: Rizzoli. Exhibition catalogue, Queens Museum, NY. The Museum was the "New York State Building" at the 1939-40 Fair.

Bloch, R. (1967). Life in somebody's times [Short story]. In *The living demons* (pp. 9–16). NY: Belmont Productions.

Boardman, J. (1973). *Greek art* (Rev. ed., p. 168, illus. #173). NY: Oxford UP.

Boatwright, T. (1994, May 29). Letters on travel: The Peak District [Travel Section]. *New York Times*, p. 18.

Boller, P. F. (1996). *Congressional anecdotes* (pp. 16–17). Oxford UP.

Bonfante, L. (1990). Etruscan. In J. T. Hooker (Ed.) *Reading the past: Ancient writing from cuneiform to the alphabet* (pp. 321–78). Berkeley: U. of California P./British Museum. Contents: J. T. Hooker, Introduction. C. B. F. Walker, Cuneiform. W. V. Davies, Egyptian hieroglyphs. J. Chadwick, Linear B and related scripts. J. F. Healey, The early alphabet. B. F. Cook, Greek inscriptions.

Boning, R. A. (1972). *The Cardiff giant.* Baldwin, NY: Barnell Loft.

The book of record of the Time Capsule of Cupaloy: Deemed capable of resisting the effects of time for five thousand years-preserving an account of universal achievements— embedded in the grounds of the New York World's Fair—1939 (1938). NY: Westinghouse Electric and Manufacturing, Inc. The Time Capsule as compliment to archaeological data is on pp. 5, 6–7. The Einstein letter is on pp. 48–49.

Borges, J. L. (1998). *Collected fictions.* NY: Viking. Two short pieces are: The fable: Museum: on exactitude in science (p. 325) and: The Library of Babel (pp. 112–18).

Borneman, L. (1990, October 16). Time capsule buried in Rauch. *The Brown and White* [Newspaper]. (Lehigh U., Bethlehem, PA), p. 2.

Botanists dig up weed seeds buried 101 years. (1980, May 12). *Chemical and Engineering News*, p. 50.

Bower, B. (1989, April 1). Iraqi dig uncovers Mesopotamian city. *Science News, 135*, 198.

Bowersock, G. (1999, April 18). Open house for the ancients. *New York Times* [Arts and Leisure Section], pp. 33–39.

Brace, H. (1938). Composition and properties of Cupaloy in the Time Capsule. *Metals and Alloys, 9*, 311–13.

Brand, S. (1998-1999). February 1999 posting: *<www.longnow.com>* Originally published as: Written on the wind. (1998, November). *Civilization Magazine.*

_____. (1999). *The clock of the long now: Time and responsibility* (pp. 81–92). NY: Basic Books.

Braudel, F. (1981). *Civilization and capitalism 15th–18th Century* (Vol. 1, S. Reynolds, Trans.). *The structures of everyday life: The limits of the possible.* London: Collins (p. 61). Olfactory-culinary adage is cited in: Wright,

C. A. (1999). Introduction (p. xv). *A Mediterranean feast.* NY: William Murrow.

Breasted, J. H. (1948). *Egyptian servant statues* (Bollingen Series XIII). NY: Pantheon.

Bremmer, J., & Roodenburg, H. (Eds) (1997). *A cultural history of humour: From antiquity to the present day.* Oxford, Malden, MA: Cambridge, Polity P., Blackwells.

Brereton, J. (1987). Sacred places. In *Encyclopedia of religion* (Vol. 12, pp. 526–35). M. Eliade (Ed.) Chicago: Macmillan.

Brewer, D. E. (1940, May 26). Oglethorpe Crypt sealed amid gloomy forecast. *Atlanta Journal* [Newspaper], p. 1. One of numerous articles from Atlanta, GA, newspapers. Another source of frequent news articles from the 1936–40 Crypt project days is *The Stormy Petrel*, the Oglethorpe U. campus newspaper.

Britain Building Millennium Dome. (1998, October 20). *Associated Press via New York Times on the Web: <www.nytimes.com/>* See also: *The Millennium experience* packet including: *The Millennial Dome* brochure, etc. issued by: The New Millennium Experience Company Ltd., 110 Buckingham Palace Road, London SW1W 9SB.

British Library. (1999). National Preservation Office. *Time capsules* [Leaflet].

British Museum (1999, November 11). [Personal information]. Faxed staff correspondence]. From Hillary Dixon, Ethnology Department, November 11, 1999, to W. E. Jarvis.

Britton, J. (1836). *Cathedral antiquities. Historical and descriptive accounts, with 311 illustrations, of the following English cathedrals. Canterbury, York, Salisbury, Norwich, Winchester, Lichfield, Oxford, Wells, Exeter, Peterborough, Gloucester, Bristol, Hereford, and Worcester* (5 vols.). The engravings, mostly by J. Le Keux, from drawings by E. Blore [and others]. London: M. A. Nattali. Vol. 1. *Canterbury and York.* Vol. 2. *Salisbury, Norwich, and Oxford.* Vol. 3. *Winchester, Lichfield, and Hereford.* Vol. 4. *Wells, Exeter, and Worcester.* Vol. 5. *Peterborough, Gloucester, and Bristol.* Stone laying at York Cathedral in (Vol. 1, p. 3).

Broad, W. J. (1998, September 29). Astronomers revive scan of the heavens for signs of life. *New York Times*, p. 1.

Brooke, J. (1999, March 26). Deep desert grave awaits first load of nuclear waste. *New York Times*, pp. 1, 17. Waste Isolation Pilot Plant in New Mexico.

Brower, M. A. (1972, January 9). How to dedicate a building. *American Institute of Architects Journal, 57*, 29.

Brown, M. W. (1990, July 13). Computers help fill in the gaps of Pompeii's past. *New York Times*, p. B 6.

Brunvand, J. H. (1984). *The choking Doberman and other new urban legends.* NY: Norton.

_____. (1989). *Curses, broiled again!: The hottest urban legends going.* NY: Norton.

_____. (1999). *Too good to be true: The colossal book of urban legends.* NY: Norton.

Building ceremonies. (1949-1950). In *Funk and Wagnalls standard dictionary of folklore, mythology and legend* (1972 ed., Vol. 1, p. 169). 1972 reprint of the 1949-50 2 vols. ed. bound in one physical volume. Index added (1972).

Building inscription. (1988). *A dictionary of ancient Near Eastern architecture.* London: Routledge. Features Mesopotamian building inscriptions and foundation deposits (pp. 38–39).

Bunker, J. (1966, November 23). Edwards records in a capsule: items stored in mine for historical evaluation. *Desert Wings* [Newspaper]. (Edwards USAF Base, CA), p. 3.

Burdick, L. D. (1901). *Foundation rites with some kindred ceremonies: A contribution to the study of beliefs, customs, and legends connected with buildings, locations, landmarks, etc., etc.* NY: The Abbey P.

The Bureau of Atomic Tourism. (1999). <*http://www.oz.net/%7Echrisp/atomic.html*>

Burrows, E. G., & Wallace, M. (1999). *Gotham: A history of New York City to 1898* (p. 923). NY; Oxford: Oxford UP.

Cady, S. A. (1990, July). The electronic revolution in libraries: microfilm deja vu? *College & Research Libraries, 51,* 374–86.

The Calendar. (1996). Johnson, O. (Ed.) *Information please almanac, atlas & yearbook* (49th ed., pp. 584–85). Boston & NY: Houghton Mifflin.

Cameron, C. M., & Gatewood, J. B. (1998). Excursions into the un-remembered past: what people want from visits to historical sites. Presented at the *57th annual meeting of the Society for Applied Anthropology, April 21–25, 1998,* San Juan, PR.

Caney, S. (1990). *Make your own time capsule.* NY: Workman. Book kit included plastic time capsule container.

Canfora, L. (1989). *The vanished library.* London: Vintage. Tales compared.

Canto, C., & Falin, O. (1993). *History of the future: Images of the 21st century.* The "Travelator," prototype of various "people movers," was a harbinger of the (at least envisioned) future of transportation for visitors to the 1900 Paris Exposition Universelle (p. 11, illus. #6). Paris: Flammarion.

Cantor, N. F. (1991). *Inventing the Middle Ages: The lives, works, and ideas of the great medievalists of the twentieth century* (pp. 28–39). NY: William Morrow.

_____. (1997). *The American century: Varieties of culture in modern times.* NY: HarperCollins. Rev. ed. of 1988: *Twentieth-century culture.*

_____, & Werthman, M. S. (Eds.) (1968). *The history of popular culture.* NY: Macmillan.

Capsule for 6939 A. D.: rubber objects preserved for posterity. (1938, October). *India Rubber World,* 99, 52.

Cardinal and Gray Column. (1957, July). *Technology Review, 59,* 506–507. News item describes the 1957–2957 MIT millennially deposited time capsule.

Carne-Ross, D. S. (1985). *Pindar.* Yale UP.

Centennial Safe [Brochures]. (1976). Title, two handouts, Office of the Architect of the Capitol: [1 p. , n.d.] and [7 pp.], Art and Reference Division.

Centennial Time Capsule fact sheet [Brochure]. (1990, March 15). 1989 Washington Centennial Commission Documentary Report, compiler, M. Craig.

Ceram, C. W. (1965). *Archaeology of the cinema.* NY: Harcourt, Brace & World.

Churchill library in 5 inch time capsule. (1967, January 15). *Library Journal, 92,* 182.

Clarity, J. F., & Weaver, W. (1985, June 28). Pryor's Dime [Washington Talk Column]. *New York Times,* p. A12.

Clarke, A. C. (1959). History lesson [Short story]. In *Across the sea of stars; An omnibus containing the complete novels Childhood's end and Earthlight and eighteen short stories.* NY: Harcourt, Brace.

_____. (1973). *Rendezvous with Rama* [Novel]. NY: Harcourt Brace Jovanovich.

_____. (1999). *A Space Odyssey* [Novel]. NY: New American Library.

Clarke, J. Popular culture and libraries. (1973, May). *College & Research Libraries, 34*, 215–218.

Clarke, S., & Engelbach, R. (1930). *Ancient Egyptian masonry: The building craft* (pp. 60–61). London: Oxford UP. Dover reprint (1990) is entitled: *Ancient Egyptian construction and architecture.*

Clock ticks twice a year; living cornerstone laid in Chicago. (1953, September 6). *Science Newsletter*, p. 148.

Codrington, A. (1993, January-February). Archives: time capsules built to last. *I. D.: Magazine of International Design, 40*, 22.

Coffin is a Corvette [Caption of a photograph]. (1994, May 26). *New York Times*, p. A12 (via *Associated Press*).

Cohen, B. (1989). *Trylon and Perisphere: The 1939 New York World's Fair.* NY: Abrams.

Cohen, R. (1986, November 23). What price charity? *Washington Post Magazine*, p. w9.

Collins, G. (2000). Mother lode of TV comedy is found in forgotten closet [Arts Section]. *New York Times on the Web: <www.nytimes.com>*

Collins, W. Our queerest building custom. (1931, March). *Pencils Points, 12*, 178–182. Journal title changed to: *Progressive Architecture.*

Compton's in the Year 8113 A. D.: Encyclopedia filmed for Crypt of Civilization [n.d.]. Chicago, IL: F. E. Compton & Company, [4 pp.]. Pamphlet from *Compton's* publisher, one of numerous promotional stories on the Crypt.

Condemns "despotism" in "Time Capsule" message (1938, October 1). *Science News Letter*, p. 215. Brief item on Robert A. Millikan's letter in: *The book of record of the Time Capsule of Cupaloy*, with the then-novel term "time capsule."

Contact [Film]. (1997). Burbank, CA: Warner Home Video. Novel by Carl Sagan.

Cook, R. M. (1972). *Greek painted pottery* (pp. 253–60). London: Methuen; NY: Harper & Row.

Cope, W. (1940, May?). Oglethorpe Curator expects to be present when Crypt is opened 6000 years hence: Dr. Peters believes people are reborn after their death. [Personal information: research file photocopy]. *Atlanta Constitution*? [Newspaper]. [n.d.; p.?]. Undated and unpaginated (apparent) newspaper article clipping-photocopy obtained from Oglethorpe University representative in the mid–1980s. Layout of clipping has photograph of T. K. Peters. Photocopy in author's files. (Oglethorpe University Archives, Atlanta.)

Cornerstone. (1901-02). In R. Sturgis (Ed.) *A dictionary of architecture and building: Biographical, historical, and descriptive.* NY, London: Macmillan.

Cort, D. (1959, November). Our ephemeral civilization. *Nation, 28*, 397–399.

Cowell, A. (1988, December 24). Grave yields Psalms: world's oldest? *New York Times*, p. 11.

Cox, R. J. (2001). *Managing records as evidence and information.* Westport, CT:

Quorum Books. Expounds the centrality of record management and archival administration to modern life.

Crashing into the Millennium Dome on a bulldozer and throwing smoke bombs, thieves expected to snatch 500 million worth of diamonds and zoom away in a boat waiting on the Thames. (2000, November 7). *Associated Press via New York Times on the Web: <www.nytimes.com/>*

Crowley, J. (1986). In *The world of tomorrow* [Film]. Directors, L. Bird & T. Johnson. Screenplay, J. Crowley. NY: Media Study.

Crypt of Civilization [Brochure]. Oglethorpe University pamphlet [n.d.]. It contains a large inventory of Crypt items. Atlanta.

Crystal, D. (2000). *Language death.* Cambridge, England, & NY: Cambridge UP. The general dynamics of the processes of language obsolescence are traced.

Dale, J. L. (1876). *What Ben Beverly saw at the Great Exposition, by a Chicago lawyer.* Chicago: Centennial Publishing Co. Fictional character visits real 1876 International Centennial Exposition in Philadelphia.

Daly, L. (1986, April). Dutch "archaeologists" with a heart. *Smithsonian, 17, 1,* 106–15.

David, A. R., Archbold, R., & Brand, P. (2000). *Conversations with mummies: New light on the lives of ancient Egyptians.* NY: Morrow.

Davies, J. G. (1987). Architecture. In M. Eliade (Ed.) *Encyclopedia of religion* (Vol. 1, pp. 382–92). Chicago: Macmillan.

Deiss, J. J. (1968). Roman luxury—the "Villa of the Papyri" (pp. 4, 8, 47–57); Houses and shops of the Plebs (pp. 94–99). *Herculaneum: A city returns to the sun.* London: Souvenir P. Earlier ed. (1966) was: *Herculaneum: Italy's buried treasure.* NY: Crowell.

Delgado, J. P. (1996, May/June). Lure of the deep. *Archaeology, 49, 3,* 40–42.

Del Tredici, R. (1987). *At work in the fields of the bomb* (illus. #101, text p. 189). NY: Perennial Library. Photograph captioned: Hiroshima Peace Park, August 6, 1985. Shows the granite cenotaph memorial deposit receiving added names on Hiroshima Day.

Denes, A. (1979). Rice/Tree Burial Project: ArtPark 1977–79. *ArtPark 1979 visual arts catalogue.* Lewiston, NY: ArtPark. Artist describes her time capsule.

Design is selected for *New York Times* Capsule [Arts Section]. (1999, December 2). *New York Times on the Web: <www.nytimes.com/>*

Deul, L. (1965). The Cairo Geniza. *Testaments of time: The search for lost manuscripts and records* (pp. 351–381). NY: Knopf. A wide survey.

Deutsch, R. (1999). *Mesarim min he-{176}avar.* English. *Messages from the past: Hebrew bullae from the time of Isaiah through the destruction of the First Temple.* Tel Aviv: Archaeological Center.

Dickson, H. (1988, May 21). Time capsule recalls WWI. *Boston Herald* [Newspaper], p. 12.

Diehm, Mrs. C. F. (Ed.) (1882). *President James A. Garfield's memorial journal: Giving a short sketch of his life, from his childhood to his death. With sketches and portraits of all the Presidents of the United States from Washington to Arthur* (pp. 194–200). NY: C. F. Diehm.

dMarie Time Capsule. (1998). *<dMarie.com/asp/history.asp>*

Donbaz, V., & Grayson, A. K. (1984). *Royal inscriptions on clay cones from Ashur now in Istanbul.* U. of Toronto P. Catalogue of clay cone, knob, bosse, pegs and nail foundation deposits.

Doresse, J. (1960). *Secret books of the Egyptian Gnostics.* NY: Viking. Texts analyzed.

Dorian, N. C. (1981). *Language death: The life cycle of a Scottish Gaelic dialect.* Philadelphia: U. of Pennsylvania P. Analyzes the demise of a Scottish Gaelic dialect.

Dowling, D. (1987). *Fictions of nuclear disaster.* Basingstoke, Hampshire, England: Macmillan.

Dragoni, G., & Fichera, G. (1997). (Eds) *Fountain pens: History and design* (p. 68). Antique Collectors Club: Suffolk, England. This Pompeii 1 AD era fresco variously titled "Portrait of a magistrate and his wife" or "The Baker Paquio Proculo and his Wife," National Museum, Naples.

Draper, H. (1963). *Ms.* found in a Libry [sic] [Short story]. In G. Conklin (Ed.) *17X infinity* (pp. 52–58). NY: Dell.

Drosnin, M. (1997). *The Bible code.* NY: Simon & Schuster.

Dukas, H., & Hoffmann, B. (Eds.) (1979). *Albert Einstein: The human side: new glimpses from his archives* (p. 105). Princeton UP.

Duncan, D. E. (1998). *Calendar: Humanities epic struggle to determine a true and accurate year.* NY: Avon. Caption to illustration: Early Greeks greet spring (p. 13). A comprehensive treatise.

Dunn, J. T. (1954). *The true, moral, and diverting tale of the Cardiff giant or the American Goliath* (2nd ed.). Cooperstown, NY: Farmers' Museum.

Dunning, J. (1999, April 13). Saving the human details of Jerome Robbins' art [Arts Section]. *New York Times on the Web: <www.nytimes.com/>*

Durrans, B. (1992). Posterity and paradox: some uses of time capsules. S. Wallman (Ed.), *Contemporary futures: Perspectives from social anthropology* (ASA Monographs Series # 30, pp. 51–67). London & NY: Routledge. Anthropological aspects of time capsules in relation to social, futurist forecasting are analyzed. See also: Durrans, B. (1990, April 2–5). The dialectics of time capsules [Unpublished paper, *Ms.* copy]. *Anthropology and the Future Conference.* ASA Edinburgh, Scotland. Dr. Durrans is: Keeper, East Asia Collections, The British Museum.

_____. (1993). A box of tricks: collecting as magic. *Social History in Museums, 20,* 50–59.

_____. (1998, November). Altruism and escape from circulation: the significance of BESTCapsule 2001. *BESTCapsule 2001 Symposium* [Unpublished paper]. Osaka, Japan.

_____. (1998, December 21). [Personal information]. Fax to W. E. Jarvis of miscellaneous ITCS–directed correspondence. Dr. Brian Durrans, the British Museum, Anthropologist, time capsule studies, and co-founder ITCS.

_____. British Museum. (1995, February 10). [Personal information]. Faxed cover letter to ITCS members *re* the *British Design Council Project 2045.*

_____. (2000, January 11). Re: What if anything has happened w/ the (British) *Design Council's survey of Time Capsules*? [E-mail response to author]. From: B. Durrans, *B.Durrans@british-museum.ac.uk,* To: *jarvis@wsu.edu,* et al.

Dwyer, J. (1999). *Subway lives: 24 hours in the life of the New York subway* (pp. 147–48, 234, 235). NY: Crown Publishers.

East and West: completion of the Great Line spanning the continent. (1869, May 11). *New York Times*, p. 1.

Easterman, D. (1994). *The Judas Testament.* NY: HarperCollins.

Edmonds to open, bury time capsules. (1998, May 26). *Seattle Times* [Newspaper]. (WA), p. B2.

Edsman, C.-M. (1987). Boats. In M. Eliade (Ed.) *Encyclopedia of religion* (Vol. 1, pp. 257–262). Chicago: Macmillan.

Egan, T. (1992). *Breaking blue.* NY: Knopf.

8 tips on how to organize a time capsule. (1999). International Time Capsule Society (ITCS). <*www.oglethorpe.edu/itcs*> (ITCS, Oglethorpe University, Atlanta.)

8113 A. D. (1936, November). *Scientific American, 155*, 259. Orson Munn's editorial endorsement of Jacobs' project.

Eiseman, C. J., & Ridgeway, B. (1987). *The Porticello shipwreck: A Mediterranean merchant vessel of 415–385 B. C.* Texas A & M UP.

Elder, W. (1956, January). Our own epic of man. *Mad* [Humor Magazine].

Eliade, M. (1954). *The myth of the eternal return: or, Cosmos and history.* Princeton UP. (This classic has also been published as *Cosmos and history.*) A key history of religions study on the archetypal functions of time, history and renewal in archaic and modern societies. Hindu construction-foundation examples are on pp. 18–19. Construction rites in general, including foundation rites are discussed on pp. 18–21, 30, 76–77. Boundary delineation consecration and symbolic world creation are covered on pp. 9–11.

_____. (1972). *Zalmoxis the vanishing god: Comparative studies in the religions and folklore of Dacia and Eastern Europe* (pp. 162–69, 170, 172–73, 175, 179–83, 183–87, 195–99, 204). U. of Chicago P.

Ellis, A., & Highsmith, A. (1990, May). Popular culture and libraries. *College & Research Library News, 51*, 410–13.

Ellis, R. S. (1968). *Foundation deposits in ancient Mesopotamia.* Yale UP. There are numerous examples and analyzes throughout this definitive treatise. P. 103 covers Esarhaddon's deposits. Fig. 21 shows an Ur III brick box for deposits and the final fig. 35 is a typological-histogram of all these Mesopotamian deposits.

Empereur, J.-Y. (1999a, March/April). Diving on a sunken city. *Archaeology, 52, 2*, 36–43. This is an article regarding excavations of Cleopatra's sunken palace.

_____. (1999b). *Alexandria rediscovered.* NY: George Braziller. The Sarapieon metallic foundation tablets are on pp. 27, 89, 96–97. The five-acre ruin field of the Ptolemies palace and also remains of the island Pharos Lighthouse, one of the fabled ancient "Seven Wonders of the World," is on pp. 62–85. Archaeological aspects of the whole Sarapieon Daughter Library site are on (pp. 96–97). The archaeological finding aid value of that City's nineteenth century Water Board archives is on (pp. 124–44).

Epicurus. (1937). P. Harvey (Ed.) *The Oxford companion to classical literature* (pp. 161–62). Oxford UP.

Erlanger, S. (1999, April 17). In Kosovo, empty towns, burned homes and shops. *New York Times*, p. A1.

Fagan, B. M. (1998). *From black land to fifth sun: The science of sacred sites.* Reading, MA: Addison-Wesley. Various time frameworks in the cultural life at numerous ancient sacred sites are on pp. 143–48, 146, 160, 165, 168–73, 228. See the Preface on the contrast between living folkloric informants and archaeological traces of ritual. Chapter One deals with Paleolithic cave paintings and possible rituals in Pleistocene Europe. The intriguing comment about clay figures in brick Neolithic house walls is on p. 96. Mound-builders of eastern North America are on pp. 184–219.

Family time capsule. *Holiday 1999 catalogue* [Time Capsule Container Advertisement]. Boston: Museum of Fine Arts, p. 49.

Field, B. P. (1989, May). U.S. history in a box. *National Geographic, 175, 5,* 652–660.

Findling, J. E., & Pelle, K. D. (Eds) (1990). *Historical dictionary of world's fairs and expositions, 1851–1988.* Westport, CT: Greenwood.

Fischler, S. (1976). *Uptown, downtown: A trip through time on New York's subways* (pp. 19–27). NY: Hawthorn.

Five million years to Earth [Film review, TV Section]. (1984, February 12). *Call-Chronicle Newspapers.* (Syracuse, NY), p. 54. See also: *Quatermass and the Pit* [Film].

5000-year journey. (1940, September 30). *Time, 36, 14,* 59.

For 8113 A.D. Oglethorpe University builds a crypt to preserve culture of 1936. (1936, October 31). *Literary Digest,* pp. 19–20. T. K. Peters in his January 1940 *Oglethorpe Bulletin* article credits G. E. Pendray as the author of this unsigned science section note from the *Literary Digest.*

For travelers, Y2K starts now. (1999, February 4). *CNN* website: <*www.cnn.com*>

Forbidden Planet [Film]. (1956). Santa Monica, CA: MGM/UA Home Video: Turner Entertainment, 1997. Newly remastered ed. on a 99-minute videodisc. See also: Stuart, W. J. (1956). *Forbidden Planet* [Novel].

Forsees our civilization rated barbaric by future: archaeologist believes clay records of Babylonians will give later scientists more favorable picture. (1938, October 1). *Science News Letter,* p. 215.

Foster, D. (2000). *Author unknown.* NY: Henry Holt.

Foundation deposit. (1988). *A dictionary of ancient Near Eastern architecture* (pp. 80–81). London: Routledge. Features Mesopotamian building inscriptions and foundation deposits.

Foundation stone ceremonies. (1936, November 21). *Journal of the Royal Institute of British Architects, 44,* 1–85.

Franco, B. (1969). *The Cardiff giant: A hundred-year-old hoax.* Cooperstown, NY: New York State Historical Association. Reprinted from *New York History,* October 1969.

Fraser, H. (1992). *The time capsule: Repository of the past or romantic notion* (AASLH Technical Leaflet no. 182)? Nashville, TN: American Association for State and Local History. A supplement to the 1992 volume of the AASLH's *History News.*

Frazer, J. G. (1922). *The golden bough: A study in magic and religion* (1 vol., abridged ed. 1958 reprint, pp. 1–7+). NY: Macmillan.

Frazer, M. (1972). *Ptolemic Alexandria.* Oxford UP. Major study includes many segments on the Libraries, including the Ship Books. Numerous foundation plaques are also cited.

Freudenthal, H. (1960). *Lincos; Design of a language for cosmic intercourse.* Amsterdam: North-Holland.

From Los Angeles of 1952 to Los Angeles of 2052. (1952, May). *The American City*, p. 7.

Fromkin, D. (1999). *The way of the world: From the dawn of civilizations to the eve of the twenty-first century.* NY: Knopf: Distribution: Random House.

Gallo, I. (1986). The Herculeanum papyri. *Greek and Latin papyrology: Classical Handbook #1* (pp. 36–45). Institute of Classical Studies, U. of London. Includes valuable inventory of categories among the then 1,826 papyri.

Garcia, G. X. (1991, January 13). Old safe-deposit boxes producing items of history. *Spokesman-Review* [Newspaper]. (Spokane, WA), p. H1.

Garrett, W. E. (Ed.) (1985, October). From the Editor. *National Geographic, 168, 4*, 421. This preface has the classic metaphorical comment on sunken ships as time capsules in that issue's article on the *HMS Pandora.*

Geer, R. M. (Ed.) (1964). *Epicurus: Letters, principal doctrines, and Vatican sayings.* NY: Bobbs-Merrill.

Geist, C. D., et al. (Eds.) (1984). *Directory of popular culture collections.* Phoenix, AZ: Oryx.

Gelernter, D. H. (1991). *Mirror worlds, or, the day software puts the universe in a shoebox— how it will happen and what it will mean.* NY: Oxford UP.

_____. (1995). *1939: The lost world of the Fair.* NY: Simon & Schuster. The Preface and the Bibliography on (pp. 269–70) list some key books on the 1939-40 New York and other World's Fairs. Use of fictional composite characters to narrate actual, factually based Fair remembrances is an interesting way to bring this lost, missing world period from the past to life.

Gerster, G. (1963, October). Threatened treasures of the Nile. *National Geographic, 124, 4*, 587–621.

_____. (1966, May). Saving the ancient temples at Abu Simbel. *National Geographic, 129, 5*, 694–742. Sanctuary solar illumination citation is on (p. 717).

_____. (1969, May). Abu Simbel's ancient temples reborn. *National Geographic, 135, 5*, 724–774. Foundation deposit ceremony is on (p. 728). Limited filling in of just the surfaces of cracks is on (p. 744).

Gies, F., & Gies, J. (1998). *A Medieval family: The Pastons of fifteenth-century England.* NY: HarperCollins (p. 3). Pastons' family archive from fifteenth century Midlands' English dialect of late Middle English.

A gift to the future: time capsules are preserving history for tomorrow. (1987, July). *Chrysler-Plymouth Spectator* [Corporate magazine], pp. 6–7.

Glantz, J. (2000, November 28). Testing the aging stockpile in a test ban era. *New York Times on the Web*: *www.nytimes.com*

Gleick, J. (1987, October 10). Air from dinosaurs' age suggests dramatic change. *New York Times*, p. D2, D7.

_____. (1999). *Faster: The acceleration of just about everything.* NY: Pantheon. The 1964 state of the art wristwatch is on (p. 39) and the "future packaging" world of commercial time capsule sellers on (pp. 253–54).

Glob, P. V. (1969). *The Bog People: Iron-age man preserved.* NY: Barnes.

Goddio, F. (1994, July). The tale of the *San Diego. National Geographic, 186, 1,*

33–57. That "archaeological time capsule" bears unexpected evidence of Spanish life then.

Goffman, E. (1974). *Frame analysis: An essay on the organization of experience.* Cambridge: Harvard UP.

Goldsmith, D., & Owen, T. (1980). *The search for life in the universe* (pp. 366, 369, 379, 381, 386, 393–97). Menlo Park, CA: Benjamin/Cummings.

Gone with the wind, a certificate returns. (1990, June 22). *New York Times*, p. A10.

Gorman, J. (2000). Making stuff last: Chemistry and materials science step up to preserve history, old and new. *Science News, 158, 24*, 378–380. Includes one-page box: Gorman, J. (2000). Locking away tomorrow's history. *Science News, 158, 24*, 379. It features the "National Millennium Time Capsule, 2001–2101."

Goudy, F. W. (1946). *A half century of type design and typography* (Vol. 2, pp. 195–196). NY: The Typophiles. A 2-vol. *catalogue raisonee* includes an entry on "Village No.2" typeface used to print most of the 1938 *The book of record of the Time Capsule of Cupaloy.*

Gould-Hilliard, N. (1994, September 26). [Personal information]. [Untitled] e-mail. Washington State University *News* posting of an open invitation to a cement pouring ceremony at Riverside Higher Education Park, Spokane, WA).

Gracy, D. B. (1977). *Archives and manuscripts: Arrangement and description* (Basic Manual Series, pp. 2–3). Chicago: Society of American Archivists.

Grant, M. (1958). Pt. 1. New evidence for the past: unknown people (pp. 58–63). Pt. 2. Art, politics, religion, economics (pp. 63–65, Plates 10, 22). *Roman history from coins: Some uses of the Imperial coinage to the historian.* Cambridge UP. It is easy to see the use of Roman Imperial numismatics in many of Grant's other books as well, especially after noting his focus on the theme in that title.

_____. (1982). *From Alexander to Cleopatra: The Hellenistic world* (pp. 38, 70, 138, 153, 197, 231, 254, 258, 263). NY: Charles Scribner's Sons. The period between the death of Alexander (III) the Great in (323 BC) and the end of the Egyptian reign of Cleopatra VII (30 BC) is analyzed, including the great Alexandrine "*Mouseion*" and the Libraries.

_____. (1990). *The visible past: An archaeological reinterpretation of ancient history* (p. 20). NY: Macmillan. Etruscan gold foil tablets, Chapter 5, #2, pp. 78–80. Vindolanda wooden tablets, Chapter 8, #2 (pp. 129–33). Hellenistic Egyptian papyrus finds, Chapter 8, #5 (pp. 141–43). See also: Appendix II, (i) (p. 179).

Graves, R. (1934). *I, Claudius: From the autobiography of Tiberius Claudius: born B. C. X: murdered and deified A. D. LIV* (pp. 3–13). NY: Random House. See also the scholarly reprint: Graves, R. R. Francis (Ed.) (1998). *I, Claudius and Claudius the god* (pp. 8–9). London: Carcanet.

Greenhaigh, P. (1988). *Ephemeral vistas: The expositions universelles, great exhibitions, and world's fairs, 1851–1939.* Manchester, England: Manchester UP. Distribution: St. Martin's.

Greer, W. R. (1987, February 12). New York takes photos of itself for posterity. *New York Times*, pp. A1, C8.

Grescoe, T. (2000, November 19). Secrets of the Paris Metro. *New York Times on the Web*: *<http://www.nytimes.com>*

Grossman, L. M. (1987, August 20). Future generations won't forget videos, Bic pens or catalogues. *Wall Street Journal*, pp. 1, 12. Interview with the author.

Haas, C. (1997). *Alexandria in late antiquity: Topography and social conflict*. Baltimore: Johns Hopkins UP.

Hafner, K. (1999, March 25). In love with technology, as long as its dusty: a collector tracks down antiques, but the paraphernalia of the Digital Age Leave him cold [Technology/Circuits Section]. *New York Times on the Web:* *<www.nytimes.com/>*

_____. (1999, April 8). Books to bytes: the electronic archive: research libraries grapple with the difficult task of preserving the digital present [Technology/Circuits Section]. *New York Times*, pp. D1, D5.

Harrington, P. (1999, March 7). UW time capsule spans yawning gap. *Seattle Times* [Newspaper]. (WA), p. B2.

Harrison, H. A. (1985, July 11). 20-year perspective on World's Fairs. *New York Times*, p. C3.

_____. (Ed.) (1980). *Dawn of a new day*. NY: HarperCollins.

Harrison, J. E. (1962). *Epilegomena to the study of Greek religion, and: Themis; A study of the social origins of Greek religion* (1st American ed., p. 98, Fig. 15). New Hyde Park, NY: University Books.

Hazzard, S. (1983, August 29). Our far-flung correspondents: papyrology at Naples. *New Yorker, 59*, 81.

_____. (1987, May 10). Quest for a fabled ancient library. *New York Times*, pp. H1, 34.

Henniger, J. (1987). Sacrifice. In M. Eliade (Ed.) *Encyclopedia of religion* (Vol. 12, pp. 544–557). Chicago: Macmillan.

Hettel, J. N. (1952, 18 November). The cornerstone: its significance and ceremony. *Journal of the American Institute of Architects*, pp. 209–216.

Higham, N. (2001, January 2). Nick Higham on why the Millennium Dome really went wrong. *BBC News*: *<http://news.bbc.co.uk/hi/english/static/in_depth/world/2000/review_of_the_year/jan.stm>*

Highet, G. (1965). The survival of records (pp. 257–75). *The light of the past*. NY: American Heritage. This renowned scholar and interpreter's fundamental essay on the survivability of written records, primarily from the Greco-Roman classical tradition, has been published in a variety of slightly different layouts over the years. Citations here are from *Light*. Highet's: The survival of records (pp. 290–311) also appears in the anthological work: G. Highet (Ed.) (1979). *The discovery of lost worlds*. NY: American Heritage. Citations include the following:

_____. Kush, Iraq tablet image (p. 257).

_____. (1965). Vergil's *Aeneid* edging out Ennius' epic poem the *Annals* (p. 262).

_____. (1965). "Complete Pindar" anecdote (pp. 262, 273).

_____. (1965). Hypothetical analogy of microfilm replacing paper cited. Today the joint access-preservation issue is digital electronic-based computation media vs. paper-based written media (p. 265).

_____. (1965). Aristotle's missing work analyzing comedy (p. 268).

_____. (1965). Pindar's *Victory Odes* (p. 271).

_____. (1965). Time capsule metaphor regarding the container of a previously lost Greek comedy (p. 270).

_____. (1965). Epicurus' principles inscribed on a monument (p. 272).

Hine, T. (1986). *Populuxe* (pp. 101–02). NY: Knopf.

Hiss Grand Jury archive ordered unsealed. (1999, May 13). *Associated Press via New York Times on the Web: <www.nytimes.com/>*

Histories of the future: Studies in fact, fantasy and science fiction. (2000). A. Sandison & R. Dingley. (Eds) NY: Palgrave.

History of the Doomsday Clock. (1999). Posted on: *The Bulletin of Atomic Scientists. http://www.bullatomsci.org/clock.html*

Hoban, R. (1980). *Riddley Walker* [Novel]. London: Picador.

Hoffman, E. (1999, December 26). Time and again: counting the years to make sense out of Life. *New York Times on the Web: <www.nytimes.com/>*

Hoffmann, F. W. (1984). *Popular culture and libraries* (pp. vii–9, 16–20). Hamden, CT: Library Professional Publications.

Hogan, J. P. (1939, February). Up from the ashes: New York World's Fair 1939 a glittering Cinderella...engineering difficulties of filling in and building upon ash-filled swamp muck. *Scientific American, 160,* 76–78.

Hoge, W. (1999, September 12). A changed Thames and a Millennium Dome. *New York Times,* p. 13+.

Hood, C. (1993). *722 miles: The building of the subways and how they transformed New York* (pp. 42–48, 50, 78). NY: Simon & Schuster.

Hornung, E. (1999). *The ancient Egyptian books of the afterlife* (D. Lorton, Trans.). Ithaca, NY: Cornell UP.

Howgego, C. (1995). *Ancient history from coins* (p. 4). London & NY: Routledge. Votive foundation deposit of coins from sixth century BCE Persepolis.

Hoyle, F., & Elliot, J. (1962). *A for Andromeda* [Novel]. Greenwich, CT: Fawcett.

Hudson, P. S. (1991, spring). Georgia history in pictures: The "archaeological duty" of Thornwell Jacobs: the Oglethorpe Atlanta Crypt of Civilization Time Capsule. *The Georgia Historical Quarterly, LXXV, 1,* 121–138. Brief prefatory remarks and 22 captioned photographs.

_____. (1998, fall). Notes and documents: "the end of the world — and after": the cosmic history millenarianism of Thornwell Jacobs. *Georgia Historical Quarterly, LXXXII, 3,* 594–607. Essay expounding the significance of President Thornwell Jacob's Cosmic History course for senior students at Oglethorpe U. in the 1930s and 1940s, including syllabus and essay questions.

Hughes, M. A., & Jarvis, W. E. (1999, summer). [Personal information]. Inspection: M. A. Hughes, Neill Public Librarian and this author at capsules' site, Neill Public Library, Pullman, WA.

Hunter, G. S. (2000). *Preserving digital information: A how-to-do-it manual.* NY: Neal-Schuman. 2000. Rothenberg is cited on (pp. 42–44+).

Hus, A. (1961). *The Etruscans* (J. U. Duell, Trans., pp. 77–86). NY: Grove. The slim amount of their written record is discussed throughout.

Hyman, S. E., & McLelway, S. C. (1953, December 5). Onward and upward with business and science. *New Yorker, 29,* 194, 196–206, 209–16, 219. This irreverent article on the 1938 Westinghouse Time Capsule of Cupaloy includes interview material with Pendray, traces the genesis of the Time Capsule and coinage of the term Time Capsule and it excerpts the 1938 *The book of record of the Time Capsule of Cupaloy.*

In Illinois: cigars and bottled history. (1979, December 17). *Time, 114, 25,* 8, 9, 12. Presumably the "Time Capsule" label is a modern one for this deposit of relics.

In West New York, a time capsule is proving to be an elusive buried treasure. (1998, April 12). *New York Times,* p. A17.

International Time Capsule Society. (1999). ITCS website: <*www.oglethorpe.edu/itcs*> ITCS, Oglethorpe University, Atlanta. A variety of time capsule, Society, and Crypt of Civilization information postings are featured.

Iron Mountain/National Underground Storage, Inc. (1999). *http://www.national-underground.com*

Ise Daijingu. (1979). *Jingu: The grand shrine of Ise.* [Ise?]: The Shrine.

Ise Shrine. (1983). *Kodansha encyclopedia of Japan* (Vol. 3, pp. 338–39). Tokyo: Kodansha International.

It's hooray for Hollywood. (1987, January 30). *Boston-Herald* [Newspaper], p. 11.

Jackson, S. L. (1974). *Libraries and librarianship in the West: A brief history.* NY: McGraw-Hill. Ashurbanipal's ancient library at Nineveh on (pp. 4–5). Alexandrian libraries on (pp. 9–17). Pergamon Library of Asia Minor on (pp. 17–18).

Jacobs, T. (1936, November). Today-tomorrow: archaeology in A. D. 8113: preserving records for posterity. *Scientific American, 155,* 260–61.

_____. (1942, September 27). What will the World be like in 8113 A. D.: when the Crypt of Civilization is opened? *Atlanta Journal Magazine,* pp. 1–2.

_____. (1945). *Step down, Dr. Jacobs: The autobiography of an autocrat.* Atlanta: Westminster. This autobiography of former Oglethorpe University President Thornwell Jacobs has a few brief diary entries about the Crypt project. It also contains (on pp. 880–992) articles and speeches about the Crypt, including T. K. Peters' January 1940 *Oglethorpe U. Bulletin* article, Jacobs' 1936 *Scientific American* "call" and his 1942 *Atlanta Journal* article. Transcripts of his 1937 NBC national radio broadcast and 1940 Crypt sealing ceremony speeches are included.

Japan Information Network Website link to: <*http://210.235.30.41/atlas/architecture/arc09.html*>, 1999.

Jarvis, A. C. H. (1996, August 19). [Personal information]. [*Untitled* postcard]. Cassini Program submittal. Author's research photocopy of postcard submittal by the author's ten-year-old daughter Anna with this message: "Please put my name on the Cassini Probe's CD-ROM." Mailed to: Cassini Program, JPL, Pasadena, CA 91109.

Jarvis, W. E. (1979, August 1). [Personal information]. Author's inspection of site and plaque, MONY Plaza, Syracuse, NY.

_____. (1985, winter). Do not open until 8113 A. D.: the Oglethorpe Crypt and other time capsules. *World's Fair,* pp. 1–4. Apparently the first published discussion of the priority aspects of the 1935–40 time capsule period, with the exception of Peters (1940b) and Jacobs (1945) brief comments. See also the detailed discussion in Jarvis, 1988, pp. 338–40.

_____. (1987a). [Personal information]. Discussion between author and (now deceased) informant about the late 1930s Time Capsule of Cupaloy project. The informant claimed no awareness of the Crypt of Civilization until 1987!

_____. (1988, January). Time capsules. In *Encyclopedia of library and information science* (Vol. 43, *Suppl. 8*, pp. 331–555). NY: Marcel Dekker. First major article approaching time capsule phenomena from the perspectives of a variety of auxiliary sciences of history, including archival, archaeological, ethnological and popular cultural aspects. The history and dynamics of deliberately deposited target-dated vessels and other categories of time capsule phenomena are compared.

_____. (1990-1991). Washington State University Time Capsule, 1990–AD 2040 Project [Personal information: Project notes]. Pullman, WA. Various in-house activities, consultations, and files of the author.

_____. (1991, April). *A three-minute history of time capsules* [Personal information: Speech notes]. Author's Crimson and Gray Founder's Day speech at the WSU Centennial Time Capsule, 1990–2040 sealing.

_____. (1992a). The time capsule as a way for the future to acquire popular culture items. *The Acquisitions Librarian, 8*, 33–45. Reprinted monographically in B. Katz (Ed.). (1992). *Popular culture and acquisitions* (pp. 33–45). Binghamton, NY: Haworth.

_____. (1992b, summer). Modern time capsules—repositories of civilization. *Libraries and Culture, 127, 3*, 279–295.

_____. (1993a). [Personal information]. Authors inspections and oral history interpretive presentations by tour guides, June 1993 at two St. Louis Parish cemeteries, New Orleans, LA.

_____. (1993b). [Personal information]. Attendance by the author at the official footrace and groundbreaking ceremony of the Atlanta (GA) 1996 Olympics Stadium site, Saturday, July 11, 1993.

_____. (1997, October 14). [Personal information]. Public service time capsule project of the author at Neill Public Library, Pullman, WA 99163.

_____. (1999a). *Long Now Foundation Website discussion boards* [E-mail]. Posting to *<www.longnow.org>*

_____. (1999b). [Personal information]. E-mail & telephone consultations with America Online Inc. Special Projects staff, March 1999-ongoing. Also including other International Time Capsule Society, (Oglethorpe University, Atlanta) member-consultants.

_____. 1999c). [Personal information]. E-mail discussions between the author and staff]. Experimenta Media Arts. *<http://www.experimenta.org>*

_____, & Marak, T. (1987, October 31). [Personal information: Speech & project notes]. The author helped project organizer Tom Marak pack the Troy Hill Capsule on October 31, 1987, and speaker-participant at closing ceremonies on November 1, 1987. We served as Troy Hill Time Capsule, November 1, 1987–November 1, 2037, project general advisor for that Pittsburgh, Pennsylvania, neighborhood time capsule, 1987.

_____, & Perino, S. E. (1986, March 10) [Personal information]. Correspondence from Perino at the Boston U. Medical Center Library in response to author's earlier time capsule query.

_____, Hudson, P., & other ITCS members. [Personal information: Millennial discussions *via* e-mail]. (1998-1999). Miscellaneous discussions, e-mails, communications and consultations.

Jequier, G. (1924). *Manuel d' archeologie egyptienne* (pp. 33–60). See esp.: Rites de foundation d'un temple (figs. 10–13). Paris: August Picard. Those four frames illustrate the sequence of an ancient Egyptian foundation dedication ceremony. After: de Rochemonteix, M., & Chassinat, E. (1884, decembre). *Le temple d'Edfou. Vol. X: Memoires ... de la Mission archaelogique francaise au Caire* (Plate XL, b. c. d. e.). Paris.

Jingu, the grand shrine of Ise. (1970?, 1979). Japan: Grand Shrine Office, Kogeisha.

Jinkins, F. (2000, February 7). *Update on Opening of the Sharpstown, TX Time Capsule* Personal information]. E-mails from Sharpstown Civic Association, Member of the Planning Committee for the Opening of the "Sharpstown Time Capsule" *hapyom@yahoo.com* Sharpstown, TX, to W. E. Jarvis, E-mail from Hendricks, Mary Kay (2000, February 8). *RE: Sharpstown Time Capsule Opening* [E-mail]. Sharpstown, TX, to W. E. Jarvis.

Johnson, E. D. (1970). *History of libraries in the Western world.* Scarecrow. Libraries of Alexandria on (pp. 54–61) and the ancient library at Pergamon on (pp. 61–62).

Johnson, G. (2000, December 31). The Future is coming faster: "A virtual space odyssey." *New York Times on the Web: <www.nytimes.com>*

Johnson, T., & Bird, L. (1984). *The World of Tomorrow* [Film]. 78-minute documentary of the 1939-40 New York World's Fair, Media Study/Buffalo, NY.

Jonas, H. (1963). *The Gnostic religion: The message of the alien God and the beginnings of Christianity* (2nd ed. enlarged). Boston: Beacon P. The classic treatise-sourcebook.

Journey into time: the Time Capsule buried in 1938 on the site of the New York World's Fair has now passed ten of its 5001 years underground. (1948, autumn). *Archaeology, 1,* 165–68.

Kale, P. (1959). *The Cairo Geniza* (2nd ed.). Oxford: Blackwells.

Kamiizumi, Y. (1998, February 21). For some Eternity, time capsules in Antarctica [Arts Section]. *New York Times on the Web: <www.nytimes.com/>*

Karlson, N. (1998). *American art tile, 1876–1941* (pp. 76, 91, 95, 109). NY: Rizzoli.

Keats, J. Ode on a Grecian urn. In E. R. Wasserman (Ed.) (1953). *The finer tone: Keats' major poems* (pp. 11–12). Baltimore: Johns Hopkins UP.

Kellerman, L. S. (1999, July). Combating whole-book deterioration: the rebinding program & mass deacidification program at the Penn State U. Libraries. *Library Resources & Technical Services, 43, 3,* 170–77.

Kemp, P. (1997). *U-boats destroyed: German submarine losses in the World Wars.* Annapolis, MD: Naval Institute P.

Kenyon, F. G. (1970). *The palaeography of Greek papyri* (pp. 3–5, 32–33, 70–79). Chicago: Argonaut Publishers. Reprint of the 1898 classic. Herculeanum papyri discussions, stylistic descriptions, finds, techniques and scholarship.

Kern, E. P. H. (1979, April 22). A "time capsule" from ancient Rome. *New York Times,* pp. C1, C13.

Kidder, J. T. (1985). *House* (pp. 140–43). Boston: Houghton Mifflin.

Kihlstedt, F. T. (1986). Utopia realized: the world's fairs of the 1930's. In J. J. Corn (Ed.) *Imagining tomorrow* (pp. 97–118). MIT P.

Kimball, G. (1966). *The Cardiff Giant.* NY: Dwell, Sloan, and Pearce.

Kimmel, A. (1979, March). When news is not news: a psychological look at rumor in the media. (March 1979). Paper presented at the *1979 Conference on Culture and Communication*. Philadelphia.

_____. (1985, March). The ethics of gossip: the right to know versus the right to privacy. Paper presented at the *56th meeting of the Eastern Psychological Association*. Boston.

_____. (1989, June). Psychological correlates of the transmission and acceptance of rumors about AIDS. Research presented at the *V International Conference on AIDS*. Montreal, Quebec, Canada.

_____. (1993, October). Rumor in the marketplace. Paper presented at the *Joint Seminar of ESSEC, HEC, and INSEAD*, Cergy-Pontoise, France.

_____. (1997). Managing marketplace rumors. *Keystone: The International Business Administration Publication of the American U. of Paris, 7*, 8–11.

_____. (1999). Commercial rumors: The role of the media. Paper presented for the symposium *Commercial rumors: What makes them come — and what makes them go?* 23rd International Congress of Applied Psychology, Madrid, Spain.

_____, & Keefer, R. (1991). Psychological correlates of the transmission and acceptance of rumors about AIDS. *Journal of Applied Social Psychology, 21*, 1608–28.

_____, & Levin, J. (1979). Gossip columns: media small talk. *Journal of Communication, 27*, 169–75. Reprinted in: Gray, W. S. (1979). *Research collection in reading*. Alvina Treut Burrows Institute.

_____, & Rosnow, R. L. (1979, December). Lives of a rumor. *Psychology Today*, pp. 88–92. (Reprinted in part as: Roots of rumors. (1979, December). *Reader's Digest*.

_____, & Rosnow, R. L. (2000). Rumors. *Encyclopedia of psychology*. Washington, D.C.: American Psychological Association.

Kirkpatrick, D. D. (2000, December 17). The literary puzzle involving a certain jolly old elf. *New York Times on the Web: www.nytimes.com*

Kitagawa, J.M. (1987). Japanese religion: an overview. In M. Eliade (Ed.) *Encyclopedia of religion* (Vol. 7, p. 530). Chicago: Macmillan. Symbolic character of the Ise complex in context of traditional practices.

Klein, J. (1958, May). Time capsules and what they hold. *The American Mercury*, pp. 80–81.

Kleine, M. (1967). #7. 1 The Alexandrian world. In *Mathematics for the nonmathematician* (pp. 153–58). Reading, MA: Addison-Wesley. Descriptions of the study of gases, including the use of automatic steam action devices in temples' statues, automat coin-driven, vending machine-operated temple doors, dove-figures that rose and fell by means of steam jets and compressed ("BB gun") air guns. Remarkably, steam power was used to drive automobiles in the annual religious parade in Alexandria.

Klinger, E. (1987). Vows and oaths. In M. Eliade (Ed.) *Encyclopedia of religion* (Vol. 15, pp. 301–05). Chicago: Macmillan.

Knight, V. J., & Steponaitis, V. P. (Eds.) (1998). *Archaeology of the Moundville chiefdom*. Washington, D.C.: Smithsonian Institution P.

Knox, B. (Ed.) (1993). *The Norton book of classical literature* (pp. 24, 25–26). NY: Norton.

Knutson, L. L. (1996, December 22). He's having a great time as White House clock man: career; former chief electrician and longest serving employee at the presidential residence keeps 85 timepieces ticking; Bulldog edition. *Los Angeles Times* [Newspaper]. *Electronic Library. <http://www.elibrary.com/edumark/getdoc…docid=1464472@library_a&dtype=0-0&dinst=0>.*

Koningsberg, I. (1987). Mutograph, Mutoscope. *The complete film dictionary* (p. 229). NY: NAL Penguin.

Kotlowitz, R. (1987). *Before their time: A memoir.* NY: Knopf. WW II combat autobiography.

Kouwenhoven, A. P. (May/June 1996). Largest, heaviest book. *Archaeology, 49, 3,* 24.

Kramer, S. N. (1993). Sumerian literature. In *Microsoft Encarta* [Online encyclopedia]. Microsoft; Funk & Wagnall's. A classic sketch.

Kruta, V. et al. (Ed). (1999). F. E. Barth. The Hallstatt Salt Mines (pp. 191–94). *The Celts.* NY: Rizzoli. Essay illustrates various artifactual finds.

Kusterer, J. E., & Hind, J. D. (1972, November 21). *Gaseous diffusion paper deacidification.* U.S. Patent 3,703,353, filed April 15, 1971 in: *US Patent Gazette,* pp. 365–66.

Lambert, J. B. (1987). *Traces of the past: Unraveling the secrets of archaeology through chemistry.* Reading, MA: Addison-Wesley. Soil analyses on p. 33. Dietary analysis of bone on pp. 214–22. Chapter 8 covers various human chemical traces (pp. 214–57).

Lang, M. (1974). *Graffiti in the Athenian Agora: Excavations of the Athenian Agora.* Picture Book No. 14 (p. 3). Princeton, NJ: American School of Classical Studies at Athens.

Languages of the world: English: Basic English. (1963, summer). *The Monotype Recorder, 42,* 34.

Large, A., & Jarvis, W. E. (1999). [Personal information]. Conversations and correspondence of informant Allen Large with the author, summer 1999 concerning Large's Bicentennial logbook entry expressing hope for future human progress. Logbook at Onondaga County Public Library, Syracuse, NY, 1976. (Allen Large, Redmond, WA.)

Lathrop, M. (1998, May 14). Last nursing class seals mementoes in cornerstone. *The Morning Call* [Newspaper]. (Allentown, PA), p. B13.

Leary, W. E. (1999, February 7). New framers of the Nation's Constitution work to preserve a heritage. *New York Times on the Web: www.nytimes.com/*

_____. (2000, December 5). Mighty Moon suits are falling apart. *New York Times,* pp. 1–2.

Ledgard, L. (1981, September 20). Suffolk U. unveils 12-story addition. *Boston Sunday Globe* [Newspaper], p. 43.

Leick, G. (1988). Foundation. In *A dictionary of ancient Near Eastern architecture* (p. 79). London & NY: Routledge.

Lelyveld, J. (1986, June 18). English thinker (1748–1832) preserves his poise. *New York Times,* p. A2.

Lem, S. (1973). *Memoirs found in a bathtub* [Novel]. NY: Seabury P.

Lenihan, D. J. (1983). Rethinking shipwreck archaeology: a history of ideas and considerations for new directions. In R. A. Gould (Ed.) *Shipwreck anthropology* (pp. 37–64). U. of New Mexico P. Methodological perspectives applicable to time capsule concerns.

Lerner, F. (1998). *The story of libraries: From the invention of writing to the computer age.* NY: Continuum.
Lesko, L. H. et al. (1994). *Pharaoh's workers: The villagers of Deir el Medina* (pp. 7–8). Cornell UP.
Levarie, N. (1968). *The art & history of books* (p. 1). NY: J. H. Heineman.
Lewis, P. (1989, April 19). Ancient king's instructions to Iraq: fix my palace. *New York Times*, p. A4.
Liberty: The French-American statue in art and history. (1986). New York Public Library, and the Comite officiel franco-americain pour la celebration du centenaire de la Statue de la Liberte, with P. Provoyeur and J. Hargrove. NY: Perennial Library.
Library of Congress (U.S.). (1975). C: auxiliary sciences of history. *L.c. classification outline* (p. 4). Washington, D.C. Detailed sections of various call numbers *Schedules* are revised over time, general *Outline* remains fundamentally the same.
Life-form samples sealed for two-century siege. (1967, September 27). *Science News Letter*, p. 197.
Lifeline column: New-Age Eve. (1999, December 31). *USA Today*, p. D1.
Lifting the lid on Civilization's shoebox [Arts Section]. (1998, February 21). *New York Times on the Web: <www.nytimes.com>*
Long Now Foundation Website link to Ise Shrine web pages (1999): *<http://www.longnow.com/timelinks/timelink.htm>*). (See also *Japan Information Network* web site links to Ise Shrine web pages.)
A look at Boston of years gone by. (1980, September 16). *The Boston Globe* [Newspaper], p. 27. Thanks to A. Large.
Lovelock, J. (1998, May 8). Essays on science and society — a book for all seasons. *Science, 280*, 832–833.
Lovinger, C. (1998, December 27). How not to prepare a time capsule. *New York Times on the Web: <www.nytimes.com>*
Lowenthal, D. (1985). *The past is a foreign country*. Cambridge UP.
_____. (1998). *Possessed by the past.* Cambridge UP.
Lucas, A. (1962). *Ancient Egyptian materials and industries* (4th ed., rev., enl. by J. R. Harris). London: Arnold.
Lueck, T. J. (1966, December 2). In pickpocket's stash, a peek at life in 60's. *New York Times*, pp. A1, A13.
Lukas, J. A. (1987, August 30). Class reunion: Kennedy's men relive the Cuban missile crisis. *New York Times Sunday Magazine*, p. 22.
Lynes, R. (1954). *The tastemakers.* NY: Harper.
M & M's Time Capsule Kit [Chocolate candy "tin" Millennial promotion]. (1999). Mars Candy Co.
Maass, J. (1973). *The glorious enterprise: The Centennial Exhibition of 1876 and H. J. Schwarzmann, architect-in-chief.* Watkins Glen, NY: Published for the Institute for the Study of Universal History Through Arts and Artifacts, by the American Life Foundation. "Semantic note" defining various sources and usages of the interchangeable terms "World's Fair" on p. 6. Terms "Exposition," "World's Fair," "Exposition International et Universelle," "Weltausstellung" and "Expo."

MacAlister, S. (1996). *Dreams and suicides: The Greek novel from Antiquity to the Byzantine Empire.* London & NY: Routledge.

Macaulay, D. (1979). *Motel of the mysteries.* Boston: Houghton Mifflin.

Maddox, B. (1998, December 27). Where time began [Travel Section]. *New York Times on the Web: <www.nytimes.com/>*

Malamud, C. et al. (1996). *1996 Internet World Exposition.* Internet production realized at MIT and other server platform sites, including especially Japan's.

_____. (1997). *A world's fair for the global village.* MIT P.

Maples, W. R., & Browning, M. (1984). *Dead men do tell tales: The strange and fascinating cases of a forensic anthropologist* (pp. 3, 207–08, 209–22). NY: Doubleday. Various tales of forensic anthropology, including the interplay of crime archives and archaeological forensics of Francisco Pizzaro's skeletal remains.

Marathon man [Film]. (1976). Hollywood, CA: Paramount Studios.

Marden, L. (1985, October). Wreck of HMS *Pandora* found on Australian Great Barrier Reef. *National Geographic, 168, 4*, 423–50. Describes the ca. 1984 marine archaeological expedition.

Martin, D. (1996, November 17). Under New York, the tracks that time forgot: subway planners' lofty ambitions of the 1920s are buried as dead-end curiosities. *New York Times*, p. Y19.

Maruyama, M., & Harkins, A. M. (Eds.) (1973). *Cultures of the future.* Papers at 9th International Congress of Anthropological and Ethnological Sciences, Chicago, The Hague: Mouton, Chicago: Distribution: USA and Canada, Aldine, 1978.

_____. (Eds.) (1975). *Cultures beyond the earth.* NY: Vintage. A 1974 symposium at annual meeting of American Anthropological Association.

Matthews, J., & Matthews, C. (1998). *The Winter Solstice: The sacred traditions of Christmas.* Wheaten, IL: Quest Books, Theosophical Publishing House.

Matthews, K. D. (1957). *Cities in the sand, Leptis Magna and Sabratha in Roman Africa.* Philadelphia: U. of Pennsylvania P.

Matz, D. (1995). *Ancient world lists and numbers: Numerical phrases and rosters in the Greco-Roman civilizations.* Jefferson, NC: McFarland.

Maxim, G. W. (1998, December 10). Time capsules: tools of the classroom historian. *The Social Studies: via: <http://www.elibrary.com/s/edumark/getdoc... rydocid=37893@library-f&dtype=0-0%dinst=0>1998> Electric Library* document. Maxim, G. W. (1998, December 10).

Maytag celebrates 80th anniversary of its first washing machine with washing machine tub time capsule festivities [Press release]. (1987, May 7). Maytag Corporation, Newton, IA. DIALOG database posting.

McCabe, J. D. (1876). *The illustrated history of the Centennial Exhibition held in commemoration of the one hundredth anniversary of American independence: With a full description of the great buildings and all the objects of interest in them, embracing also a concise history of the origin and success of the exhibition, and biographies of the leading members of the Centennial Commission: to which is added a complete description of the city of Philadelphia.* Philadelphia: National Publishing Co.

McCall's Time Capsule. (1976, July). *McCall's Magazine*, pp. 50–51.

McGill, D. C. (1987, October 18). Museums bringing a mass of art out of hiding: The Metropolitan. *New York Times*, p. E28.

McIver, T. (1999). *The end of the world: An annotated bibliography*. Jefferson, NC: McFarland. Cites ca. 3,500 works mostly Christian orientation, including customary themes. Eschatological beliefs of other religions, popular cultures, various psychic, etc. belief systems, and secular-oriented (Y2K chaos, etc.) are listed too. Chronological range from pre–1800s works, including other periods of 1800–1910, 1910–70, and 1970 on.

McKenn, R. (1996). *Real time*. Cambridge: Harvard U.

M'Clintock, J., & Strong, J. (1890). Corner, Corner-gate, Corner-stone. *Cyclopedia of Biblical, theological, and ecclesiastical literature* (Vol. 2, pp. 518–19).

McLuhan, M. (1964). *Understanding media: The extensions of man*. NY: McGraw-Hill.

Meighan, C. W. (Ed). (1981). *Messages from the past: Studies in California rock art*. Los Angeles: Institute of Archaeology, U. of California, Los Angeles. University of California. LA Institute of Archaeology Series Vol. 20.

Menen, A. (1993). *Cities in the sand*. NY: Dial.

Merrifield, R. (1987). *The archaeology of ritual and magic*. London: Batsford. A key analytic survey of the vast topic of votive offering deposits and rituals. Chapter 2: Offerings to earth and water in pre–Roman and Roman times on pp. 22–57. The Romano-British discussion is on pp. 51–55. Roman and post–Roman land boundary, wall foundations and gate marking deposits dedicated precincts protected by distinctive deliberate deposits of animal sacrifices are on p. 119. Dark age and medieval foundation deposits are on pp. 116–19. Late medieval and post-medieval building deposits are on pp. 119– 21. Wax-string votive forms of horse and human portions were found in the fifteenth century Exeter, England, Cathedral tomb of Bishop Lacey (p. 90, fig. 28). English museum exhibits on desiccated chickens, domestic cats or well-worn shoes, once secreted under floors, thresholds, inside walls, chimney recesses or roofs deposited from the seventeenth through the nineteenth centuries are on pp. 128–36. Chapter 6: Written spells and charms, including building deposits of written incantation squares, witch-bottles and maledictory-curse tablets are on pp. 137–58.

Michel, J. L.; Ballard, R. D. (1994). The RMS *Titanic* 1985 discovery expedition. *Ocean, 3*, III-132–III-137.

Millenios Time Capsule [Cereal food cardboard-boxed product]. (1999). Special "Millenios" addition of Cheerios brand cardboard cereal box and #2's cereal piece shapes in addition to "Cheerios" 0s shapes, Betty Crocker, Inc.

Miller, W. M. (1959). *A canticle for Leibowitz*. Boston: Gregg.

Mine becomes unique Time Tunnel. (1966, [November?, Date?]). *Los Angeles Times*, [p.?]. Handout copy. (Goldcamp Museum of Burton's Tropico Gold Mine Tour, Rosamond, CA.)

Miner, H. (1956). Body ritual among the Nacirema. *The American Anthropologist, 58*, 503–07.

Moncrieff, A. (1984). *Messages to the future: The story of the BBC Time Capsule*. London: Futura Publications.

Moore, J. D. (1992, July-August). Bumper crop. *Archaeology, 45*, 4, 52–55.

Mulford, H. B. (1950a). Research on cornerstones. *Wilson Library Bulletin, 26*, 66–67.

_____. (1950b, February 11). Noah also laid cornerstones. *School and Society, 1834*, 84–85.

_____. (1952, June). Adventures with cornerstones. *Hobbies — The Magazine for Collectors*, pp. 60–61, 75–80.

Murdock, M. (1952). *Your memorials in Washington* (pp. 162–65). Washington, D.C.: Monumental P.

Murphy, L. (1983). Shipwrecks as data base for human behavioral studies. R. A. Gould (Ed.) *Shipwreck anthropology* (pp. 65–89). U. of New Mexico P. Perspectives applicable to our time capsule concerns.

Naofusa, H. Shinto. (1987). In M. Eliade (Ed.) *Encyclopedia of religion* (Vol. 13, p. 284). Chicago: Macmillan. Shinto character of the Ise complex.

Nathan, R. (1974). *The Weans*. NY: Knopf.

The National Environmental Specimen Bank: Proceedings of the Joint EPA/NBS Workshop on Recommendations and Conclusions on the National Environmental Specimen Bank. (1978). National Bureau of Standards, Gaithersburg, MD, August 19–20, 1976. H. L. Rook & G. M. Goldstein (Eds.) Washington, D.C.: U.S. Department of Commerce, NBS.

National Geographic Society. Preparation of a painted tomb-chapel — the Egyptian Artist and his methods (pp. 158–59). (1951). *Everyday life in ancient times*. Washington, D.C.: National Geographic P. One of the series of historical reconstructions painted by H. M. Herget.

"National Millennium Time Capsule" (2000). U.S. White House Millennium Council's project exhibited and stored by the U.S. National Archives and Records Administration. *http://www.nara.gov/index.html*

Neary, L. (1994, October 13). [*Untitled*, radio news item]. Neary was the announcer of this NPR (U.S.) news item, regarding a 100-year-old cornerstone.

Neolithic figurines: idols or toys? (1985). *The world atlas of archaeology* (pp. 66–67). Boston: G.K. Hall.

The New York Times Magazine. (1999). "Times' Capsule" project. *<http://www.nytimes.com/library/magazine/millennium/timecapsule/index.html>*

The New York Times Magazine. (1999). These six "Special Millennium Issues" include: The Best of the Millennium. April 18, 1999; Women: The shadow story of the Millennium. May 16, 1999; Into the unknown. June 6, 1999; Old eyes and new. September 19, 1999; The Me Millennium. October 17, 1999; and the final issue: The Times Capsule: Will they get it? December 5, 1999. These six Special Millennial Issues were coordinated with the advancement activities of the *New York Times*' Times Capsule project, a year 2000 to year 3000 effort that is to be deposited in the year 2000. For example: "The Best of the Millennium" on April 18, 1999, features the subtitle "The best: ideas, stories, and inventions of the last thousand years" Each of these "Special Millennium Issues" was included in the Times Capsule.

New York World's Fair [1939-40]. (1939). *Official guidebook of the New York World's Fair, 1939* (3rd ed.). NY: Exposition Publications.

New Zealand Millennial Vault & Time Capsules. (1999). TimeVault 2000 Corporation Ltd, NZ. <*http://www.timevault-2000.co.nz/index_0.html*> E-mail: *office@timevault-2000.co.nz*

Newly unearthed Time Capsule just full of useless old crap. (1999, October 13). *The Onion: America's Finest News Source* Website: <*http://www.theonion.com/onion3537/time_capsule.html*> Thanks to U. of Idaho archivist Michael Tarabulski for noticing this satire.

Nine minutes to Midnight: The Bulletin of the Atomic Scientists has moved the minute hand of the Doomsday Clock, its symbol of nuclear peril, five minutes closer to midnight (1998, June 11, Press Release, Chicago). *The Bulletin of Atomic Scientists.* <*http://www.bullatomsci.org/clock.html*>

1902 mementos found under White House entrance. (1950, March). *Hobbies—The Magazine for Collectors*, p. 463.

1939: President Roosevelt laid the cornerstone of the Jefferson Memorial in Washington, D.C. [On this day]. (1999, November 14). *New York Times on the Web:* <*http://www.nytimes.com/learning/general/onthisday/991115onthisday.html*>

Norsam Technologies. (1999). *HD-ROSETTA ion beam system provides eye-readable permanent information and images on a 2 metal disk.* <*http://www.norsam.com/*>

_____. (1999). *MEMS & micromachining devices and systems based on surface, bulk and/or focused ion beam micromachining processes.* <*http://www.norsam.com/*>

NPR (National Public Radio). (2000, August 22). "Jennifer Schmidt reports residents of Walpole, New Hampshire are attempting to record everything that happens in their town this year. The idea is to leave future citizens with a complete understanding of what life was like in Walpole at the dawn of the millennium." [Radio news item].

Nussbaum, M. C. (1994). *The therapy of desire: Theory and practice in Hellenistic ethics* (pp. 102–279). Princeton UP. Epicurus' work is analyzed.

O'Connell, K., Director. (1999). *Time capsule: Message in a bottle* [Film]. 53 minutes. Zia Films, Seattle, WA. <*www.bigfoot.com/~timecapsule*> First full-length documentary feature exclusively on time capsules.

O'Donnell, J. J. (1998). *Avatars of the word: From papyrus to cyberspace.* Cambridge, MA: Harvard UP.

The official record of Time Capsule Expo 70: A gift to the people of the future from the people of the present day. (1980). Kodama, Japan: Matsushita Electrical Industrial Co. Chronicles the project and contents in Time Capsules no.1 and no. 2.

Ogden, D. Pt. I. *Binding spells: Curse tablets and voodoo dolls in the Greek and Roman worlds (pp. 1–90).* (Eds) Ankarloo and S. Clark. *Witchcraft and magic in Europe. Ancient Greece and Rome* (1999). Philadelphia: U. of Pennsylvania P.

Ohmura, T. (2000). The Process of opening the EXPO 70 Time Capsule and problems encountered [Unpublished paper and subsequent Symposium discussions with Jarvis et al. Japanese language document]. National Ethnology Museum. *Symposium, Time Capsules in the Modern World*, September 2000. Paper included extensive technical data from Matsushita Technoresearch, Inc. (Takuichi Ohmura is a Member of the Board and General Manager, Matsushita Technoresearch, Inc., Matsushita Electric Industrial Co., Ltd., Osaka, Japan.)

Oikonomides, A. N. (Ed.) (1964.) *Ancient coins illustrating lost masterpieces of Greek art.* Chicago: Argonaut, Inc. Publishers, New enlarged ed. with Introduction, Commentary and Notes. Includes in full the classic work by Imhoof, F. W. and Gardner, P. *Numismatic commentary to Pausanias.*

Olmert, M. (1992). *The Smithsonian book of books* (pp. 202–03). Washington, D.C.: Smithsonian Institution P.

100 dailies to be placed in "capsule." (1949, October 15). *Editor & Publisher*, p. 26.

O'Neil, W. M. (1975). *Time and the calendars.* Sydney, Australia: Sydney UP. An excellent concise tour of the history of calendar studies and chronologies.

Opie, I. A. (1959). *The lore and language of schoolchildren.* St Albans: Paladin.

Oppenheim, A. L. (1964). *Ancient Mesopotamia: Portrait of a dead civilization* (pp. 26, 147, 234). U. of Chicago P.

Oravec, J. A. (1999 *ms.*). Technologists as prophets and preservationists: the Long Now Foundation [Unpublished *ms.*]. Author is at U. of Wisconsin-Whitewater. *<oravecj@uwwvax.uww.edu>*

Ovason, D. (2000). *The secret architecture of our nation's capital: the Masons and the building of Washington, D.C.* NY: HarperCollins. See these and other extensive index entries on Masonic-astrological symbolism of the capital district: Cornerstone ceremonies (pp. 71, 73, 76–79, 121, 123–25, 239, 264+); Capitol, cornerstone ceremony of (pp. 67–89, 91, 103, 129, 173, 223, 304+); Foundation ceremonies (pp. 74, 76–79, 87, 98, 359+).

Pagels, E. H. (1979). *The Gnostic Gospels.* NY: Random House.

Parrot, A. (1955). *Discovering buried worlds.* NY: Philosophical Library. Mesopotamian mound site which yielded at a Temple of Dagon a foundation deposit consisting of a copper nail driven through a sort of peg, associated with uninscribed silver and stone tablets on p. 30. Another Mesopotamian tell's *via sacra's* hundreds of votive offerings on p. 78. Deposit at Jerusalem found in 1871 in the form of an inscribed block embedded in the Temple wall that bears an injunction against transgressors on p. 106.

Parsons, E. A. (1952). *The Alexandrian Library, glory of the Hellenic world: Its rise, antiquities, and destructions.* Amsterdam, NY: Elsevier P. Temple of Serapis and its Daughter Library on pp. 86, 346–47, 349, 352–55, 358–70. Destruction stories about the Alexandrian Libraries on pp. 273–432.

Pauketat, T. R., Bozell, J. R., & Dunavan, S. L. (1993). *Temples for Cahokia Lords: Preston Holder's 1955-1956 excavations of Kunnemann Mound.* Ann Arbor: Museum of Anthropology, U. of Michigan.

Pendray, G. E. (1939). The story of the Time Capsule. *Smithsonian Institution Annual Report.* Also published monographically under corporate authorship of Westinghouse Inc. as: *The story of the Time Capsule.* (1939). Pittsburgh, PA: Westinghouse Electric and Manufacturing, Inc.

Perrot, G., & Chipiez, C. (1884). *A history of art in Chaldaea & Assyria* (W. Armstrong, Trans. Vol. 1, pp. 311–22). NY: A. C. Armstrong & Son. Note also figs. 146–50 there.

Peters, T. K. (1940a). The preservation of history in the Crypt of Civilization. *Journal of the Society of Motion Picture Engineers, 44,* 206–11. Peters describes audio-visual media preservational aspects and also some autobiographical background as the Crypt technical archivist.

_____. (1940b, January). The story of the Crypt of Civilization. *Oglethorpe University Bulletin, 25*, 1–32. Atlanta.

_____, & Pendray, G. E. (1940, January 5, & 1940, February 9). [Apparently unpublished correspondence]. A two-letter exchange between that Oglethorpe U. Crypt project archivist T. K. Peters and G. E. Pendray, Assistant to the President (1938). NY: Westinghouse Electric and Manufacturing, Inc. (Oglethorpe University Archives, Atlanta.)

Petrie, F. (1938). Foundations. *Egyptian architecture* (entry #38, pp. 46–49). London: British School of Archaeology in Egypt.

Petronius Arbiter. (1996). *The Satyricon*. (G. Walsh, Trans.). Oxford UP.

Petroski, H. (1999). *The book on the bookshelf*. NY: Knopf. Distribution: Random House.

Pindar. (1997). *Pindar: Works. English & Greek* (W. H. Race, Trans., Ed. 2 vols., Loeb classical library ed.). Cambridge: Harvard UP.

Pinker, S. (1997). *How the mind works*. NY: Norton.

Pivaro, A. (1995, February 3). *British Design Council Project 2045* [Mass-mailing cover letter and nine pp. documentation].

Popham, P. (1990). *Wooden temples of Japan*. London: Tauris Parke. The native tradition (pp. 19–31) describes the Ise Shrine complex in pre–Buddhist Japan.

Post, R. C. (1976). (Ed.) 1876: *A Centennial Exhibition*. Washington, D.C.: National Museum of History and Technology. Smithsonian Institution P.

Povich, E. S. (1987, January 8). The Liberty Bell will be gently rung and 50 state replicas, along with church bells across the nation, will peel at noon January 19 to celebrate the second annual Martin Luther King Holiday. *United Press International*. Washington, D.C. DIALOG File 261, online record No. 0328444.

Preservation of library & archival materials: A manual (3rd ed.). (1999). S. Ogdon (Ed.) Andover, MA: Northeast Document Conservation Center.

Preserving the present. (1967, January 29). *New York Sunday News*, p. 27.

Professor searching for new angle on fluorocarbon sources. (1976, January). *Chemecology*, pp. 1–2.

Quatermass and the Pit [Film]. (1998, 1967). Troy, MI: Distribution: Anchor Bay Entertainment. Videodisc release of the 1967 motion picture previously released as *Five Million Years to Earth*. Based on an earlier BBC TV "Dr. Quatermass" series that included a version of this tale. See also *Five Million Years to Earth* [Film review, TV Section].

Rabuzzi, K. A. (1987). Home. In M. Eliade (Ed.) *Encyclopedia of religion* (Vol. 6, pp. 438–42). Chicago: Macmillan.

Rathje, W. L., & Murphy, C. (1992). *Rubbish!: The archaeology of garbage*. NY: HarperCollins.

Reagan-Mondale Presidential debates [Transcription]. (1984, October 23). *New York Times*, p. A29.

"Real" new Millennium approaches. (2000, December 23). *Associated Press via New York Times on the Web: <www.nytimes.com/>*

Reardon, B. P. (Ed.) (1989). *Collected ancient Greek novels*. Berkeley: U. of California P.

_____. (1991). *The form of Greek romance*. Princeton UP.

Recaptured. (1956, February 25). *New Yorker, 31*, 26–27.

Recordor. (1952). *Cassell's Latin-English and English-Latin dictionary* (p. 471). NY: Funk & Wagnalls.

Rediscovering Pompeii Exhibition by IBM-ITALIA, New York City, IBM Gallery of Science and Art (1990, 12 July–15 September). Ministero per i beni culturali e ambientali, Soprintendenza archeologica di Pompei, IBM. Roma, Italy: L'Erma di Bretschneider. Text: English and Italian.

Reif, R. (1988, December 24). Scholars see problems. *New York Times*, p. 11. Cites interview of scholars on question of most ancient codices.

Reinhardt, R. (1978). *Treasure Island 1939-1940: San Francisco's Exposition years* (p. 38). Mill Valley, CA: Squarebooks.

Religion, study of. (1994–1999). *Encyclopædia Britannica Online. <http://search.eb.com/bol/topic?eu=117379&sctn=22>*

Remains to be seen. (1964, September 28). *Newsweek, 64*, 92.

Remington, F. (1954, May). Filing cabinets for posterity. *Think*, pp. 16–17.

Reynolds, L. D., & Wilson, N. G. (1974). *Scribes and scholars: A guide to the transmission of Greek & Latin literature* (2nd Rev. ed.). Oxford UP. Alexandrian Museum and Library, as well standardizing of Greek texts by their scholars (pp. 5–15). Examples of ancient works still extant after 900 AD, surviving into our twentieth century in only one copy, if any survive at all. Numerous Latin works extant in but a single copy during the Carolingian copyist heyday of the ninth century AD, and hence that close to oblivion to our modern readership (p. 90). Herculeanum papyri finds are briefly noted on pp. 32, 177.

The Reynolds Metals Company Bicentennial Time Capsule [Brochure]. (1976). Reynolds Metals, Inc.

Richter, G. M. A. (1936). *Red-figured Athenian vases in the Metropolitan Museum of Art* (2 vols. , Vol. 1, pp. xxviii–xxxiv, 26, 147, 234). Yale UP; London: H. Milford, Oxford UP.

Ritual, performance, media (1998). (Eds.) F. Hughes–Freeland. London & NY: Routledge. ASA monographs No. 35. Papers presented at ASA Conference, University of Wales, Swansea, March 1996.

Roads, V. (1998). Welcome to tomorrow. *The iconography of hope: The 1939-40 New York World's Fair. http://xroads.virginia.edu/~1930s/DISPLAY/39wf/frame.htm*, May 1998, "America in the 1930s" project, American Studies Program, U. of Virginia.

Rogers, A., & Allen, F. L. (1947). *I remember distinctly: A family album of the American people.* NY & London: Harper and Brothers. Personal style narrative on all aspects of American life November 11, 1918, to December 7, 1941.

Rogers, J. D., & Smith, B. D. (Eds.) (1995). *Mississippian communities and households.* Tuscaloosa: U. of Alabama P.

Romain, W. F. (2000). *Mysteries of the Hopewell: Astronomers, geometers, and magicians of the eastern woodlands.* Akron, OH: U. of Akron P.

Rose, C. A. (1988, May). *Consecration of an Egyptian temple according to foundation scenes on the outer precinct wall of the temple of Edfu.* This Brandeis U. dissertation analyzes the 14 scenes of the foundation ceremonial (figs. 2–3). Ann Arbor, MI: UMI.

Rothenberg, J. (1995, January). Ensuring the longevity of digital documents. *Scientific American, 272, 1,* 42. Five-year digital shelf life is discussed.

_____. (1999). *Avoiding technological quicksand: Finding a viable technical foundation for digital preservation.* Washington, D.C.: Council on Library and Information Resources: <*text/html http://www.clir.org/pubs/reports/rothenberg/contents.html*> This RAND, Inc. expert's report analyzes various extant and proposed digital preservation methodology to cope with the key long-term preservational issues. He concludes that extensive annotations, fully digitized encapsulation, and complete, successive software emulation of digital documentary contexts are the most cogent preservational approaches.

Rothenbuhler, E. W. (1998). *Ritual communication: From everyday conversation to mediated ceremony.* Thousand Oaks: Sage Publications. Chapter 6, section 6.9: Backward and forward references (pp. 63–64); Chapter 10, section 10.3: Public festivals and ceremonies (pp. 103–04).

Rothenstein, J., & Gooding, M. (1998). *The Redstone diary 1999: Messages to a future.* London: Redstone P. This appointment diary is itself an anthological missive to possible futures, full of colorful illustrations of time capsule–type phenomena and concludes with a 16-page supplement illustrating, explaining and defining time capsule containers, effects, and giving advice. Captions (in English-French-German-Spanish) to these "Picture Credits": Illus. 30 is: Message to a future found behind wall during building work at Tate Gallery, London 1985. Tate Gallery Archive, 1985. Illus. 33 is: Coffins for a driver and for a farmer [Caption & Photograph by Kane Kwei, Ghana]. Illus. 43 is: Spoerri, D., (burying of dining table loaded with remains of dedication's meal) at Foundation Cartier, Jouy-en-Josas, France, 1983.

Rowe, A., & Rees, B. R. (1956–1957). A contribution to the archaeology of the western desert: IV. The great Serapeum of Alexandria. *Bulletin of the John Rylands Library, XXXIX,* 485–520. Manchester, England. Archaeologist Rowe is author of Pt. I: The archaeological evidence (pp. 485–512). Rees the philologist of Classical Greek is author of Pt. II: The literary and other evidence (pp. 513–20).

Ryan, M. (1998, January 25). A message from the child you once were. *Parade Magazine,* pp. 8–9.

Rydell, R. W. (1984). *All the world's a fair.* U. of Chicago P.

_____, Findling, J. E., & Pelle, K. D. (2000). *Fair America: World's Fairs in the United States.* Washington, D.C.: Smithsonian Institution P.

Saeve-Soederbergh, T. (1987). *Temples and tombs of ancient Nubia: The international rescue campaign at Abu Simbel, Philae and other sites.* London: UNESCO/Thames and Hudson.

Sagan, C. (Ed.) (1973). *Communication with extraterrestrial intelligence (CETI).* Soviet-American Conference on the Problems of Communication with Extraterrestrial Intelligence (1st: 1971: Byurakan Astrophysical Observatory): MIT P.

_____et al. (1978). *Murmurs of Earth: The Voyager interstellar record.* NY: Random House. Contents are: C. Sagan. For future times and beings; F. D. Drake. The foundations of the Voyager Record; J. Lomberg. Pictures of Earth; L. S. Sagan. A Voyager's greetings; A. Druyan. The sounds of Earth; T. Ferris. Voyager's music; C. Sagan; The Voyager Mission to the Outer Solar system; C. Sagan. Epilogue.

_____. (1985). *Contact* [Novel]. NY: Simon & Schuster.

Salzman, L. F. (1952). *Building in England down to 1540: A documentary history* (pp. 82, 87, 380–86, 391, 407, 523, 527, 538). Oxford: Clarendon.

Sanger, D. E. (1993, October 7). Ise journal: a sojourn for a Shinto Sun Goddess. *New York Times*, p. A4.

Satinover, J. B. (1997). *Cracking the Bible code.* NY: William Morrow.

Sawyer, R. J. (1996). *Starplex* (pp. 131+). NY: Berkeley Publishing Group.

Schilling, P. Numen. (1987). In M. Eliade (Ed.) *Encyclopedia of religion* (Vol. 11, pp. 21–22). Chicago: Macmillan.

Schmandt-Besserant, D. (1992). *Before writing: From counting to cuneiform* (Vol. 1). Austin: U. of Texas P.

Schulman, S. (1999). *Owning the future.* Boston: Houghton-Mifflin.

Schuster, A. M. H. Mapping Alexandria's royal quarters. (1999, March/April). *Archaeology, 52, 2*, 44–46.

Schwartz, S. I. (Ed.) (1998). *Atomic audit: The costs and consequences of U.S. nuclear weapons since 1940.* Washington, D.C.: Brookings Institution. Washington, D.C.: Brookings. Apparently the first systematic economic audit-study of U.S. atomic weapons, nuclear propulsion and nuclear generation of electric power ever conducted. This Mt. Pony site was once designated as a key continuity of government facility (pp. 213, 317). Defending against the bomb: civil defense section outlines some of these "continuity of government" structures and plans (pp. 309–25). Many key "continuity of government" facilities are featured.

Scientific events: the sealing of the Time Capsule. (1940, September 27). *Science, 92*, 280–81. News note on its final ceremonials.

Scientists probe tomb of emperor. (1998, November 2). *Associated Press via New York Times on the Web: www.nytimes.com*

Seattle's New Year's Eve celebration canceled. (1999, December 28). *Associated Press via New York Times on the Web: <www.nytimes.com/>*

Sebeok, T. A. (1984, April). *Communication measures to bridge ten Millennia.* U.S. Department of Energy Contract Report BMI/ONWI-532. Also published as: Sebeok, T. A. (1984). Keeping Pandora's Box shut: a relay-system in the care of an atomic-priesthood (Nuclear Waste Disposal). *Zeitschrift fuer Semiotik*, 6, 229–51.

Secular ritual. (1977). (Eds.) S. F. Moore & B. G. Myerhoff. Assen: Van Gorcum. Papers presented at conference: *Secular rituals considered*, August 24–September 1, 1974, Burg Wartenstein, Austria.

Segal, H. P. (1985). *Technological utopianism in American culture* (pp. 125–127). U. of Chicago P.

Seniors put their past 6-feet under. (1998, June 5). *The Chronicle of Higher Education*, p. A8.

SETI Institute. (1999). *<http://www.seti.org/>*

SETI: Search for extra-terrestrial intelligence. (1990). Washington, D.C.: NASA; Moffett Field, CA: Ames Research Center, SETI Office; Pasadena, CA: JPL, California Institute of Technology, SETI Office; Washington, D.C.: NASA

Headquarters, Office of Space Sciences and Applications, Life Sciences Division.

Shanks, H. (Ed.) (1992). *Understanding the Dead Sea Scrolls: A reader from the Biblical Archaeological Review.* NY: Random House. One of many sources, extensively annotated.

Sheeler, C. G. (1995). *Tour map of northern Berks County along Dutch Hex Highway: Hex signs & barn signs in Berks.* Lenhartsville, PA: The Association.

Shepherd, C. Oops! (1999, September). *Funny Times: Humor, Politics & Fun* [Humor-cartoon magazine; News of the Weird Column]. (Cleveland Heights, OH), p. 21.

_____. Also in the last month [sixth of eight untitled short comments]. (2000, May). *Funny Times: Humor, Politics & Fun* [Humor-cartoon magazine: News of the Weird Column]. (Cleveland Heights, OH), p. 13.

Shinbunsha, A. (1965). *Ise, prototype of Japanese architecture.* MIT P.

Shoumatoff, A. (1985). *The mountain of names: A history of the human family.* NY: Simon & Schuster.

Shrock, R. R. (1965). *Geology at MIT 1865–1965* (Vol. 2, pp. 195–208). MIT P. The two-volume work surveys some MIT capsules.

Shute, N. (1957). *On the Beach* [Novel]. NY: New American Library.

Silver-gelatin film, etc. [Index entries]. (1996). In L. L. Fox (Ed.) *Preservation microfilming: A guide for librarians and archivists* (2nd ed.). For ARL. Chicago: ALA.

Singh, S. (1999). *The code book: The evolution of secrecy from Mary Queen of Scots to quantum cryptography.* NY: Doubleday. The 1999 British imprint has a distinct subtitle: *The science of secrecy from ancient Egypt to quantum cryptography.* London: Fourth Estate.

Sleeper [Film]. (1996). Director, W. Allen. Santa Monica, CA: MGM/UA Home Video, 1973.

Smithsonian Center for Materials Research and Education. (2000). Smithsonian Institution. Washington, D.C.: <*www.si.edu/scmre/timecaps.html*>

Smithsonian New Millennium Time Capsule Kit (1999). Smithsonian Institution. Washington, D.C. Sale item #2025.

Sniffing through history [Editorial]. (1989, February 19). *New York Times,* p. E18.

Snook, S. A. (2000). *Friendly fire: The accidental shootdown of U.S. Black Hawks over Northern Iraq.* Princeton UP.

Some cracks in the foundation; The top area news stories of 2000 centered around an economy, an environment and a population under pressure. (2000, December 31). *Lewiston (ID) Tribune:* <*http://www.lmtribune.com/*>, p. 1+.

Sources of Japanese tradition (1958). NY: Columbia UP. Ise Shrine discussed on (pp. 1, 24, 34, 268, 271, 332, 870); "vertical-horizontal: time-to-space: Japan-Western Worlds, etc. topic by: Kitaro, N. The problem of Japanese culture (pp. 857–72).

Span, P. (1986, October 29). The real Centennial; a low-key celebration of the Lady's 100th.... *Washington Post,* p. D1.

Spare times: attractions: museums and sites: Capturing time: The New York Times Capsule [Leisure/Weekend Section]. (1999, December 10). *New York Times on the Web:* <*www.nytimes.com*> Exhibition, American Museum of Natural History, New York City.

Specter, M. (1992, August 16). The tomb of Caiaphas unearthed? *New York Times*, p. 2 E.
Sproul, B. C. (1987). Sacred time. In M. Eliade (Ed.) *Encyclopedia of religion* (Vol. 12, pp. 535–544). Chicago: Macmillan.
Stambaugh, J. E. (1972). *Sarapis under the early Ptolemies* (p. 7). Leiden, Netherlands: E. J. Brill. Through study of the Sarapis cultus, patron god of the Ptolemic dynasty, and of megapolitian Alexandria.
Staski, E., & Sutro, L. D. (Eds.) (1991). *The ethnoarchaeology of refuse disposal.* Arizona State U. Anthropological Research Papers No. 42.
Staszkow, N. (2000, January 1 and 2). Moscow youth help with time capsule. *Moscow-Pullman Daily News* [Newspaper: Weekend ed.]. (Pullman, WA), pp. 1A, 2A.
Steel, F. (1927, May). City planning in Moscow. *Garden Club of America Bulletin, 15*, 24–25.
Stern, R. A. M. (1987). *New York 1930* (p. 730). NY: Rizzoli.
Stocking, G. W. (1987). *Victorian anthropology.* NY & Oxford: Free P., Maxwell Macmillan.
Stockwell, F. (2001). *A history of information storage and retrieval.* Jefferson, NC, & London: McFarland. Sketches ancient records as well as modern writings, documents and information retrieval.
Stone, E. C., and Zimansky, P. (1995, April). The tapestry of power in a Mesopotamian city. *Scientific American, 272*, 118+.
Stuart, W. J. (1956). *Forbidden Planet* [Novel]. NY: Farrar, Straus. Novel on which the 1956 film was based.
Suzuki, K. (1980). *Early Buddhist architecture in Japan.* Tokyo & NY: Kodansha International; Distribution: Harper & Row.
Swartzburg, S. G. (1995). *Preserving library materials: A manual* (2nd ed.). Metuchen, NJ: Scarecrow P.
Swerdlow, J. L. (1998, January). Making sense of the Millennium. *National Geographic, 193, 1*, 2–32.
Szirmai, J. A. (1999). *The archaeology of medieval bookbinding.* Aldershot: Hants; Brookfield, VT: Ashgate. Covers physical bibliography, the leaved book as artifact, their antique construction and how to repair them are all analyzed. Coptic Codices of Nag-Hamaddi, cross-cultural Medieval bookbinding, Arabic, other Medieval culture areas Western European periods are cited.
Talk of the town column — notes and comment: Postscript. (1963, June 29). *New Yorker, 39*, 18–19.
Talk of the town column — notes and comment: Ceremonies. (1964, September 26). *New Yorker, 40*, 37–39.
Talk of the town column — notes and comment: [Untitled]. (1965, October 1965). *New Yorker, 41*, 47.
Talos, I. (1987). Foundation rites. In M. Eliade (Ed.) *Encyclopedia of religion* (Vol. 5, pp. 395–401). Chicago: Macmillan.
Taylor, J. A. (1997). *The 500 year delta: What happens after what comes next.* Oxford: Capstone.
Taylor, P. (1989, August 27). In France, the remembrance of things present. *New York Times*, pp. 31–33.

Teeuwen, M. (1996). *Watarai Shinto: An intellectual history of the outer shrine in Ise.* Leiden, The Netherlands: Research School CNWS.

10 lost time capsules [Press release]. (1991, June 28). Oglethorpe University News—ITCS. Item #2. See also: *The 9 most wanted time capsules.* (1999, July). ITCS. <*www.oglethorpe.edu/itcs/wanted.html*> (ITCS, Oglethorpe University, Atlanta.)

30 leading drugs buried in medical time capsule. (1963, October 12). *Science News Letter, 84,* 231.

This heavy door of shining stainless steel to seal Georgia Crypt until year 8113. (1938, July-August). *Ingot Iron Shop News,* p. 3. Typical trade magazine story.

Thomas, D. N. (1983). Jacobs, Thornwell. *Dictionary of Georgia biography* (Vol. 1, pp. 517–19). Athens, GA: U. of Georgia P.

Thompson, D. B. (1993). *An ancient shopping center: The Athenian Agora.* Princeton, NJ: American School of Classical Studies at Athens. Excavations of the Athenian Agora. Picture Book no. 12.

Thompson, E. M. (1893). *Handbook of Greek and Latin palaeography* (pp. 113–14). NY: D. Appleton. An indispensable work by the then chief librarian of Great Britain. See also his standard treatise: *An introduction to Greek and Latin paleography* (1912). Oxford UP.

Thompson, J. W. (1940). *Ancient libraries* (p. 83). Hamden, CT: Archon.

Thompson, L. S. (1975). Libraries, imaginary and imaginary books. *Encyclopedia of library and information science* (Vol. 14, pp. 304–10). NY: Marcel Dekker.

311 microfilmed pages cached for 2048 folk. (1948, October 30). *Editor & Publisher,* p. 39.

Time capsule. (1989). *The Oxford English dictionary.*

Time Capsule II. (1965). A supplemental one-leaf insertion for the 1938 *The book of record of the Time Capsule of Cupaloy.* This one-side printed page provides basic data about the 1964-65 twin (called "Time Capsule II") of the 1938 Time Capsule I.

Time Capsule II deposited for 5000 years at Fair. (1965, October 23). *Science News Letter,* pp. 260.

A time capsule helps archivists to look back [Campus Life]. (1991, July 14). *New York Times,* p. 131.

Time capsules: Archival protection. (1999). <*http://www.simsc.si.edu/cal/timecaps*> Smithsonian Institution. Conservation Analytical Laboratory. Washington, D.C.

Time Capsules in the Modern World Symposium. (September 2000). Osaka, Japan: National Museum of Ethnology. [Unpublished papers and subsequent Symposium discussions.] Thirteen abstracts in Japanese and eight in English.

Time immemorial. (1999, February 1). *Popular Mechanics, 176, 2,* 68+.

Time is on Marilyn's side. (1987, December 18). *Boston Herald* [Newspaper], p. 11.

Time-Life Books, The Editors. (1964). *Official guide: New York World's Fair 1964/1965.* NY: Time, Inc.

Time Zone 2000: Project overview [ca. 1998, May]. A two-sided commercial circular, MilleniEvents Ltd., Fornby, Merseyside, England.

The Titan Missile Museum. (1999). *http://clui.zone.org/clui/database/museums/titan1.html*

To the immortal name and memory of George Washington: The United States Army Corps of Engineers and the construction of the Washington Monument (pp. 870). (1984). U.S. Army Corps of Engineers. SuDoc D103.48.

Tompkins, P. (1981). *The magic of obelisks.* NY: Harper & Row. The Obelisk now in Central Park, New York City, is on pp. 282–307. The Washington Monument obelisk in Washington, D.C., is on pp. 321–23, 329–37.

Travis, J. (1999, June 12). Prehistoric bacteria revived from buried salt. *Science News, 155*, 373.

Treasure!: Tomb of the Terra Cotta Warriors [Film]. (1999). A&E Network, 50-minute video, Item Number: AAE-13041.

Tropico Time Tunnel Sealing Ceremonies [Program for ceremony]. (1966, November 20). Tropico Gold Mine, Rosamond, CA.

Troy Hill Time Capsule: November 1, 1987: November 1, 2037 [Program for ceremony]. The Program for the November 1 deposits events, Troy Hill neighborhood, Pittsburgh, PA.

Turner, E. G. (1968). *Greek papyri: An introduction.* Princeton UP. See index entry: Herculeanum (pp. 17, 18, 39, 41, 56, 171, 175). Waxen tablet entry on p. 39. See also entries on carbonized rolls on pp. 1, 18, 39, 43, 56, 173, 174.

2001: A Space Odyssey [Film]. (1968). Director, Stanley Kubrick. Santa Monica, CA: MGM/UA Home Video, 1994.

An unexpected find at Maryland College [Going on in the Northeast Column]. (1986, November 16). *New York Times*, p. 58.

UP eye on Illinois: blast from the past. (1998, November 6). *United Press International* posting.

Update: Halley Time Capsule. (1985, October). *Halley's Comet Watch Newsletter*, p. 2.

Van Buren, E. D. (1931). *Foundation figurines and offerings.* Berlin: Hans Schoetz, G. M. B. H., Verlagsbuchhandlung. Photographs of 40 such Mesopotamian figurines and offerings are provided at the end of this (English) text in Plates I–XX. See also Van Buren: 1952a. Foundation rites for a new temple. *Orientalia, N. S., 21*, 293–306; (1952b). The building of a temple-tower. *Revue d' assyriologie orientale, 46*, 65–74.

van Buren, P. M. (1998). The *Old Testament*, not *Tanak* or *Hebrew Bible. According to the Scriptures: The origin of the Gospel and of the Church's Old Testament* (pp. 83–93). Grand Rapids MI, Cambridge, UK: Eerdmans.

Vault for the Future. (1956, July 6). *Science, 124*, 22.

Verdery, K. (1999). *The political lives of dead bodies: Reburial and postsocialist change.* NY: Columbia UP.

Vietnam Veterans Memorial. (2000). Washington, D.C.: *<http://www.nps.gov/vive/index2.htm>*

Viskochil, L. A. (1976). Chicago's Bicentennial photographer: Charles D. Mosher. *Chicago History 5, 2*, 95–104.

Visser, M. (1986). *Much depends on dinner.* NY: Grove. The Underground Vaults and Storage Company's salt-mined based facility on pp. 58–60. Ancient "Salzburg Salt Men" on pp. 56–58.

Wald, M. L. (1998, February 9). Leap Day 2000 might pose big problems for some computers' software. *New York Times*, p. C3.

Walker, J. B. (1970). *Fifty years of rapid transit: 1864–1917* (pp. 87–104). NY: *New York Times* Company/Arno P. Includes photographs of the 1870 subway tube car and the subway tunnel at its unearthing in 1912. A reprint of the 1918 Law Printing Co. imprint.

Wallich, P. (1999, October). Cyber View: to err is mechanical. *Scientific American, 281, 4*, 50.

Ward-Perkins, J., & Claridge, A. (1978). *Pompeii A. D. 79* (2 vols.). Boston: Museum of Fine Arts. Exhibition catalogue, itself a fine "time capsule."

Warner, R. [Personal information]. E-mails, miscellaneous correspondence and telephone conversations of the author with local historian Dick Warner, Tulsa, OK, March 2001 about the 1957 and 1998 car deposits there. Thanks to the Tulsa (OK) Historical Society for that referral.

Watson, P. J., LeBlanc, S. A., & Redman, C. A. (1984). *Archeological explanation* (p. 257). NY: Columbia UP.

Watterson, B. (1998). *The House of Horus at Edfu: Ritual in an ancient Egyptian temple*. See especially the foundation and consecration of Edfu Temple (pp. 85–92). Gloucestershire, England: Tempus.

Weber, E. (1999). *Apocalypses: Prophecies, cults, and millennial beliefs through the ages*. Harvard UP.

Weldon, J., et al. (1998). *Decoding the Bible code: Can we trust the message?* (pp. 47–55). Eugene, OR: Harvest House. Critical analysis of the Bible Code controversies, including the expositions of Satinover, 1997, and Drosnin, 1997.

"The West Worlock Time Capsule" [TV Story broadcast]. (1957). *Alfred Hitchcock Presents* [TV Program Series].

Westcott, T. (1876). *Centennial portfolio*. Philadelphia: Thomas Hunter.

The Westinghouse Time Capsule [Brochure]. ([1938?]. One of two promotional brochures by Westinghouse Electric and Manufacturing, Inc. This [1938?] one is just a single sheet folded into a four-sided leaflet. It only treats the 1938 Time Capsule of Cupaloy.

The Westinghouse Time Capsules [Brochure]. ([1964?]). Second of two promotional brochures by Westinghouse Electric and Manufacturing, Inc. This second, [14 pp.] glossy brochure [ca. 1964] lists the years "1938, 1964, 1965, 6939" on it, with "1964" highlighted. Its featured Time Capsule II was done for the 1964-65 New York World's Fair, but it also discusses the 1938 Time Capsule.

Wexler, R. (1986, September 26). Big bash honors new bank and park. *Albany Times-Union* [Newspaper]. (Albany, NY), pp. A1, A8.

White, E. B. (1997). The world of tomorrow (pp. 71–79). *One man's meat*. Gardiner, ME: Tilbury House. White's May 1939 trip to the New York World's Fair laid bare.

White, F. (1990). *The SETI factor: How the search for extraterrestrial intelligence is changing our view of the universe and ourselves*. NY: Walker.

Wilford, J. N. (1996, July 26). Ancient Egypt's beer, a sophisticated brew. *New York Times*, p. A5.

_____. (1999a, April 6). Who began writing?: many theories, few answers. *New York Times on the Web: www.nytimes.com/*

_____. (1999b, November 14). Finds in Egypt date alphabet in earlier era. *New York Times*, pp. Y1, Y10.

_____. (1999c, February 17). A last meal for the Iceman. *New York Times on the Web: <www.nytimes.com/>*

Willetts, R. F. (1965). *Ancient Crete: A social history* (pp. 12–15, 40, 55, 66, 73, 75, 77–81, 83–85, 87–90, 92–94, 96–97, 99–102, 113, 147). London: Routledge & Kegan P. The Code, or "Law of Gortyn," is a centerpiece of this work.

Williams, D. (1996). *The reach of Rome* (pp. 76–78). NY: St. Martins.

Williams, M., & Elliott, D. T. (Eds.) (1998). *A world engraved: Archaeology of the Swift Creek Culture.* U. of Alabama P. Chapter One: Swift Creek research: history and observations (pp. 1–11).

Wiseman, J. (1999, May/June). Challenge of the deep. *Archaeology, 52, 3,* 10–12.

Woodbridge, R. (1969, August). Acoustical recordings from Antiquity. *IEEE Proceedings,* pp. 1465–66. See also: Benford, 1986.

Woolley, C. L. (1926, October). Babylonian prophylactic figures. *Journal of the Royal Asiatic Society,* pp. 688–713. Vernacular, domestic buildings' apotropaic figurines of the Neo-Babylonian era are depicted.

_____, & Moorey, R. (1982). *Ur of the Chaldees* (Rev. updated ed., pp. 227–31). Ithaca, NY: Cornell UP. Foundation deposits section.

Wright, H. C. (1970, summer). Metallic documents of antiquity. *Brigham Young U. Studies, 10, 4,* 18, 21, 457–77.

_____. (1982, December). Ancient burials of metallic foundation documents in stone boxes. *U. of Illinois SLIS Occasional Papers, 157,* 4–5, 17–18.

Wu, C. (1999, June 26). Old Glory, new glory: the Star-Spangled Banner gets some tender loving care. *Science News, 155, 26,* 408–409.

Wurts, R. et al. (155 photographs by), & Appelbaum, S. (selection, arrangement, and text by) (1977). *The New York World's Fair 1939/1940.* NY: Dover

Y2K glitch identifies new cars as "horseless carriages." (1999, October 13). *The Daily Evergreen* [Newspaper]. (Washington State University, Pullman, WA, via *Associated Press*), p. 5.

Yes Minister: The diaries of a Cabinet Minister by the Rt. Hon. James Hacker, M. P. (1981). London: British Broadcasting Corporation. Program scripts of the BBC-TV series *Yes Minister.*

Yoder, D., & Graves, T. E. (2000). *Hex signs: Pennsylvania Dutch barn symbols and their meaning.* Mechanicsburg, PA: Stackpole Books.

Youngholm, D. S. (1940, October 4). The Time Capsule. *Science, 92,* 301–02. Westinghouse VP's sealing ceremony speech.

Zaleski, C. G. (1987). *Otherworld journeys* (p. 18). Oxford UP.

Zero Effect [Film]. (1998). Burbank, CA: Warner Home Video.

Index